Instructor's Resou
for

Wood and Wood

The World of Psychology

Third Edition

Prepared by
Fred W. Whitford
Montana State University

Allyn and Bacon
Boston • London • Toronto • Sydney • Tokyo • Singapore

Copyright © 1999, 1996, 1993 by Allyn and Bacon
A Viacom Company
160 Gould Street
Needham Heights, Massachusetts 02494
Internet: www.abacon.com

All rights reserved. The contents, or parts thereof, may be reproduced for use with *The World of Psychology*, Third Edition, by Samuel E. Wood and Ellen Green Wood, provided such reproductions bear copyright notice, but may not be reproduced in any form for any other purpose without written permission from the copyright owner.

ISBN 0-205-28566-X

Printed in the United States of America

10 9 8 7 6 5 4 3 2 1   02 01 00 99 98

Contents

Preface — xi

Part One: Introduction

Teaching Strategies — xv

    Teaching Strategies for the Multicultural Classroom, by Joyce Bishop, Golden West College — xv

Transparencies for Introductory Psychology — xviii

Digital Image Archive — xxv

Videodisc Table — xxxi

Part Two: Chapter Resources

Chapter 1 Introduction to Psychology

Chapter-at-a-Glance	1
What's New	2
Learning Objective Questions	3
Chapter Overview	4
Key Terms	5
Annotated Lecture Outline	
A. Introduction to Psychology	6
B. Descriptive Research Methods	7
C. The Experimental Method: Searching for Causes	9
D. Other Research Methods	11
E. Participants in Psychological Research	12
F. Exploring Psychology's Roots	15
G. Psychology Today	16

Chapter 2 Biology and Behavior

Chapter-at-a-Glance	21
What's New	22
Learning Objective Questions	23
Chapter Overview	24
Key Terms	25

Annotated Lecture Outline
- A. The Neurons and the Neurotransmitters — 25
- B. The Central Nervous System — 27
- C. The Cerebral Hemispheres — 29
- D. Discovering the Brain's Mysteries — 33
- E. Brain Damage: Causes and Consequences — 34
- F. The Peripheral Nervous System — 34
- G. The Endocrine System — 35

Chapter 3 Sensation and Perception

Chapter-at-a-Glance	37
What's New	38
Learning Objective Questions	39
Chapter Overview	40
Key Terms	41
Annotated Lecture Outline	
A. Sensation: The Sensory World	41
B. Vision	43
C. Hearing	45
D. Smell and Taste	45
E. Our Other Senses	46
F. Perception: Ways of Perceiving	48
G. Additional Influences on Perception	53
H. Subliminal Persuasion and Extrasensory Perception	54

Chapter 4 States of Consciousness

Chapter-at-a-Glance	57
What's New	58
Learning Objective Questions	59
Chapter Overview	60
Key Terms	61
Annotated Lecture Outline	
A. What Is Consciousness	61
B. Circadian Rhythms: Our 24-Hour Highs and Lows	62
C. Sleep: That Mysterious One-Third of Our Lives	63
D. Sleep Disorders	66
E. Altering Consciousness through Concentration and Suggestion	67
F. Altered States of Consciousness and Psychoactive Drugs	68

Chapter 5 Learning

Chapter-at-a-Glance		73
What's New		74
Learning Objective Questions		74
Chapter Overview		75
Key Terms		76
Annotated Lecture Outline		
A.	Classical Conditioning	76
B.	Operant Conditioning	80
C.	Cognitive Learning	87

Chapter 6 Memory

Chapter-at-a-Glance		91
What's New		92
Learning Objective Questions		93
Chapter Overview		93
Key Terms		95
Annotated Lecture Outline		
A.	Remembering	95
B.	Measuring Memory	99
C.	Forgetting	100
D.	The Nature of Remembering and Forgetting	101
E.	Factors Influencing Retrieval	105
F.	Biology and Memory	106
G.	Improving Memory	106

Chapter 7 Cognition and Language

Chapter-at-a-Glance		109
What's New		110
Learning Objective Questions		111
Chapter Overview		111
Key Terms		112
Annotated Lecture Outline		
A.	Imagery and Concepts: Tools of Thinking	112
B.	Deductive and Inductive Reasoning	114
C.	Decision Making: Making Choices in Life	114
D.	Problem Solving: Beyond Decision Making	116
E.	Language	118

Chapter 8 Intelligence and Creativity

Chapter-at-a-Glance	123
What's New	124
Learning Objective Questions	125
Chapter Overview	125
Key Terms	126
Annotated Lecture Outline	
A. The Nature of Intelligence	127
B. Measuring Intelligence	128
C. The IQ Controversy: Brain Dispute	132
D. Emotional Intelligence	133
E. Creativity: Unique and Useful Productions	134

Chapter 9 Child Development

Chapter-at-a-Glance	137
What's New	139
Learning Objective Questions	139
Chapter Overview	140
Key Terms	140
Annotated Lecture Outline	
A. Developmental Psychology: Basic Issues and Methodology	142
B. Heredity and Prenatal Development	142
C. Physical Development and Learning in Infancy	145
D. Emotional Development in Infancy	146
E. Piaget's Theory of Cognitive Development	147
F. Vygotsky's Sociocultural View of Cognitive Development	149
G. Cognitive Development: The Information Processing Approach	149
H. Language Development	149
I. Socialization of the Child	150

Chapter 10 Adolescence and Adulthood

Chapter-at-a-Glance	153
What's New	154
Learning Objective Questions	155
Chapter Overview	156
Key Terms	157
Annotated Lecture Outline	
A. Adolescence: Physical and Cognitive Development	157
B. Adolescence: Moral and Social Development	159
C. Erikson's Psychosocial Theory: Adolescence through Adulthood	160
D. Other Theories of Adulthood	162

	E.	Early and Middle Adulthood	162
	F.	Later Adulthood	165

Chapter 11 Motivation and Emotion

Chapter-at-a-Glance	169
What's New	170
Learning Objective Questions	171
Chapter Overview	172
Key Terms	173
Annotated Lecture Outline	
A. Introduction to Motivation	173
B. Theories of Motivation	173
C. The Primary Drives: Hunger and Thirst	175
D. Social Motives	177
E. The What and Why of Emotions	178
F. The Expression of Emotion	181
G. Experiencing Emotion	182

Chapter 12 Human Sexuality and Gender

Chapter-at-a-Glance	185
What's New	186
Learning Objective Questions	187
Chapter Overview	188
Key Terms	189
Annotated Lecture Outline	
A. What Makes a Male, a Male and a Female, a Female?	189
B. Gender-Role Development	190
C. Gender Differences: Fact or Myth?	190
D. Sexual Attitudes and Behavior	191
E. Sexual Orientation	192
F. Sexual Dysfunctions	193
G. Sexually Transmitted Diseases: The Price of Casual Sex	194

Chapter 13 Personality Theory and Assessment

Chapter-at-a-Glance	195
What's New	196
Learning Objective Questions	197
Chapter Overview	198
Key Terms	199

Annotated Lecture Outline
- A. Sigmund Freud and Psychoanalysis — 199
- B. The Neo-Freudians — 202
- C. Trait Theories — 203
- D. Learning Theories and Personality — 205
- E. Humanistic Personality Theories — 206
- F. Personality: Is It in the Genes? — 208
- G. Personality Assessment — 208

Chapter 14 Health and Stress

- Chapter-at-a-Glance — 211
- What's New — 212
- Learning Objective Questions — 212
- Chapter Overview — 213
- Key Terms — 214
- Annotated Lecture Outline
  - A. Two Approaches to Health and Illness — 214
  - B. Theories of Stress — 215
  - C. Sources of Stress: The Common and the Extreme — 215
  - D. Coping with Stress — 217
  - E. Evaluating Life Stress: Major Life Changes, Hassles, and Uplifts — 217
  - F. Health and Disease — 219
  - G. Your Lifestyle and Your Health — 221

Chapter 15 Psychological Disorders

- Chapter-at-a-Glance — 223
- What's New — 224
- Learning Objective Questions — 225
- Chapter Overview — 225
- Key Terms — 226
- Annotated Lecture Outline
  - A. What Is Abnormal — 227
  - B. Schizophrenia — 230
  - C. Mood Disorders — 233
  - D. Anxiety Disorders: When Anxiety Is Extreme — 235
  - E. Somatoform and Dissociative Disorders — 237
  - F. Other Psychological Disorders — 238

Chapter 16 Therapies

Chapter-at-a-Glance		239
What's New		240
Learning Objective Questions		240
Chapter Overview		241
Key Terms		242
Annotated Lecture Outline		
A.	Insight Therapies	242
B.	Behavior Therapy: Unlearning the Old, Learning the New	245
C.	Cognitive Therapies: It's the Thought That Counts	248
D.	The Biological Therapies	249
E.	Therapies and Therapists: Many Choices	250

Chapter 17 Social Psychology

Chapter-at-a-Glance		253
What's New		255
Learning Objective Questions		255
Chapter Overview		256
Key Terms		257
Annotated Lecture Outline		
A.	Introduction to Social Psychology	257
B.	Social Perception	258
C.	Attraction	260
D.	Conformity, Obedience, and Compliance	262
E.	Group Influence	263
F.	Attitudes and Attitude Change	265
G.	Prejudice and Discrimination	266
H.	Prosocial Behavior: Behavior That Benefits Others	268
I.	Aggression: Intentionally Harming Others	269

Appendix: Statistical Methods

Appendix-At-A-Glance		273
Annotated Lecture Outline		
A.	Descriptive Statistics	273
B.	Inferential Statistics	277

Part Three: Handout and Transparency Masters

Handout Masters

- Introduction (INTRO)
- Research Methods (METHODS)
- Biology (BIO)
- Sensation and Perception (S&P)
- Consciousness (CONSC)
- Learning (LEARN)
- Memory (MEM)
- Cognition (COG)
- Language (LANG)
- Intelligence (INTELL)
- Development (DEV)
- Motivation (MOT)
- Emotions (EMOT)
- Health, Stress, and Coping (HEALTH)
- Personality (PERS)
- Abnormal (ABN)
- Therapy (THER)
- Social (SOCIAL)
- Statistics (STAT)
- Diversity Topics (DT)

Preface

The goal of the *Instructor's Resource Manual to Accompany Wood and Wood's The World of Psychology,* Third Edition, is to provide an integrated, comprehensive manual for the instructor. The manual's arrangement of information, visual material, and student-focused activities is a great support for both the seasoned professor and the new instructor.

Part One contains introductory material. In the introductory section, Joyce Bishop, of Golden West College, has prepared suggestions for teaching in a multicultural setting called "Teaching Strategies for the Multicultural Classroom." The introduction also includes a complete list of transparencies provided by Allyn and Bacon, the list of Videodisc topics and the Digital Image Archive list.

As a companion to the *Annotated Instructor's Manual* of Wood and Wood's *The World of Psychology,* Third Edition, this manual includes the Chapter-at-a-Glance, What's New, Learning Objectives Questions, Chapter Overview, Key Terms, and the Annotated Lecture Outline for each chapter.

Part Two, the Chapter Resources feature, is the core of this manual. At the heart of the Chapter Resources is the Chapter-at-a-Glance which correlates and integrates all the available instructional ideas and supplemental materials. The Chapter-at-a-Glance provides a quick reference by showing each item in its place in the chapter outline. As you use the Chapter-at-a-Glance, you will find that it helps you organize the following materials: Classroom Demonstrations, Lecture Examples, Critical Thinking Opportunities, Critical Thinking Forum, Learning Objectives, Test Questions, Transparencies, Digital Image Archive PowerPoint Slides, and Internet Web Sites.

The second major section of the Chapter Resources is the Annotated Lecture Outline Section for each chapter, which includes classroom demonstrations, with appropriate handouts, lecture examples, diversity topics ,and student chalkboards all arranged according to the major headings of each chapter. The following is a detailed description of the materials contained in the Annotated Lecture Outline:

Classroom Demonstrations and Handouts: Lists each demonstration and student chalkboard. The demonstration includes the description of the activity and how to use it in class. Information contained in these demonstrations are arranged by objectives, materials, procedures and conclusions. Many of these demonstrations are updated and referenced to the Internet. The Internet references will allow the instructor to explore each topic in more detail and in terms of the latest information available.

Lecture Examples: Contains the full version of the lecture example ready to use in the classroom. It contains both bibliographic references and a new feature, Internet references. The Internet references will allow the instructor to explore each topic in more detail and in terms of the latest information available.

Student Chalkboards: Their primary role is to help the student organize ideas and notes.

Diversity Topics: Text of the diversity topic feature, with bibliographic and Internet references, is supplied. These materials were developed by David Matsumoto, of San Francisco State University.

Critical Thinking Section: Text of critical thinking forum and critical thinking opportunity features.

Part Three of the Instructor's Resource Manual contains the Handout Masters arranged according to topics. Each topic includes the Student Chalkboard and the Handouts for the Demonstrations.

As you plan your term, you may want to browse through the Handout and Transparency masters. There are 175 masters for Student Chalkboards and Demonstrations. Advanced planning will be necessary to select the activities appropriate for your course. The Student Chalkboards can be used in several ways, but their primary role is to help the students organize ideas and notes.

Some of the material from the Second Edition *Instructor's Resource Manual* by Mark Garrison of Kentucky State University has been retained or modified for this edition. I hope that these resources help make your class more enjoyable to teach, and more exciting and informative for the students.

Fred W. Whitford
Montana State University
Whitford@montana.edu

Part One

Introduction

TEACHING STRATEGIES FOR THE MULTICULTURAL CLASSROOM

Joyce Bishop, Golden West College

Course Design

- A written schedule of assignments and exams provides a visual backup for language disadvantaged students.
- Key terms written on the chalkboard or overhead transparency will be more easily understood by students than those terms only given orally. This also helps students focus on what is most important in the material, since many cultures emphasize pure memorization of material rather than analysis and application.
- Variety in class activities gives students of various learning styles and backgrounds the opportunity to experience and master the information in many ways. Infusing material on effective study skills throughout the course can be very useful to disadvantaged students.
- Study worksheets for exams (such as the student chalkboard exercises provided in the Instructor's Resource Manual) help students focus on what is most important, especially since some students have no prior exposure to psychological concepts.

Teaching Methods

- Visual aids (such as the blackboard, overhead transparencies, videos, demonstrations, and handouts) reinforce verbal presentations for students with limited language skills in English.
- Content relevant to other cultures may be introduced in each chapter (see the chart of multicultural discussion topics which follows).
- Student participation can increase the relevance of material in the course:
    - Journal writing or keeping a scrapbook
    - Demonstrations that involve students
    - Classroom discussions
    - Small group discussions (notes may be taken on transparencies and shared with the rest of the class)
    - Personal anecdotes to illustrate content may be written in a journal, shared in a dyad, or shared with the whole class. Your class examples can be multicultural.
- Limit use of language and examples that are strongly dependent on American culture or a deep understanding of English unless thorough explanations are included. The following are just a few examples of idioms or colloquialisms with which many students express difficulty:

umbrella of psychology	to get high	stems from
coined the term	narrow brush with	pay dearly
enhanced environment	underpinnings	Monopoly
tide has turned	absenteeism	off the wall
rollercoaster history	at odds with	the "in" thing to do

Testing Methods

•During an exam, allow students to quietly ask for a word to be explained. Let them know in advance that you may have to decline their request if the word in question is a technical term they should have learned from the text or lecture. Write the word and definition on the chalkboard or overhead so that all students can benefit from the information and do not sense any favoritism.
•Proofread your exam prior to administration to eliminate any difficult-to understand, non-essential terms.

Outside Resources

•If your campus has a tutoring center, recruit students from various cultures to tutor. Make your students aware of this resource.
•Make contact with campus or community intercultural organizations. These can provide ideas for discussion questions, guest speakers, and perhaps mentors for your students.
•Develop a support system of counselors and psychologists from many cultures.

EXAMPLES OF MULTICULTURAL DISCUSSION TOPICS

1. Introduction to Psychology	Who provides emotional support and counseling in other cultures? How is psychology viewed in other cultures?
2. Biology and Behavior	Are medications used to treat depression in other countries?
3. Sensation and Perception	In what ways is beauty perceived differently in other countries?
4. States of Consciousness	How are dreams viewed in various cultures?
5. Learning	Describe what school was like in your native country.
6. Memory	Describe memory techniques used in your country.
7. Cognition and Language	In your native culture, how would you tell someone that you are angry with him or her?
8. Intelligence and Creativity	How do different cultures define intelligence?
9. Child Development	How is parenting different in your native culture?
10. Adolescence and Adulthood	Describe the adolescent years in your culture. How is aging viewed?
11. Motivation and Emotion	What are the most motivating things or activities in your culture? Are emotions expressed openly in your native culture?
12. Human Sexuality and Gender	Why might psychological testing be unfair to people of various cultures?
13. Personality Theory and Assessment	List positive and negative personality traits as viewed in your native culture.
14. Health and Stress	What methods of coping are used in your native culture?
15. Psychological Disorders	How are psychological disorders viewed in your native culture?
16. Therapies	How are psychological disorders treated in various cultures?
17 Social Psychology	Describe authority within a family in your native culture.

TRANSPARENCIES

ALLYN AND BACON TRANSPARENCY LIST FOR INTRODUCTORY PSYCHOLOGY

RESEARCH METHODS

METHODS 1 Comparison Between Cross-Sectional and Longitudinal Research (Part I)
METHODS 2 Comparison Between Cross-Sectional and Longitudinal Research (Part II)
METHODS 3 Correlations Do Not Show Causation
METHODS 4 The Hawthorne Project: Some Surprising Results

BIOLOGY

BIO 1	A Stereotaxic Apparatus
BIO 2	The Functions of the Parasympathetic and Sympathetic Nervous System (ANS)
BIO 3	The Human Nervous System
BIO 4	Major Subdivisions of the Human Nervous System (Part I)
BIO 5	Major Subdivisions of the Human Nervous System (Part II)
BIO 6	The Functions of Afferent and Efferent Neurons
BIO 7	The Basic Structure of Neurons
BIO 8	The Action Potential: How Neurons Fire
BIO 9	Synaptic Transmission
BIO 10	Neurotransmitters That Excite or Inhibit the Postsynaptic Neuron
BIO 11	Synapses Between Several Neurons
BIO 12	Characteristic Electrical Activity Patterns in the EEG's of Healthy Humans in Different States of Excitation
BIO 13	Computerized Axial Tomography (CAT Scan)
BIO 14	The Twelve Cranial Nerves
BIO 15	The Three Major Sections of the Brain
BIO 16	The Divisions of the Brain Stem
BIO 17	The Four Lobes of the Cerebral Cortex
BIO 18	The Primary Sensory and Motor Areas of the Brain
BIO 19	The Seven Components of the Wernicke-Geschwind Model
BIO 20	How the Wernicke-Geschwind Model Works
BIO 21	Wernicke's Area and Broca's Area in Human Speech
BIO 22	The Split-brain Operation
BIO 23	Lateralization of Brain Functioning
BIO 24	Identification of an Object in Response to an Olfactory Stimulus by a Person with a Split-brain
BIO 25	The Pituitary Gland
BIO 26	The Endocrine Glands

BIO 27	The Major Endocrine Glands, the Hormones they Secrete, and their Principal Function (Part I)
BIO 28	The Major Endocrine Glands, the Hormones they Secrete, and their Principal Function (Part II)
BIO 29	Brain Activity During Stages of Sleep

SENSATION AND PERCEPTION

S&P 1	A Traditional Model of Sensory System Organization
S&P 2	A Cross-Section of the Human Eye
S&P 3	The Receptive Field of "Simple" Cortical Cells
S&F 4	Major Components of the Visual System
S&P 5	Information from Each Eye Crosses at the Optic Chiasm
S&P 6	Transduction of Light into Neural Activity and the Transmission of Information to the Brain
S&P 7	The Densities of Rods and Cones Across the Retina
S&P 8	The Cells of the Retina
S&P 9	The Electromagnetic Spectrum
S&P 10	The Spectral Sensitivity Curve
S&P 11	The Muller-Lyer Illusion
S&P 12	The Wundt Illusion and the Poggendorf Illusion
S&P 13	The Ponzo Illusion and the Zollner Illusion
S&P 14	Laws of Perceptual Grouping
S&P 15	Examples of Top-down Processing
S&P 16	Illusory Contours
S&P 17	The Gestalt Principle of Proximity
S&P 18	Illusions: Errors in Perception of the Physical World
S&P 19	Twelve Sources of Information about an Object's Distance
S&P 20	Color Coding in the Retina
S&P 21	Psychological Responses to Various Sound Intensities
S&P 22	Responses to Sound Waves
S&P 23	Anatomy of the Auditory System
S&P 24	Papillae on the Surface of the Tongue: A Taste Bud
S&P 25	The Olfactory System
S&P 26	Sensory Receptors in Hairy Skin and in Hairless Skin
S&P 27	Muscle Spindles

LEARNING

LEARN 1	Halo Effects: Their Basic Nature
LEARN 2	Riskiness in Decision-Making
LEARN 3	A Comparison of the Effectiveness of Four Kinds of Stimulus, Presentation in Classical Conditioning
LEARN 4	Key Factors in Observational Learning

LEARN 5	Reinforcement-Affect Theory: Conditioned Feelings (Part I)	
LEARN 6	Reinforcement-Affect Theory: Conditioned Feelings (Part II)	
LEARN 7	Learned Helplessness-The Procedure by Anderson, Crowell, Cunningham, and Lupo	
LEARN 8	Pavlov's Classical Conditioning Experiment	
LEARN 9	Spontaneous Recovery	
LEARN 10	Types of Learning (Building Table)	

MEMORY

MEM 1	The Stroop Effect
MEM 2	The Articulatory Loop
MEM 3	Basic Memory Process
MEM 4	Short-Term Memory
MEM 5	Long-Term Memory
MEM 6	Model for Sensory/Short-Term/Long-Term Memory
MEM 7	Schemas and Memory Distortions
MEM 8	Sternberg's Triarchic Theory of Intelligence
MEM 9	Knowledge Needed to Produce Meaningful Speech

DEVELOPMENT

DEV 1	DNA's Double Helix Structure
DEV 2	The Journey of the Ovum Toward the Uterus
DEV 3	Critical Periods in Prenatal Development
DEV 4	Progress Through the Birth Canal During the First Two Stages of Labor
DEV 5	Dominant and Recessive Traits
DEV 6	Each Parent Contributes Half of a Child's Genetic Material
DEV 7	Milestones in Motor Development (Part I)
DEV 8	Milestones in Motor Development (Part II)
DEV 9	Visual Scanning of Simple and Complex Targets by Young Infants
DEV 10	The Procedure and Results of the Experiment by Watson and Ramey
DEV 11	Children's Perception of Conservation of Liquid
DEV 12	Children's Perception of Conservation of Mass
DEV 13	Assimilation and Accommodation in Cognitive Development
DEV 14	Viewing Box for Newborns (Fantz)
DEV 15	Aging and Physical Decline
DEV 16	Differentiation and Development of the External Genitalia
DEV 17	The Genitourinary System
DEV 18	A Nation Growing Older
DEV 19	Major Changes in Important Domains of Adult Functioning (Building Table)

MOTIVATION, EMOTION, AND STRESS

MOTIV 1	The Components of Motivation
MOTIV 2	The Metabolic Pathways Used When the Digestive System Contains Food and When It Is Empty
MOTIV 3	Self-Esteem and Attributions for Successes and Failures
MOTIV 4	Social Facilitation: A Drive Theory Approach
MOTIV 5	Mayer's Glucostatic Hypothesis
MOTIV 6	Maslow's Hierarchy of Needs
MOTIV 7	Discounting and Augmenting: Two Basic Principles of Causal Attribution
MOTIV 8	Kelley's Theory of Causal Attribution
MOTIV 9	Drive, Expectancy, Cognitive, and Humanistic Theories of Motivation

EMOTIONS

EMOT 1	Comparison: Cannon and James-Lange Theories
EMOT 2	Schachter-Singer Theory of Emotion
EMOT 3	Media Violence: Mechanisms Underlying Its Affects

HEALTH, STRESS, AND COPING

HEALTH 1	Sources of Work-Related Stress
HEALTH 2	Physiological Reactions to Stress
HEALTH 3	Optimists and Pessimists: Contrasting Strategies for Coping with Stress
HEALTH 4	Burnout: An Overview
HEALTH 5	Fighting the Effects of Stress: Hardiness and Fitness

PERSONALITY, ABNORMAL, AND THERAPY

PERS 1	Schematic Summary of Trait Theories of Personality
PERS 2	TAT Measurement of Four Groups' Need to Achieve After Performance on a Test During Various Conditions
PERS 3	Example of a TAT Figure
PERS 4	Eysenck's Theory Illustrated for Two Factors
PERS 5	Freud's View of the Human Mind: The Mental Iceberg
PERS 6	Freud's Psychosexual Stages of Development
PERS 7	Kohlberg's Theory of Morality
PERS 8	The Stages of Piaget, Erikson, Levinson, and Freud
PERS 9	Psychoanalytic, Humanistic, Trait, Behavioral, and Cognitive Theories (Building Table)

ABNORMAL

ABN 1	Psychological Perspectives on Disorders
ABN 2	Obsessive-Compulsive Disorders
ABN 3	Depression: Control and Cognitive Perspective
ABN 4	Major Classifications in DSM-III-R
ABN 5	Some Common Forms of Object Phobias
ABN 6	The Risk of Developing a Schizophrenic Disorder

THERAPY

THER 1	The Goals of Psychoanalysis
THER 2	Summary of Key Issues in Psychoanalytic, Humanistic, Trait, Behavioral, and Cognitive Theories
THER 3	Primary Orientation of Clinical Psychologists in the APA

SOCIAL

SOCIAL 1	Sleeper Effects: The Disassociation Explanation
SOCIAL 2	Dissonance and Attitude Change
SOCIAL 3	Prejudice and the Processing of Social Information
SOCIAL 4	Prejudice as the Result of Intergroup Conflict
SOCIAL 5	Interpersonal Attraction: Liking and Disliking Other People
SOCIAL 6	The Three Components of Passionate Love
SOCIAL 7	To Help Or Not To Help: Prosocial Behavior as a Series of Decisions
SOCIAL 8	The Effects of Media Violence: Some Underlying Processes
SOCIAL 9	Escalation of Commitment: An Overview
SOCIAL 10	The Confirmation Bias and Theory in Social Psychology
SOCIAL 11	Group Decision-Making: Advantages and Disadvantages
SOCIAL 12	The Three Major Components of Attitudes
SOCIAL 13	The Tendency to Obey: Some Key Contributing Factors
SOCIAL 14	Results of Milgram's Studies of Obedience
SOCIAL 15	OB: Three Levels of Analysis

SOURCES

The following transparencies are from Baron and Byrne's *Social Psychology: Understanding Human Interaction*, Sixth Edition:

METHODS 4   (Source: Based on data from Roethusberger & Dickson, 1939.)
HEALTH 5   (Source: Based on data from Roth et al, 1989.)
SOCIAL 1   (Source: Based on suggestions by Kelman & Hovland, 1953.)
SOCIAL 2   (Source: Based on suggestions by Festinger, 1957.)
SOCIAL 7   (Source: Adapted by Byrne & Kelley, 1981.)
SOCIAL 14   (Source: Data from Milgram, 1963.)

The following transparencies are from Carlson's *The Physiology of Behavior*, Third Edition:

BIO 22   (From Fundamentals of Psychology by M. S. Gazzaniga, copyright 1973 by Harcourt Brace Jovanovich, Inc. Reprinted by the permission of the publisher.)

S&P 8   (Redrawn by permission of the Royal Society and the authors from Dowling, J.E., and Boycott, B. B., Proceedings of the Royal Society [London], 1966, Series B, 166, 80-111.)

S&P 15   (From McClelland, J. J., Rumelhart, D. E., and Hinton, G. E., in *Parallel Distributed Processing Vol. I: Foundations*, edited by D. E. Rumelhart, J. J. McClelland, and the PDP Research Group, Cambridge, MA: The MIT Press, 1986.)

PERS 4   (From Eysenck, H. *J. The Inequality of Man*, San Diego, CA: Edits Publishers, 1975.)

The following transparencies are from Lefton's *Psychology*, 6th Edition:

LEARN 9   (Data from Pavlov, 1927, p.58.)
DEV 14   (Source: Fantz, 1961; photo by David Linton.)
DEV 19   (Source: Adapted and modified from Korchin, 1975, table 14.2.)
THER 2   (Source: Adapted and modified from Korchin, 1976, table 14.2.)
THER 3   (Source: Based on data from Norcross, Prochaska, and Gallagher, 1989.)

The following transparencies are from Baron and Greenberg's *Behavior in Organizations: Understanding and Managing the Human Side of Work*, Third Edition:

HEALTH 2   (Source: Based on suggestions by Selye; Selye, H. [1976]. *Stress in Health and Disease.* Boston: Butterworths.)

HEALTH 3   (Source: Based on suggestions by Scheier, Weintraub, & Carver, 1986; Scheier, M. F., Weintraub, J. K., & Carver, C. S. [1986]. Coping with Stress: Divergent Strategies of Optimists and Pessimists. *Journal of Personality and Social Psychology*, 37, 1-11.)

Digital Image Archive

METHODS

PSMT001a: Comparison Between Cross-Sectional and Longitudinal Research (Part I)
PSMT001b: Comparison Between Cross-Sectional and Longitudinal Research (Part II)
PSMT002: Correlations Do Not Show Causation
PSMT003: Mean Intensity of Shock Chosen
PSMT004: Interpreting Scores by Means: The Normal Curve
PSMT005: What Psychologists Do

BIOLOGY

PSBI001: A Stereotaxic Apparatus
PSBI002: Autonomic Nervous System
PSBI003: Basic Divisions of the Nervous System
PSBI004a: Major Subdivisions of the Human Nervous System (Part I)
PSBI004b: Major Subdivisions of the Human Nervous System (Part II)
PSBI005: Functions of Afferent and Efferent Neurons
PSBI006: Neuron Structure
PSBI007: Action Potential: How Neurons Fire
PSBI008: Synaptic Transmission
PSBI009: Neurotransmitters That Excite or Inhibit Neurons
PSBI010: Synapses Between Several Neurons
PSBI011: The Synapse
PSBI012a: How Drugs Affect Synaptic Transmission (Part I)
PSBI012b: How Drugs Affect Synaptic Transmission (Part II)
PSBI013: Characteristic Electrical Activity in the EEG's of Healthy Humans in Different States of Excitement
PSBI014: Computerized Axial Tomography (CAT Scan)
PSBI015: The Twelve Cranial Nerves
PSBI016: Structures of the Brain
PSBI017: Principal Structures of the Limbic System
PSBI018: The Human Brain: A Cross-Section
PSBI019: The Four Lobes of the Cerebral Cortex
PSBI020: The Primary Sensory and Motor Areas of the Brain
PSBI021: Seven Components of the Wernicke-Geschwind Model
PSBI022: How the Wernicke-Geschwind Model Works
PSBI023: Wernicke's Area and Broca's Area in Human Speech
PSBI024: The Split-Brain Operation
PSBI02S: Lateralization of Brain Functioning
PSBI026: Two Views of the Cerebral Hemisphere
PSBI027: Testing a Split-Brain
PSBI028: The Pituitary Gland
PSBI029: The Endocrine Glands

PSBI030a: The Major Endocrine Glands, Their Hormones, and Their Principal Functions (Part I)
PSBI030b: The Major Endocrine Glands, Their Hormones, and Their Principal Functions (Part II)
PSBI031a: Brain Activity During Stages of Sleep (Part I)
PSBI031b: Brain Activity During Stages of Sleep (Part II)
PSBI032: Typical Sleep Cycles

SENSATION AND PERCEPTION

PSSP001: A Traditional Model of Sensory System Organization
PSSP002: A Cross-Section of the Human Eye
PSSP003: Major Components of the Visual System
PSSP004: Information from Each Eye Crosses at the Optic Chiasm
PSSP005: Transduction of Light into Neural Activity and the Transmission of Information to the Brain
PSSP006a: The Densities of Rods and Cones Across the Retina and the Blind Spot (Part I)
PSSP006b: The Densities of Rods and Cones Across the Retina and the Blind Spot (Part II)
PSSP007: The Cells of the Retina
PSSP008: The Electromagnetic Spectrum
PSSP009: The Spectral Sensitivity Curve
PSSP010: The Muller-Lyer Illusion
PSSP011: The Wundt Illusion and the Poggendorf Illusion
PSSP012: The Zollner Illusion and the Ponzo Illusion
PSSP013: The Ponzo Illusion
PSSP014: Laws of Perceptual Grouping
PSSP015: Examples of Top Down Processing
P55P016: The Gestalt Principle of Proximity
PSSP017: Illusions: Errors in Perception of the Physical World
PSSP018: Twelve Sources of Information About an Object's Distance
PSSP019a: Color Coding in the Retina (Part I)
PSSP019b: Color Coding in the Retina (Part II)
PSSP019c: Color Coding in the Retina (Part III)
PSSP020: Psychological Responses to Various Sound Intensities
PSSP021: Responses to Sound Waves
PS5P022: Frequency and Amplitude of Sound Waves
P55P023: The Human Ear
P5SP024: Papillae on the Surface of the Tongue: A Taste Bud
P55P025: The Olfactory System
PSSP026a: Sensory Receptors in Hairy Skin and in Hairless Skin (Part I)
PSSP026b: Sensory Receptors in Hairy Skin and in Hairless Skin (Part II)
PSSP027: Muscle Spindles

LEARNING

- PSLN001: Halo Effects: Their Basic Nature
- PSLN002: Riskiness in Decision-Making
- PSLN003a: A Comparison of the Effectiveness of Four Kinds of Stimulus Presentation in Classical Conditioning (Part I)
- PSLN003b: A Comparison of the Effectiveness of Four Kinds of Stimulus Presentation in Classical Conditioning (Part II)
- PSLN004: Pavlov's Classical Conditioning
- PSLN005: Key Factors in Observational Learning
- PSLN006a: Reinforcement-Affect Theory: Conditioned Feelings (Part I)
- PSLN006b: Reinforcement-Affect Theory: Conditioned Feelings (Part II)
- PSLN007a: Learned Helplessness: An Experimental Procedure (Part I)
- PSLN007b: Learned Helplessness: An Experimental Procedure (Part II)
- PSLN008a: Four Basic Types of Reinforcement Schedules (Part I)
- PSLN008b: Four Basic Types of Reinforcement Schedules (Part II)
- PSLN009: Spontaneous Recovery
- PSLN010: Latent Learning
- PSLN011: Types of Learning

MEMORY

- PSME001: The Stroop Effect
- PSME002: The Articulatory Loop
- PSME003: Basic Memory Process
- PSME004: The Three Memory Systems
- PSME005: Short-Term Memory: A Traditional View
- PSME006: Short-Term Memory: Working Memory View
- PSME007: Long-Term Memory
- PSME008: Model for Sensory/Short-Term/Long-Term Memory
- PSME009: Schema Development
- PSME010: Sternberg's Triarchic Theory of Intelligence
- PSME011: Guilford's Structure of Intellect
- PSME012: Knowledge Needed to Produce Meaningful Speech
- PSME013: Retroactive and Proactive Interference

DEVELOPMENTAL

- PSDV001: The Journey of the Ovum Toward the Uterus
- PSDV002: Progress Through the Birth Canal During the First Stages of Labor
- PSDV003: Dominant and Recessive Traits
- PSDV004: Each Parent Contributes Half of a Child's Genetic Material
- PSDV005a: Milestones in Motor Development (Part I)
- PSDV005b: Milestones in Motor Development (Part II)
- PSDV006: The Procedure and Results of the Experiment by Watson and Ramey (1972)

PSDV007: Children's Perception of Conservation of Liquid
PSDV008: Children's Perception of Conservation of Mass
PSDV009a: Piaget's Stages of Cognitive Development (Part I)
PSDV009b: Piaget's Stages of Cognitive Development (Part II)
PSDV009c: Piaget's Stages of Cognitive Development (Part III)
PSDV009d: Piaget's Stages of Cognitive Development (Part IV)
PSDV010: Assimilation and Accommodation in Cognitive Development
PSDV011: Differentiation and Development of the External Genitalia
PSDV012: The Genitourinary System
PSDV013: Aging and Physical Decline
PSDV014: Age Differences in Mental Ability
PSDV015: A Nation Growing Older
PSDV016: Major Changes in Important Domains of Adult Functioning
PSDV017: Major Stages of Bereavement

MOTIVATION

PSMO001: The Drive Theory of Motivation
PSMO002: Overview of Food Metabolism
PSMO003: Mayer's Glucostatic Hypothesis
PSMO004: Self-Esteem and Attributions for Successes and Failures
PSMO005: Social Facilitation: A Drive Theory Approach
PSMO006: Maslow's Hierarchy of Needs
PSMO007: Discounting and Augmenting: Two Basic Principles of Causal Attribution
PSMO008: Kelley's Theory of Causal Attribution
PSMO009: Theories of Motivation

EMOTION

PSEM001: The James-Lange and Cannon-Bard Theories of Emotion
PSEM002: The Schachter-Singer Theory of Emotion
PSEM003: Sternberg's Triangular Theory of Love
PSEM004: Media Violence: Mechanisms Underlying its Effects

HEALTH, STRESS AND COPING

PSHL001: Sources of Work-Related Stress
PSHL002: Optimists and Pessimists: Contrasting Strategies for Coping with Stress
PSHL003: Effects of Stress: The Three Variables
PSRL004: Three Types of Conflict
PSHL005: Burnout: An Overview
PSHL006: Effect of Cognitive Appraisal
PSHL007: Developing a Stress Reduction Program

PERSONALITY

PSPR001:   Schematic Summary of Trait Theories of Personality
PSPR002:   Eysenk's Theory Illustrated for Two Factors
PSPR003:   Freud's View of the Human Mind
PSPR004:   Freud's Psychosexual Stages of Development
PSPR005:   Kohlberg's Theory of Morality
PSPR006:   The Stages of Piaget, Erikson, Levinson, and Freud
PSPR007:   Jung's Conception of Personality
PSPR008:   Rogers's View of Adjustment
PSPR009a: Theoretical Approaches to Understanding Personality (Part I)
PSPR009b: Theoretical Approaches to Understanding Personality (Part II)

ABNORMAL

PSAB001:   Abnormal Behavior: A Psychological Perspective
PSAB002:   Obsessive-Compulsive Disorders
PSAB003:   Depression: Control and Cognitive Perspectives
PSAB004:   Depression: Negative View of the Social World
PSAB005:   Lewinsohn's View of Depression
PSAB006:   Major Classifications in DSM-IV
PSAB007:   Some Common Forms of Object Phobias
PSAB008:   The Risk of Developing a Schizophrenic Disorder
PSAB009:   Bipolar Disorder
PSAB010:   Prevalence of Psychiatric Disorders

THERAPY

PSTH001:   The Goals of Psychoanalysis
PSTH002a: Approaches to Therapy (Part I)
PSTH002b: Approaches to Therapy (Part II)
PSTH003:   Primary Orientation of Clinical Psychologists in the APA
PSTH004:   Goals of Psychotherapy

SOCIAL PSYCHOLOGY

PSSC001:   Sleeper Effects: The Disassociation Explanation
PSSC002:   Cognitive Dissonance and Attitude Change
PSSC003:   Prejudice and the Processing of Social Information
PSSC004:   Prejudice as the Result of Intergroup Conflict
PSSC005a: Interpersonal Attraction: Liking and Disliking Other People (Part I)
PSSC005b: Interpersonal Attraction: Liking and Disliking Other People (Part II)
PSSC006:   The Three Components of Passionate Love
PSSC007:   To Help or Not to Help: Prosocial Behavior as a Series of Decisions
PSSC008:   The Effects of Media Violence: Some Underlying Processes
PSSC009:   Escalation of Commitment: An Overview
PSSC010:   The Confirmation Bias and Theory in Social Psychology
PSSC011:   Group Decision-Making: Advantages and Disadvantages

PSSC012:   The Three Major Components of Attitudes
PSSC013:   The Tendency to Obey: Some Key Contributing Factors
PSSC014:   Results of Milgram's Studies of Obedience
PSSC015:   Organizational Behavior: Three Levels of Analysis
P55C016:   Elaboration Likelihood Model
PSSC017a: Attributional Thinking (Part I)
PSSC017b: Attributional Thinking (Part II)
PSSC018:   Need Theory Versus Goal-Setting Theory
PSSC019a: Expectancy Theories (Part I)
PSSC019b: Expectancy Theories (Part II)
PSSC020a: Equity Theory (Part I)
PSSC020b: Equity Theory (Part 11)

VIDEODISC

Introductory Psychology Videodisc

Chapter	Introductory Psychology Videodisc I	Introductory Psychology Videodisc II	Introductory Psychology Videodisc III	Child Developmental Videodisc IV
1. Introduction to Psychology	Segment 1			
2. Biology and Behavior	Segments 2-4, 17	Segment 19	Segments 1, 5-13, 18, 19, 25-28	Segment 1
3. Sensation and Perception	Segments 5-7			
4. States of Consciousness	Segments 8-10		Segments 14-17	
5. Learning			Segment 2	Segment 8
6. Memory	Segments 11, 12		Segments 20-24	
7. Cognition and Language	Segment 3			
8. Intelligence and Creativity	Segments 13, 14			
9. Child Development	Segments 14, 15	Segment 21	Segments 3-11, 18, 19	Segments 2-6
10. Adolescence and Adulthood	Segments 4, 16, 17			
11. Motivation and Emotion		Segments 18, 19, 24		
12. Human Sexuality and Gender		Segment 20		
13. Personality Theory and Assessment		Segment 19		
14. Health and Stress		Segments 21-24		
15. Psychological Disorders		Segments 25-27		Segments 7, 9, 10
16. Therapies		Segments 28, 29		
17. Social Psychology		Segments 30, 31		

Part Two

Chapter Resources

1 Introduction to Psychology

Chapter-at-a-Glance

Chapter Outline	Instruction Outline	Multimedia
Psychology: An Introduction p. 4 Psychology: Science or Common Sense? • The Goals of Psychology • Critical Thinking: Thinking Like a Scientist	**Student Chalkboard** METHODS 1 **Demonstration** INTRO 1, 3, 4 **Critical Thinking Forum** 1.1 **Lecture Examples** 1.1 **Test Questions** 1-12	**Web Site** http://www.psych-web.com/ Many links to psychology sites
Descriptive Research Methods p. 7 Naturalistic Observation: Caught in the Act of Being Themselves • The Case Study Method: Studying a Few Subjects in Depth • Survey Research: The Art of Sampling and Questioning	**Demonstration** METHODS 1, 2 **Lecture Examples** 1.2-1.3, 1.4 **Learning Objectives** 1.1-1.6 **Test Questions** 13-28	**Web Site** http://www.indiana.edu/~gasser/experiments.html Causal relationships and experimental research
The Experimental Method: Searching for Causes p. 10 Independent and Dependent Variables • Experimental and Control Groups: The Same Except for the Treatment • Generalizing the Experimental Findings: Do the Findings Apply to Other Groups? • Potential Problems in Experimental Research • Advantages and Limitations of the Experimental Method	**Demonstration** METHODS 5 **Lecture Examples** 1.5, 1.6 **Critical Thinking Opportunities** 1.1-1.2 **Diversity Topics** 1.1-1.2 **Learning Objectives** 1.7-1.12 **Test Questions** 29-61	*Discovering Psychology: Understanding Research* **PsychScience** Scientific Inquiry **Transparencies** METHODS 4, SOCIAL 10 **Digital Image Archive** PSMT0001a&b **Web Site** http://www.york.ac.uk/depts/psych/www/etc/whatispsych.html A description of experimental psychology
Other Research Methods p. 15 The Correlational Method: Discovering Relationships, Not Causes • Psychological Tests: Assessing the Subject • Meta-analysis: Combining the Results of Many Studies	**Demonstration** METHODS 3, 4 **Learning Objectives** 1.13-1.15 **Test Questions** 62-79	**Transparency** INTRO 3 **Digital Image Archive** PSMT002 **Web Site** http://www.cas.lancs.ac.uk/glossary_v1.1/main.html Statistical concepts and terms

Chapter Outline	Instruction Outline	Multimedia
Participants in Psychological Research p. 19 Ethics in Research: Protecting the Participants • Human Participants in Psychological Research • Bias in Psychological Research • The Use of Animals in Research	**Demonstration** METHODS 6, 7, 8, 9 **Lecture Examples** 1.7-1.8, 1.1.9 **Critical Thinking Forum** 1.2 **Journal Entry** 1.1 **Diversity Topic** 1.3 **Learning Objectives** 1.16-1.18 **Test Questions** 80-86	Video Disc I Segment 1 Web Site http://methods.fullerton.edu/chapter3.html Ethics in Research
Exploring Psychology's Roots p. 22 Wilhelm Wundt: The Founding of Psychology • Titchener and Structuralism • Functionalism: The First American School of Psychology • Gestalt Psychology: The Whole Is More Than Just the Sum of Its Parts • Behaviorism: Never Mind the Mind • Psychoanalysis: It's What's Down Deep That Counts • Humanistic Psychology: Looking at Human Potential • Cognitive Psychology: Focusing on Mental Processes	**Student Chalkboard** INTRO 1 **Demonstration** INTRO 2, 5, 6 **Lecture Examples** 1.10, 1.11 **Critical Thinking Opportunity** 1.3 **Journal Entry** 1.2 **Learning Objectives** 1.19-1.26 **Test Questions** 87-117	*Psychology and Culture*: Ch. 18 Web Site http://paradigm.soci.brocku.ca/~lward/TIME/TIME_PSY.HTML Timetable of Significant Events in Psychology 1846 to 1935
Psychology Today p. 29 Modern Perspectives in Psychology: Current Views on Behavior and Thinking • Psychologists at Work	**Demonstration** INTRO 7, 8, 9 **Lecture Examples** 1.12-1.13, 1.14 **Diversity Topics** 1.4-1.6 **Learning Objectives** 1.27-1.28 **Test Questions** 118-135	Digital Image Archive PMST005 *Discovering Psychology: New Directions* *Discovering Psychology: Past, Present, and Promise* *Psychology and Culture*: Ch. 1-6 Web Site http://www.psych-web.com/resource/deptlist.htm A listing of psychology departments on the Internet

What's New in Chapter 1

New Content

- New text section on critical thinking—thinking like a scientist
- Updated demographics of diversity
- The animal rights controversy
- Role of cognitive psychology and neuroscience

Expanded Content

- The scientific method
- Survey research
- Experimental methods

Organizational Changes

- Ethics was moved to the forefront of the section on participants in psychological research.
- Gestalt psychology was moved to fall in a more appropriate chronological order in the history of psychological thought.

New Special Features

- New chapter opening vignette—McCaughey septuplets
- New *Try It!*
- Revised *Remember It's*

New Key Terms

- scientific method
- critical thinking
- neuroscience

Learning Objective Questions

1.1 What is the scientific method?
1.2 What are the four goals of psychology?
1.3 What is naturalistic observation, and what are some of its advantages and limitations?
1.4 What is the case study method, and for what purposes is it particularly well suited?
1.5 What are the methods and purposes of survey research?
1.6 What is a representative sample, and why is it essential in a survey?
1.7 What is the main advantage of the experimental method?
1.8 What is the difference between the independent variable and the dependent variable?
1.9 How do the experimental and control groups differ?
1.10 What is selection bias, and what technique do researchers use to control for it?
1.11 What is the placebo effect, and how do researchers control for it?
1.12 What is experimenter bias, and how is it controlled?
1.13 What is the correlational method, and when is it used?
1.14 What is a correlation coefficient?
1.15 What is meta-analysis?
1.16 What are some ethical guidelines governing the use of human participants in research?
1.17 Why are animals used in research?

1.18 What was Wundt's contribution to psychology?
1.19 What were the goals and method of structuralism, the first school of psychology?
1.20 What was the goal of the early school of psychology known as functionalism?
1.21 What is the emphasis of Gestalt psychology?
1.22 How did behaviorism differ from previous schools of psychology?
1.23 What is the role of the unconscious in psychoanalysis, Freud's approach to psychology?
1.24 What is the focus of humanistic psychology?
1.25 What is the focus of cognitive psychology?
1.26 What are seven major perspectives in psychology today?
1.27 What are some specialists in psychology, and in what settings are they employed?

CHAPTER OVERVIEW

Though the definition of psychology has changed over the years, first focusing on mental processes and then on observable behavior, we now define psychology as the scientific study of behavior and mental processes. Three types of research methods that make psychology scientific are described in this chapter:

(1) Descriptive methods include naturalistic observation, the case study method, and survey research. Surveys typically require the selection of a sample of possible participants from the broader population. The authors describe how a sample can be selected using a representative or random selection, how questionnaires are used, and why interviews often have an advantage because of the elaboration of details that is possible when a good rapport exists between the subject and the interviewer.

(2) The experimental method is the research method that meets the conditions necessary to establish that a cause-effect relationship exists. Experiments are meant to test a hypothesis about the causal relationship between the independent and dependent variables. If an experiment confirms the hypothesis, the next question that must be addressed is whether the results apply to other situations. Several problems can occur in an experiment that influence, or bias, the results. These problems include bias caused by how the control and experimental groups are chosen; the placebo effect, in which the subject behaves according to his or her expectations about the experiment; and experimenter bias, in which the experimenters' expectations influence the participants' responses. Sometimes the control used in an experiment makes the setting contrived or unnatural. Also, some experiments cannot be conducted on human participants because of ethical considerations.

(3) The correlational method is the research method that analyzes data in order to discover the relationships between variables (relationships other than cause-effect). The authors describe the correlation coefficient, distinguish between positive and negative correlations, and introduce the concept of strength. When a correlation is high, the presence or absence of one variable predicts the presence or absence of the other variable. Psychologists have used a variety of tests to collect data, and many of the tests are used in correlational research.

Research findings are verified by the replication of psychological studies. If the findings are valid, the replication of the study will yield similar results. When human participants are used in research, they are most often college students. This raises questions about the appropriateness of generalizations about behavior based on this limited population. Animals are also used in research. This has become controversial because of the perception of how research animals are treated. Concerns about the rights and welfare of participants in psychological studies have led to the development of specific research standards.

The history of psychology is reviewed. Wilhelm Wundt founded psychology as a formal academic discipline, and structuralism was the first formal school of thought in psychology. William James was very influential in the development of functionalism, the first American school of psychology. The development of the Gestalt school of psychology is then discussed. Behaviorism focused on the study of observable behavior, drawing first on the work of John B. Watson and then on the work of B. F. Skinner. The authors also describe the foundation of psychoanalysis and the emergence of humanistic psychology with its focus on the uniqueness of human beings and human abilities. A discussion of cognitive psychology concludes this section.

The contemporary perspectives that are predominant in psychology today are the biological perspective, the psychoanalytic perspective, the behavioral perspective, the cognitive perspective, and the humanistic perspective. Psychologists work in a variety of specialties, including clinical, counseling, physiological, experimental, developmental, educational, school, social, industrial, and organizational specialties. Their work includes research, counseling, consulting, and teaching.

Key Terms

applied research (p. 6)
basic research (p. 6)
behavioral perspective (p. 29)
behaviorism (p. 24)
biological perspective (p. 29)
case study (p. 8)
cognitive perspective (p. 29)
cognitive psychology (p. 26)
control group (p. 12)
correlation coefficient (p. 16)
correlational method (p. 16)
critical thinking (p. 6)
dependent variable (p. 11)
descriptive research methods (p. 7)

double-blind technique (p. 14)
evolutionary perspective (p. 30)
experimental group (p. 12)
experimental method (p. 10)
experimenter bias (p. 14)
functionalism (p. 23)
Gestalt psychology (p. 24)
humanistic perspective (p. 29)
humanistic psychology (p. 25)
hypothesis (p. 10)
independent variable (p. 11)
meta-analysis (p. 17)
naturalistic observation (p. 7)
placebo (p. 14)

placebo effect (p. 13)
population (p. 8)
psychoanalysis (p. 25)
psychoanalytic perspective (p. 29)
psychology (p. 5)
random assignment (p. 13)
reliability (p. 16)
replication (p. 17)
representative sample (p. 9)
sample (p. 9)
selection bias (p. 13)
sociocultural perspective (p. 30)
structuralism (p. 23)
survey (p. 8)
theory (p. 5)
validity (p. 16)

Annotated Lecture Outline

A. Psychology: An Introduction

Classroom Demonstrations and Handouts

Student Chalkboard METHODS 1: Strengths and Weaknesses of Research Methods

Demonstration INTRO 1: Previewing the Contents of the Course.

Objective: To think critically about our notions of psychology and behavior, and to "preview" the contents of the course.
Materials: None
Procedure: Ask students to form groups of no larger than four. Each group is to generate four questions about behavior that have been asked by the members of the group at some point in their lives. Each question is to be prefaced with the phrase "Inquiring minds want to know…" (e.g.: "Inquiring minds want to know why we dream"; "Inquiring minds want to know what is schizophrenia"). As each group presents their questions to the entire class, you may wish to rouse their interest and "tease" them with an answer. Point out the questions that will be fully answered in a particular chapter.
An alternative procedure is to direct students to develop answers, right or wrong, to these questions based upon their own experiences, logic, imagination, and preconceived notions. You may wish to follow this Demonstration with *Demonstration INTRO 4 Commonsense Psychology Quiz*. At the end of the semester, return these questions to the students and allow them to apply their new knowledge to correctly answer the questions. This will provide a chance to review and a sense of coming full circle.
Conclusions: Psychology as a science relies upon inquiring. However, it must go beyond mere inquiry to acquire knowledge using the various research tools described in the chapter. Let your students know that inquiry is a healthy trait, and should be expected from them throughout the semester. Use http://trochim.human.cornell.edu/ to help prepare this demonstration.

Demonstration INTRO 4: Commonsense Psychology Quiz

Objective: To demonstrate that commonsense is not a reliable source of information about behavior.
Materials: Commonsense Psychology Quiz (**Handout INTRO 4**)
Procedure: An important difference between science and non-science is the reliance upon scientific methods and techniques to test a hypothesis or theory before actually believing it. It is rare when a student walks into a class bearing no notions about psychology and science. This is a good icebreaker and allows students to evaluate their level of knowledge of psychology before getting into the heart of the course. There are various versions of the *Commonsense Psychology Quiz* floating around. Use **Handout INTRO 4**, which contains an item for each chapter in the text, or synthesize your own *Commonsense Psychology Quiz*. Note that under most conditions,

all the statements are false.
Conclusions: Psychologists cannot rely upon something as undependable as commonsense. You should mention to students the conditions under which the statements might be true (Brown, 1984).

Brown, L. T. (1984). Misconceptions about psychology aren't always what they seem. *Teaching of Psychology, 11*, 75-78.

Lamal, P. A. (1979). College students' common beliefs about psychology. *Teaching of Psychology, 6*, 155-158.

Ruble, R. (1986). Ambiguous psychological misconceptions. *Teaching of Psychology, 13*, 34-36.

Demonstration INTRO 3: Popular Press and Psychology

Objective: To demonstrate how the popular press can distort psychological research.
Materials: Have the student collect examples of psychology in the popular press—anything from tabloids to *People* or *Glamour* magazines will work.
Procedure: Have each student summarize one article of their own choosing in a short paper. Have each student use the information about the scientific method in Chapter 1 to describe the inaccuracies in their article. The students can present this material to the class, or you can collect the paper as homework.
Conclusions: The students will learn how easy it is to distort the science of psychology through misquoting, misrepresenting findings or misinterpretation of the results of psychological research.

Lecture Examples

Lecture Example 1.1: Perception of Psychology

During your first lecture, ask the students what they think psychology is all about and what they expect to learn in the course. As part of my first lecture, I display a very large image of Freud (available in the Digital Image Archive) as I describe psychology. During this first lecture, I find that many students' views are either very narrow or very broad.

B. Descriptive Research Methods

Classroom Demonstrations and Handouts

Demonstration METHODS 2: Representative Sample

Objective: To demonstrate the importance of representative samples in research as well as to show the effect of increasing sample size.
Materials: Sample Data Sheet (**Handout METHODS 2**)
Procedure: Identify a "population" (e.g., everyone sitting in the two rows next to the windows). Calculate the mean height of that population. Next, draw a sample of 10 percent from the

population and determine the mean height. Compare the two means. Increase the size of the sample gradually and note how the sample mean becomes a more accurate statistic of the population mean. Your last sample should be the entire population.
Conclusions: Psychologists rely heavily on inferential statistics and acknowledge the importance of representative samples and sample sizes.

Demonstration METHODS 1: Naturalistic Observation

Objective: To demonstrate naturalistic observation in the field.
Materials: Overhead projector
Procedure: Assign students into small groups of four or five students. Ask each to collect data on personal space in two distinct social situations. I send my students to the Student Union Building or other public areas on campus. Other social situations include a party, a bar, or another area where individuals are talking. Ask the students to estimate the distance that individuals stand apart when they talk in this public area, noting any differences between same sex and opposite sex individuals. Students should be encouraged to be creative in their data collection; for example, they could approach the participants with a yardstick, or they could count the number of tiles on the floor. Students will come up with their own ideas on the best methods of data collection.
Conclusions: Summarize each group's findings in terms of the mean distances individuals stand apart while talking. Break out the data by sex and situation. Discuss any problems the students encountered with this type of data collection. See http://panther.bsc.edu/~gspitts/descript.htm for more on descriptive research methods.

Lecture Examples

Lecture Example 1.2: Case Study of Phineas Gage

Phineas Gage's tragic railroad accident is a classic example of a case study. A portion of Gage's brain was destroyed when a spike traveled through his skull. Before the accident Gage was a good family man and conscientious worker; after the accident his work habits and personality changed dramatically. For more on Phineas Gage see http://www.mc.maricopa.edu/academic/cult_sci/anthro/origins/phineas.html.

Harlow, J. M. (1869). Recovery from the passage of an iron bar through the head. *Massachusetts Medical Society Publication, 2,* 329-347.

Lecture Example 1.3: Sex Surveys

The most famous sex survey ever conducted in the United States is the Kinsey report, which consists of two volumes *Sexual Behavior in the Human Male* (Kinsey, Pomeroy, & Martin, 1948) and *Sexual Behavior in the Human Female* (Kinsey, Pomeroy, Martin, & Gebhard, 1953). Over 10,000 men and women were interviewed in this survey, which revealed that behaviors considered abnormal or deviant—masturbation, oral sex, and homosexual activity—were far more common than most people had imagined. The Kinsey sample was flawed because it did not include African Americans, and it underrepresented the poor and the elderly. Consequently it provides a more accurate picture of the sexual behavior of white, middle class America in the 1940s and 1950s than of the whole population. Furthermore, Kinsey used all male interviewers with female subjects, and this might have served to inhibit the responses of some of the women. For information on the Kinsey Institute got to http://www.indiana.edu/~kinsey/mission.html.

Kinsey, A. C., Pomeroy, W. B., & Martin, C. E. (1948). *Sexual behavior in the human male.* Philadelphia: Saunders.

Kinsey, A. C., Pomeroy, W. B., Martin, C. E., & Gebhard, P. H. (1953). *Sexual behavior in the human female.* Philadelphia: Saunders.

Lecture Example 1.4: Laboratory versus Naturalistic Research

Students are often skeptical about the artificial nature of laboratory experimentation. This provides the opportunity during your lecture on this topic to compare and contrast laboratory and naturalistic research. Natural research avoids the problem of artificiality but sacrifices the controls necessary to establish cause-and-effect relationships. Good examples can be found in social psychological research. At this point you could also consider discussing quasi-experiments from social psychology. The laboratory allows the control needed for causality, but the findings are not certain to generalize to the real world. Explain to the students that the ideal situation would involve both laboratory and naturalistic research to establish causal relationships that work in the real world. Use http://panther.bsc.edu/~gspitts/ct1.htm#descript as a reference for laboratory versus naturalistic research.

C. The Experimental Method: Searching for Causes

Classroom Demonstrations and Handouts

Demonstration METHODS 5: Designing an Experiment

Objective: To design an experiment.
Materials: Designing an Experiment (**Handout METHODS 5**)
Procedure: Ask students to form groups. Each group should select a cliché or old wives' tale (e.g., "an apple a day...," "you can't teach an old dog..."). Have them construct a correctly worded hypothesis, specify the variables, identify the population, and differentiate the subject groups. You may extend this by asking how they would interpret the results if there were a difference between subject groups. In addition, the students should consider any ethical problems in the experiment. Expect dependent variables that are not operationally defined. For example, how would we go about measuring health in the case of "an apple a day..."?
Conclusions: Students should come to appreciate the difficulties and concerns of designing an experiment. Moreover, it is excellent practice in identifying the parts of the scientific method. Consider using Demonstration **METHODS 7** on writing informed consent forms as a logical extension of this activity. Use http://panther.bsc.edu/~gspitts/ct1.htm#descript for some critical thinking consideration for this demonstration.

Lecture Examples

Lecture Example 1.5: Independent and Dependent Variables

A study examining the effects of colorization of black-and-white movies is a simple yet effective case of the difference between independent and dependent variables and subject groups. Cutler et al. (1988) presented the movie *It's a Wonderful Life* to two subject groups. The experimental group saw the colorized version; the control group saw the original black-and-white version. The participants rated their version on humor, interest, action, and acting (dependent variables). (There was no significant difference!) Use http://www.oseda.missouri.edu/hickmanmillsc1.k12.mo.us/smithhale/staff/dickey/depindep.html as a reference.

Cutler, G. H., Dalseide, A. R., Plummer, V. H., & Bacon, C. R. (1988). Subjective reactions to a colorized movie vs its original black/white version. *Perceptual and Motor Skills, 66,* 677-678.

Lecture Example 1.6: The Placebo Effect

The power of suggestion is powerful indeed. Consider this example of the placebo effect: During the 1950s surgeons routinely performed a simple operation to relieve chest pain suffered by patients with angina pectoris. An amazing number of the patients—nearly 90 percent—reported relief from pain. An experimental study divided angina patients into two groups and informed them that they were going to have an operation that had a very high success rate in relieving angina pain. The actual surgery was performed on only half the patients. What was done with the other half would no longer be allowed according to ethical medical standards. The surgeons took the remaining half of the patients, put them under anesthesia, made the surgical incision in their chests, and then simply sewed them up again. When the patients awakened in the recovery room, they were told that the operation had been performed (Cherry, 1981). The patients who had had the sham surgery did even better than the patients who had undergone the real operation! Their pain had been relieved simply by the power of suggestion. Use http://cybertowers.com/selfhelp/articles/depress/antidprs.html in your preparation of this lecture example.

Cherry, L. (1981, September). Power of the empty pill. *Science Digest,* 60-67, 116.

Diversity Topics

Diversity Topic 1.1: Psychological Constructs

Can a psychological construct be measured in the same way across different cultures? Pick any construct in psychology (e.g., intelligence, self-concept, etc.) and bring a measure of it to class. Give students time to examine it and get some feel for the measure. Then engage in a discussion regarding whether they feel it actually measures that construct according to how they would define it.

Discussion/Description: The definition of many constructs we take for granted in American psychology can differ quite substantially in other cultures. For example, how we define intelligence may or may not be the same as how people of another culture will define it. Cultural differences in the conceptual definitions of a psychological construct will naturally lead to differences in the ways in which they should be measured appropriately across cultures. The methods of measuring constructs in American psychology and using these measurements in American research are developed from a particular way of defining those constructs. These definitions and their operationalizations are culture bound. Use http://trochim.human.cornell.edu/tutorial/young/eiweb2.htm as a reference.

Matsumoto, D. (1994). *Cultural influences on research methods and statistics.* Pacific Grove, CA: Brooks Cole Publishing Co.

Diversity Topic 1.2: Cultures and Acceptance of Science

Do people of different cultures accept the findings from scientific research to the same degree? Have students engage in a discussion/debate concerning the degree to which they personally allow findings from scientific research to alter their lives.

Discussion/Description: In the U.S., Americans are particularly well primed not only to believe in results of research, but to make changes in their lives according to findings from research. Changes in diet (e.g., lowering cholesterol intake), smoking, and lifestyle (e.g., increasing exercise) are just a few of the examples in American life that most people have engaged in because of the results of studies and the dissemination of those results. Still, people of other cultures and countries differ quite substantially in the degree to which they will believe the results from scientific studies in the first place, let alone make changes in their lives. This difference does not result from skepticism in these other cultures; rather, it is a difference in cultural attitudes and values is based in culture regarding research.

Matsumoto, D. (1994). *Cultural influences on research methods and statistics.* Pacific Grove, CA: Brooks Cole Publishing Co.

D. Other Research Methods

Classroom Demonstrations and Handouts

Demonstration METHODS 3: Classroom Correlation

Objective: To understand correlations.
Materials: Correlation (**Handout METHODS 3**)
Procedure: This is a relatively simple activity to perform in which the correlation between two variables is plotted. Select two variables that are innocuous and lend themselves to easy data collection. Two time-honored variables are students' heights and shoe sizes. Collect the data and plot the data on a graph. If you have time, you may want to compute Pearson's *r* on the data. Students record their hypothesized correlations on **Handout METHODS 3**.
Conclusions: Ask students to speculate on the relationship between height and shoe size. Stress

the fact that we cannot show cause and effect relationships with correlation.

Demonstration METHODS 4: Correlation versus Causation

Objective: To compare correlation and causation.
Materials: Correlation versus Causation (**Handout METHODS 4**)
Procedure: Ask students to provide a possible cause and effect relationship using the blank spaces in Part B, 1) on the handout (do not allow height and shoe size if you have used Demonstration **METHODS 3**). Students then should volunteer their causal relations. Other students can offer prior causes of both factors, thus illustrating that sometimes causation is only apparent. In Part B, 2) students are to provide additional correlated factors with a hypothesized third, possibly causal, factor, similar to that illustrated in Part A, 2).
Conclusions: Quite a number of apparent causal relations should be offered; some may be quite correct. Discuss the kind of research needed to demonstrate a causal relationship and how these intervening variables must be eliminated. Use http://stat.tamu.edu/stat30x/node42.html in your preparation of this demonstration.

E. Participants in Psychological Research

Classroom Demonstrations and Handouts

Demonstration METHODS 6: Research Ethics

Objective: To become familiar with ethical dilemmas related to research.
Materials: Judging the Ethics of Research (**Handout METHODS 6**)
Procedure: First, students are to read each of these vignettes and rate their responses on each. Then, have them form small groups to discuss the judgments they made. Each group should report its discussions and conclusions.
Conclusions: People may agree on some of these, but they may also disagree strongly with each other on some. To extend the activity, ask students to describe the principles by which they made their judgments. Use http://ccme-mac4.bsd.uchicago.edu/CCMEdocs/Research as a reference for this demonstration.

Demonstration METHODS 7: Informed Consent

Objective: To write an informed consent form and to become sensitive to the ethics of research.
Materials: Sample Informed Consent Form (**Handout METHODS 7**); instead you may wish to provide a copy of an informed consent form typically used at your institution
Procedure: After forming groups of no more than four, students are to write their own informed consent form. This activity is a great adjunct to Demonstration **METHODS 5** on designing experiments.
Conclusions: Psychologists are very concerned about the ethics of research. In general, participants must give informed consent before participating in research.

Demonstration METHODS 8: Animal Rights Committee

Objective: To enhance the sensitivity of students regarding the issue of animal rights and animal research.
Materials: Animal research vignettes (**Handout METHODS 8**)
Procedure: Students are asked to role-play members of an institutional animal rights committee and must decide whether or not to approve four research projects involving animals. Divide students into small groups. Each group represents a committee and must discuss the merits of each research proposal arriving at a general consensus. Consult Herzog (1990) for further details regarding this class activity as well as a summary of the two arguments (i.e., utilitarian versus rights).
Conclusions: According to Herzog, each vignette offers a different perspective on the issue of using animal research. Through this activity, your students will learn that there are no easy answers to this controversy. For the radical side of this issue look at http://www.envirolink.org/arrs/peta/.

Herzog, Harold. (1990). Discussing animal rights and animal research in the classroom, *Teaching of Psychology, 17*, 90-94.

Demonstration METHODS 9: Animal Resource Center

Objective: To enhance the sensitivity of students regarding the issue of animal rights and animal research.
Materials: Permission to tour animal resource center
Procedure: If possible, take your class (if small enough) on a tour of the animal resource center on your campus. If you have a large class, perhaps the laboratory or recitation sections could take the tour. As an alternative, allow students to sign up for extra credit for this tour.
Conclusions: Students will gain an appreciation for the animals' care and the procedures that are imposed for humane treatment.

Lecture Examples

Lecture Example 1.7: Ethical Issues

An important consideration for psychologists is the ethical treatment of research participants. There are many potential problems in research, such as deception and invasion of privacy, especially in studies using naturalistic observation. Let students generate other ethical issues; point out that it is the task of science to balance its own needs to collect data with the rights of participants. Supplement your lecture with a discourse on the ethical guidelines set down by the American Psychological Association (APA). Ask your students whether these principles are too liberal or too conservative. Are psychologists held to a higher standard than other professionals (e.g., lawyers, stockbrokers, clergy) are? You could also tie in the use of animals in research. Go to http://www.buffalo.edu/~raulin/apaethic.html for more information about ethical issue with human research participants.

Lecture Example 1.8: APA Research Guidelines

Bring to class a copy of the American Psychological Association's (APA) guidelines for research and share a few of them with your students. Occasionally the APA publishes a list of members who have been sanctioned for violation of these guidelines; bring this list and read aloud an example or two. It is important for students to understand that psychology, as a profession and as a science, is very dedicated and sensitive to ethical issues. For more information on the use of human participants in research go to http://www.buffalo.edu/~raulin/apaethic.html.

Lecture Example 1.9: Ethical Issues of Control

Students will probably be sensitive to the issue of control as a goal of psychology. They often believe it involves the control of their own behavior. They will probably be quite accepting of control in other sciences. In your lectures on this topic, point out that control in psychology is not a bad goal. People are constantly engaging in behaviors designed to control the behaviors of others (teaching, advertising, compliments, increasing production, or self-promotion). A similar goal of many types of therapy is to help individuals institute control in their lives.

Diversity Topic

Diversity Topic 1.3: Psychologists Views

How do people of different cultural backgrounds view psychologists? For the most part, psychology has become a well-accepted profession in the U.S. Is this true in other cultures and countries as well? Have students engage in a discussion about how they view psychology as a profession. Make a special attempt to gather information from people who have experienced living in other cultures.
Discussion/Description: Psychology is a well-accepted profession in the U.S. In some areas of the country, it is almost fashionable to have your own psychologist! Still, psychology as a profession does not enjoy the same privileges of acceptance in many other countries and cultures. This lack of recognition and acceptance manifests difficulties not only in the study of psychology, but also in the serious consideration of psychology as a career. A discussion of these issues may be informative to many students in the U.S. who do not see the world, and psychology, in this manner.

F. Exploring Psychology's Roots

Classroom Demonstrations and Handouts

Student Chalkboard INTRO 1: Perspectives in Psychology

Demonstration INTRO 2: Introspection

Objective: To experience the shortcomings of introspection.
Materials: Any object (e.g., piece of paper, watch, pencil, candy) that can be held, seen, or otherwise experienced
Procedure: Ask students to use introspection, Wundt's technique to "measure" conscious experience. Have them either hold an object or look at an object. Ask for a report of their sensation or experience of the object.
Conclusions: Since descriptions of the object do not count, point out the obvious flaws of this approach and note that these flaws led to the demise of structuralism. For a downloadable picture of Wundt see http://www.psy.kuleuven.ac.be/labexp/wundt.html.

Demonstration INTRO 5: Early Psychologists: Role Playing

Objective: To understand early psychologists.
Materials: None
Procedure: Ask students to form small groups of three to five students. To each group assign one early psychologist—Wundt, James, or any others that you cover in your lectures. Ask students to research the individuals in the library and on the Internet in order to find as much information as possible. Then ask the groups to appoint one individual to role-play the psychologists. Have this person be prepared to answer questions from the class and to discuss his or her philosophy.
Conclusions: This longer, term project will allow the students to investigate an historical psychologist in depth and try to understand how this individual conducted research. For more on early psychologists see http://lonestar.texas.net/~jgr/Wundt.htm.

Demonstration INTRO 6: Today in the History of Psychology

Objective: To explore the history of psychology.
Materials: Internet access
Procedure: Go to http://www.cwu.edu/~warren/today.html and explore three different dates in the history of psychology. This site will allow the individual to explore dates that are relevant to the individual, such as a birthday, wedding day, or graduation day.
Conclusions: Have each student investigate this site and prepare to discuss the historical figures that were born on their favorite days. Lead a discussion using the following two questions: Which of the many individuals on your favorite day was the most significant? Which of the many individuals on your favorite day was the most interesting? This demonstration will allow the students to begin to see the common threads that are laced throughout the history of psychology.

Lecture Examples

Lecture Example 1.10: Structuralism

Preface your discussion of structuralism with a question on the basic structure of a fireplace (bricks), a song (notes), an ocean beach (sand), a book (words), or words (letters). Explain that Wundt was attempting to ascertain the same thing, but for consciousness.

If Wundt held a yellow pencil before your eyes and asked you to describe what you see—your conscious experience of the event—he would not expect you to say, "I see a pencil." Wundt taught that an immediate experience is not according to the object's use or function (the pencil), but instead is the experience of a slender, cylindrical object that is yellow and has a sharp point. The immediate experience would also include any emotional reactions to the pencil and any other images it evoked. How could Wundt study conscious experience scientifically?

When we look at an apple, we see an apple, not a round object with a red hue, which may be polished to a high gloss, and is edible. Furthermore, we do not introspect each time we take a step, put on a coat, or open a door. We just do it. Use http://spsp.clarion.edu/history/Structuralism.html as a reference for this lecture example.

Lecture Example 1.11: Behaviorism and the Discipline of Psychology

Behaviorism both narrowed and extended the field of psychology. It narrowed the field because all but observable, measurable behavior was eliminated. It extended the field because organisms other than human adults were studied. Animals cannot introspect, and neither can infants, young children, or the mentally impaired. But all living animals (including humans) behave, so their behavior could be studied. The behavioral approach has been referred to as a blackbox theory because its proponents do not speculate about what is going on within the organism; rather, they seek to explain behavior only in terms of stimulus and response. Use http://www.biozentrum.uni-wuerzburg.de/genetics/behavior/learning/behaviorism.html as an area to obtain more information on this topic.

G. Psychology Today

Classroom Demonstrations and Handouts

Demonstration INTRO 7: Critical Thinking—How Many Squares Are There?

Objective: To demonstrate critical thinking.
Materials: Critical Thinking Squares (**Handout INTRO 7**)
Procedure: As you are discussing critical thinking, present your students with **Handout INTRO 7**. Ask them how many squares they see. A typical response is 16. Request from your students a reevaluation of their answer. Are there more than 16 squares?
Conclusions: Critical thinking requires careful assessment and objective examination. Did your

students practice critical thinking? Use http://www.kcmetro.cc.mo.us/longview/ctac/psychexer1.htm as a resource for critical thinking materials.

Bell, J. (1991). A Note to the Student: Critical thinking: Taking a first look and then a second look. *Inside Psych: Exploring the News*. Needham Heights, MA: Allyn & Bacon.

Demonstration INTRO 8: Careers in Psychology

Objective: To allow students to explore career opportunities in psychology.
Materials: Internet access
Procedure: Go to http://www.psych-web.com/careers/index.htm and explore three different career choices in the field of psychology. The students will have the major areas of specialization in psychology from which to choose.
Conclusions: Have each student investigate this site and prepare to discuss his or her career choices in the next class meeting. Students will find that there are many career choices under the heading of psychology. Lead a discussion using the following questions: Which of the many types of career choices do you find the most interesting? Which specific career was the most interesting and why? After exploring this page, do you think you would like to choose psychology as a career?

Demonstration INTRO 9: Careers in Psychology II

Objective: To explore an alternative method to **INTRO 8** above to allow students to explore career opportunities in psychology.
Materials: Library access
Procedure: School that have limited access to the Internet can have students research the role of a particular psychological field of specialization such as school, industrial, counseling, developmental, community, clinical, forensic, health, academic, and other areas of psychological specialty, by interviewing an individual faculty member or member of the community.
Conclusions: This demonstration can also be a good starting point for using library resources as their primary source of materials. The students can prepare papers or make class presentations on the tasks performed by the individual, the training and experiences needed to enter the area, and other unique characteristics of the individual areas.

Lecture Examples

Lecture Example 1.12: Clinical Psychology in the Persian Gulf

Psychology can be applied in many settings, including the military. According to an article in *APA Monitor*, in early 1991, at the start of the Gulf War, there were about 370 military psychologists stationed in the Persian Gulf. These psychologists dealt with hundreds of serious psychological disturbances. In addition, workshops on stress management and posttraumatic stress disorder were conducted to help U.S. soldiers cope with the tension.

DeAngelis, T. (1991, February). "Role of psychologists in Gulf is demanding." *APA Monitor, 22,* 1, 19.

Lecture Example 1.13: Different Perspectives on Treating Anxiety

The differences in training and orientation among mental health professionals are apparent in the treatment of anxiety disorders. The psychologist might suggest relaxation training, the psychiatrist might prescribe Valium, and the psychoanalyst might examine unresolved childhood conflicts.

Lecture Example 1.14: Types of Psychologists

Play the game "Twenty Questions"; most students will know this game, although foreign students may need a short explanation. Tell students that you are thinking of a certain type of psychologist—this could range through any of the major areas of study. The students are to determine what type by asking you questions to which you can respond only "yes" or "no." Through this process, students are soon able to identify the characteristics that distinguish the various types of psychologists. Use http://gort.canisius.edu/canhp/departments/canpsych/employ.htm as a resource for your lecture on types of psychologists.

Diversity Topics

Diversity Topic 1.4: Defining the Scope of Psychology

Are these the areas about which psychology should be mostly concerned? Are there other areas that are equally or more important that are not described here? Have students engage in a discussion about these areas that define the scope of psychology. Challenge the students not only to defend their viewpoints, but also to discuss other ways of defining the scope of psychology, and to understand those other views as well.
Discussion/Description: The areas that describe the scope of psychology as defined here are bound generally to western psychology and, more particularly, to American psychology. They define what we believe are important to psychology. People of other cultures, however, will define psychology in different ways, which ultimately lead to a focus on different aspects of human functioning. One area of human functioning that is particularly important in the study of psychology across cultures is human social interaction. This receives little attention in the above description. The welfare of interrelationships is a prime concern of people of many different cultures, and this topic should arise in classroom discussion with a diversity of viewpoints.

Diversity Topic 1.5: Cross-Cultural Study

Have students design a simple cross-cultural study that compares any aspect of human behavior across cultural groups. Then engage in a discussion about the study, especially with regard to the samples and the measurement of the variables of interest.
Discussion/Description: This activity should demonstrate to the students the trials and tribulations of cross-cultural research. Two issues that are especially germane to consider in cross-cultural research are sampling and measurement equivalence (see previous annotation for discussion of measurement equivalence). With regard to sampling, cross-cultural researchers often need to be concerned with whether or not their samples are adequate representatives of their culture, and whether the samples themselves are equivalent. Engaging in this discussion will make

real for the students the inherent difficulties in conducting this type of research well.

Matsumoto, D. (1994). *Cultural influences on research methods and statistics.* Pacific Grove, CA: Brooks Cole Publishing Co.

Diversity Topic 1.6: Visiting Lecturer

Have a psychologist from a different country or culture come and give a lecture on what psychology is like in his or her own country or culture.
Discussion/Description: It is often very informative to have psychologists from other countries and cultures talk not only about their field of expertise in psychology, but also about what it is like to be a psychologist in their culture—to do psychological research, or to practice psychology as a therapist or as a consultant. These discussions are often informative about psychology in other cultures as are their knowledge about their content field of expertise.

2 Biology and Behavior

Chapter-at-a-Glance

Chapter Outline	Instruction Outline	Multimedia
The Neurons and the Neurotransmitters p. 38 The Neurons: Billions of Brain Cells • Neurotransmitters: The Chemical Messengers of the Brain • The Effects of Drugs on Neural Transmission • The Variety of Neurotransmitters • The Rate of Neural Firing and the Speed of the Impulse • Glial Cells: The Neurons' Helper Cells	**Student Chalkboard** BIO 1-3 **Demonstration** BIO 1 **Lecture Examples** 2.1, 2.3, 2.4 **Learning Objectives** 2.1-2.6 **Test Questions** 1-46	**Transparencies** BIO 7-11 **Video Disc I** Segment 3 **Video Disc II** Segment 19 **Digital Image Archive** PSBI005-012a&b **Web Site** http://www.csuchico.edu/psy/BioPsych/neurotransmission.html Tutorial on the basics of neurotransmission
The Central Nervous System p. 45 The Spinal Cord: An Extension of the Brain • The Brainstem: The Most Primitive Part of the Brain • The Cerebellum: A Must for Graceful Movement • The Thalamus: The Relay Station between Lower and Higher Brain Centers • The Hypothalamus: A Master Regulator • The Limbic System: Primitive Emotion and Memory	**Student Chalkboard** BIO 4,6 **Demonstration** BIO 2, 8, 9, 5 **Lecture Examples** 2.5, 2.6 **Learning Objectives** 2.7-2.12 **Test Questions** 47-67	**Transparencies:** BIO 3-5, 16 **Video Disc I** Segment 4 **Video Disc III** Segments 1, 2, 6-13, 25-28 **Digital Image Archive** PSBI017 **Web Site** http://www.med.harvard.edu/AANLIB/home.html The Whole Brain Atlas
The Cerebral Hemispheres p. 49 The Lobes of the Brain • Specialized Functions of the Left Hemisphere: Language, First and Foremost • Specialized Functions of the Right Hemisphere: The Leader in Visual-Spatial Tasks • The Split Brain: Separate Halves or Two Separate Brains?	**Lecture Examples** 2.7-2.8 **Diversity Topic** 2.1 **Learning Objectives** 2.13-2.20 **Demonstration** BIO 4, 6, 7, 10 **Lecture Examples** 2.2, 2.7, 2.8 **Critical Thinking Opportunity** 2.1 **Journal Entry** 2.1 **Learning Objectives** 2.18-2.20 **Test Questions** 68-104	*Discovering Psychology: The Behaving Brain* **Transparencies** BIO 15, 17 *Discovering Psychology: The Responsive Brain* **Transparencies** BIO 22-24 **Digital Image Archive** PSBI0024-027, 018-020 **Web Site** http://ezinfo.ucs.indiana.edu/~pietsch/split-brain.html Split Brain

Chapter Outline	Instruction Outline	Multimedia
Discovering the Brain's Mysteries p. 63 The EEG and Microelectrode • The CT Scan and Magnetic Resonance Imaging • The PET Scan, fMRI and Other Imaging Techniques	**Demonstration** BIO 11, 12 **Lecture Examples** 2.9-2.10 **Learning Objectives** 2.21-2.22 **Test Questions** 105-120	**Transparencies:** BIO 1, 12, 29 **Video Disc I** Segment 2 **Digital Image Archive** PSBI013 **Web Site** http://www.bic.mni.mcgill.ca/demos/ Brain Imaging
Brain Damage: Causes and Consequences p. 62 Stroke • Head Injury • Recovering from Brain Damage	**Learning Objectives** 2.23-2.24 **Lecture Examples** 2.11 **Test Questions** 121-124	**Video Disc I:** Segment 17 **Web Site** http://www.mbnet.mb.ca/scip/health/h&sfound.html Stroke
The Peripheral Nervous System p. 64	**Student Chalkboard** BIO 5 **Demonstration** BIO 3 **Journal Entry** 2.2 **Learning Objectives** 2.25-2.26 **Test Questions** 125-128	**Transparency** BIO 2 **Digital Image Archive** PSBI002 **Web Site** http://www.mic.ki.se/Diseases/c10.772.html Peripheral Nervous System
The Endocrine System p. 66	**Diversity Topic** 2.2 **Learning Objective** 2.27 **Test Questions** 129-135	**Transparencies** BIO 25-28 **Digital Image Archive** PSBI028-029, 030a&b **Web Site** http://www3.hmc.edu/~clewis/endocrine/endocrin.htm Describes the glands and functions of the endocrine system

What's New in Chapter 2

New Content

- The effects of drugs on neural transmission
- Neuromodulators
- "Runner's high"
- Multiple sclerosis
- Appearance of the cortex
- The cortex in musicians
- Functional MRI (fMRI)

Expanded Content

- The synapse
- Strokes

Organizational Changes

- Specialization of hemispheres has been incorporated under coverage of the hemispheres.

New Special Features

- Improved anatomical drawings
- Revised *Remember It's*

New Key Terms

- functional MRI (fMRI)

Learning Objective Questions

2.1   What is a neuron, and what are its three parts?
2.2   What is a synapse?
2.3   What is the action potential?
2.4   What are neurotransmitters, and what role do they play in the transmission of signals from one neuron to another?
2.5   What are some of the ways in which neurotransmitters affect our behavior, and what are some of the major neurotransmitters?
2.6   How can the body tell the difference between a very strong stimulus and a very weak stimulus?
2.7   Why is an intact spinal cord important to normal functioning?
2.8   What are the crucial functions handled by the brainstem?
2.9   What are the primary functions of the cerebellum?
2.10 What is the primary role of the thalamus?
2.11 What are some of the processes regulated by the hypothalamus?
2.12 What is the role of the limbic system?
2.13 What are the cerebral hemispheres, the corpus callosum, and the cerebral cortex?
2.14 What are some of the main areas within the frontal lobes, and what are their functions?
2.15 What are the primary functions of the parietal lobes in general and the somatosensory cortex in particular?
2.16 What are the primary functions of the occipital lobes in general and the primary visual cortex in particular?
2.17 What are some of the major areas within the temporal lobes, and what are their functions?
2.18 What are the specialized functions of the left hemisphere?

2.19 What are the specialized functions of the right hemisphere?
2.20 What is the significance of the split-brain operation?
2.21 What are some methods that researchers have used to learn about brain function?
2.22 What is the electroencephalogram (EEG), and what are three of the brain-wave patterns it reveals?
2.23 Why is a stroke so serious?
2.24 What must occur in the brain for there to be some recovery from brain damage?
2.25 What is the peripheral nervous system?
2.26 What are the roles of the sympathetic and parasympathetic nervous systems?
2.27 What is the endocrine system, and what are some of the glands within it?

Chapter Overview

All of our behavior is rooted in biological events, and this chapter examines the connections between biology and behavior. The activity of neurons is at the basis of all thought, feeling, and behavior, and the structure of the neuron is carefully described. The neural impulse involves a change in the electrical potential of the cell membrane. This impulse, called the action potential, causes a neuron to release neurotransmitters across the synaptic cleft, thus communicating to the next neuron. Neurotransmitters lock into receptor sites on the neuron, either stimulating or inhibiting the neuron, depending on the type of neurotransmitter and whether drugs are present. The rate of firing of the neuron conveys the critical information. Glial cells provide nutrients and serve other helping functions for neurons.

The central nervous system is composed of the spinal cord and the brain. The spinal cord descends from the brain and transmits messages between the brain and the peripheral nervous system. The authors provide a detailed description of the function of each part of the brain, the brainstem, the cerebellum, the thalamus, the hypothalamus, the limbic system, and the cerebral hemispheres (including the frontal, parietal, occipital, and temporal lobes).

The specialized functions of the hemispheres are described. Language and logical thought are associated with the left hemisphere, and emotions and visual-spatial tasks are associated with the right hemisphere. The authors examine issues and research relating to split-brain surgery and its implications about hemispheric specialization. They also examine the ways of recording and observing brain activity, including the EEG, the microelectrode, the CT scan, MRI, the PET scan and the fMRI.

Information about the brain is also gathered from cases of injury and damage to the brain. Strokes and head injuries can have serious consequences for brain function. An important role of psychology is the discovery of means to recover from brain damage.

The peripheral nervous system is composed of two parts, the somatic nervous system, responsible for muscle and sensory information, and the autonomic nervous system, responsible for the involuntary or automatic actions of body organs. The autonomic nervous system is divided into the sympathetic nervous system, which mobilizes resources for action, and the parasympathetic nervous system, which calms the body after activity.

The endocrine system is another communication system in the body, involving the release by glands of hormones, specific chemicals that influence bodily function. The pituitary gland, the thyroid gland, the adrenal glands, the pancreas, and the gonads all have important roles in the function of the body that in turn influence behavior.

Key Terms

acetylcholine (p. 42)
action potential (p. 39)
adrenal glands (p. 67)
alpha wave (p. 60)
amygdala (p. 48)
aphasia (p. 52)
association areas (p. 51)
axon (p. 38)
beta wave (p. 60)
brainstem (p. 46)
Broca's aphasia (p. 52)
Broca's area (p. 52)
cell body (p. 38)
central nervous system (p. 45)
cerebellum (p. 46)
cerebral cortex (p. 51)
cerebral hemispheres (p. 49)
cerebrum (p. 49)
corpus callosum (p. 49)
CT scan (p. 61)
delta wave (p. 60)
dendrites (p. 38)
dopamine (p. 42)
electroencephalogram
(EEG) (p. 60)
endocrine system (p. 67)
endorphins (p. 43)
fMRI (p. 61)
frontal lobes (p. 51)
glial cells (p. 44)
hippocampus (p. 48)
hormone (p. 67)
hypothalamus (p. 47)
lateralization (p. 55)
left hemisphere (p. 55)
limbic system (p. 48)
medulla (p. 46)
microelectrode (p. 60)
motor cortex (p. 51)
MRI (p. 61)
myelin sheath (p. 44)
neuron (p. 38)
neurotransmitter (p. 41)
norepinephrine (p. 42)
occipital lobes (p. 54)
parasympathetic nervous system (p. 65)
parietal lobes (p. 52)
peripheral nervous system (p. 64)
PET scan (p. 61)
pituitary gland (p. 67)
plasticity (p. 63)
primary auditory cortex (p. 54)
primary visual cortex (p. 54)
receptor site (p. 41)
resting potential (p. 39)
reticular formation (p. 46)
reuptake (p. 41)
right hemisphere (p. 56)
serotonin (p. 42)
somatosensory cortex (p. 52)
spinal cord (p. 45)
split-brain operation (p. 58)
stroke (p. 62)
sympathetic nervous system (p. 65)
synapse (p. 39)
temporal lobes (p. 54)
thalamus (p. 46)
Wernicke's aphasia (p. 54)
Wernicke's area (p. 54)

Annotated Lecture Outline

A. The Neurons and the Neurotransmitters

Classroom Demonstrations and Handouts

Student Chalkboard BIO 1: The Basic Structure of the Neuron

Student Chalkboard BIO 2: Transmission at the Synapse

Student Chalkboard BIO 3: Neurotransmitters

Demonstration BIO 1: Human Neuronal Chain

Objective: To illustrate that the transmission of messages in the nervous system is not instantaneous.
Materials: 20 students standing, facing forward, in a line; a stopwatch
Procedure: Ask the last student to tap either shoulder of the next person and each subsequent person to continue the process through the entire line, always using the same shoulder and never crossing the body (i.e., left hand to right shoulder). Use the stopwatch to time how long it takes for the last person to receive the stimulus.
Conclusions: Using the stopwatch, it becomes apparent that reacting to a stimulus and the transmission of messages do take time.

Harcum, E. R. (1988). Reaction time as a behavioral demonstration of neural mechanisms for a large introductory psychology class. *Teaching of Psychology, 15*, 208-209.

Lecture Examples

Lecture Example 2.1: Leading Off the Chapter

Only when there is damage (through stroke, disease, or brain trauma) do we realize the importance of the nervous system. If there is an example from your personal life that is apropos here, such as a family member with a neurological disease, consider sharing it with your students. Students may add their own stories as well, highlighting the importance of studying biology in a psychology class.

Lecture Example 2.3: Action Potential as a Stadium Wave

Use "The Wave," an activity at sport arenas, as an analogy for the action potential. Like "The Wave," the action potential travels the length of the neuron; the neuron doesn't experience the action potential all at once. To extend the analogy, mention that right after people stand up in "The Wave," they are somewhat tired and must recover (i.e., refractory period) to be prepared for the next go-round (i.e., action potential). Use http://fig.cox.miami.edu/Faculty/Tom/bil255/action_potential.html for a detailed discussion of the action potential.

Lecture Example 2.4: Acetylcholine and Serotonin

Acetylcholine (ACh) is a neurotransmitter that plays an important role in transmitting the electrical impulse from motor neurons to the skeletal muscles, enabling our muscles to contract. ACh is involved in a variety of functions, including "arousal, attention, and memory as well as a host of more specific motivated behaviors such as aggression, sexuality, and thirst" (Panksepp, 1986, p. 86). Its crucial role in the formation of memories can be seen in Alzheimer's patients, who have a deficiency in acetylcholine and suffer from severe memory loss (Mishkin & Appenzeller, 1987; Silberner, 1985). Use http://www.lfc.edu/~rigitjp/acetylcholine.html as a reference.

Serotonin is a neurotransmitter that inhibits behaviors ranging from feeding, play, and aggression to sexual and maternal behaviors, and its presence promotes sleep (Panksepp, 1986). Adequate levels of both serotonin and norepinephrine are related to positive feelings (Carlson, 1990), and a deficiency in the two has been linked to depression. A class of antidepressant drugs called tricyclics relieves the symptoms of depression in many of its victims by blocking the reuptake of these neurotransmitters, thus increasing their availability in the synapses. Use the site http://www.ed.uiuc.edu/COE/EDPSY/counseling/pa-drug/ssri.htm as a general reference.

Carlson, N. R. (1990). *Physiology of behavior* (4th ed.). Boston: Allyn and Bacon.

Mishkin, M., & Appenzeller, T. (1987). The anatomy of memory. *Scientific American, 25,* 680-89.

Panksepp, J. (1986). The neurochemistry of behavior. *Annual Review of Psychology, 37,* 77-107.

Silberner, J. (1985). Alzheimer's disease: Source searching. *Science News, 12,* 824.

B. The Central Nervous System

Classroom Demonstrations and Handouts

Student Chalkboard BIO 4: The Human Nervous System

Student Chalkboard BIO 6: The Human Brain (Limbic System and Brain Stem)

Demonstration BIO 2: The Biceps Stretch Reflex

Objective: To demonstrate a monosynaptic reflex.
Materials: Three or four textbooks; a volunteer
Procedure: To demonstrate the bicep's stretch reflex, ask someone to hold their forearms straight out in front of them with their elbows close to their body. Ask the subject to close their eyes. Next drop the textbooks on their arms. Their arms should dip then return to their original position.
Conclusions: The weight of the books stretches the bicep, and this ultimately activates the reflexive shortening of the bicep. The arms return to their horizontal position before the brain has realized what has happened. See http://www.umds.ac.uk/physiology/mcal/sreflex.html for more information.

Demonstration BIO 8: Neuroscience

Objective: To allow exploration of the field of neuroscience.
Materials: Internet access
Procedure: Go to http://weber.u.washington.edu/~chudler/ehceduc.html and explore three different neuroscience links. This is an extremely detailed site that consists of links for education and research. This site is large enough to spend several days exploring and is a must for anyone interested in the neuroscience field. Have students investigate this site and prepare to discuss their findings in the next class meeting.
Conclusions: Students will have discovered many different neuroscience links. Lead a discussion using the following questions: Which of the many types of links did you find the most interesting? Which specific area of the study of neuroscience was the most interesting and why? After exploring this page would you consider a career in the neurosciences?

Demonstration BIO 9: Human Brain

Objective: To expose students to the human brain.
Materials: A human brain from your department or the biology department on your campus; rubber gloves; paper towels; overhead transparencies of the brain
Procedure: If possible, obtain a human brain or as a second choice, a sheep brain. This brain can be in a bio-mount encased in plastic. If the brain is in formaldehyde and can be handled, bring rubber gloves and sufficient newspapers or paper towels to clean up. As you lecture on brain function and structure, point out the areas of the brain as you discuss them. Use overhead transparencies to accompany your lecture. At the end of the lecture, allow time for the students for explore the brain on their own. (Make sure you have enough rubber gloves.)
Conclusions: The students will have the opportunity to see that the brain structures are much more difficult to identify in a real brain. Additionally, students will be exposed to the colorful overhead transparencies, which can enhance your lecture. Use http://www.hbp.scripps.edu/Home.html as a reference to the Human Brain Project.

Demonstration BIO 5: Whole Brain Atlas

Objective: To allow the students to explore the brain on the Internet.
Materials: Internet access
Procedure: Go to http://www.med.harvard.edu/AANLIB/home.html. This site contains information, images, and QuickTime movies all related to the brain. Included is a discussion on the pathology of Alzheimer's disease as well as a complete reference to the brain. Have the students explore several of the links. Students could write a short summary of their experiences at this site and their understanding of these links.
Conclusions: After this assignment, be prepared for students' questions about the brain and the study of neuroscience.

Lecture Examples

Lecture Example 2.5: Monosynaptic Reflexes

The patellar reflex (knee jerk) is an example of a monosynaptic reflex because there is only one synapse in the reflex arc, which is composed of afferent and efferent neurons. The patellar reflex takes about 50 milliseconds from start to end. If the brain became involved, with sensory information going to the brain and then the motor message from the brain going to the muscle, the action would take about 200 milliseconds to complete. That's a long time in the world of reflexes. It would take longer for the same response to happen because the brain is multisynaptic, and transmission of neural information is more time-consuming in the brain compared to the monosynaptic reflex arc of the spinal cord. Consider using Demonstration **BIO 2** to illustrate a monosynaptic reflex. For a more detailed discussion see http://www.umds.ac.uk/physiology/mcal/sreflex.html.

Galluscio, E. H. (1990). *Biological psychology.* New York: Macmillan.

Lecture Example 2.6: The Hippocampus

Studies with animals have confirmed the role of the hippocampus in learning, and autopsies performed on patients suffering from Alzheimer's disease have revealed extensive damage to neurons in the hippocampus (Wolozin, 1986). A tragic experimental surgical procedure performed on a man known as H. M. provides the most dramatic evidence of the critical role the hippocampus plays in human memory. Brenda Milner (1972), who made an extensive study of H. M.'s case, reported that his general intelligence suffered not at all, and the information stored in his memory before the surgery was not affected either. But H. M. could no longer learn new information and store it in memory for later recall. He could not remember what he had said, done, read, or experienced from one day to the next. He would read the same magazines over and over, and each time the material was completely unfamiliar to him. H. M.'s memory was forever imprisoned in his past. Use http://www.medinfo.ufl.edu/year2/neuro/v11611.html as a reference for the hippocampus and memory.

Milner, B. (1972). Disorders of learning and memory after temporal lobe lesions in man. *Clinical Neurosurgery, 19,* 421-446.

Wolozin, B. L., Pruchnicki, A., Dickson, D. W., & Davies, P. (1986). A neuronal antigen in the brains of Alzheimer patients. *Science, 232,* 648-650.

C. The Cerebral Hemispheres

Classroom Demonstrations and Handouts

Demonstration BIO 4: A Tour of the Brain

Objective: To introduce the brain to students.
Materials: None
Procedure: Ornstein and Thompson (1984) write about a simple way to introduce the basic brain structures.

> Place your fingers on both sides of your head beneath the ear lobes. In the center of the space between your hands is the oldest part of the brain, the brain stem. Now, form your hands into fists. Each is about the size of one of the brain's hemispheres, and when both fists are joined at the heel of the hand they describe not only the approximate size and shape of the entire brain but also its symmetrical structure. Next, put on a pair of thick gloves preferably light gray. These represent the cortex...the newest part of the brain and the area whose functioning results in the most characteristically human creations, such as language and art (Ornstein & Thompson, 1984, pp. 21-20).

Conclusions: This activity serves as an excellent introduction to the basic brain structure. Refer to http://www.med.harvard.edu/AANLIB/home.html, the Whole Brain Atlas web site, for additional information for this demonstration.

Ornstein, R., & Thompson, R. F. (1984). *The amazing brain*. Boston: Houghton Mifflin.

Demonstration BIO 6: Lateralization Activities

Objective: To demonstrate the lateralization of the brain.
Materials: None
Procedure: Several demonstrations that illustrate the lateralization of the brain have been described by Kemble, Filipi, and Gravlin (1985). A variant by Morton Gernsbacher requires students to move their right hand and right foot simultaneously in a clockwise direction for a few seconds. Next ask that the right hand and left foot be moved in a clockwise direction. Then, have students make circular movements in opposite directions with right hand and the left foot. Finally, have students attempt to move the right hand and right foot in opposite directions. A simple alternative activity is to ask students to pat their head and to rub their stomach clockwise and then switch to a counterclockwise motion. The pat will show slight signs of rotation as well.
Conclusions: The brain is lateralized to some extent, and this makes some activities difficult to perform. Challenge your students to explain why activities of these types are difficult to execute. An advanced discussion of cerebral lateralization and schizophrenia can be found at http://www.ama-assn.org/sci-pubs/journals/archive/psyc/vol_54/no_5/oa4315a.h.

Kemble, E. D. (1987). Cerebral lateralization. In V. P. Makosky, L. G. Whittemore, and A. M. Rogers (Eds.). *Activities handbook for the teaching of psychology* (Vol. 2) (pp. 33-36). Washington, D.C.: American Psychological Association.

Kemble, E. D., Filipi, T., & Gravlin, L. (1985). Some simple classroom experiments on cerebral lateralization. *Teaching of Psychology, 12*, 81-83.

Demonstration BIO 7: Looking Left, Looking Right

Objective: To demonstrate that lateral eye movements are associated with thinking.
Materials: Left and Right Hemisphere Questions (**Handout BIO 7**)
Procedure: It has been theorized that when language-related tasks are being performed in the left hemisphere, the eyes look to the right; when non-language, spatial abilities are being used in the right hemisphere, the eyes look to the left. This is a relatively easy class activity. After pairing up, one student asks the questions and records lateral eye movements, while the other attempts to answer the questions.
Conclusions: Compare the lateral eye movements with the type of question asked. Is there a relationship? Make sure you remind students that the relationship between hemisphere functioning and lateral eye movements is still questionable.

Bakan, P. (1971). The eyes have it. *Psychology Today, 4*, 64-67, 96.

Erlichman, H., & Weinberger, A. (1979). Lateral eye movements and hemispheric asymmetry: A critical review. *Psychological Bulletin, 85*, 1080-1101.

Weitan, W., & Etaugh, C. R. (1974). Lateral eye-movements as a function of cognitive mode, question sequence and sex of subject. *Perceptual and Motor Skills, 38*, 439-444.

Demonstration BIO 10: Demonstration of Hemispheric Specialization

Objective: To demonstrate hemispheric specialization.
Materials: Drawing on the Right Side of the Brain, Edwards, published by JP Tarcher
Procedure: Find a simple line drawing that you like and make enough copies for each student. As outlined in Edwards' book, ask each student to try and copy the line drawing upside down. This task will allow the right side of the brain to dominate. As the students finish, ask them not to look at their drawings until everyone has finished, then have all the students look at their drawings at the same time; many will find them funny. Allow students to share their drawing with other students.
Conclusions: This demonstration allows the right, typically non-verbal. side of the brain to express itself. Lead a discussion on the other types of functions the right side of the brain controls. Use the site http://www.superlearning-asia.com/bookstore/drawing.htm a reference for this topic

Lecture Examples

Lecture Example 2.7: Parietal Lobes

If a digit (finger) of a monkey is amputated, the part of the somatosensory cortex that serves that finger is taken over by the fingers on either side. Also, the more sensitive a part of the body is to touch, pressure, and temperature, the larger the area of the somatosensory cortex that serves it. The whiskers on rats and cats, for example, are extremely sensitive and therefore have a disproportionate share of those animals' somatosensory cortexes. Use http://www.uni.edu/walsh/parietal.html as a reference for this lecture example.

Lecture Example 2.8: Aphasia

Most individuals with aphasia retain their reasoning ability, concepts, and experiences, but they have lost the ability to express themselves with language. How well a patient can recover from aphasia depends on the severity of the loss. The prognosis is best for those who are motivated and intelligent, and who previously had a good command of language. Cerebral blood-flow studies have provided evidence that the right hemisphere is involved in recovery from aphasia (Knobman, et al., 1984). Left-handers typically fare better than right-handers do because their language abilities are less strongly lateralized (Luria, 1970; Subirana, 1958). Use this site http://www.tesarta.com/www/resources/library/aphasia.html as a reference for your lecture example on aphasia.

Knopman, D., Rubens, A., Seines, O., et al. (1984). Evidence from several xenon 133 cerebral blood flow studies. *Ann Neurol, 15,* 530-535.

Luria, A. R. (1970). *Traumatic aphasia.* Hawthorne, New York: Mouton.

Subirana, A. (1958). The prognosis in aphasia in relation to cerebral dominance and handedness. *Brain, 81,* 415-425.

Lecture Example 2.2: Misuse of Research

Efron (1990) suggests that the ideas of hemispheric duality have been exaggerated. Normal individuals do not operate with only half a brain, that is, a dominant, active hemisphere that does the lion's share of the mental work, while beside it sits a minor, mostly idle, hemisphere that contributes only a bit of mental work from time to time on command from the dominant hemisphere. Neither do normal people have two brains, each performing its own tasks in isolation, each doing its own thing as it chooses and exercising a separate consciousness. See some comments on this book at http://www.erlbaum.com/444.htm.

Efron, R. (1990). *The decline and fall of hemispheric specialization.* Hillsdale, NJ: Erlbaum.

Diversity Topic

Diversity Topic 2.1: Learned Patterns of Behavior

Where are learned patterns of behavior stored in the brain? After students have been introduced to the basic functions of the various brain areas, have them make guesses about where language, ritualistic behaviors, and other learned aspects of behavior may be stored.
Discussion/Description: In the past, scientists interested in the brain attempted to associate behaviors with specific areas of the brain they believed stored the information related to those behaviors. Of course, in many cases they are correct, such as in the areas controlling language. Fibers from the motor cortex also are directly related to behavior, because their firing is necessary for behaviors to occur. But what happens below the motor cortex is still much of a mystery, especially with respect to culture. If we believe that culture is a set of learned action patterns that are communicated from one generation to the next, then what is learned must be represented in the brain somehow, and that representation would reflect culture in the brain. However, these

representations may not necessarily be related to specific brain areas; rather, they may be represented only in functional relationships between brain areas, that is, how brain areas talk to each other. This type of interassociation and interrelationships among brain areas are the focus of new and exciting research on the brain. This may serve to highlight to students how scientists are actually beginning to understand the brain and brain-behavior relationships.

D. Discovering the Brain's Mysteries

Classroom Demonstrations and Handouts

Demonstration BIO 11: Brain Imaging

Objective: To demonstrate brain imaging techniques.
Materials: Internet access
Procedure: Go to http://www.bic.mni.mcgill.ca/ to see the web site for the McConnell Brain Imaging Center (BIC), one of the largest scientific communities in North America dedicated solely to researching imaging of the human brain. This web site contains both links and video presentations. Have the students investigate this site and explore the different kinds of brain imaging techniques. They should be prepared to discuss their findings at the next class meeting.
Conclusions: The students will be exposed to the latest techniques in the field of brain imaging. Several will encounter these techniques during their lifetime. Lead a discussion using the following questions: Which of the many types of brain imaging techniques do you find the most interesting? Which specific technique was the most interesting and why?

Demonstration BIO 12: Trip to the Hospital

Objective: To demonstrate brain imaging techniques.
Materials: Local or regional hospital
Procedure: Arrange a trip to the local or regional hospital to see their CAT, PET, MRI and fMRI facilities. Being able to see and hear about this equipment firsthand far exceeds what students can gain from the text. Such a trip can be undertaken only if you have a small class, recitation, or laboratory sections. A voluntary sign-up list can also be used. You will have to make your plans well in advance and at the convenience of the hospital staff. If the size of your class precludes this field trip, you could invite a local physician or one of the technicians to discuss these procedures. It will be helpful if he or she can arrange to bring examples of the records or scans that are produced for evaluation of neurological disorders. You should plan to ask your guest speaker to compare these procedures to earlier procedures.
Conclusions: Student will gain valuable first-hand knowledge of the types of procedures and their uses currently avaliable in your area. For a detailed discussion of brain imaging see http://www-pet.cc.nih.gov/brainpet97/abstracts/032.html.

Lecture Examples

Lecture Example 2.9: Monitoring Neuronal Activity

Bring to class an EEG record or a CT, MRI, fMRI or PET scan. Show your students how our literal view of the brain has changed in the last 20 years. Discuss what might be in store for the future.

Lecture Example 2.10: Measurement of Brain Activity

Sophisticated PET scans allow neuroscientists to explore the working brain and to determine what areas are being used during the performance of a verbal task. The Brain Imaging site at http://www.bic.mni.mcgill.ca/demos/ is an excellent source to use in the preparation of your lecture.

E. Brain Damage: Causes and Consequences

Lecture Examples

Lecture Example 2.11: The Hippocampus and H. M.

The role of the hippocampus in the formation of memories can be dramatized through the case of H.M. who had brain surgery that damaged the hippocampus. Brenda Milner (1972), who made an extensive study of H. M.'s case, reported that his general intelligence had not suffered not at all, and the information stored in his memory before the surgery was not affected either. But H. M. could no longer learn new information and store it in memory for later recall. He could not remember what he had said, done, read, or experienced from one day to the next. In effect, H. M. became unable to form new long-term memories. His old long-term memories were intact and his short-term memory operated normally, but the transfer of information from STM to LTM could not be made. This is a good example of the types of problems that can be associated with any type of brain injury. Learn more about H. M. at http://unr.edu/homepage/otto/CH7/n_stm.html.

Milner, B. (1972). Disorders of learning and memory after temporal lobe lesions in man. *Clinical Neurosurgery, 19,* 421-446.

F. The Peripheral Nervous System

Classroom Demonstrations and Handouts

Student Chalkboard BIO 5: The Autonomic Nervous System

Demonstration BIO 3: Measuring Sympathetic Responses

Objective: To measure sympathetic responses and compare data from several subjects.
Materials: Effects of Mental Activity on Physiological Responses (**Handout BIO 3a**); Data Graph (**Handout BIO 3b**)
Procedure: Provide **Handouts BIO 3a** and **BIO 3b** for each student. In class, have them imagine an activity and then record their physiological responses (by counting heartbeats per minute). After collecting their self-data in class, each student should then collect the same data using a friend as a subject. The students should then graph the data on **Handout BIO 3b**. Data from the entire class can then be collected and graphed together. The students should also record what it was that they imagined during the activity (using the bottom half of **Handout BIO 3a**).
Conclusions: Using the descriptions of the activities, patterns of activity should emerge that depend on the type of activity imagined. The results should illustrate how mental activity influences human physiology. To see an in depth discussion of the autonomic nervous system, go to http://cme.med.mun.ca/~thoekman/autonom/ans1.htm.

G. The Endocrine System

Diversity Topic

Diversity Topic 2.2: Culture and Body Differences

Ask a physician or physiological psychologist who has done work in different countries to give a presentation on whether the body operates in exactly the same way in different environments. It would be extremely helpful to arrange if this person has experience in an environment that is dramatically different from the students' environment.
Discussion/Description: Different cultures seem to promote different physiological bases for behaviors, and this phenomenon has been witnessed in medical anthropology literature. An examination of differences in health statistics in developing countries and cultures across time (e.g., Asia and Southeast Asia, post-World War II until now), and of research investigating the bases for these differences, will lead one to the conclusion that people's bodies may not necessarily provide the same bases for human behavior as we thought in the past. For example, the relationship between the hormonal system and the incidence of certain types of diseases is different depending on the environment. Another example is that we believe that calcium ingestion is essential for the prevention of bone fractures and osteoporosis, but this relationship does not necessarily exist in other cultures.

3 Sensation and Perception

Chapter-at-a-Glance

Chapter Outline	Instruction Outline	Multimedia
Sensation: The Sensory World p. 74 The Absolute Threshold: To Sense or Not to Sense • The Difference Threshold: Detecting Differences • Signal Detection Theory • Transduction: Transforming Sensory Stimuli into Neural Impulses • Sensory Adaptation	Demonstration S&P 1 Lecture Examples 3.1, 3.2, 3.3, 3.4 Learning Objectives 3.1-3.3 Test Questions 1-16	*Discovering Psychology Sensation and Perception* **PsychScience** Signal Detection **Transparency** S&P 1 **Digital Image Archive** PSSP005 **Web Site** http://psych.hanover.edu/krantz/sen_tut.html Tutorials for S&P
Vision p. 77 Light: What We See • The Eye: Window to the Visual Sensory World • Color Vision: A Multicolored World	Student Chalkboard S&P 1 Demonstration S&P 3, 4 & 147 Lecture Examples 3.5, 3.6 Learning Objectives 3.4-3.9 Test Questions 17-57	**Transparencies** S&P 2-10, 20 **Digital Image Archive** PSSP002-004, 006-009, 019abc **Web Site** http://www.exploratorium.edu/learning_studio/cow_eye/index.html Cow Eye Dissection
Hearing p. 85 Sound: What We Hear • The Ear: More to It than Meets the Eye • Theories of Hearing: How Hearing Works • Bone Conduction: Hearing Sound Vibrations through the Bones • Hearing Loss: Kinds and Causes	Student Chalkboard S&P 3 Demonstration S&P 9 Critical Thinking Opportunity 3.1 Learning Objectives 3.10-3.13 Lecture Example 3.12 Test Questions 58-81	**Transparencies** S&P 21-23 **Video Disc** I Segment 6 **Digital Image Archive** PSSP020-024 **Web Site** http://lecaine.music.mcgill.ca/~welch/auditory/Auditory.html Auditory Perception
Smell and Taste p. 89 Smell: Sensing Scents • Taste: What the Tongue Can Tell	Demonstration S&P 10 Lecture Example 3.7 Critical Thinking Opportunity 3.2 Diversity Topic 3.2 Learning Objectives 3.14-3.15 Test Questions 82-89	**Transparencies** S&P 24-25 **Video Disc** I Segment 7 **Digital Image Archive** PSSP024, 025 **Web Site** http://www.psychology.sdsu.edu/ISOT/ International Symposium on Olfaction

Chapter Outline	Instruction Outline	Multimedia
Our Other Senses p. 93 The Skin Senses: Information from Our Natural Clothing • Pain: Physical Hurts • The Kinesthetic Sense: Keeping Track of Our Body Parts • The Vestibular Sense: Sensing Up and Down and Changes in Speed	Demonstration BIO 5, S&P 12 Lecture Examples 3.8, 3.9 Journal Entry 3.1 Learning Objectives 3.16-3.21 Test Questions 90-104	Transparency S&P 26 Digital Image Archive PSSP026a,026b Web Site http://www.latitudes.org/learn01.html Kinesthetic Child
Perception: Ways of Perceiving p. 97 The Gestalt Principles of Perceptual Organization • Perceptual Constancy • Depth Perception: Perceiving What's Up Close and Far Away • Perception of Motion • Extraordinary Perceptions: Puzzling Perceptions • Cultural Differences in the Perception of Visual Illusions	Demonstration S&P 2, 5, 8, 13, 14, 15-18 Lecture Examples 3.10, 3.11, 3.13, 3.17 Diversity Topic 3.3 Learning Objectives 3.22-3.25 Test Questions 105-125	*Psychology and Culture*: Ch. 19 Transparencies: S&P 11, 13, 14, 16-19 Digital Image Archive PSSP010-014, 016-018 Web Site http://www.yorku.ca/research/vision/eye/ Visual Perception: A Web Book
Additional Influences on Perception p. 107 Bottom-Up and Top-Down Processing • The Role of Psychological Factors in Perception	Demonstration S&P 6, 19 Lecture Example 3.14 Journal Entry 3.2 Learning Objectives 3.26◻3.27 Test Questions 126-131	Transparency S&P 15 Video Disc I Segment 5 Digital Image Archive PSSP015 Web Site http://mambo.ucsc.edu/ UCSC Perceptual Science Laboratory
Subliminal Persuasion & Extrasensory Perception p. 108 Subliminal Persuasion: Does It Work? • Extrasensory Perception: Does It Exist?	Demonstration S&P 11, 20 Critical Thinking Forum 3.1 Learning Objectives 3.28◻3.29 Lecture Example 3.15 Test Questions 132-135	Web Site http://giant.sequoias.cc.ca.us/personal/Tony_Presser/english1/nosubs.html Subliminal Persuasion

What's New in Chapter 3

New Content

- Keratotomy
- Individuality of the iris
- Genetic findings on color blindness
- Sensorineural hearing loss
- Pheromones
- Psychological and cultural influences on the experience of pain

- Stereograms
- Backmasking in subliminal messages

Expanded Content

- Sensory adaptation
- The mechanics of smell

New Special Features

- New *Try It's*
- Revised *Remember It!*

New Key Terms

- pheromones

Learning Objective Questions

3.1 What is the difference between sensation and perception?
3.2 What is the difference between the absolute threshold and the difference threshold?
3.3 How are sensory stimuli in the environment experienced as sensations?
3.4 How do the cornea, the iris, and the pupil function in vision?
3.5 What are the lens and the retina?
3.6 What roles do the rods and cones play in vision?
3.7 What path does the neural impulse take from the retina to the visual cortex?
3.8 What are the three dimensions that combine to provide the colors we experience?
3.9 What two major theories attempt to explain color vision?
3.10 What determines the pitch and the loudness of a sound, and how is each quality measured?
3.11 How do the outer, middle, and inner ears function in hearing?
3.12 What two major theories attempt to explain hearing?
3.13 What are some major causes of hearing loss?
3.14 What path does a smell message take on its journey from the nose to the brain?
3.15 What are the four primary taste sensations, and how are they detected?
3.16 How does the skin provide sensory information?
3.17 What beneficial purpose does pain serve?
3.18 What is the gate-control theory of pain?
3.19 What are endorphins?
3.20 What kind of information does the kinesthetic sense provide, and how is this sensory information detected?
3.21 What is the vestibular sense, and where are its sensory receptors located?
3.22 What are the Gestalt principles of perceptual organization?
3.23 What is perceptual constancy, and what are its four types?
3.24 What are the binocular depth cues?

3.25 What are seven monocular depth cues?
3.26 In what types of situations do we rely more on bottom-up processing or top-down processing?
3.27 What are some psychological factors that affect our perceptions?
3.28 Is subliminal persuasion effective in influencing behavior?
3.29 What is extrasensory perception, and have the claims of psychics been verified?

Chapter Overview

Sensation and perception are the processes involved in detecting stimuli in the world around us, transmitting them to the brain, and then organizing and interpreting them. The study of psychophysics has led to the measurement of absolute thresholds and difference thresholds, which define the levels of stimuli needed in order for sensation to occur. Sensory experiences are translated into neural messages in a process known as transduction.

In describing each of the senses, the chapter focuses on vision and hearing, describing in detail the structure and function of the visual and auditory systems, the theories about color vision, and the place and frequency theories of hearing. The authors then describe smell, taste, touch, the kinesthetic (position) sense, and the vestibular (balance) sense. The gate control theory of pain and the role of endorphins in the relief of pain are also examined.

Perception is the process of actively organizing and interpreting sensory information. The Gestalt approach to perception suggests that analyzing perceptions into their smallest elements will not lead to an understanding of perception. Instead, perception must be understood according to organizing principles, such as figure-ground, similarity, proximity, continuity, and closure. Other perceptual phenomena at work in the interpretation of sensory stimuli include perceptual constancy, a phenomenon occurring in the perception of size, shape, brightness, and color; depth perception, based on both binocular and monocular cues; and the perception of motion. The chapter examines the role of illusions—the Müller Lyer illusion and the Ponzo illusion—and of ambiguous and impossible figures in understanding perception.

The chapter closes with a discussion of bottom-up and top-down processing and factors that influence perception, including our perceptual set (what we *expect* to perceive). The authors discuss subliminal perception. The chapter ends with a discussion of extrasensory perception and its relationship to parapsychology, the study of psychic phenomena.

Key Terms

absolute threshold (p. 75)
accommodation (p. 79)
afterimage (p. 83)
amplitude (p. 85)
apparent motion (p. 103)
audition (p. 86)
binocular depth cues (p. 101)
binocular disparity (p. 102)
bone conduction (p. 88)
bottom-up processing (p. 107)
brightness (p. 82)
brightness constancy (p. 100)
cochlea (p. 87)
color blindness (p. 83)
color constancy (p. 100)
cones (p. 80)
convergence (p. 101)
cornea (p. 79)
dark adaptation (p. 81)
decibel (p. 86)
depth perception (p. 101)
difference threshold (p. 75)
endorphins (p. 94)
extrasensory perception (ESP) (p. 109)
feature detectors (p. 82)
figure-ground (p. 98)
fovea (p. 81)
frequency (p. 85)
frequency theory (p. 87)
gate-control theory (p. 94)
Gestalt (p. 98)
gustation (p. 91)
hair cells (p. 87)
hue (p. 82)
illusion (p. 105)
inner ear (p. 87)
just noticeable difference (p. 75)
kinesthetic sense (p. 94)
lens (p. 79)
middle ear (p. 86)
monocular depth cues (p. 103)
naloxone (p. 94)
olfaction (p. 90)
olfactory bulbs (p. 90)
olfactory epithelium (p. 90)
opponent-process theory (p. 83)
optic nerve (p. 81)
outer ear (p. 86)
parapsychology (p. 109)
perception (p. 97)
perceptual constancy (p. 99)
perceptual set (p. 109)
pheromones (p.90)
phi phenomenon (p. 105)
place theory (p. 87)
retina (p. 79)
retinal image (p. 99)
rods (p. 80)
saturation (p. 82)
semicircular canals (p. 96)
sensation (p. 75)
sensory adaptation (p. 76)
sensory receptors (p. 76)
shape constancy (p. 100)
signal detection theory (p. 76)
size constancy (p. 99)
subliminal perception (p. 109)
subliminal persuasion (p. 109)
tactile (p. 93)
taste buds (p. 91)
timbre (p. 86)
top-down processing (p. 109)
transduction (p. 96)
trichromatic theory (p. 82)
vestibular sense (p. 96)
visible spectrum (p. 79)
Weber's law (p. 75)

Annotated Lecture Outline

A. Sensation: the Sensory World

Classroom Demonstrations and Handouts

Demonstration S&P: 1: Stimulus Change

Objective: To demonstrate stimulus change.
Materials: Lamp with a three-way, 50-100-150 watt light bulb
Procedure: Turn the light from 50 to 100 watts. This will seem like a much brighter increase than turning the light from 100 to 150 watts, although both were increases of 50 watts.
Conclusions: Discuss how we interpret our psychologically experience. A jump from 50 to 100 watts is a 100 percent increase (50 over 50 watts), but a jump from 100 to 150 watts is only a 50 percent increase (50 over 100 watts). Regardless of the absolute stimulus change (in wattage), we experience a relative change in perception.

Lecture Examples

Lecture Example 3.1: Absolute Threshold for the Visual System

As you lecture on the visual system's absolute threshold, put the smallest magnitude into concrete terms. Refer to the candle being seen 30 miles on a clear, dark night. Suggest this would be like you going to the top of a tall dorm on campus and lighting a candle, while the rest of the class goes to a town about 30 miles away to look at the visual stimulus! Go to http://pavlov.psyc.queensu.ca/~symonsl/sensperc/psychophysics.html for a general discussion of thresholds.

Lecture Example 3.2: Eye Exams and the Difference Threshold

If you have ever been fitted for eyeglasses, you have experienced a type of difference threshold. As you sat in the chair, the doctor probably had you look through a large pair of "binoculars" to check for the best lenses. Do you remember being asked as you looked at the visual display, "Can you tell the difference between Lens 1 and Lens 2? Lens 1? Lens 2?" The doctor was, in effect, checking for just noticeable difference (JND). Go to http://pavlov.psyc.queensu.ca/~symonsl/sensperc/psychophysics.html for a general discussion of thresholds.

Lecture Example 3.3: Sensory Adaptation

Adaptation works with smell too. Imagine that you are visiting a friend who has a cat and, of course, a litter box. When you first enter the house, the cat odor is overpowering. After about 30 minutes, the odor becomes less noticeable, and you wonder if your friend got rid of the cat and its litter box. The answer is that your olfactory system has simply become less sensitive to the odor, which is just as strong as when you first walked in. This is sensory adaptation.

Lecture Example 3.4: Psychophysics

Originally psychophysics virtually ignored the subjective characteristics of the perceiver. In your lecture try to explain *why* this was the case and how the early results might have been influenced by factors such as emotion, motivation, and personality. For an advanced class this would be a good place to introduce signal-detection theory. See http://iweb.spawar.navy.mil/services/sti/publications/pubs/td/627/behavioral.html for an annotated bibliography of psychophysics.

B. Vision

Classroom Demonstrations and Handouts

Student Chalkboard S&P 1: The Structure of the Eye

Demonstration S&P 3: Differences between Rods and Cones

Objective: To illustrate that the differences between rods and cones affect our visual behavior.
Materials: Pencil or pen; book
Procedure: First, take a pencil or pen and put it at arm's length to your side. Can its color or writing on it be perceived? Slowly bring it forward. As the cones detect the image, the color and other detail will become apparent. When you read, letters and words are focused onto the fovea, where cones are concentrated. Try reading words using the periphery; it's much more difficult. Finally, people who enjoy fishing suggest that if it is after dusk and you want to watch a fishing bobber, do not look directly at it, but to the side. Cones in the fovea don't work best in dim light; rods located in peripherally do.
Conclusions: The differences in function and location of rods and cones are evident in how we look at things. See http://www.innerbody.com/text/nerv08.html for more information.

Demonstration S&P 4: The Blind Spot

Objective: To demonstrate the blind spot.
Materials: **Handout S&P 4** or a standard letter size paper cut in half with a small capital X and small capital Y written about four inches apart on one half and a small capital X, Y, and Z written about three inches apart on the other half
Procedure: Using the top half of **Handout S&P 4**, students are to hold the side of paper at arm's length while covering one eye. If the left eye is covered, focus on the X. Bring the paper close to the eye. They should notice that the Y will disappear and reappear as the distance of the paper from the eyes is adjusted; that is, as they slowly bring the paper forward, the Y disappears. Next use the bottom half of **Handout S&P 4** and repeat the procedures, focusing on the Y in the middle. This time, however, a gap in the thick line will disappear and the line becomes one. The students can also experience this blind spot by focusing on a mark on the chalkboard and walking slowly towards the mark as you hold a candle to either side of their starting point. Students will report that the candle disappears.
Conclusions: Ask your students to explain what happens in the first part of the experiment as the letter disappeared and then reappeared in the context of the blind spot. Is the same explanation valid for the second part of the experiment? The activity demonstrates that we add to the picture to fill in the blind spot. Use the information at
http://www.exploratorium.edu/snacks/blind_spot.html to build apparatus to detect your blind spot.

Duda, J. J. (1981). The blind spot. In L. T. Benjamin and K. D. Lowman (Eds.), *Activities handbook for the teaching of psychology* (Vol. 1) (p. 43). Washington, D.C.: American Psychological Association.

Demonstration S&P 7: Ocular Dominance

Objective: To demonstrate each student's dominant eye.
Materials: None
Procedure: Ask each student to point at your nose with his or her finger and then close one eye. If your face seems to jump to the side, the student is looking at you with his or her non-dominant eye. The non-moving eye will be the student's dominant eye. Most individuals are right eye dominant (much like handedness) with a smaller number being left eye dominant. There will be several individuals whose eyes have equal dominance. As the students point at you, identify each student's eye dominance as right, left, or equal. The students will be amazed that you can identify their dominant eye, but it is very simple; just line up their fingers with their eyes.
Conclusions: Lead a discussion on the importance of using your dominant eye, especially when looking through a telescope or microscope or shooting a rifle. Ask for comment from students who have been in the military and have been forced to shoot a rifle after aiming using their non-dominant eyes. Ask students for other examples where ocular dominance has made a difference in performance. Jack Nicklaus the golfer is left eye dominant and moves his head before each shot to position his dominant eye over the ball. This looks odd but if you are a great golfer it is just good technique. See a simple test at http://w3.ime.net/~phillips/laboratory/exp2.html to determine your dominant eye.

Lecture Examples

Lecture Example 3.5: Stabilized Retina Images

Our perception systems have a great need for constant variation in stimulation. Pritchard (1961), in a classic experiment, stabilized different images on the retina using a special contact lens; he reported that these images began to fade and finally disappeared. When words that had been stabilized vanished, they did so in a logical and meaningful way. You could supplement this lecture with an effective, albeit crude, replication of Pritchard's study. Ask students to stabilize one eye by pushing very gently the outside upper corner of the eye. Their visual field should start to deteriorate. A discussion of the eye's normal, nystagmus movements would be helpful; one can detect these by having a subject stare at an object.

Pritchard, R. M. (1961). Stabilized images on the retina. *Scientific American, 204,* 72-78.

Lecture Example 3.6: What Is the Pupil?

An intriguing answer to the question, "What is the pupil?" is that the pupil is nothing but a hole in your eye. The answer to the next question, "What does one see, then?" is the retina. "Why is it black?" Very little light gets inside, and the back of the eye is pigmented. Finally, if you consider the retina to be an extension of the brain, what you see as you gaze into a person's eye is really his or her brain! An excellent QuickTime movie of the anatomy of the eye is at http://www.imagiq.com/clients/PSO/Anatomy.html, or see http://www.yorku.ca/eye/eye1.htm for a detailed text description.

C. Hearing

Classroom Demonstrations and Handouts

Student Chalkboard S&P 3: Anatomy of the Auditory System

Demonstration S&P 9: Audition

Objective: To explore auditory perception on the Internet.
Materials: Internet access
Procedure: Go to http://www.music.mcgill.ca/auditory/Auditory.html. This site contains a multimedia presentation on selected topics in auditory perception, including auditory demonstrations, discussions, and experiments. Assign the students to explore several topic areas in this site.
Conclusions: Students could write a short summary of their experiences at this site. Their understanding of these auditory principles will be enhanced. Lead a discussion of what aspects of auditory perception at this site the students found most interesting.

Lecture Example

Lecture Example 3.12: The Loudest Sound

Ask your students to describe the loudest sound they have ever heard. Some of your students may have been in the military and will have some good examples. Other examples will range from rock concerts to jet airplanes. Use these examples as a lecture lead-in to your lecture on hearing damage. What is the loudest natural sound? Find out at http://www.learningkingdom.com/press/coolfact/s10-15-97.html.

D. Smell and Taste

Classroom Demonstrations and Handouts

Demonstration S&P 10: Effects of Color on Taste

Objective: To demonstrate the power of vision on taste.
Materials: Various foods; food colorings
Procedure: Have students sample a meal you have prepared using food coloring to make the food different colors. Have the students collect data on their reactions to this new colored food. Possible examples are purple potatoes, green bread, blue butter, and black milk.

Conclusions: Have the students discuss in class their reactions to the differently colored foods. Which did they find the most disturbing combination? Why are the reactions so strong to these color changes? Did the color affect the students' perception of the taste?

Lecture Example

Lecture Example 3.7: Carrier Proteins and Smell

Schofield (1988) found that the nose emits from its tip proteins that bind to airborne odorants as they enter the nose. Apparently the proteins facilitate the delivery of these bound odors to the olfactory receptors in the epithelium. For more on olfaction see http://bioinfo.weizmann.ac.il/_ls/doron_lancet/doron_lancet.html.

Schofield, P. R. (1988). Carrier-bound odorant delivery to olfactory receptors. *Trends in Neuroscience, 11,* 471-472.

Diversity Topic

Diversity Topic 3.2: Cultural Differences in Taste and Smell

Objective: To demonstrate how culture affects taste and smell.
Materials: Have students from different cultural backgrounds bring a representative food dish to class to share for potluck
Discussion/Description: Tastes are very much culturally acquired. What we may think of as gross and distasteful may be the next person's delicacy, and vice versa. By having students sample foods from other cultures, they will get a first-hand adventure in the influence of culture on our palates (and they will probably have a good time). It has been my experience that students get the most out of this activity if, as each food is introduced to the class, students receive an explanation of not only what the food is, but why it is a representative food of the culture, how it is made, any sacred or religious meanings it may have, and eating etiquette.

E. Our Other Senses

Classroom Demonstrations and Handouts

Demonstration BIO 5: Two-Point Thresholds

Objective: To reveal the varying sensitivities of body areas as a function of nerve density and the amount of somatosensory cortex devoted to the body area.
Materials: Compass or calipers; **Handout BIO 5**
Procedure: Put students into groups of three; in each group there should be a data recorder, experimenter, and subject. The experimenter should apply the calipers to the subject's elbow. The calipers should be slightly opened and the data recorder should note and record the span. Does the subject report feeling only one point? Gradually, the calipers should be opened and applied to

the elbow until the subject reports feeling two points (e.g., two-point threshold). Next, repeat the procedure to the subject's forearm, palm, and index finger. The data recorder should carefully record the distance of the calipers at each point. Are there differences between these body areas with regard to two-point thresholds? Why? Nazzaro (1981) describes a similar activity. There is a variation of the first activity that has the same effect (Motiff, 1987). With students paired up, one member should hold and press a number of fingers against the other's back. It is very difficult to identify the number of fingers held to the back. Next, do the same procedure, except press the fingers to the subject's shoulder, forearm, and finally hand with the subject's eyes closed.
Conclusions: Areas of the body that are the most sensitive have more brain area devoted to them in the somatosensory cortex and have proportionately more nerve endings. In addition, there are implications for these differences; for example, a cut on the thumb is more painful than a cut on the forearm or back. To find out more about touch go to http://haptic.mech.nwu.edu/links/psychophysics.html.

Motiff, J. P. (1987). Physiological psychology: The sensory homunculus. In V. P. Makosky, L. G. Whittemore, and A. M. Rogers (Eds.). *Activities handbook for the teaching of psychology* (Vol. 2) (pp. 51-52). Washington, D.C.: American Psychological Association.

Nazzaro, J. R. (1981). Cutaneous two-point thresholds. In L. T. Benjamin, Jr., & K. D. Lowman (Eds.). *Activities handbook for the teaching of psychology* (Vol. 1) (pp. 31-32). Washington, D.C.: American Psychological Association.

Demonstration S&P 12: Kinesthetic Challenge

Objective: To demonstrate the kinesthetic sense.
Materials: None
Procedure: Close your eyes and bring the tip of your finger to the tip of your nose. You probably touched the tip right on target or were very close. Now with your eyes closed, put your head as far back as possible with your nose high in the air. Touch it with the tip of your finger.
Conclusions: Even though your nose is in a different position, you are still able to guide your fingertip to your nose.

Lecture Examples

Lecture Example 3.8: How Do You Measure Pain?

The West Haven-Yale Multidimensional Pain Inventory (WHYMPI) is an assessment tool used by clinicians to measure several dimensions of pain, including how other people respond to a patient's pain. Another common tool is the McGill Pain Questionnaire. A component of the McGill is to present patients with a list of words (e.g., *dull, cramping, vicious*) and ask them to circle whichever words describe the pain. Go to http://gasbone.herston.uq.edu.au/teach/su602/docs/f28_0pn.html for more on the measurement of pain.

Kerns, R. D., Turk, D. C., & Rudy, T. E. (1985). The West Haven-Yale Multidimensional Pain Inventory WHYMPI. *Pain, 23,* 345-356.

Melzack, R. (1975). The McGill pain questionnaire: Major properties and scoring methods. *Pain, 1,* 277-299.

Lecture Example 3.9: Synesthesia

Synesthesia is a fascinating phenomenon in which an individual experiences "spill-over" effects among the sensory systems, for example, seeing sounds or smelling colors. One of the most fascinating accounts of synesthesia is that of S., a man who was known for his exceptional memory. He used synesthesia to help him encode, store, and retrieve extensive lists of words. In fact, the synesthetic reactions gave him "extra information" to help his retrieval. During questioning, S. commented that whenever he retrieved a list of words, the experimenter would respond yes or no depending on S.'s accuracy. According to S., these yes's and no's produced a blur on his mental images of the list. The same thing happened when he heard background noises in auditoriums or halls; he would see those noises as "puffs of steam" or "splashes." For more on synesthesia see http://www.lijn.demon.co.uk/scantxt/marks75a.htm.

Lemley, B. (1984). Synesthesia: Seeing is feeling. *Psychology Today,* 65.

Luria, A. R. (1968). *The mind of a mnemonist.* New York: Basic Books.

F. Perception: Ways of Perceiving

Classroom Demonstrations and Handouts

Demonstration S&P 2: Differences in Perception—Expectancy

Objective: To show that our expectations affect our perceptions of the world around us.
Materials: **Handout S&P 2** (use as an overhead master)
Procedure: Prior to presenting the nonsense words on **Handout S&P 2**, secretly inform one group that the words will be related to animals, and inform a second group to expect words related to sailing. Next present the words as fast as you can to both groups. Ask them to write down the words they saw. The former group will probably report that they saw seal, whale, and duck, whereas the latter will say sail, wharf, and deck as the words. Make sure you stress both groups saw the same words yet had different expectations. Be sure to stress that both groups saw the same stimuli.

Just so your students don't think that the activity was just a fluke, use the following demonstration to establish different sets:

> "What does s-i-l-k spell?"
> "What do cows drink?" (A typical response is milk.)

> "What does r-o-a-s-t spell?"

"What do you put on bread?" (Typically, they respond "toast.")

"What does s-p-o-t spell?"
"What do you do at a traffic light?" (A typical response is "stop.")

Conclusions: In these crude demonstrations, the expectations of what was upcoming affected how subjects perceived nonsense words and responded to questions.

Fisher, J. (1979). *Body magic.* New York: Stein and Day.

Demonstration S&P 5: What Do You See?

Objective: To illustrate the active perception.
Materials: **Handout S&P 5a; Handout S&P 5b**
Procedure: According to White and Broekel, our brain "sees," and sometimes it sees more than what is really there. Present **Handout S&P 5a** to your students. Objectively, the stimuli are merely lines with no real meaning, but our brains do not see it that way! In fact, the brain can interpret incomplete stimuli and perceive something whole. Are your students confident that what they "see" is actually the word "science?" Show them **Handout S&P 5b**.
Conclusions: Perception is a not a passive process. It takes into account experience and reason and sometimes will guess incorrectly.

White, L. B., Jr., & Broekel, R. (1986). *Optical illusions.* New York: Franklin Watts.

Demonstration S&P 8: Brightness Constancy

Objective: To show the limits of brightness constancy.
Materials: **Handout S&P 8**
Procedure: Give students **Handout S&P 8**. Ask them to place a piece of paper or notebook upright on the dotted, center line. Make sure that the barrier does not allow light to pass through. Position the handout so that the light source is in the direction indicated on the handout. Your students should place the tip of their nose on the top edge of the barrier so that the single grey circle is seen with the left eye and the four grey circles with the right eye. Which of the four circles on the right most closely matches the circle on the left? At this point, remove the barrier so that all the circles are illuminated equally. Now which of the four circles best matches the one on the left?
Conclusions: When there is an unequal change in lighting between object and its surrounding, the perception of brightness does not remain constant.

Demonstration S&P 13: Art and Distance Cues

Objective: To show how artists use their excellent understanding of distance cues in their works.
Materials: A picture from an art book that shows the distance cues (If your class is large, consider making an overhead or slide of it so all can see. Often, Art History departments have the capability to produce slides of works from books for classroom use; they may even have the picture you want to show.)

Procedure: Optionally, ask students to get into groups. Analyze and describe how different artists use cues to convey distance and depth. Point out to your students that in art there have been trends or styles of one kind or another, each giving different emphasize on using distance and depth cues. Consider these works:

>Salvador Dali: *Perspectives* (1937), *The Invisible Man* (1929)
>Rene Magritte: *Les Promenades d'Euclide* (1955)
>M.C. Escher: *Day and Night* (1938), *Waterfall* (1961)

Conclusions: Distance is conveyed through monocular distance cues. These monocular distance cues are sometimes called pictorial cues. And in some paintings, these cues are used to mislead the viewer and cause an illusion. Consult Livingstone (1988) for more information.

Livingstone, M. S. (1988). Art, illusion, and the visual system. *Scientific American, 258*, 78-85.

Demonstration S&P 14: Simple Binocular Demonstration

Objective: To demonstrate binocular disparity.
Materials: One pencil
Procedure: With both eyes open, hold a pencil (or a finger) at arm's length in front of your face. Each student should focus his or her view beyond the pencil, to a point on a distant wall (you may wish to place a visual target on the wall). They will now see two pencils. If the students focus directly on the pencil, the point on the wall will become two points.
Conclusions: The two points are the result of the slightly different view of each eye, known as binocular disparity. Ask the students to explain the phenomenon. Go to http://www.vision3d.com/fftext.html to view the famous frankfurter experiment.

Demonstration S&P 15: Seeing Isn't Believing

Objective: To demonstrate the power of illusions.
Materials: Internet access
Procedure: Go to http://www.illusionworks.com/ and explore three different kinds of illusions. There are both classic and newer illusions at this site..
Conclusions: Have students investigate this site and prepare to discuss their findings in the next class meeting Lead a discussion using the following questions. Which of the many types of illusions do you find the most interesting? Which specific illusion was the most interesting and why? After exploring this page do you think seeing is believing?

Demonstration S&P 16: Exploratorium

Objective: To allow the students to explore sensation and perception on the Internet.
Materials: Internet access
Procedure: Go to the site http://www.exploratorium.edu/imagery/exhibits.html. This site contains digital versions of Exploratorium exhibits. It is important to understand that these versions, in most cases, are only adequate replacements for the real experiences that you will have if you are able to visit the Exploratorium in San Francisco. Most of these exhibits are electronic versions

from the museum floor; a few are unique to the web site. **Assign the students to explore several of the exhibits.**
Conclusions: Students could write a short summary of their experiences at this site. Their understanding of these exhibits and principles behind the exhibits will be enhanced. After this assignment, be prepared for students to ask questions about the principles behind the exhibits.

Demonstration S&P 17: Moon Illusion

Objective: To illustrate why the moon appears larger at the horizon than at the zenith.
Materials: None
Procedure: During your lecture on size constancy, you can set the stage for an interesting demonstration. In this lecture describe how at the zenith the sky appears to be a flattened dome and discuss the apparent distance theory of Kaufman and Rock (1962) on size constancy. Also discuss contextual clues and how they affect this illusion as described by Baird (1982). Now that you have set the stage, ask the students to do an experiment. On the night of a full moon, ask students to go to a vantage point (you should check the moon rise time) and attempt to disrupt the environmental cues that could be contributing to the illusion. A paper towel tube used as a "spy glass" will disrupt the cues and make the moon appear smaller. Students could also try standing on their heads to disrupt the cues. You could also take two pictures, one at moonrise and the other at the zenith, then bring the photographs or slides to class to compare sizes.
Conclusions: This powerful illusion can be partially explained by Kaufman and Rock and Baird. Ask students for any of their hypotheses to further explain this illusion. Go to http://rpssg3.psychologie.uni-regensburg.de/peter/psychology/vision/moon_illusion/moon_illusion.html for a site that explains the moon illusion and ponders many unanswered questions.

Demonstration S&P 18: Autokenetic Effect

Objective: To demonstrate the autokenetic effect.
Materials: Small pen light with red filter
Procedure: Make the classroom light proof, or move the class to a room that can be made light proof. Take a yardstick and tape it to a table as the students watch. Make the room dark and ask students to judge how far the light will move. Stand the light with the red filter on the table and do not move the light. Allow the students to observe the light for several minutes. Turn off the red light, turn on the room lights, and ask students to write down how much the light moved. Ask each student to announce how far the light moved in terms of the following blocks of movement: 1-3 inches, 4-6 inches, 7-9 inches, and finally 0 inches, then figure the mean for the class. Then announce that the light did not move. As an alternative, particularly if you split the class into groups for this demonstration, use a confederate to suggest an amount of movement; for example, suggest to one group two inches and suggest to the other group nine inches. Make sure your confederate is the first to announce the results.
Conclusions: Discuss the autokenetic effect and ask students if they could think of an application for this illusion in an experiment. Review this demonstration when you discuss the work of Sherif (1936) and conformity in your social psychology lectures. To learn more about the autokenitic effect see http://www2.tltc.ttu.edu/SCHNEIDER/IUteach/sopsy/conform.htm.

Lecture Examples

Lecture Example 3.10: The Amazing Cosmos of the Black Hills

Most illusions that we think of are drawings. But according to a brochure for The Amazing Cosmos, a tourist attraction in South Dakota, the Cosmos is where the "whole world seems topsy turvy, with the laws of nature gone completely berserk." A person seems to be able to sit on a chair on a wall, stand on a wall and lean into the room, or even see a ball running up hill. The rooms are constructed to present cues that are ostensibly of right angles and perpendicularity, but in fact they are not.

Lecture Example 3.11: Gestalt Psychologists

The Gestalt psychologists described perception as something in which "the whole is more than the sum of its parts." Be prepared to explain this statement; students might find it troublesome. For example, our perceptions, according to the Gestaltists, are more than adding up each individual light, as in the case of the phi effect (e.g., marquees). The perception we experience when watching a motion picture is more than the simple addition of frame 1 plus frame 2 plus frame 3 and so on. Show that, on very close examination, a newspaper photograph or a document produced with a dot matrix printer is just a bunch of dots; yet we perceive much more. The phi effect can be replicated in class by cutting three small holes about two inches apart in construction paper. Darken the room and quickly pass a flashlight behind the holes. For more information see http://unr.edu/homepage/otto/CH15/gestalt.html.

Lecture Example 3.13: Everyday Illusions

Develop a lecture that discusses illusions that occur in the real world. One good example is the Doppler effect involving the apparent pitch of the siren from a moving vehicle. Another example is that when you first see a mountain range on the horizon it appears much larger than it really is. Perception in everyday life can be an interesting topic for this lecture.

Lecture Example 3.17: Color Constancy and Make-Up Mirrors

As part of your lectures on perceptual constancies include the following information on color constancy. Objects are not perceived to change color from daytime to nighttime or under different lighting conditions despite the fact that the message to the receptors is changed. As an example, most students will have had an experience of buying an item of clothing in a store under conditions of fluorescent lighting. Later, in the sunlight or under incandescent lights, the item may turn out to be a quite different shade. Some students may have seen facial make-up mirrors with light that could be changed to change the wavelength of the light emitted. A knob usually had positions like business, (fluorescent), daylight, and after five (incandescent). For a site with references for color constancy got to http://tiger.eng.uci.edu/projects/color_constancy.html.

G. Additional Influences on Perception

Classroom Demonstrations and Handouts

Demonstration S&P 6: Mirror Writing

Objective: To demonstrate that our experience with writing can prove useless when we change the rules of perception and motion.
Materials: A mirror; paper; pencil (if you have a mirror tracer, it will work very well for this activity)
Procedure: Ask students to write using a mirror.
Conclusions: Initially, this is very difficult, but just like writing for the first time, the coordination between vision, vestibular, and kinesthetic senses improves with experience. A variation of this is the classic maze-tracing activity.

Demonstration S&P 19: Perceptual Set

Objective: To illustrate the effect perceptual set has on tactile perception.
Materials: An article on Lyme disease with a discussion of ticks
Procedure: You should covertly inform the students in the back of the classroom (or another "select" group of students) to act as observers and to take note of the behavior of others in the classroom. Ask them to watch for itching prior to and during the reading of the article on Lyme disease. Suggest to the rest of your students that an activity on the perception of language will be performed, and therefore close attention to what is being read is critical. Begin to read the article on Lyme disease focusing on ticks and their behavior. As you read, watch your students show an increase in itching and rubbing behavior.
Conclusions: Establishing perceptual sets can affect olfactory and visual perception. As this activity demonstrates, our tactile perception may also be influenced. Normal skin sensations now are interpreted in the context of ticks. For more information see http://www.lymenet.org/.

Lecture Examples

Lecture Example 3.14: Speed Reading?

Ask if any of the students in your class have taken a speed-reading course. Then ask them what they learned. Many will think they have increased their reading comprehension and speed. Many scientific studies indicated that speed-reading courses are largely ineffective because these courses fail to train students to better comprehend what they are reading. A classic joke by Woody Allen sums up this topic, "I read *War and Peace* in 20 minutes—it is about Russia." See another guaranteed method of speed reading at http://www.proportionalreading.com/comprehension.html.

H. Subliminal Persuasion and Extrasensory Perception

Classroom Demonstrations and Handouts

Demonstration S&P 11: Testing Students for ESP

Objective: To give students an opportunity to examine their extrasensory perception (ESP).
Materials: Zener Cards (**Handout S&P 11a**); Recording Sheet (**Handout S&P 11b**)
Procedure: Conduct this activity after lecturing on ESP. Give each of your students a copy of **Handout S&P 11b** and tell them to record their responses on this handout. Zener cards, consisting of five symbols (**Handout S&P 11a**) are frequently used in extrasensory perception research to detect telepathy, clairvoyance, and precognition. Each symbol is presented five times in a typical run with at least 10 runs in serious research. You'll probably have time for only one or two runs, however. Reproduce and cut enough cards. It is helpful to mount each symbol on an index card to make shuffling easier and the cards more durable. You may wish to select a student to act as experimenter.

Before you or your assistant shuffles the deck, ask your students to write down the cards in the order that they will appear using **Handout S&P 11b**. This is a test of precognition. Run through the cards asking students to determine their accuracy. To test for clairvoyance, reshuffle the deck. Place the deck face down and ask subjects to record the cards in order. A variation of this test is to lift each card off the deck face down and them face down beside the deck. Subjects are to record their responses. In these tests, the experimenter does not look at the card face. Telepathy may be assessed with the experimenter examining each card face and then sending one's thoughts to subjects. Statistically, with chance alone we would expect one correct response out of every five cards. So in a run of 25 trials, a hit rate of five would be a chance occurrence. Are there any students with hit rates of above 20 in class? Ask students to point out the methodological flaws of these tests as they were conducted in class.
Conclusions: If we practice the values of science and conduct systematic research, chance success must be ruled out before we conclude that someone possesses ESP.
Follow Up, Outside Class Project: Give students a copy of the Zener cards (**Handout S&P 11a**) and ask them to replicate this class activity. Do their subjects' responses indicate ability beyond chance? For more information on ESP see
http://www.hope.edu/academic/psychology/myerstxt/esp/esp.html.

Demonstration S&P 20: Questioning ESP

Objective: To develop skepticism in students regarding paranormal phenomena.
Materials: None
Procedure: Invite a magician/mentalist to class to demonstrate some techniques. Challenge students to develop hypotheses to account for these apparent paranormal abilities.
Conclusions: Discuss with students the idea that skepticism is a healthy trait that scientists should have especially when they deal with paranormal abilities. For more information on ESP see
http://www.hope.edu/academic/psychology/myerstxt/esp/esp.html.

Lecture Examples

Lecture Example 3.15: Subliminal Messages

Ask your students what they think about the current practice of playing subliminal messages in stores to stop shoplifters. Also ask what they think of the practice to deter employee theft. How would they feel if those messages tried to convince them to buy a certain product? This has been tried with little success. What if the messages tried to convince the students to vote for the store owner's favorite political candidate?

4 States of Consciousness

Chapter-at-a-Glance

Chapter Outline	Instruction Outline	Multimedia
What Is Consciousness? p. 116	Diversity Topic 4.1 Learning Objective 4.1 Lecture Examples 4.4 Test Questions 1-5	Discovering Psychology: The Mind Awake and Asleep **Web Site** http://sol.zynet.co.uk/imprint/chalmers.html Journal of Consciousness Studies
Circadian Rhythms: Our 24-Hour Highs and Lows p. 117 The Suprachiasmatic Nucleus: The Body's Time Keeper • Jet Lag: Where Am I and What Time Is It? • Shift Work: Working Day and Night • Taking Melatonin as a Sleep Aid	Lecture Examples 4.1, 4.2 Learning Objectives 4.2-4.4 Test Questions 6-16	**Video Disc I** Segment 8 **Web site** http://www-nw.rz.uni-regensburg.de/~.tam14205.zoologie.biologie.uni-regensburg.de/CHRONO.HTM Circadian Rhythms
Sleep: That Mysterious One-Third of Our Lives p. 120 NREM and REM Sleep: Watching the Eyes • Sleep Cycles: The Nightly Pattern of Sleep • Variations in Sleep: How We Differ • Sleep Deprivation: How Does It Affect Us? • The Functions of Sleep: The Restorative and Circadian Theories • Dreaming: Mysterious Mental Activity While We Sleep	**Student Chalkboard** CONSC 1 **Demonstration** CONSC 2, 3, 7 & 9 **Lecture Examples** 4.3- 4.9 **Critical Thinking Opportunity** 4.1 **Learning Objectives** 4.5-4.14 **Test Questions** 17-58	**Transparency** BIO 29 **Web Site** http://www.dreamgate.com/dream/resources/online97.htm Dreams
Sleep Disorders p. 128 Parasomnias: Unusual Behaviors during Sleep • Major Sleep Disorders	**Demonstration** CONSC 8 **Lecture Examples** 4.10-4.12 **Learning Objectives** 4.15-4.20 **Test Questions** 59-75	**Wes Site** http://www.sleepnet.com/disorder.htm Sleep Disorders

Chapter Outline	Instruction Outline	Multimedia
Altering Consciousness through Concentration and Suggestion p. 131 Meditation: Expanded Consciousness or Relaxation? • Hypnosis: Look into My Eyes • Culture and Altered States of Consciousness	Lecture Example 4.13-4.15, 23, 24 Critical Thinking Opportunity 4.2 Journal Entry 4.1 Diversity Topic 4.2 Learning Objectives 4.21-4.23 Test Questions 76-88	*Psychology and Culture*: Ch. 8 **Video Disc I** Segment 9 **Web Site** http://www.psych-web.com/asc/asc.html States of Consciousness
Altered States of Consciousness and Psychoactive Drugs p. 136 Variables Influencing Individuals' Responses to Drugs • Drug Addiction: Slave to a Substance • Stimulants: Speeding Up the Nervous System • Depressants: Slowing Down the Nervous System • World of Psychology: The Use and Abuse of Alcohol • Hallucinogens: Seeing, Hearing, and Feeling What Is Not There • How Drugs Affect the Brain	**Student Chalkboard** CONSC 2 **Demonstration** CONSC 4-6 & 10 Lecture Examples 4.16-4.23 Critical Thinking Forum 4.2 Journal Entry 4.2 Diversity Topic 4.4 Learning Objectives 4.24-4.32 Test Questions 89-139	*Psychology and Culture*: Ch. 11 **Video Disc I** Segment 10 **Web Site** http://orion.it.luc.edu/~pcrowe/375link.htm Substance Use and Abuse

What's New in Chapter 4

New Content

- Role of the suprachiasmatic nucleus in circadian rhythms
- Melatonin as a sleep aid
- REM sleep behavior disorder
- The restorative and circadian theories of sleep
- Sociocognitive and neodissociation theories of hypnosis
- Hypnosis as an altered state of consciousness
- MDMA (Ecstasy) as a "designer drug"
- Binge drinking on college campuses
- Inhalants

Expanded Content

- Daydreaming
- Shift work
- Sleep deprivation

Organizational Changes

- Hallucinogens have been moved to follow depressants, so that stimulants and depressants are discussed consecutively.

New Special Features

- Revised *Remember It's*

New Key Terms

- suprachiasmatic nucleus (SCN)
- melatonin
- restorative theory
- circadian theory
- meditation (concentrative)
- sociocognitive theory of hypnosis
- neodissociation theory of hypnosis
- MDMA (Ecstasy)

Learning Objective Questions

4.1 What are some different states of consciousness?
4.2 What is a circadian rhythm, and which rhythms are most relevant to the study of sleep?
4.3 What is the Suprachiasmatic Nucleus?
4.4 What are some problems experienced by employees who work rotating shifts?
4.5 How does a sleeper react physically during NREM sleep?
4.6 How does the body respond physically during REM sleep?
4.7 What is the progression of NREM stages and REM sleep that a person follows in a typical night of sleep?
4.8 How do sleep patterns change over the life span?
4.9 What factors influence sleep patterns?
4.10 What are the two main theories that attempt to explain the function of sleep?
4.11 What factors influence our sleep needs?
4.12 How do REM and NREM dreams differ?
4.13 In general, what have researchers found regarding the content of dreams?
4.14 What function does REM sleep appear to serve, and what happens when people are deprived of REM sleep?
4.15 What are the characteristics common to sleepwalking and sleep terrors?
4.16 What is a sleep terror?
4.17 How do nightmares differ from sleep terrors?
4.18 What are the major symptoms of narcolepsy?
4.19 What is sleep apnea?

4.20 What is insomnia?
4.21 For what purposes is meditation used?
4.22 What is hypnosis, and when is it most useful?
4.23 What are the two main theories that have been proposed to explain hypnosis?
4.24 What is the difference between physical and psychological drug dependence?
4.25 How do stimulants affect the user?
4.26 What effects do amphetamines have on the user?
4.27 How does cocaine affect the user?
4.28 What are some of the effects of depressants, and what drugs comprise this category?
4.29 What are the general effects of narcotics, and what are several drugs in this category?
4.30 What are the main effects of hallucinogens, and what are two psychoactive drugs classified as hallucinogens?
4.31 What are some harmful effects associated with heavy marijuana use?
4.32 What effect on the brain do all addictive drugs have in common?

Chapter Overview

Consciousness refers to our states of awareness, and the chapter explores altered states of consciousness that result from sleep, dreaming, meditation, hypnosis, and drugs. The chapter begins by explaining the relevance of some circadian rhythms to our understanding of sleep and daydreams. The chapter then defines the suprachiasmatic nucleus and describes its function as the body's timekeeper. The sleep cycles are discussed along with individual variations in patterns of sleep and the effects of sleep deprivation, particularly concerning work. The taking of melatonin as a sleep aid is then discussed. The chapter turns to a discussion of how the body reacts physically during REM and NREM sleep. Sleep cycles and variations in sleep cycles are considered. The function of sleep in terms of the restorative and circadian theories is then explored. The topic of dreaming is examined, and the authors discuss theories about the meaning and interpretation of dreams. This section of the chapter ends with a discussion of the function of REM sleep and why it is necessary.

Some sleep disturbances (parasomnias), like sleepwalking, sleep terrors, nightmares, and sleeptalking, may be minor problems. Sleep disorders, however, like narcolepsy (uncontrollable falling asleep), sleep apnea, and insomnia can be severe.

Hypnosis and meditation are also altered states, induced by concentration or suggestion. A *Try It!* section presents a relaxation technique. The authors discuss myths about and criticisms of hypnosis. The authors discuss the application of hypnosis especially medical and surgical applications. The two main theories of hypnosis (sociocognitive and the neodissociation) are discussed at length.

Psychoactive drugs (both legal and illegal) are responsible for a wide variety of altered states of consciousness. The authors discuss several protective factors that can lower the risk of young people using drugs. Drug addiction can be both physical and psychological. Stimulant drugs like caffeine, nicotine, amphetamines, cocaine, and crack speed up the nervous system. Hallucinogens, a group of drugs that includes LSD, PCP, MDMA (Ecstasy), and marijuana, alter mood and perception and cause hallucinations. Depressants include alcohol, barbiturates, minor tranquilizers, narcotics (morphine and heroin), and inhalants. Depressants slow nervous system activity.

Key Terms

alcohol (p. 140)
altered state of
    consciousness (p. 117)
amphetamines (p. 139)
barbiturates (p. 140)
circadian rhythm (p. 117)
Circadian theory (p.124)
cocaine (p. 140)
consciousness (p. 116)
crack (p. 140)
crash (p. 140)
delta wave (p. 122)
depressants (p. 140)
drug tolerance (p. 138)
flashback (p. 143)
hallucinogens (p. 142)
heroin (p. 142)
hypnosis (p. 132)
illicit drug (p. 136)
insomnia (p. 131)
LSD (p. 143)

lucid dream (p. 126)
marijuana (p. 143)
MDMA (Ecstasy) (p. 144)
meditation (p. 131)
melatonin (p.118)
microsleep (p. 124)
minor tranquilizers
    (p. 140)
narcolepsy (p. 130)
narcotics (p. 142)
Neodissociation theory of
    hypnosis (p.134)
nightmare (p. 129)
NREM dreams (p. 124)
NREM sleep (p. 121)
physical drug dependence
    (p. 138)
psychoactive drug (p. 136)
psychological drug
    dependence (p. 138)
REM dreams (p. 124)

REM rebound (p. 128)
REM sleep (p. 121)
Restorative theory (p. 124)
sleep apnea (p. 130)
sleep cycle (p. 122)
sleep terror (p. 129)
slow-wave sleep (p. 122)
Sociocognitive theory of
    hypnosis (p 134)
somnambulism (p. 129)
Stage 4 sleep (p. 122)
stimulants (p. 138)
subjective night (p. 118)
Suprachiasmatic Nucleus
    (p.117)
THC (p. 143)
Theory of dissociated
    control (p. 135)
withdrawal symptoms
    (p. 138)

Annotated Lecture Outline

A. What Is Consciousness?

Lecture Examples

Lecture Example 4.4: Descriptions of Consciousness

The difficulties faced in defining and researching consciousness will become apparent to students when you ask them to describe their own subjective experiences. This can either be in a verbal form for a small class or in a written form for larger sections. This is also a good activity for lab or recitation sections. Ask students to describe what they "feel" when they daydream, when they drift off to sleep, or when they consume mind-altering substances such as alcohol. If any students have been hypnotized, have them describe the experience. For more information go to the University of Arizona's web site http://www.consciousness.arizona.edu/.

Diversity Topic

Diversity Topic 4.1: Awareness

How are we aware of our own cultural background? While we are being raised, we are also being enculturated and socialized into our own cultures and societies. Yet, we are not always aware of the effects of that enculturation and socialization process. Have students engage in a discussion about the degree to which they may be aware of their own cultural backgrounds, and relate that discussion to the text presentation on defining consciousness.

Discussion/Description:

As discussed in my review, we are not always aware of our own cultural backgrounds. As adults, we operate on much of what we have learned in the enculturation process automatically, without thinking about it. We become very aware of our own culture when we engage with a different culture, for example, when on a trip to a different culture or country. Because culture operates within us at different levels, it provides the perfect opportunity for instructors to engage in a discussion about culture and consciousness together.

B. Circadian Rhythms: Our 24-Hour Highs and Lows

Lecture Examples

Lecture Example 4.1: Impact of Shift Work

Several studies have documented the detrimental health effects of shift work. One study conducted by Gordon et al. (1986) found that males who work variable work schedules had higher rates of heavy drinking, job stress, and emotional problems than did males working nonvariable schedules. Females who worked variable shifts reported more use of sleeping pills, tranquilizers, and alcohol, as well as more job stress and emotional problems. One interesting finding was that no difference was found in heavy cigarette smoking or coffee drinking between straight-shift workers and variable-shift workers. The authors suggest that more attention should be placed on health promotion at variable shift worksites. For more information on shift work, go to http://www.cami.jccbi.gov/AAM-400A/am95-19.html.

Gordon, N. P., Cleary, P. D., Parker, C. E., & Czeisler, C. A. (1986). The prevalence and health impact of shiftwork. *American Journal of Public Health, 76,* 1225-1228.

Lecture Example 4.2: Working Shifts

Some of your students are future managers and supervisors who will manage other people's work schedules; therefore, this topic will be especially important to them. Ask students who have worked on rotating shifts to describe the length of time they spent on each shift and how often they would rotate to the next shift. How did shift work affect their job satisfaction, productivity, and personal relationships? For more information of Circadian Rhythms and shift work, go to http://www.acep.org/ns-search/POLICY/PR004166.HTM?NS-search-set=\351ad\ s97.1ada83&NS-doc-offset=0&.

C. Sleep: That Mysterious One-Third of Our Lives

Classroom Demonstrations and Handouts

Student Chalkboard CONSC 1: Brain Activity during Stages of Sleep

Demonstration CONSC 2: Dream Journal

Objective: To become more aware of dreams and dreaming.
Materials: Sleep and Dreaming Record (**Handout CONSC 2**)
Procedure: Ask students to keep a sleep and dream journal for a week. Give them enough copies of **Handout CONSC 2**. Some students might argue that they do not dream; inform them that they probably have poor dream recall. Offer the following hint to improve recall: As you fall asleep, tell yourself that you want to and will remember your dreams the next morning. As soon as you get up in the morning, jot your dream down, or at least several keywords that you can use later to jog your memory. You might set the alarm clock about 30 minutes earlier than usual to awaken yourself during a REM period. As you review your dreams, think about how they may relate to the events and people in your life right now. Is there a relationship between the dream and the previous day's events? Later collect the Records, summarize the data, and present the results to your students.
Conclusions: Students will be interested in the dreams of their classmates. These data can be presented in such a way that no one student can be identified. For an example of a dream journal see http://www.willa.com/dreams/dreams.htm.

Demonstration CONSC 3: Discussion of Dream Journal

Objective: To analyze dreams.
Materials: Student dream journals
Procedure: In groups of no larger than five, students should share and discuss the dreams they have experienced in the last week. Each student must realize that sharing a dream is voluntary and not compulsory. This Demonstration is an appropriate supplement to Demonstration CONSC 2.
Conclusions: Students should become more attuned to their dreams and to realize the similarity in the dreams of others.

Demonstration CONSC 7: Electroencephalograph (EEG)

Objective: To demonstrate the use of the Electroencephalograph (EEG).
Materials: Electroencephalograph or field trip
Procedure: If your department has a working EEG and it is portable, take it to the classroom and ask for a volunteer or pre-arrange for your TA or graduate students to volunteer. If no EEG is available, plan a field trip to your local hospital. After preparing the volunteer, record EEG data. It might be a good idea to screen your volunteer to be sure that the individual will have a reasonably normal EEG.
Conclusions: Discuss the different wave patterns and how they are interpreted in a clinical setting.

If you have access to abnormal EEG data, compare the two sets of data. Students will have first-hand knowledge of the process of EEG recording. For more information on EEG, go to http://dizzy.library.arizona.edu/images/caron/chp3elec.html.

Demonstration CONSC 9: Dreams

Objective: To allow the students to explore material on dreams on the Internet.
Materials: Internet access
Procedure: Go to http://www.dreamgate.com/dream/resources/online97.htm. Have the students explore this massive site which contains the following Mail List, Usenet Newsgroups and Web sites by category: Dream Sharing, Magazines and Journals, Information, Education and Organizations, Personal Dream Journals, Religion, Spirituality and Healing (and Shamanism), Lucid Dreaming, Psi, Paranormal, Telepathic Dreaming, Dream Science and Research, Dreams and Anthropology, Dream Bibliography Collections, Dream Art, Dream Software, Jung and Dreams, Freud and Dreams, Books and Articles Online and Lists of Links. Assign the students to explore several of the links.
Conclusions: Students could write a short summary of their experiences at this site. Their understanding of these dream related links and principles behind them will be enhanced. After this assignment be prepared for students asking questions about the dreaming.

Lecture Examples

Lecture Example 4.3: What Goes on during NREM?

Some students might wonder what goes on in NREM sleep if most dreaming occurs in REM. Thoughtlike mentation is generally experienced in NREM. Point out that this type of mental activity is less vivid, more plausible, and less emotional. Go to http://www.sawka.com/spiritwatch/function.htm for more information of NREM sleep.

Lecture Example 4.5: Sleep Deprivation

After a few nights without sleep, people usually experience fine hand tremors, drooping eyelids, difficulty focusing their eyes, and increased sensitivity to pain (Webb, 1975). After four nights without sleep, a few people exhibit symptoms of severe disturbance—paranoid delusions and bizarre hallucinations. According to Hobson (1989), "After we go five to ten days without sleep, our brain loses its bearings altogether and madness takes over: The trusting become paranoid; the rational, irrational; and the sane begin to see and hear things that aren't there." For recent findings see http://www.kron.com/nc4/healthbeat/stories/sleep.html or
http://www.ail.org/Media/Dreams/VisualDreams/disorders/deprivation.html.

Hobson, J. A. (1989). *Sleep.* New York: Scientific American.

Webb, W. B. (1975). *Sleep: The gentle tyrant.* Englewood Cliffs, NJ: Prentice-Hall.

Lecture Example 4.6: Putting Sleep into Perspective

We spend about one-third of our lives asleep. If your students live to be 75 years old, they will have slept about 25 years. An average 20-year-old college student has spent about 6 years asleep. Moreover, if we spend about 25 percent of our sleep time dreaming, then the 20-year-old student has spent about one and one-half years dreaming! What behavior, other than wakefulness, is so prevalent?

Lecture Example 4.7: Incorporating Ongoing Stimuli into Dreams

Several researchers have found that subjects can bring external stimuli into their dreams (e.g., Foulkes et al., 1969). One subject, after having a puff of air directed to her face, recalled a dream of sailing. Bedwetters often report dreaming of urinating prior to bedwetting. However, it has been suggested that the dream actually comes after urinating. The physical sensations of being wet are then incorporated into the dream. Your students may want to conduct a mini-experiment using their roommates, friends, or spouses (after obtaining the participant's consent). As they observe the person in REM, introduce a stimulus, such as a mist of water, a bright light, or other stimulation. Ask the participant upon awakening to recount his or her dream. Did the person incorporate the stimulus into his or her dreams?

Foulkes, D., Larson, J. D., Swanson, E. M., & Radin, M. (1969). Two studies of childhood dreaming. *American Journal of Orthopsychiatry, 39*, 627-643.

Lecture Example 4.8: Lucid Dreaming

Lucid dreaming is the experience of being able to control the activities and characters in one's dreams. The earliest written reference to lucid dreaming dates back to 415 A.D. in a letter written by St. Augustine; however, scientific study of lucid dreaming has existed only since the 1970's. Stephen LaBerge (1980) asserts that lucid dreaming can be learned through motivation and good dream recall. LaBerge (1985) suggests a method called Mnemonic Induction of Lucid Dreams (MILD), which teaches people to wake up *in* a dream rather than *from* it. In MILD, people learn to memorize a dream they've just had (preferably in the early morning hours) and verbally as well as visually put themselves back into the dream. As the individual is learning to dream lucidly, he or she must be able to control emotional arousal. At the moment of recognizing that one is in control of a dream, there tends to be an immediate increase in arousal, which leads to awakening. For more on lucid dreaming, go to http://www.sawka.com/spiritwatch/individu.htm or http://library.advanced.org/11189/nflucid.htm.

Gackenbach, J., Heilman, N., Boyt, S., & LaBerge, S. (1985). The relationship between field independence and lucid dreaming ability. *Journal of Mental Imagery, 9*, 9-20.

LaBerge, S. P. (1980). Lucid dreaming as a learnable skill: A case study. *Perceptual and Motor Skills, 51*, 1039-1042.

LaBerge, S. P. (1985). *Lucid dreaming.* New York: Ballantine Books.

Lecture Example 4.9: Why Do We Sleep?

One of the questions sleep research does not yet answer is "Why do we sleep?" Begin by asking students to describe their conscious experiences when they have been deprived of sleep. Most students will probably report negative effects. When asked why we sleep, many students will give a variation of the restorative theories. Contrast that view with the notion of sleep as evolutionary adaptation; for example, animals sleep to avoid predators.

D. Sleep Disorders

Classroom Demonstrations and Handouts

Demonstration CONSC 8: DSM IV and Sleep Disorders

Objective: To analyze sleep disorders.
Materials: DSM IV
Procedure: Form groups of about five or six students, and then distribute a photocopy of a disorder from the sleep disorders section of the DSM IV. Ask each group to summarize the behaviors associated with each disorder. Encourage students to volunteer any personal examples of sleep disorders. Have a spokesperson from each group present the summaries to the class.
Conclusions: Students will gain valuable experience from exposure to the summaries of DSM IV symptoms. Lead a discussion of the types of sleep disorders and examples provided by the students. Ordering information for the DSM-IV http://www.tetondata.com/DSMFLhome.html. All the DSM-IV disorders can be found at http://134.68.135.89/abnormal/dsm/dsm-main.htm.

Lecture Examples

Lecture Example 4.10: Sleepwalking (Somnambulism)

About 15 percent of children between the ages of 5 and 12 have had some sleepwalking episode, but adult somnambulism is more serious and is often related to extreme stress or psychological problems (Kales et al., 1980). For additional information on sleepwalking, see http://www.ail.org/Media/Dreams/VisualDreams/disorders/walking.html.

Kales, A., Soldatos, C. R., Bixler, E. O., et al. (1980). Hereditary factors in sleepwalking and
      night terrors. *British Journal of Psychiatry, 137,* 111-118.

Lecture Example 4.11: Treatment for Sleep Apnea

Often individuals with sleep apnea are reported to have loud snoring and are very sleepy the following day. Treatment approaches may involve weight loss, surgery, antidepressants, or mechanical devices such as the Tongue Retaining Device; it looks much like a mouth guard and is designed to prevent the tongue from falling backward (Cartwright et al., 1988). For additional information see http://www.gulf1.com/shehee/apnea.htm.

Cartwright, R., et al. (1988). Toward a treatment logic for sleep apnea: The place of the tongue retaining device. *Behaviour Research and Therapy, 26,* 121-126.

Lecture Example 4.12: Link between Insomnia and Depression

A recent epidemiological study (Ford & Kamerow, 1989) examined the relationship between sleep disturbances and behavioral disorders. It found that sufferers of insomnia are twice as likely as the general population to have some psychiatric disorder. The strongest link with insomnia was major depression, followed by anxiety disorders and alcohol abuse. The authors suggest that early diagnosis and treatment of insomnia may reduce the likelihood of developing psychiatric disorders. For additional information see http://www.mhsource.com/expert/exp1102896l.html.

Ford, D., & Kamerow, D. (1989). Epidemiologic study of sleep disturbances and psychiatric disorder. *Journal of the American Medical Association, 262,* 1479-1484.

E. Altering Consciousness through Concentration and Suggestion

Lecture Example

Lecture Example 4.13: Mesmerism

Demonstrations by Franz Mesmer (1734-1815) of animal magnetism were effective because of hypnotic suggestion, not because of the "magnetic forces." Though he demonstrated a real psychological phenomenon, he had the explanations entirely wrong. He did however, make a living in Europe traveling between royal courts and displaying his animal magnetism.

Lecture Example 4.14: Hypnosis

Hypnosis has been used in the criminal justice system to induce eyewitness recall of details relating to a crime. There has been some very controversial use of hypnosis in recovered memories (see web sites on Memory Chapter-at-a-Glance). Since hypnotically induced recall may be inaccurate or invented, should such eyewitness evidence be allowed in court? Also see http://home.earthlink.net/~izone/tools/hypno.htm for information on self hypnosis.

Lecture Example 4.15 Sensory Deprivation

As popularized in recent movies, sensory deprivation can lead to alteration in perception, including hallucinations, cognitive processes, and mood. This is not surprising, given that normal consciousness is achieved through the action of a normal nervous system functioning in a normal environment. Change either the nervous system, as with psychoactive drugs, or the environment, as with sensory deprivation, and you can produce altered states of consciousness. In the 1960s and 1970s many Psychology departments conducted research of sensory deprivation. If your department has a sensory deprivation chamber, take you class on a tour of the facility. As an alternative some departments have auditory research chambers. For recent findings see http://www.kron.com/nc4/healthbeat/stories/sleep.html or http://www.ail.org/Media/Dreams/VisualDreams/disorders/deprivation.html.

Diversity Topic

Diversity Topic 4.2: Meditation

Arrange for a yogi or expert in any one of the meditative systems described in the text to come to class and give a presentation, and, if possible, lead the class in a demonstration.
Discussion/Description: The best way to understand these different approaches is not to simply talk about them; it is to actually engage with them. There are a sufficient number of Zen meditation centers, TM centers, and yoga centers with experts who can give a demonstration on their art and practice and lead students through simple activities to demonstrate them.

F. Altered States of Consciousness and Psychoactive Drugs

Classroom Demonstrations and Handouts

Student Chalkboard CONSC 2: Drugs and Their Effects

Demonstration CONSC 4: Guest Speaker on Drug Abuse

Objective: To expose students to authorities on the topic of drug abuse, and to inform students of local efforts to combat the drug abuse.
Materials: None
Procedure: If you are pressed for time, consider inviting only one of the people mentioned here. Many times celebrities and athletes who have abused drugs participate in drug prevention programs as part of their rehabilitation. It may be a good idea to have this person speak to your students on the topic of drug abuse. Other individuals to consider include a member of the local police department, Drug Enforcement Administration, or a chemical dependency counselor. To make their presentations more effective, ask if real samples of drugs can be brought to class to show.
Conclusions: Depending on your purpose of having a guest speaker, students will appreciate the personal accounts of overcoming abuse, helping those with a drug problem, and those who are on the front lines of the war on drugs in enforcing law.

Demonstration CONSC 5: Antecedents and Consequences of Drug Use

Objective: To identify the stimuli that precede drug use and its effects.
Materials: Antecedents and Consequences of Drug Use (**Handout CONSC 5**)—give each student four copies
Procedure: For four days, students are to monitor their use of alcohol, caffeine, and nicotine. Using Handout **CONSC 5**, Students should record data on drug use antecedents and consequences.
Conclusions: Using these data, ask students to note any trends they see in the antecedents and consequences of their drug use. Draw conclusions in the context of the psychological mechanisms

underlying drug abuse as discussed in the text. For instance, is the use of drugs automatic in response to certain stimuli? Is social pressure present and powerful? Are the consequences of drug use pleasant and reinforcing?

Demonstration CONSC 6: Effects of Alcohol Intoxication

Objective: To demonstrate the effects of alcohol intoxication on decision making.
Materials: None
Procedure: You may have some difficulty pulling this activity off at your college or university depending on policies and the law. Because of the alcohol abuse prevalent on many campuses, it deserves a chance. The basic idea is to allow a consenting adult (over the age 21) to consume alcohol while performing tasks that measure reaction time, judgment, decision making, and other observable tasks. Often, State Highway Patrols, Campus Security, or local Police Departments put on such demonstrations. You may have to get their approval and cooperation to stage this activity. At minimum, you should check it out with your institution's administration. A scaled down version of this activity needing less preparation and clearance is to use caffeine as the consciousness-altering drug.
Conclusions: Alcohol impairs judgment as it depresses the nervous system. Discuss the blood alcohol level that is considered to be impairing in your state. What types of behaviors and mental process are affected? For specific effects, go to http://www.netxpress.com/~lannyn/alc/alcefts.html.

Demonstration CONSC 10: Substance Use and Abuse

Objective: To demonstrate substance use and abuse.
Materials: Internet access
Procedure: Go to http://orion.it.luc.edu/~pcrowe/375link.htm and explore three different links from a course at Loyola University taught on addiction/substance abuse. The students will find many diverse links from varying viewpoints on the state of consciousness.
Conclusions: Have each student investigate this site and prepare to discuss their findings at the next class meeting. Lead a discussion using the following questions: What are the pros and cons of legalizing marijuana? What is the most destructive drug in our society? Should all drugs be legalized and controlled?

Lecture Examples

Lecture Example 4.16: In Pursuit of Artificial Paradise

A professor at UCLA argues that efforts to conduct a war on drugs are futile because of an innate drive to alter consciousness. Ronald Siegel (1988) contends that human beings have consumed, are consuming, and always will consume drugs to experience optimal positive effects. In fact, according to Siegel, almost all cultures in history have consumed substances to alter their consciousness. In Siegel's view, the money that is being spent on the drug war should be used on developing "safe" drugs that still produce the desired effects but without toxicity or dangerous consequences such as dependency. Have students debate this argument.

Siegel, R. (1988). Intoxication: Life in pursuit of artificial paradise. New York: Dutton.

Lecture Example 4.17: Drugs and Behavior

Most students are knowledgeable about the effects of drugs on overt behavior. But they might not be familiar with how those effects come about through alterations of nervous system processes such as re-uptake, production, and storage of neurotransmitters, and the activity at receptor sites. A logical extension includes how pharmacological therapies (e.g., antidepressants) work on neurotransmitters and related structures, as the text briefly mentions. For a listing of student generated questions on drugs and behavior, see http://www.slu.edu/classes/ancham/drugs_viewqs.html.

Julien, R. M. (1981). *A primer of drug action.* San Francisco: W. H. Freeman.

Kimble, D. (1988). *Biological psychology.* New York: Holt, Rinehart, and Winston.

Lecture Example 4.18: Caffeinism

One of the most pervasively used psychoactive drugs is caffeine. It is difficult to escape caffeine because of its widespread use in colas and headache remedies and its natural occurrence in chocolate, tea, cola, and coffee. There has been growing concern over the abuse of caffeine. Although caffeine has long been identified as a benign, socially approved drug, researchers now know that chronic consumption of caffeine (i.e., caffeinism) is characterized by depression, disturbed sleep, agitation, delirium, and decrements in performance. The behavioral signs of severe caffeinism may be hard to distinguish from those of a psychotic state. In low to moderate doses, caffeine may facilitate performance, increase concentration, and help to arouse. So strong are these effects that many adults cannot "function" before consuming their first cup of coffee in the morning. When such adults reduce or eliminate caffeine, withdrawal symptoms are common and include anxiety, headaches, irritability, and lethargy.
Caffeinism may develop when daily ingestion reaches more than 500-600 mg of caffeine, an amount equivalent to four to seven cups of coffee or seven to nine cups of tea in a day. Symptoms of caffeinism that are similar to those of anxiety neurosis include nervous irritability, tremulousness, muscle twitches, insomnia, palpitations, flushing, cardiac arrhythmias, diuresis, and gastrointestinal disturbances (Murray, 1988).

Bolton, S., & Null, G. (1981). Caffeine psychological effects, use and abuse. *Journal of Orthomolecular Psychiatry, 10,* 202-211.

Murray, J. B. (1988). Psychophysiological aspects of caffeine consumption. *Psychological Reports, 62,* 575-587.

Sawyer, D. A., Julia, H. L., & Turnin, A. C. (1982). Caffeine and human behavior: Arousal, anxiety, and performance effects. *Journal of Behavioral Medicine, 5,* 415-439.

Lecture Example 4.19: Cocaine

Although illegal now, cocaine was once alleged to cure a plethora of ailments. In fact Sigmund Freud claimed that cocaine was a "magical drug" capable of delivering a person from depression and fatigue; so ardent was he in his belief that in 1884 he wrote and published a song praising this wonder drug. Later, however, he withdrew his support for the drug. During the same era, cocaine was widely accepted and used in teas, elixirs, and even the commercially successful Coca-Cola. (The cocaine was removed from Coca-Cola in 1903 and replaced with caffeine.) Attitudes toward use of cocaine changed as the public focused on its apparent link with criminal behavior and on issues of abuse and toxicity. The sale of cocaine was prohibited by the Pure Food and Drug Act (1906) and the Harrison Narcotic Act (1914). For an interesting investigation of cocaine abuse and modern imaging techniques, see http://www.med.harvard.edu/BWHRad/BrainSPECT/Cocaine/Cocaine_2/Coc2.html.

Ray, O. (1983). *Drugs, society, and human behavior.* St. Louis, Mo.: Mosby.

Stone, N., Fromme, M., & Kagan, D. (1984). *Cocaine.* New York: Clarkson N. Potts.

Lecture Example 4.20: Culture and Hallucinogens

Many cultures maintain their use of hallucinogenic drugs as components of essential religious and cultural rituals. For example, the Yanomamo of South America produce a drug that is blown into their noses through a long tube. The drug causes them to have green mucus and to appear ferocious as they enter their trance with the spirits. The name *Yanomamö* means "fierce people." For information on films of the *Yanomamö*, see http://www.sscf.ucsb.edu/anth/projects/axfight/updates/yanomamofilmography.html.

Lecture Example 4.21: Origins of Drug Names

Liebman (1991) gives very interesting accounts of the origin of some drug names. For example, the name *barbiturate* actually is derived from a coffeehouse waitress named Barbara. Barbara contributed her urine to Emil Fisher's attempt to condense malonic acid with urea (urea is extracted from urine). *Morphine* gets its name from the Greek god of dreams, Morpheus; the idea is that morphine induced a dreamlike altered state. *Marijuana* comes from the Hispanic names of Maria and Juan and is related to the belief that marijuana has aphrodisiac effects.

Liebman, M. (1991). *Neuroanatomy made easy and understandable* (4th ed.). Gaithersburg, MD: Aspen Publishers.

Lecture Example 4.22: Heroin Addiction

A new route to heroin addiction is now available. Drug users are now injecting, snorting, or smoking "moonrock" a mixture of heroin and cocaine used to soften the "crash" of paranoia and depression that follows cocaine's high.

Lecture Example 4.23: Standards of Intoxication

In many states, a blood alcohol level of .10 is used as the legal standard for intoxication while driving a vehicle. Recently, the United State Congress is proposing that all state be required to adopt a stricter .08 standard. Many states are resisting this effort and claming it is a states' rights issue to set the legal standard. Because the effects of drugs are individual and subjective, is an imposed arbitrary legal standard sensible? Ask students either individually or in small groups if they can develop an alternative legal definition of intoxication; some possibilities include behaviors relating to coordination and reaction time. This is a good time to discuss the advantages and disadvantages of both physiological and behavioral measures of intoxication. For specific effects, go to http://www.netxpress.com/~lannyn/alc/alcefts.html.

Diversity Topics

Diversity Topic 4.4: Drug Abuse

What is it about American culture that may make drug abuse attractive? Have students engage in a discussion about the social and cultural forces that may contribute to drug abuse problems in the U.S. today. Contrast those social and cultural factors with past history or other cultures of the world to examine whether those periods of time or those other cultures also experience drug abuse problems.

Discussion/Description: One thing that is missing from the presentation in the text on why people abuse drugs is a discussion of the social and cultural forces in the U.S. that may have contributed to the problem. From the 1960s into the 1990s, the individualistic American culture transformed itself so that there was an extreme focus on instant and immediate gratification and pleasure.

5 Learning

Chapter-at-a-Glance

Chapter Outline	Instruction Outline	Multimedia
Classical Conditioning: The Original View p. 152 Pavlov and Classical Conditioning • The Elements and Processes of Classical Conditioning • John Watson, Little Albert, and Peter • **Pioneers: John B. Watson** • Classical Conditioning: The Contemporary View • The Cognitive Perspective: Prediction Is the Critical Element • Biological Predispositions: Their Role in Classical Conditioning • Classically Conditioned Taste Aversions • Classical Conditioning in Everyday Life • Factors Influencing Classical Conditioning	**Student Chalkboard** LEARN 1 & 3 **Demonstration** LEARN 1, 2, 9 & 10 **Lecture Examples** 5.1-5.5, 5.18 **Learning Objectives** 5.1-5.10 **Test Questions** 1-57	*Discovering Psychology: Learning* *Discovering Psychology: Health, Mind, and Behavior* **Transparencies** LEARN 3, 8-9 **Video Disc I** Segment 12 **Digital Image Archive** PSLN003a&b-004 **Web Site** http://www.as.wvu.edu/~sbb/comm221/chapters/pavlov.htm History of Classical Conditioning
Operant Conditioning p. 165 Thorndike and the Law of Effect • The Elements and Processes in Operant Conditioning • **Pioneers: Burrhus Frederic Skinner** • Reinforcement: What's the Payoff? • Factors Influencing Operant Conditioning • Comparing Classical and Operant Conditioning: What's the Difference? • Punishment: That Hurts! • Culture and Punishment • Escape and Avoidance Learning • Learned Helplessness • Applications of Operant Conditioning	**Student Chalkboard** LEARN 2 **Demonstration** LEARN 3-6, 11-13 **Demonstration** INTRO 6 **Lecture Examples** 5.7-5.14 **Critical Thinking Opportunity** 5.1 **Critical Thinking Forum** 5.1 **Journal Entries** 5.1-5.2 **Diversity Topics** 5.1-5.3 **Learning Objectives** 5.11-5.23 **Test Questions** 58-122	*Psychology and Culture*: Ch. 22 *PsychScience* Behavior Modification **Video Disc IV** Segment 8 **Digital Image Archive** PSLN006a&b, 007-010 **Web Site** http://www.indiana.edu/~iuepsyc/Ch_8/C8E1.html Classical Conditioning and Operant Conditioning
Cognitive Learning p. 181 Learning by Insight: Aha! Now I Get It • Latent Learning and Cognitive Maps: I Might Use That Later • Observational Learning: Watching and Learning	**Demonstration** LEARN 7-8 **Lecture Example** 5.15, 5.16 **Journal Entry** 5.3, 5.4 **Diversity Topic** 5.4 **Learning Objectives** 5.24-5.26 **Test Questions** 123-135	**Transparency** LEARN 4 **Video Disc III** Segment 2 **Digital Image Archive** PSLN005, 010 **Web Site** http://mse.byu.edu/ipt301/jordan/learnterm_c.html Cognitive Learning Theory Terms

What's New in Chapter 5

New Content

- The cognitive perspective on classical conditioning (Rescorla)
- Biological predispositions in classical conditioning

Organizational Changes

- Topics in classical conditioning and operant conditioning have been reordered for a more logical flow from fundamentals through applications.
- B. F. Skinner has been integrated within the text.

New Special Features

- New chapter opening vignette
- Revised *Remember It's*

Learning Objective Questions

5.1 What was Pavlov's major contribution to psychology?
5.2 How was classical conditioning accomplished in Pavlov's experiments?
5.3 How does extinction occur in classical conditioning?
5.4 What is generalization?
5.5 What is discrimination in classical conditioning?
5.6 How did Watson demonstrate that fear could be classically conditioned?
5.7 According to Rescorla, what is the critical element in classical conditioning?
5.8 What two exceptions to traditional classical conditioning did Garcia and Koelling find?
5.9 What types of responses can be learned through classical conditioning?
5.10 What are four factors that influence classical conditioning?
5.11 What is Thorndike's major contribution to psychology?
5.12 What is Skinner's major contribution to psychology?
5.13 How are responses acquired through operant conditioning?
5.14 How is shaping used to condition a response?
5.15 How does extinction occur in operant conditioning?
5.16 What is the goal of both positive reinforcement and negative reinforcement, and how is the goal accomplished by each?
5.17 What are the four major schedules of reinforcement, and which schedule yields the highest response rate and the greatest resistance to extinction?
5.18 What is the partial-reinforcement effect?
5.19 What three factors, in addition to the schedule of reinforcement, influence operant conditioning?
5.20 How does punishment differ from negative reinforcement?

5.21 What are some disadvantages of punishment?
5.22 What three factors increase the effectiveness of punishment?
5.23 What are some applications of operant conditioning?
5.24 What is insight, and how does it affect learning?
5.25 What is latent learning?
5.26 What is observational learning?

Chapter Overview

Learning, the relatively permanent change in behavior acquired through experience, is one of the most important topics in psychology. In this chapter the authors examine classical conditioning, operant conditioning, and cognitive learning.

Classical conditioning originates with Ivan Pavlov's original study of the conditioned reflex. The text describes the basic process of acquisition of a conditioned response. The other basic principles discovered by Pavlov include the extinction of a conditioned response and its spontaneous recovery; the generalization of the response to stimuli similar to the conditioned stimulus; and discrimination and higher order conditioning. J. B. Watson's work with both creating and removing fears represents early applications of conditioning to life. The contemporary view of classical conditioning, the cognitive perspective, and the effect of biological predispositions are discussed. The phenomenon of taste aversion and its application to cancer treatment also illustrates the value of classical conditioning. The factors that affect conditioning, such as the number and frequency of pairings of the unconditioned and conditioned stimuli, the timing of the pairings, and the strength of the stimuli, are also described.

Operant conditioning depends on the association of a behavior with its consequences. This was first recognized by Thorndike as the law of effect and later studied by B. F. Skinner as reinforcement. Operant conditioning allows the shaping of behavior by successive approximations. Each of the phenomena found in classical conditioning—extinction, spontaneous recovery, generalization, and discrimination—have equivalent forms in operant conditioning. The authors also describe reinforcement and reinforcement schedules in detail and then distinguish punishment and its effectiveness from the effectiveness of reinforcement. The disadvantages and methods to maximize the effects of punishment are then discussed. Applications of operant conditioning are also described.

Cognitive learning includes mental processes in the study of learning. These processes include insight, latent learning, and observational learning. Observational learning has been applied to the learning of aggressive behavior through the observation of others who model the behavior.

Key Terms

avoidance learning (p. 178)
behavior modification (p. 179)
biofeedback (p. 179)
classical conditioning (p. 152)
cognitive map (p. 182)
cognitive processes (p. 181)
conditioned reflex (p. 154)
conditioned response (p. 154)
conditioned stimulus (p. 154)
continuous reinforcement (p. 170)
discrimination (p.157)
discriminative stimulus (p. 168)
drug tolerance (p. 162)
extinction (p. 156)
extinction (p. 168)
fixed-interval schedule (p. 171)
fixed-ratio schedule (p. 171)
generalization (p. 156)
higher-order conditioning (p. 157)
insight (p. 181)
latent learning (p. 181)
law of effect (p. 165)
learned helplessness (p. 178)
learning (p. 152)
model (p. 182)
modeling (p. 182)
negative reinforcement (p. 169)
observational learning (p. 182)
operant conditioning (p. 166)
partial reinforcement (p. 170)
partial-reinforcement effect (p. 173)
positive reinforcement (p. 169)
primary reinforcer (p. 170)
punishment (p. 175)
reflex (p. 154)
reinforcement (p. 169)
reinforcer (p. 166)
schedule of reinforcement (p. 170)
secondary reinforcer (p. 170)
shaping (p. 166)
Skinner box (p. 166)
spontaneous recovery (p. 156)
stimulus (p. 152)
successive approximations (p. 166)
taste aversion (p. 162)
token economy (p. 180)
trial-and-error learning (p. 165)
unconditioned response (p. 154)
unconditioned stimulus (p. 154)
variable-interval schedule (p. 172)
variable-ratio schedule (p. 171)

Annotated Lecture Outline

A. Classical Conditioning

Classroom Demonstrations and Handouts

Student Chalkboard LEARN 1: Order of Presentation

Student Chalkboard LEARN 3: Learning Theory Comparison

Demonstration LEARN 1: Classical Conditioning in Humans

Objective: To show classical conditioning as a relevant form of learning.

Materials: Straw; musical theme to Jaws; balloons; blackboard; lemon; Conditioning Record **(Handout LEARN 1)**

Procedure: Ask students to use **Handout LEARN 1** to record the components of these activities.

> A well-known demonstration involves puffing air (UCS) through a straw directed at a subject's eye which causes an eye blink (UCR). Precede the puff with a finger snap or another appropriate neutral stimulus.
>
> Consider using the theme to Jaws to elicit a CR (Smith, 1987). The activity requires students to imagine a warm sunlit beach; they cool off by dipping into the water. After stretching the imagery to around three to four minutes, "unobtrusively" play the Jaws theme (CS). Students' responses (CR) will clearly show a demonstration between the shark (UCS) with music (CS). Alternatively, try using music from Nightmare on Elm Street, Halloween, or Friday the 13th to elicit responses (using other scenes).
>
> Our responses to a balloon being twisted and handled are due to classical conditioning. That is, balloon sounds (CS) always come before the pop (UCS). The pop elicits a startle response (UCR).
>
> Say any word and then immediately make a bone chilling scratch on the blackboard. Do this for a couple of trials. Soon the mere mention of the word will cause a CR. A modification of the UCS could be an airpowered starter's horn or pistol.
>
> Bring a fresh lemon or two and a bag of lemon drops to class. What response do students experience when you mention the word "lemon" or let students smell the lemon? Do they report the activation of the salivary gland or that "puckered" feeling? Do you get the same results with lemon drops? Ask students to identify the UCS, UCR, CS, and CR. Consult Cogan and Cogan (1984) for a variation of this activity using lemonade powder.

Conclusions: In each of these activities, it is very crucial to break down the conditioning by identifying UCS, UCR, CS and CR. By performing these activities, students will acknowledge that they have been classically conditioned. See http://www.abacon.com/lefton/learning.html to answer the question, "Does the cerebellum play a role in classical conditioning in humans?"

Cogan, D., & Cogan, R. (1984). Classical salivary conditioning: An easy demonstration. *Teaching of Psychology, 11*, 170-171.

Gibb, G. D. (1983). Making classical conditioning understandable through a demonstration technique. *Teaching of Psychology, 10*, 112-113.

Smith, R. A. (1987). Jaws: Demonstrating classical conditioning. In V. P. Makosky, L. G. Whittemore, & A. M. Rogers (Eds.). *Activities handbook for the teaching of psychology* (Vol. 2) (pp. 65-66). Washington, D.C.: American Psychological Association.

Demonstration LEARN 2: The Learning Curve

Objective: To demonstrate the learning curve.
Materials: Learning Curve: Backwards Alphabet (**Handout LEARN 2**); stopwatch
Procedure: Challenge your students to write down the alphabet backwards on a sheet of paper as fast as they can. There should be at least 15 trials to allow for the learning curve to develop (each trial lasts 20 seconds). Of course, students are not allowed to view lists from prior trials; they should simply fold the paper. At the end of each trial, the number of correct letters is recorded on Handout **LEARN 2** and then plotted on the graph. Time the first and last trials, if possible.
Conclusions: In the initial trials, students will show relatively fast acquisition of the new skill. However, the increase in the curve should be followed by a gradual leveling off.

Sheldahl, L. M. (1987). Backwards alphabet. In V. P. Makosky, L. G. Whittemore, and A. M. Rogers (Eds.). *Activities handbook for the teaching of psychology* (Vol. 2) (pp. 63-54). Washington, D.C.: American Psychological Association.

Demonstration LEARN 9: Classical Conditioning

Objective: To allow the students to explore classical conditioning on the Internet.
Materials: Internet access
Procedure: Go to the web site: http://www.indiana.edu/~iuepsyc/Ch_8/C8E1.html. This site contains the components of classical conditioning and everyday examples of classical conditioning. Assign the students to explore several of the links.
Conclusions: Students' understanding of the components of classical conditioning will be greatly enhanced. Have the students write a short summary of the materials on this site and give several examples of everyday classical conditioning from their lives.

Demonstration LEARN10: Animal Resource Center

Objective: To enhance the sensitivity of students regarding the issue of animal rights and animal research.
Materials: Permission to tour animal resource center
Procedure: If possible take your class (if small enough) on a tour of the animal resource center on your campus. If you have a large class perhaps the laboratory or recitation sections could take the tour. As an alternative, allow students to sign-up for extra credit for this tour.
Conclusions: Students will gain an appreciation for the animals' care and the lengths that are taken for humane treatment. For information on one of the most famous animal laboratories in the world see http://www.jax.org/.

Lecture Examples

Lecture Example 5.1: Pavlov and Serendipity

Point out that Pavlov's discovery of classical conditioning was accidental. This example can be used to illustrate the importance of serendipity to most scientific disciplines. As a classic example, use Fleming's discovery of penicillin. Fleming noticed a mold growing on a culture of bacteria and saw that the culture around the mold was dissolving. Conducting further research, he discovered that the mold would systematically kill bacteria. He grew the mold and made it into a drug that could be given to humans with bacterial infections. Thus, penicillin was born and has saved the lives of many individuals. This accidental discovery could quite possibly be the reason everyone in the classroom is alive today. Students should be encouraged to investigate unexpected phenomena whatever their field of inquiry.

Lecture Example 5.2: Classical Conditioning in Real Life

The properties of classical conditioning have been delineated in laboratory research, but exact examples of classical conditioning are more difficult to identify in everyday life. Ask students to name some of their own behaviors that involve classical conditioning. Students might have difficulty in finding examples, so suggest any superstitions they might have. Is this form of learning important to the survival of organisms, or is it simply an interesting laboratory oddity?

A good example of classical conditioning is to ask the students what they do when a toilet flushes while they're taking a shower. In dorms and apartment buildings, especially the older ones, a flushing toilet takes away cold water from the shower and the result is very hot water (UCS). The automatic, unconditioned response to the hot water is to jump back (UCR). Over several trials we learn to associate the sound of a flushing toilet (CS) with hot water, and we respond by taking a step back (CR) before the predicted hot water arrives and scalds us.

Lecture Example 5.3: Stimulus Generalization and Discrimination

Generalization means a widening or an extending. In Pavlov's experiment, the dogs might have salivated to anything that sounded like a bell, such as a buzzer or a ringing telephone. Conversely, discrimination refers to a narrowing or constricting. The dogs perhaps only responded to a very high-pitched bell and not to other bell-like sounds.

Lecture Example 5.4: Immune System Conditioning

Glenda MacQueen and her colleagues (1989) tested whether the immune system could be classically conditioned to produce an allergic reaction to lights and sounds. The researchers produced an allergy in one group of rats by injecting egg white under their skin, which triggered a measurable allergic response. Once the allergic reaction was well established, the researchers continued with the egg-white injections while, at the same time, exposing the rats to 15 minutes of flashing lights and a noisy, humming sound. Several sessions later, the researchers were able to measure a strong immune reaction to the lights and the noise (CS) alone.

MacQueen, G., Marshall, J., Perdue, M., Siegel, S., & Bienenstock, J. (1989). Pavlovian conditioning of rat mucosal mast cells to secrete rat mast cell protease II. *Science, 243,* 83-85.

Lecture Example 5.5: Taste Aversions in Students

We can all come up with examples of learned taste aversions. According to Garb and Stunkard

(1974), many of us have long-lasting aversions to all sorts of foods. Ask your students for other examples. Relate taste aversions to anticipatory nausea/vomiting that chemotherapy patients often experience (Andrykowski et al., 1985). For more on taste aversion, go to http://141.140.8.150/diaries/diariesf95/Megan/diary5.

Andrykowski, M., Redd, W., & Hatfield, A. (1985). Development of anticipatory nausea: A prospective analysis. *Journal of Consulting and Clinical Psychology, 53,* 447-454.

Garb, J. L., & Stunkard, A. J. (1974). Taste aversions in man. *American Journal of Psychiatry, 131,* 1204-1207.

Lecture Example 5.8: Subtle Differences in UCR and CR

The text discusses the subtle differences between the UCR and CR, yet both involved salivation in classic Pavlov experiment. This may be confusing to the students; for example, how can salivation be different in two conditions? Evidence indicates, while the two responses may be the same on the surface, there are typically subtle differences. The UCR will usually be larger than the CR—more salivation in the case of Pavlov's dogs—it will usually last longer, and it tends to occur more quickly than the CR.

B. Operant Conditioning

Classroom Demonstrations and Handouts

Student Chalkboard LEARN 2: Reinforcement and Punishment

Demonstration LEARN 3: Operant Conditioning and TV Advertisements

Objective: To demonstrate the use of the principles of learning in advertising.
Materials: Videotape of several TV commercials; Tally Record (**Handout LEARN 3**)
Procedure: After your students have formed groups, present the ads. The task of the groups is to analyze what behaviors are implicitly being reinforced if the viewer buys the product or service. Use **Handout LEARN 3** to tally the pairing of stimuli (possible classical conditioning) and the implied reinforcements (operant conditioning). This activity may have observational learning implications as well, depending upon the advertisements.
Conclusions: Our buying behaviors and preferences are reinforced by carefully designed and produced TV advertisements.

Demonstration LEARN 4: Using Positive Reinforcement

Objective: To demonstrate the application of operant conditioning in modifying behavior.
Materials: **Handout LEARN 4** (twenty pieces of paper 2 x 2 inches; ten should have a straight side and the other ten should have at least one curved side)
Procedure: Spread out the pieces of paper in front of a volunteer. Ask the volunteer to select pieces of paper one at a time. Reinforce the subject for picking up a curved-edged piece with

"Yes, that is correct" while providing no response when a straight-edge piece is picked up.
Conclusions: As you discuss what learning was going on and why, ask the volunteer to verbalize what he or she was thinking as the activity was progressing.

Keith-Spiegel, P. (1988). Operant conditioning demonstration. In L. T. Benjamin, Jr., & K. D. Lowman (Eds.). *Activities handbook for the teaching of psychology*, (Vol. 1) (pp. 58-59). Washington, D.C.: American Psychological Association.

Demonstration LEARN 5: Shaping Students or the Professor

Objective: To demonstrate the principles of shaping.
Materials: One willing participant
Procedure: After removing a volunteer or yourself from the room, have the class select a simple behavior, for example, turning off a light or picking up chalk. The subject is then informed that only successive approximations of the selected behavior will be reinforced by the class's collective utterance of "Good." Another form of reinforcement may be substituted, like clapping. Some students will become somewhat frustrated; encourage them that they are doing well. A variation is to punish incorrect responses with "Bad" and note the increase in time it takes to accomplish this brand of shaping.
According to Watson (1981), a second activity may be performed by dividing the entire class into pairs. One member is the "behaviorist" who is attempting to shape the other's behavior. The response selected by the shaper should be relatively simple. The "subject" should try to hear as many reinforcements (e.g., "Good") as possible. Have the students switch their roles, and this time use "Bad" to punish incorrect responses. Is punishment more effective than reinforcement in shaping behavior? Follow-up these two activities by choosing a real-life behavior to shape. For example, how could you use shaping to improve your study habits or an exercise program?
Not only can a student's behavior be shaped, so can an instructor's. Stories of students using shaping on their instructors have been passed down through the years. One story has an instructor being shaped to stand next to the window during his lecture and even to pull down the shades. Another story concerns an instructor who was shaped to stand almost outside of the classroom. Use your own discretion in telling students about these possibilities! If you do, you'll want to make sure to instruct them that you are much too intelligent to be shaped! See Morgan (1974) for other demonstrations.
Conclusions: Shaping is a powerful technique and can be applied to all sorts of organisms from mice to people. It can be used to shape and mold many different types of behaviors. For more on shaping behavior see http://www.suite101.com/articles/article.cfm/2024.

Morgan, W. (1974). The shaping game: A teaching technique. *Behavior Therapy, 5,* 271-272.

Watson, D. (1981). Shaping by successive approximations. In L. T. Benjamin, Jr., & K. D. Lowman (Eds.). *Activities handbook for the teaching of psychology* (Vol. 1) (pp. 60-61). Washington, D.C.: American Psychological Association.

Demonstration LEARN 6: Guest Speaker on Behavior Modification

Objective: To inform students of applications of learning theory to real-life problems.
Materials: None

Procedure: Invite someone from the community who uses behavior modification in their work to speak to the class. The speaker may be a behaviorally-oriented psychologist, teacher, counselor, or group home manager. Ask the speaker to comment on the type of clients served by the techniques.
Conclusions: The students will see the relevance of learning theory to real-world concerns and problems. They will also gain valuable insight to the use of a very powerful method of changing behavior.

Demonstration INTRO 6: Seat-Belt Contract

Objective: To demonstrate the relevance of psychology by introducing students to an effective and commonly used method of contracting to modify behavior.
Materials: Seat-Belt Contract (**Handout INTRO 6**) or develop your own contract
Procedure: Psychology has various techniques to modify behavior to improve the quality of our lives. Draw up a written contract between your students and you to wear seat belts in vehicles. In exchange, you'll allow some privilege (e.g., opportunity to retake a test or hand in an assignment late without penalty). Make sure to inform students that wearing a seat belt will reduce but not eliminate the likelihood of death or sustaining injury in an accident. In addition, provide alternative ways (e.g., not drinking and driving or quitting smoking) for students to gain the above privilege if they wish not to enter an agreement about seat-belt use.
Conclusions: This is an excellent application of psychology to a real-life problem. But be prepared to face expressions of disbelief from students as they wonder how an instructor can be concerned about students!

Thyer, B. A. (1987). Contingency contracting to promote automobile safety belt use by students. *The Behavior Therapist, 10,* 150, 166.

Demonstration LEARN 11: A Real Rat

Objective: To inform students of applications of operant learning theory.
Materials: A rat and a Skinner box
Procedure: If your advanced learning course has a lab requirement of training a rat in a Skinner box, ask one of the students to bring their animal and Skinner box to class to demonstrate operant condition. This individual can describe the techniques and problem spots associated with this training. As an alternative, you can run the computer program "Sniffy the Virtual Rat," which can be obtained from Silver Fox Developments, 14-94 General Manson Way, Miramichi, New Brunswick, Canada E1N 6K8; e-mail: etheridg@nbet.nb.ca; Internet http://www.cybersmith.net/silverfox. If neither advanced students or the "Sniffy" program are available, you can locate a Skinner box and bring it to class to demonstrate how the box works.
Conclusions: Discuss the everyday implications of the applications of operant principles. This is a good demonstration to pique the interest of students who might take the advanced learning course.

Demonstration LEARN 12: Superstitious Behavior

Objective: To demonstrate superstitious behavior.
Materials: Videotape of gamblers and baseball players

Procedure: Show the videotape of the baseball player, being certain that the sequences contain shots of individuals engaging in strange behavior: rubbing the ball a certain way, tugging on one's hat, smoothing the mound. Also include hitters tugging and pulling on body parts, not stepping on the batting lines, and going through their ritual before hitting.

Conclusions: Discuss the superstitious behavior of the baseball players and try to define the reinforcers that maintain these behaviors. Explain that these individuals performed a particular behavior and something good happened (they hit a home run) so they linked this good event with the unrelated behavior that preceded it; i.e., a superstitious behavior was born. Now show the video of the gambler and have students try to identify superstitious behaviors. For a general discussion of superstitious behavior, see http://www.knownet.net/users/Ackley/writsuper.html.

Zimmer, J. (1984, July). Courting the gods of sport. *Psychology Today*, 36-39.

Demonstration LEARN 13: Positive Reinforcement

Objective: To demonstrate the power of positive reinforcement.
Materials: Internet access
Procedure: Go to http://server.bmod.athabascau.ca/html/prtut/reinpair.htm. The purpose of this demonstration is to teach the concept of positive reinforcement. In the first part of this exercise, the concept of positive reinforcement is defined and illustrated. In the second part of this exercise, students will classify 14 examples and nonexamples and are given feedback about their performance.
Conclusions: Have each student investigate this site and prepare to discuss their findings in the next class meeting. Lead a discussion on the examples at the site. Ask students for examples from their lives.

Lecture Examples

Lecture Example 5.6: Reinforcers

Have students, either individually or in small groups, list some of the reinforcers for which they are willing to "work." List these examples on an overhead transparency. Expect their specific responses to be quite different, except for money. You should have little problem distinguishing between primary and secondary reinforcers. It is likely that most of the student responses will refer to secondary reinforcers. Ask the students why these secondary reinforcers are so important to them.

Lecture Example 5.7: Animals and Shaping

At Reptile Gardens in South Dakota, shaping was used to train rabbits to play basketball and pigeons to "gun down" each other in the Wild West show. Circus animals are excellent examples of successes of operant conditioning of a variety of species. For more on dog shaping, see http://www.suite101.com/articles/article.cfm/2024.

Lecture Example 5.9: Negative Reinforcement and Punishment

Students are often confused about the difference between negative reinforcement and punishment.

Try using McConnell's approach in which students are told that there are two types of reinforcement (positive; negative) and two types of punishment (positive; negative). Using this approach minimizes the tendency students have to regard negative reinforcement as punishment. Flora and Pavlik (1990) suggest using a 2 x 2 matrix to illustrate the relationship between reinforcement and punishment. For Internet information of negative reinforcement and punishment see http://psychstan.stmarytx.edu/psysight/stuarts/stuart5-1.htm.

Flora, S. R., & Pavlik, W. B. (1990). An objective and functional matrix for introducing concepts of reinforcement and punishment. *Teaching of Psychology, 17,* 121-122.

McConnell, J. V. (1990). Negative reinforcement and positive punishment. *Teaching of Psychology, 17,* 247-249.

Lecture Example 5.10: Negative Reinforcement and Smoking

There is evidence to suggest that nicotine in cigarettes produces a subjective calm. Some smokers smoke to reduce or eliminate negative emotional states. The behavior of smoking is negatively reinforced because it takes away the negative effect (e.g., anxiety and depression).

Lecture Example 5.11: Accidental Reinforcement of Undesirable Behavior

Positive reinforcement is an effective tool to increase the likelihood that a desired behavior will recur. Unfortunately, it is also capable of strengthening undesirable behaviors. For example, a mother may unknowingly reinforce a child's temper tantrum by giving in to the child's demands. Ask students to think about examples of how their behaviors inadvertently reinforced someone else's. Consult Martin and Pear (1983) for more examples of accidental reinforcement.

Martin, G., & Pear, J. (1983). *Behavior modification: What it is and how to do it* (2nd ed.). Englewood Cliffs, NJ: Prentice Hall.

Lecture Example 5.12: Skinner's *Walden Two*

In 1948, B. F. Skinner published a novel called *Walden Two* that described a utopian community based on operant principles. In this fictional community, behavior is engineered by the technology of behavior. For example, workers do not earn money but, rather, labor credits to be exchanged for the necessities. The planners at Walden believe that children are better reared by male and female child-care experts. In the care centers, appropriate behavior is shaped by these experts. In 1967 in Virginia, a real community called Twin Oaks was established based upon the utopian-behavioral techniques fictionalized in *Walden Two*. For more on Skinner and his writings see http://www.best.com/~kia/Skinner.html.

Kinkade, K. (1973). A Walden Two experiment: The first five years of Twin Oaks Community. New York: Morrow.

Skinner, B. F. (1948). *Walden Two*. New York: Macmillan.

Lecture Example 5.13: Generalization and Discrimination

Students are often taught that generalization and discrimination occur in opposition to each other. These processes are actually complementary in many cases of learning. For example, consider the case of a child learning the concept "cat." The child learns that the animal in his house is called a cat. When the child goes outside and sees other cats, the child realizes that they do not look the same, so the child discriminates and does not consider them cats. When the child is corrected by the parents about the nature of cats, the child may generalize too broadly and include cats, squirrels, and cows in his concept of dog. Again, discrimination must take place as the child learns the features that differentiate cats from other animals.

Lecture Example 5.14: Skinner and Animals

Students often pose the question of why Skinner worked with animals in developing principles of learning that he then applied to humans. Skinner was the greatest behaviorist of this century until his death in 1990. As a behaviorist, he believed that general laws of learning apply to all organisms under all conditions. Therefore, his view was that the organism and the behavior to be studied are irrelevant, and that human and animal behavior are interchangeable. Because of the inherent problems associated with studying humans, animals are a convenient choice. White rats and pigeons have been used extensively in this century to study learning. For more on operant conditioning, see http://www.biozentrum.uni-wuerzburg.de/~brembs/diploma/operant.html.

Diversity Topics

Diversity Topic 5.1: Extinction

Have students discuss how some behaviors of theirs may have been extinguished or punished by a group or their parents in the past. Get some feel for the diversity and range of responses. Relate these responses to cultural values such as individualism v. collectivism.
Discussion/Description: Because enculturation involves the learning of rules governing behaviors, extinguishing inappropriate behavior is a major part of learning. However, individuals within cultures, as well as different cultural groups, will differ on the exact nature of the secondary punishment, which essentially is the elimination of learned, positive stimuli. In particular, people of collectivistic cultures rely much more on social harmony and feelings of in-group cohesion with others than do people of individualistic cultures. Thus, social isolation and the withdrawal of such feelings serve as a major punishment vehicle for people of this cultural background. For individualistic cultures, however, this is not as salient. Instead, the elimination of stimuli that directly result in positive feelings for the individual alone is much more salient, e.g., fines, automobile, television, etc. These types of differences result from differences in the meaning of these stimuli as acquired by the culture. For more information on extinction, see http://snycorva.cortland.edu/~andersmd/oper/extinct.html.

Diversity Topic 5.2: Reinforcers

Have students make a list of the three to five most important types of secondary reinforcers that work for them in a certain context, including home, school, work, etc. Then ask them to generate explanations from their own background and upbringing as to why those reinforcers work for them. The reinforcers and their backgrounds can be cross-tabulated with the ethnic/cultural backgrounds of the students to identify possible cultural differences in the exact manifestations of secondary reinforcers. This should cause the students to challenge the idea that the types of lists usually reported in coverage on this topic are universal to all types of students.

Discussion/Description: Because secondary reinforcers are learned by associations with other reinforcers and acquired through learning, there is the possibility that people of different cultural backgrounds value different types of secondary reinforcers differently. Money, attention, praise, and good grades may be prime examples of secondary reinforcers for people of our own culture, but they may not have the same meaning for people of other cultural backgrounds. Alternatively, they may have the same meaning for people in other cultures as well, but not to the same degree. People of other cultural backgrounds will consider some events as secondary reinforcers that people of our own would not, and vice versa. For example, a person from a collectivistic culture would be much more likely to consider praise or accomplishments, not for oneself, but for someone else in one's in-group—a work or school colleague as a secondary reinforcer. Things like money or attention may be secondary reinforcers to us, but not to others. The demonstration of these differences would allow instructors to show students the relative fluidity of the manifestations and content of principles related to learning across cultures, despite the fact that the principles themselves may be panculturally invariant. Additional information about reinforcers can be found at http://www.science.wayne.edu/~wpoff/cor/mem/opereinf.html.

Diversity Topic 5.3: Punishment

Have students make a list of the three to five most important types of secondary punishment that work for them in at home, at school, and at work. Then ask them to generate explanations from their own background and upbringing as to why those punishers "work" for them. The punishment and their backgrounds can be cross-tabulated with the ethnic/cultural backgrounds of the students to identify possible cultural differences in the exact manifestations of secondary punishment. This should cause the students to challenge the idea that the types of lists usually reported in coverage on this topic are universal to all types of students.

Discussion/Description: This annotation is exactly the same as the previous one regarding reinforcers, and for good reason. The same reasons why cultures will differ on the exact nature of reinforcers allow them to be different on punishment as well. Because secondary punishers are learned by associations with other punishment and acquired through learning, there is the possibility that people of different cultural backgrounds value different types of secondary punishment differently. Pain, disapproval, or fines may work in one culture, but may not necessarily work as well in another. Alternatively, they may work in different ways, and for different reasons. The demonstration of these differences would allow instructors to show students the relative fluidity of the manifestations and content of principles related to learning across cultures, despite the fact that the principles themselves may be panculturally invariant. For examples of reinforcement and punishment, see http://www.sfu.ca/~tbauslau/302/rp.html.

C. Cognitive Learning

Classroom Demonstrations and Handouts

Demonstration LEARN 7: Tie Your Shoes

Objective: To educate students on the prevalence of behaviors that were acquired by observational learning.
Materials: Students with shoes that have laces
Procedure: This activity involves students teaching other students to tie shoes. Have students pair up. One member of the pair should be wearing shoes with laces. Ask students to untie their shoes. The other, referred to as the "Teacher," provides instructions on how to tie shoes. Assuming nothing, the student should follow the instructions without inference of any kind (e.g., which lace to grab with which hand; how to make "bunny" ears). The teacher cannot point to the laces or do any type of prompting. After several minutes of probable frustration, ask the teacher to use vicarious or participant modeling.
Conclusions: Make sure you note that many of our behaviors (e.g., driving a car) are acquired through watching other people (e.g., parent, siblings).

Demonstration LEARN 8: Assess the Violence in Children's Cartoons

Objective: To illustrate the level and intensity of violence depicted in cartoons for children.
Materials: Videotape of several types of children's cartoons; Violent Act Tally (**Handout LEARN 8**)
Procedure: This is best presented in your discussion of Bandura's Bobo doll study. Present the cartoons to your students. Ask them to count the number of acts of violence and record them on **Handout LEARN 8**. (Clearly, you must define what constitutes a violent act; consider explicit versus implicit acts.) Note that the older cartoons are just as violent as the cartoons of today. At the end of each cartoon, determine the number of acts of violence committed per minute.
You may wish to ask students about the violence of videos shown on MTV, for example. What is their response? Do they respond in a similar way? Or do they claim "Well that's different from children's cartoons!" By the way, a recent study reported that violence was a dominant theme in nearly 60 percent of the videos shown on MTV over a 7-week period (Sherman & Dominick, 1986).
Conclusions: Ask the students what they think children are learning from watching cartoons of this nature. Typical responses might refer to violent behavior as acceptable in solving interpersonal problems and that one-upmanship is acceptable. What do viewers who watch MTV learn? For a look at the *Simpsons* and violence on TV see http://copland.udel.edu/~stevep/simpsons.htm.

Eron, L. D., Lefkowitz, M. M., Huesmann, L. R., & Walder, L. D. (1972). Does television violence cause aggression? *American Psychologist, 27*, 253-263.

Sherman, B., & Dominick, J. R. (1986). Violence and sex in music videos: TV and rock'n'roll. *Journal of Communication, 36*, 79-93.

Lecture Examples

Lecture Example 5.15: Preparation for Hospitalization

Observational learning can be used to prepare children for surgery or other invasive medical procedures. Children scheduled for elective surgery participated in a study that examined the effectiveness of a film depicting a peer being hospitalized (Melamed & Siegel, 1975). The film shows the procedures and the anxiety they generate in the peer model, who ultimately overcomes and copes with the negative emotional state. Children who viewed the film displayed significantly less anxiety prior to and following their own surgery. A recent study by Pinto and Hollandsworth (1989) extended preparation to include the parent of the hospitalized child. They reported that when the parents were present during the presentation of the videotape, children experienced less arousal. Find out what the hospitals in your area do to prepare children for surgery or invasive medical procedures.

Melamed, B. G., & Siegel, L. J. (1975). Reduction of anxiety in children facing hospitalization and surgery by use of filmed modeling. *Journal of Consulting and Clinical Psychology, 43,* 511-521.

Pinto, R. P., & Hollandsworth, J. G., Jr. (1989). Using videotape modeling to prepare children psychologically for surgery: Influence of parents and costs versus benefits of providing preparation services. *Health Psychology, 8,* 79-95.

Lecture Example 5.16: Cognitive Learning Theory Terms

Use the material at http://mse.byu.edu/ipt301/jordan/learnterm_c.html to develop a lecture on cognitive learning theory. This site can be used for definitions or as an outline for your lecture.

Diversity Topic

Diversity Topic 5.4: Learning

Have students identify a behavior (e.g., eating etiquette, greeting rituals, etc.) or value (freedom, democracy, choice, etc.) that they can agree may be influenced by their cultural backgrounds and upbringing. Then engage in a discussion about how it is such behaviors or values are learned in development, and highlight the principles of classical, operant, or observational learning when appropriate.
Discussion/Description: Although there is very little, if any, formal or systematic research in psychology on the principles of learning and conditioning across cultures, that does not necessarily mean that nothing can be learned about culture with respect to this topic. In fact, give that culture is a conglomeration of learned patterns of values, attitudes, beliefs, and behaviors tha are communicated across generations, the topic of learning and conditioning should be a natural place for students to delve into the forces that have helped to shape their own cultural backgrounds. This simple activity will address several important issues in the teaching of psychology: (1) it will help students to apply the principles of learning and conditioning to their

own behaviors or the behaviors of others, going beyond mere textbook reading and lecture presentation; (2) it will demonstrate the close interrelationship among the principles of classical, operant, and observational learning, giving the students a better perspective on these issues as they occur in real life instead of as textbook theoretical frameworks; and (3) it will serve as an important way to continue a focus on culture and the shaping and molding of behavior as a function of culture.

6 Memory

Chapter-at-a-Glance

Chapter Outline	Instruction Outline	Multimedia
Remembering p. 190 The Three Processes in Memory: Encoding, Storage, and Retrieval • The Three Memory Systems: The Long and the Short of It • The Levels-of-Processing Model: Another View of Memory	**Student Chalkboard** MEM 1 **Demonstration** MEM 1-5, 8, 9 **Lecture Examples** 6.1-6.2, 6.6, 6.7 **Critical Thinking Opportunity** 6.1 **Learning Objectives** 6.1-6.4 **Test Questions** 1-51	*Discovering Psychology:* Remembering and Forgetting *PsychScience* Iconic Memory *PsychScience* Short-term Memory Scanning Transparencies MEM 3, 4, 6 Video Disc III Segment 23 Digital Image Archive PSME003-008 Web Site http://www.mines.u-nancy.fr/~gueniffe/CoursEMN/I31/ILS/e_for_e/nodes/NODE-8-pg.html Structures in Memory
Measuring Memory p. 198 Three Methods of Measuring Memory • Hermann Ebbinghaus and the First Experimental Studies on Learning and Memory	**Demonstration** MEM 6, 7, 13 **Learning Objectives** 6.5-6.6 **Test Questions** 52-62	Video Disc I Segment 12 Web Site http://www.psychology.nottingham.ac.uk/staff/Fernand.Gobet/C82INT/verbal-learning.html Verbal Learning
Forgetting p. 202 The Causes of Forgetting • Prospective Forgetting: Forgetting to Remember	**Demonstration** MEM 14 **Lecture Example** 6.3 **Critical Thinking Opportunity** 6.2 **Learning Objectives** 6.7-6.8 **Test Questions** 63-77	Digital Image Archive PSME013 Web Site http://www.evl.uic.edu/sugimoto/psych5.html Remembering and Forgetting
The Nature of Remembering and Forgetting p. 206 Memory as a Permanent Record: The Videocassette Recorder Analogy • Memory as a Reconstruction: Partly Fact and Partly Fiction • Eyewitness Testimony: Is It Accurate? • Recovering Repressed Memories: A Controversy • Unusual Memory Phenomena • Memory and Culture	**Demonstration** MEM 10-12, 15 **Lecture Examples** 6.4, 6.5, 6.8, 6.9 **Critical Thinking Forum** 6.1 **Journal Entry** 6.1 **Diversity Topics** 6.1-6.2 **Learning Objectives** 6.9-6.13 **Test Questions** 78-103	*Psychology and Culture*: Ch. 20 Transparency MEM 7 Video Disc I Segment 11 Digital Image Archive PSME013 Web Sites http://iquest.com/~fitz/fmsf/ Site explaining the positive aspects of false memory syndrome. http://iquest.com/~fitz/csicop/si/9503/memory.html Site explaining the negative aspects of false memory syndrome.

Chapter Outline	Instruction Outline	Multimedia
Factors Influencing Retrieval p. 213 The Serial Position Effect: To Be Remembered, Be First or Last But Not in the Middle • Environmental Context and Memory • The State-Dependent Memory Effect • Stress, Anxiety, and Memory: Relax and Remember	**Demonstration** MEM 16 **Critical Thinking Forum** 6.2-6.3 **Journal Entry** 6.2 **Diversity Topic** 6.3 **Learning Objectives** 6.14-6.17 **Test Questions** 104-120	Web Site http://www.ldc.usb.ve/~poc/hci-5.html Serial Position Effect
Biology and Memory p. 216 Brain Damage: A Clue to Memory Formation • Neuronal Changes in Memory: Brain Work • Hormones and Memory	**Demonstration** MEM 17 **Learning Objectives** 6.18-6.20 **Lecture Examples** 6.10 **Test Questions** 121-128	Video Disc III Segments 20-22, 24 Web Site http://ch.nus.sg/cybermed/clinical/psychological-medicine/amnesia.html Amnestic Syndrome
Improving Memory: Some Helpful Study Habits p. 218 Study Habits That Aid Memory	**Demonstration** 18 **Lecture Examples** 6.11-6-13 **Learning Objectives** 6.21-6.22 **Journal Entry** 6.3 **Test Questions** 129-138	PsychScience Improving Your Memory Web Site http://www.gac.peachnet.edu/Student_life/study_skills/effstdy.htm Improving Memory Study Skills

What's New in Chapter 6

New Content

- Hormones and memory

Expanded Content

- Repressed memories

New Special Features

- Revised chapter opening vignette
- Revised *Remember It's*

New Key Terms

- Elaborative rehearsal
- Priming
- Prospective forgetting

Learning Objective Questions

6.1 What three processes are involved in the act of remembering?
6.2 What is sensory memory?
6.3 What are the characteristics of short-term memory?
6.4 What is long-term memory, and what are its subsystems?
6.5 What are three methods of measuring retention?
6.6 What was Ebbinghaus's major contribution to psychology?
6.7 What are six causes of forgetting?
6.8 What is interference, and how can it be minimized?
6.9 What is meant by the statement "Memory is reconstructive in nature"?
6.10 What is Bartlett's contribution to our understanding of memory?
6.11 What are schemas, and how do they affect memory?
6.12 What conditions reduce the reliability of eyewitness testimony?
6.13 Does hypnosis improve the memory of eyewitnesses?
6.14 What is the controversy over therapy used to recover repressed memories of childhood sexual abuse?
6.15 What is the serial position effect?
6.16 How does environmental context affect memory?
6.17 What is the state-dependent memory effect?
6.18 What role does the hippocampus and the rest of the hippocampal region play in episodic and semantic memory?
6.19 What is long-term potentiation, and why is it important?
6.20 How do our memories of threatening situations, which elicit the "flight or fight response," compare with ordinary memories?
6.21 What are four study habits that can aid memory?
6.22 What is overlearning and why is it important?

Chapter Overview

Memory encompasses the following processes: encoding, storage, consolidation and retrieval. Encoding is the process of transforming information into a form that can be stored in memory. Storage is the process of maintaining the information in memory. Consolidation is a physiological process that must take place for encoded information to be stored in memory. Retrieval is the process of bringing the information to mind.

Memory is divided into three systems: the sensory memory, the short-term memory, and the long-term memory. The sensory memory holds information coming from the senses for less than a few seconds. The short-term memory, also considered the working memory, has a limited capacity and retains memories for only a short period. These memories are usually displaced by new memories. The long-term memory is considered to have an unlimited capacity. Long-term memories are distinguished as declarative (explicit) and nondeclarative (implicit). Declarative memory is further classified as episodic memory and semantic memory. The levels-of-processing model of memory is also described as an alternative to the three-memory-systems approach. Memory is measured through recall, recognition, and relearning. Ebbinghaus and the first experiments in memory are then detailed.

The ability to forget information is crucial to keeping memory from being cluttered with unneeded details. Forgetting can be caused by encoding failure, or the failure to enter long-term memory in the first place; by consolidation failure, or the failure to form a permanent memory; by the decay of the memory; and by interference of one memory with another. Forgetting may also be motivated as a means of protecting oneself from painful or unpleasant memories. Forgetting may also result from errors in how the memory was framed or how it was recalled (retrieval failure).

The chapter next examines aspects of memory that relate to its nature, memory as a permanent record and memory as a reconstruction. The authors also describe eyewitness testimony and recovering repressed memories. The authors also describe unusual memory phenomena like flashbulb memories and eidetic imagery. The chapter then turns to memory and culture. The authors then describe factors like that of retrieval, like the serial position effect, environmental context, state-dependent memory, and the role of stress anxiety and depression on memory.

The role of biology is illustrated by the case of H. M., which describes the role of the hippocampus in the formation of memories, and the case of K. C., which illustrates how a specific aspect of memory can be lost, such as the ability to form episodic memories. Long-term potentiation may be the neuronal basis for memory formation. Hormones and their effect on memory is then discussed. The chapter closes with detailed descriptions of several techniques that can be used to improve memory and study habits.

Key Terms

amnesia (p. 240)
anterograde amnesia (p. 216)
consolidation (p. 191)
consolidation failure (p. 203)
decay theory (p. 203)
declarative memory (p. 195)
displacement (p. 193)
eidetic imagery (p. 211)
Elaborative Rehearsal (p. 195)
encoding (p. 190)
encoding failure (p. 202)
episodic memory (p. 195)
flashbulb memory (p. 211)
hippocampal region (p. 216)
infantile amnesia (p. 210)

interference (p. 203)
levels-of-processing model (p. 197)
long-term memory (p. 194)
long-term potentiation (p. 219)
massed practice (p. 220)
motivated forgetting (p. 204)
nondeclarative memory (p. 196)
nonsense syllable (p. 200)
overlearning (p. 219)
primacy effect (p. 213)
priming (p. 196)
prospective forgetting (p. 205)
recall (p. 198)
recency effect (p. 213)
recognition (p. 199)

reconstruction (p. 206)
rehearsal (p. 194)
relearning method (p. 199)
repression (p. 204)
retrieval (p. 191)
retrieval cue (p. 198)
retrograde amnesia (p. 203)
savings score (p. 199)
schemas (p. 207)
semantic memory (p. 195)
sensory memory (p. 191)
serial position effect (p. 213)
short-term memory (p. 193)
state-dependent memory effect (p. 215)
storage (p. 191)

Annotated Lecture Outline

A. Remembering

Classroom Demonstrations and Handouts

Student Chalkboard MEM 1: Model of Memory

Demonstration MEM 1: Memory and Forgetting

Objective: To demonstrate a number of relevant memory principles and a technique used by Ebbinghaus.
Materials: A list of words and nonsense words; **Handout MEM 1a** and **Handout MEM 1b**
Procedure: This activity is a good lead-in to get your students thinking about memory. After dividing the class into four groups, ask each group to construct a list of words and nonsense words and record it on **Handout MEM 1a**. Read several words as examples (you should spell nonsense words). Consult Wertheimer for an appropriate list (e.g., envelope, bex, fet, fulfill). Collect the lists, and then read one to the class. Following the reading, ask Group 1 to write as many of the items as possible on **Handout 1b**. After approximately three minutes, ask Group 2 to do the same. After another five minutes have passed, ask Group 3 to recall the items, then, at the end of the class, ask Group 4 to recall the list.

Conclusions: Typically, after plotting the accuracy rate, a classical, negatively accelerated forgetting curve appears. Moreover, other principles, like serial position effect, are demonstrated. See Wertheimer for more ideas. Students will also experience the difficulty of making truly meaningless nonsense words. For more information on Ebbinghaus, see http://www.science.mcmaster.ca/Psychology/psych2h03/memory1.html, or go to http://pangaea.pratt.edu/~jlampin/LEC3.html for information of memory models.

Wertheimer, M. (1981). Memory and forgetting. In L. T. Benjamin, Jr. and K. D. Lowman (Eds.), *Activities handbook for the teaching of psychology*, (Vol. 1) (p. 75). Washington, D.C.: American Psychology Association.

Demonstration MEM 2: A Grocery List

Objective: To demonstrate the primacy and recency effect and von Restorff effect.
Materials: A list of sixteen common grocery items to be read to students; Grocery List Response Sheet (**Handout MEM 2**)
Procedure: Instruct the students not to write anything until they have been told to, then slowly read a list of grocery items. Consider throwing in some exotic food to demonstrate the von Restorff effect. Ask the students to recall and write down as many of these grocery items as they can. Then have them check the accuracy of their recall and whether their recall was better for early, middle, or later words.
Conclusions: According to the serial position effect, the first and last couple of items should be the easiest to recall. The exotic food should also be easy to recall because it stands out. For a short discussion of the von Restorff effect, see http://www.cpl.uiuc.edu/cpl/abstracts/memory.html.

Demonstration MEM 3: Chunking to Increase Meaningfulness

Objective: To demonstrate the importance of meaning in encoding and retrieval.
Materials: **Handout MEM 3** as an overhead or copied and cut in half
Procedure: Present the first sentence to students (if you hand it out, only give out the top half). Give them about 30 seconds to memorize this first string of letters in order. Next challenge them to recall the letters by writing them down on paper. Inquire as to whether it would make a difference to present the letters in chunks, then show the second string of letters, which are clearly chunked into meaningful units. There are many other examples of the effects of chunking (e.g., IBMCBSCNNDOA becomes IBM, CBS, CNN, DOA). Think about putting your school's initials (e.g., UCLA; UM; UNI; NDSCS) in this example. The military also has a habit of using chunks (e.g., Bomb Damage Assessment with three chunks now becomes BDA with one chunk).
Conclusions: Encoding becomes more efficient when the data that we are attempting to remember has meaning for us. Chunking makes the data meaningful.

Demonstration MEM 4: Short-term Memory

Objective: To illustrate the storage capability of short-term memory (i.e., Miller's Magical Number).
Materials: Pennies; a box; **Handout MEM 4**

Procedure: Throw a random number (between 1 and 13) of pennies into a box and present it to students for about two seconds. Students are asked to determine the number without actually counting but simply observing the pennies. Do this for several trials. A less involved method is to use **Handout MEM 4**, and put the sections on index cards in order to flash them to students. In addition, you may wish to have students recall a list of with spans of 2 to 12 digits. Inform your students that when you say "write," they should write down in order as many of the digits as they can recall, then read the next digit span and repeat the procedure. An example follows:

    Digit span of 2: 5 2 write
    Digit span of 3: 9 4 1 write
    Digit span of 4: 8 7 3 1 write
    Digit span of 5: 4 1 7 6 9 write
    Digit span of 6: 2 6 9 2 5 8 write
    Digit span of 7: 7 3 9 8 3 6 1 write
    Digit span of 8: 1 5 4 5 6 7 8 4 write
    Digit span of 9: 2 6 3 1 9 4 3 1 5 write
    Digit span of 10: 8 5 1 8 3 7 4 6 3 1 write
    Digit span of 11: 9 4 2 7 5 6 3 6 3 1 9 write
    Digit span of 12: 8 3 9 7 9 6 3 4 6 4 8 5 write

Conclusions: When the number of pennies, dots, or digits approaches the storage capacity of STM, the number of errors increase. Most students will have no problem determining the number of pennies, dots, or digits when they number from one to about nine, but less than one-third of them will be able to accurately estimate the number when it approaches 11 or 12. A hybrid activity is to add structure and organization to the dots' location (e.g., putting the dots in rows or other geometric design) and examine how recall is affected. See http://onesun.cc.geneseo.edu/~intd225/memmodls.htm for more on models of memory.

Shaffer, L. S. (1982). Hamilton's marbles or Jevon's beans: A demonstration of Miller's magical number seven. Teaching of Psychology, 9, 116-117.

Demonstration MEM 5: Countries and Memory

Objective: To show how knowledge is stored in long-term memory.
Materials: None
Procedure: Ask your students to write the names of as many countries as they can.
Conclusions: Typically, there is organization in the manner in which they recall them. Take an informal poll and determine how many students used the following organizational formats: 1) by alphabetical order, 2) geographic region, and 3) by physical location. This activity suggests that memories aren't stored randomly, but logically and with organization.

Demonstration MEM 8: U.S. Presidents

Objective: To demonstrate the serial position effect and the spreading activation theory.
Materials: List of Presidents (**Handout MEM 8**)

Procedure: Ask students to write down as many presidents of the United States as they can in five minutes. After that time, go through the presidents in order asking students to raise their hands if their answer is correct. **Handout MEM 8** lists the presidents in order.

Conclusions: Students are most likely to recall the first several and last several presidents. Why are students likely to remember Lincoln, an apparent exception to the serial position effect? Ask them to explain this apparent anomaly based upon what they know about memory, spreading activation theory, and meaningfulness. There is a link between presidents in the "Presidential network." Unfortunately, the link breaks down around Madison, reappears at Lincoln then disappears again, and then finally reappears around Eisenhower or Kennedy.

Roediger, H. L., & Crowder, R. G. (1976). A serial position effect in recall of United States Presidents. Bulletin of the Psychonomic Society, 8, 275-278.

Demonstration MEM 9: Sensory memory

Objective: To demonstrate sensory memory.
Materials: Overhead projector; two blank transparencies
Procedure: On one transparency, make a 3x3 matrix using random letters. On the other transparency, draw a black border that will enclose the matrix. Tell the students that you are going to show them nine letters in a matrix for a very short duration on the overhead projector. Show the students the border without the letters, so that they will know where to look on the overhead screen. Turn off the overhead and put the letters over the border. Tell students that you want them to write down as many letters as they can remember in any order. Turn the projector off and on very rapidly. You may want to practice this before class.
Conclusions: After the students have had an opportunity to write down as many letters as they can recall, turn the projector on and ask the students to score their results. Ask for a show of hands for students who wrote the first letter in the upper left quadrant of the matrix first. Most students will say they wrote this letter first. Ask for a show of hands of how many got three correct, how many got four correct, until no one raises their hands. Discuss the effect of processing and culture. In the West, we are taught to start reading from the upper left corner of a display. Ask the students for other examples from different cultures that would allow for different processing strategies. For more information of sensory memory, go to http://onesun.cc.geneseo.edu/~intd225/sensmem.html.

Lecture Examples

Lecture Example 6.1: Chunking ZIP Codes and Phone Numbers

When the U.S. Postal Service proposed the new, nine-digit ZIP codes, there was some opposition to them; some people felt that nine digits were too many to remember. Telephone numbers tend to be chunked into two bits of information instead of into seven bits. Companies and organizations attempt to give telephone numbers significance by assigning words to them. For example, 1-800-826-CARS (automobile manufacturer), 1-800-PUBLYSH (desktop publishing company), and 1-800-IBM-2468.

Lecture Example 6.2: Elaborative Rehearsal

Every teacher knows the importance of examples, but why are examples so important? Connecting new material to experiences students are familiar with allows them to attach the new material to information already present in long-term memory. For more information, see http://web.psych.ualberta.ca/~mike/Pearl_Street/OldDictionary/E/elaborative_reh.html.

Lecture Example 6.6: Really Long-term Memory

Ask students to remember the first time they were kissed, and I don't mean by their grandmother. Many students will have a smile come to their face. For most of us this was a pleasant experience and one that we cannot forget. For many of us, this also happened a very long time ago, but we remember it like it just happened. Use this as a lecture starter for your discussion of long-term memory.

Lecture Example 6.7: PowerPoint Slides for Memory

At http://psych.hanover.edu/classes/hfnotes2/sld052.html you will find a very good set of slides that can be downloaded and used to make overheads or PowerPoint presentations.

B. Measuring Memory

Classroom Demonstrations and Handouts

Demonstration MEM 6: Hierarchical Organization and Recall

Objective: To illustrate the importance of organization and structure in retrieval.
Materials: **Handout MEM 6a** and **Handout MEM 6b**
Procedure: Present half the class with the hierarchical list (**Handout MEM 6a**) and the other half with the random list (**Handout MEM 6b**). Give them about four minutes to memorize the list, then ask them to recall as many words as they can. The group given the list with organization will likely recall more words than the other group although some students from this second group may actively impose structure on the random list. Following the assessment of recall, discuss with your students the importance of organization and meaningfulness in the context of studying and test taking.
Conclusions: Organization imposes meaning on data and allows better retrieval.

Bower, G. H., Clark, M., Winzenz, D., & Lesgold, A. (1969). Hierarchical retrieval schemes in recall of categorized word lists. *Journal of Verbal Learning and Verbal Behavior, 8*, 323-343.

Demonstration MEM 7: Using Retrieval Cues

Objective: To illustrate the use of retrieval cues.
Materials: Recall versus Recognition (**Handout MEM 7**)
Procedure: It is important for students to understand the difference between strategies that use little or no cue (e.g., recall) and many cues (e.g., recognition). Develop some everyday situations that require one of these types of memory retrieval.
Conclusions: By developing examples, students should better understand recall and recognition. For more on retrieval cues and blocking, see http://www2.artsci.wustl.edu/~ebergman/rtblock.htm.

Demonstration MEM 13: Which One Is the Correct Drawing?

Objective: To demonstrate the role of attention in memory.
Materials: **Handout MEM 13**
Procedure: Present **Handout MEM 13** to students and ask them to select the correct drawing of a penny. Most students may experience a type of the "tip of the tongue" phenomenon knowing that a profile of Lincoln, some writing, and perhaps a date are present, but not remembering the specific locations. A variation of the activity that requires recall rather than recognition is to ask students to draw the front side of a penny.
Conclusions: When there is little or no attention given to a stimulus, it is very difficult to later recall or recognize it. For the most part, what a penny looks like is not important to us and does not have much meaning. Would a coin collector consider the features on a penny important and meaningful? Surely, the collector attends to this stimulus. To see an article on the "tip of the tongue" phenomenon, go to http://www.psych.ufl.edu/~levy/96_6.htm.

Nickerson, R. S., & Adams, M. J. (1979). Long-term memory for a common object. *Cognitive Psychology, 11,* 294.

C. Forgetting

Classroom Demonstrations and Handouts

Demonstration MEM 14 Amnesia

Objective: To explore the topic of amnesia.
Materials: Internet access
Procedure: Go to http://hermes.cns.uiuc.edu/ARLHomePage.html. This site contains FAQs and links to related sites on the topic of amnesia. Have the students explore three related links.
Conclusions: After students have investigated this site, ask them to prepare to discuss their findings in the next class meeting. Lead a discussion using the following questions: Which of the many types of amnesia do you find the most interesting?

Have you ever known anyone who had the symptoms of amnesia? Describe what you might feel if you woke up one morning and had amnesia.

Lecture Examples

Lecture Example 6.3: If You Graduated 35 Years Ago

Bahrick, Bahrick, and Wittlinger (1974, 1975) took names and pictures out of the high school yearbooks of 392 graduates who ranged in age from 17 to 74. The researchers used recall and recognition tests to measure their subjects' memories for the names and pictures of former classmates. The researchers reported that recent graduates could recognize 90 percent of their classmates' names and pictures, but so could subjects who had graduated 35 years earlier. Even subjects who had graduated 40 or more years earlier could recognize 75 percent of their classmates.

Bahrick, H. P., Bahrick, P. O., & Wittlinger, R. P. (1975). Fifty years of memory for names and faces: A cross-sectional approach. *Journal of Experimental Psychology: General, 104,* 54-75.

Bahrick, H. P., Bahrick, P. O., & Wittlinger, R. P. (1974, December). Those unforgettable high-school days. *Psychology Today, 8,* 50-56.

D. The Nature of Remembering and Forgetting

Classroom Demonstrations and Handouts

Demonstration MEM 10: Distortion and Construction in Memory

Objective: To exhibit how memories are distorted and reconstructed using social memory (i.e., rumor transmission).
Materials: **Handout MEM 10**, make-up a story, or take several paragraphs from a newspaper article.
Procedure: Ask 10 or so students to leave the room. Bring the first student back in and read the article. When the second student comes in, have the first student try to recite the article from memory. Do this until the last student has had the article recited to her or him. Compare the original version to the last version. Advise the rest of the students who are watching the activity not to give any clues or to laugh. Ask your students to identify the schema present in the article. If you used **Handout MEM 10**, did the schema of "teaching" enhance the retrieval of the article?
Conclusions: Discuss how rumors get started and how they seem to change as a function of our reconstructive memory system. Point out that memory is not like an automatic recorder of events or information. For a book review on this topic, go to http://www.aronson.com/ppp/constru.htm.

Demonstration MEM 11: Eyewitness Memory

Objective: To replicate a study examining how the wording of a question can influence a memory of an event.
Materials: A drawing of an automobile accident (**Handout MEM 11a**); **Handout MEM 11b**; **Handout MEM 11c**
Procedure: Show the drawing to all students. Next, give half of the class **Handout MEM 11b** and the other **Handout MEM 11c**. Ask them to answer the questions.
Conclusions: The answers that students give will be consistent with the wording of the question. Follow-up with a discussion on leading questions in criminal court cases and the merits of eyewitness memory. Interesting information on police and eyewitness memory can be found at http://www.vuw.ac.nz/psyc/hudson_police/title.html.

Loftus, E. F., & Palmer, J. (1974). Reconstruction of automobile destruction. *Journal of Verbal Learning and Verbal Behavior, 13*, 585-589.

Demonstration MEM 12: Class Interruption

Objective: To demonstrate eyewitness memory.
Materials: A colleague or willing student; **Handout MEM 12a**; **Handout MEM 12b**.
Procedure: Have the assistant come into your classroom during a lecture and write "hi" on the board and leave. Following this, give half of the class **Handout MEM 12a** and the other **Handout MEM 12b**. Ask them to answer the questions.
Conclusions: Some students will actually report "facts" about the intruder that are not valid. Again, this activity shows the importance of asking appropriate and neutral questions.

Demonstration MEM 15: Memory of your Environment

Objective: To demonstrate the importance of attention.
Materials: None
Procedure: Have students close their eyes and try to remember exactly what the students to their right and left are wearing. Some students will show good memory because they paid attention to Chuck's or Sandy's clothes. These memories will be selective—a shirt, blouse, skirt, hat, or shoes are good examples. Some students will have no recollection at all, these are often the most interesting cases because the information registered on sensory receptors but was not retained in memory. As a follow-up for the next class period, ask students what their neighbors were wearing at the previous class period. Many will recall better because of the attention you called to the clothes during the previous class.

Lecture Examples

Lecture Example 6.4: Flashbulb Memory

Ask students to write down what they were doing when the following events occurred: (1) President Reagan's attempted assassination; (2) the space shuttle *Challenger*'s explosion; (3) John

Lennon's murder; (4) the Berlin Wall's destruction; (5) the first day of the 4th grade; (6) July 11, 1986; (7) *Time* magazine named the computer as the Machine of the Year. Why is there a difference in our ability to recall these events (i.e., age, meaningfulness, invoked emotion, attention)? To view a very comprehensive site on flashbulb memories, go to http://ego.psy.flinders.edu.au/webpages/learning/jgpd/page6.html.

Lecture Example 6.5: More on Extraordinary Memory

As the text notes, Luria (1968) examined and wrote about S., an individual with a fantastic memory. S. developed a technique of eidetic imagery and a shorthand system for his images by converting long lists of nonsense words into intelligible images. The master conductor Toscanini possessed a remarkable ability to remember musical scores. For example, when a performer realized that the key on his bassoon for the lowest note was broken, Toscanini said not to worry the note was not needed for the concert. On another occasion, when Toscanini misplaced a score, he wrote down the entire score from memory, committing only one error. According to his biographer, Toscanini "knew every note of every instrument of about 250 symphonic works" (Marek, 1975, p. 414).

Other cases of extraordinary memory are those of mentally retarded individuals who possess one or more special talents that exceed the norm. They are referred to as savants and, like S., are likely to cause your students to take note. Darold Treffert has written a fascinating book describing savants and new theories that attempt to account for their atypical behaviors. For more on extraordinary memory, see http://www.idiom.com/~drjohn/memory.html.

Baddeley, A. (1981). *Your memory: A user's guide.* New York: Macmillan.

Luria, A. R. (1968). *The mind of a mnemonist.* New York: Basic Books.

Marek, G. R. (1975). *Toscanini.* London: Vision Press.

Miller, L. K. (1989). Musical savants: Exceptional skill in the mentally retarded. Hillsdale, NJ: Lawrence Erlbaum.

Treffert, D. A. (1989). Extraordinary people: Understanding "idiot savants." Harper & Row: New York.

Lecture Example 6.8: Context and Memory

Context is a potential aid for memory retrieval when one is actively attempting to recall something such as the details of a crime. Ask a student to volunteer describe the experience of going back to an old hometown or a former home and being flooded with memories. Many students will have accounts of this type. Some examples they are likely to have are seeing an old school, an old friend, or old pictures, or hearing a song. Context is important enough as a retrieval cue that it is often included in study tips. One tip is to urge students to study for a test in the same room in which it will be given.

Lecture Example 6.9: Repressed Memories

Many students believe that repressed memories are valid expressions of past events. Develop a lecture on this topic. Many of the original court cases concerning repressed memories have recently been overturned. Use http://iquest.com/~fitz/csicop/si/9503/memory.html as a reference for this lecture.

Diversity Topics

Diversity Topic 6.1: Memory and Language

Conduct a simple study on the relationship between memory and language. Use the material in **Handout MEM 10**. Have students present that material to people who are bilingual. Have all the students present the material in English. Ask half of the respondents to give responses in English, the other half in another language. Check to see whether there are differences in the amount remembered when recall is in English (the language of original encoding) and when the recall is in the other language.
Discussion/Description: I do not know of any research that examines the effects of language on recall tasks (but I would not be surprised if such research exists). This simple activity may be difficult to do, and is entirely dependent on the availability of multilingual students and friends who can serve as subjects. This activity allows students to actively participate in their learning, bring research activities to life, and allow them to get first hand knowledge about an unknown area of psychology. The results, when discussed in class, should be interesting, especially if students are able to discuss the possible reasons why differences, if found, occur.
Appendix: Need to use **Handout MEM 10** or something similar.

Diversity Topic 6.2: Eyewitness Testimony

Obtain a set of facial stimuli of people of different races. Present half of them one at a time to the class at the beginning of a class session. Then, present the entire set to the class at the end of class, asking the students to judge whether or not they saw that person earlier. Provide students with simple judgment sheets to mark their responses. Tally the correct responses in between classes, and examine whether there is a difference according to the race of the person being judged.
Discussion/Description: Some research does exist to suggest that face recognition skills differ depending on the race congruity between the person being judged and the person who is doing the judging. These types of findings have implications for eyewitness testimony research findings, especially when people must make recognition judgments of people of different racial backgrounds. The research as I understand it is relatively new, however, and it may be that these findings are applicable only under certain conditions; for example, it may depend on the degree of exposure of the subjects to people of different racial backgrounds. This activity provides students with an exciting opportunity to do an activity relevant to memory studies and cross-ethnic comparisons.

E. Factors Influencing Retrieval

Classroom Demonstrations and Handouts

Demonstration MEM 16: Context and Its Affect on Memory

Objective: To demonstrate the effects of context on memory.
Materials: An overhead transparency with the following matrix on it, making sure the number 13 looks like a cross between a B and 13:

```
      12
  A   13   C
      14
```

Procedure: Use the same procedure as in **MEM 9** above, except divide the room in half by identifying an individual in the middle and telling one half to start from the top of the display and process downward and the other half to process from left to right. If you have used the **MEM 9** display, tell them that this display is different.
Conclusions: Ask for a show of hands and ask, "Who saw 12, 13 and 14?" Most of one side will raise their hands. The other half will look puzzled. Now ask, "Who saw A, B, and C?" The other half will respond. Now show them the matrix again, and discuss the effect of psychological set on processing. For additional information on context and memory, see
http://ego.psy.flinders.edu.au/webpages/learning/jpdbkc/page2.html.

Diversity Topic

Diversity Topic 6.3: Primacy and Recency Effects

Although the serial position effects are well established in American psychological literature, they are not as well established in the cross-cultural literature. Discuss cross-cultural research that challenges this literature.
Discussion/Description: Although serial position effects are well established in the U.S., Cole and Scribner (1974) found no relationship between serial position and the likelihood of being remembered in studying the memories of Kpelle tribespeople in Liberia. Wagner (1981) suggested that the primacy effect is dependent on rehearsal or the silent repetition of things one is trying to remember, which is a memory strategy related to schooling. Wagner's research supported this notion. Other research by Scribner and Cole (1981) suggests that people of other cultures learn specific memory skills in different context that change their memory performance. Altogether, these types of studies seem to suggest that people in cultures with oral traditions are better at remembering things than do people in cultures within written traditions such as our own. This effect, however, seems to be localized to meaningful material as conveyed in stories, rather than lists of items as usually presented in memory research. Other effects due to culture cannot disentangle the effects of European type schooling on memory ability. Go to http://pangaea.pratt.edu/~jlampin/LEC3.html for information on memory models.

References/Additional Readings:

Cole, M., & Scribner, S. (1974). *Culture and thought: A psychological introduction.* New York: Wiley.

Scribner, S., & Cole, M. (1981). *The psychology of literacy.* Cambridge, MA: Harvard University Press.

Wagner, D. A. (1981). Culture and memory development. In H.C. Triandis and A. Hermon (Eds.), Handbook of Cross-Cultural Psychology, Volume 4. Boston: Allyn and Bacon.

F. Biology and Memory

Demonstration MEM 17: Enhance Your Memory with Hormones and Herbs?

Objective: To explore enhancing your memory with hormones and herbs
Materials: Internet access
Procedure: Go to http://www.asktom-naturally.com/naturally/pregnen.html and read the discussion of enhancing your memory with hormones and herbs.
Conclusions: Ask students to prepare to discuss their findings at this site at the next class meeting. Lead a discussion using the following questions: Is this a method of memory enhancement? Could this be just another "scam" against people with failing memory? Have you ever known anyone who has tried this method of memory enhancement? What were the results?

Lecture Examples

Lecture Example 6.10: Brain Damage and Memory

Ask students to volunteer to describe the behaviors of a friend or relative who has suffered brain damage. This damage could have occurred through stroke, trauma, surgery, or cancer. Use these descriptions throughout your lectures on the biology of memory. For more on brain damage, see http://www.iue.indiana.edu/psych/P326_COURSE/P326L_5.html.

G. Improving Memory

Classroom Demonstrations and Handouts

Demonstration MEM 18: Improving Memory Study Skills

Objective: To explore the topic of improving memory.
Materials: Internet access
Procedure: Go to http://www.gac.peachnet.edu/student_/study_skills/effstdy.htm. There are a

variety of study systems available, but all are organized in basically the same way and are designed to accomplish the same end: maximizing one's retention of information. Have the students explore three related links.

Conclusions: After each student has investigated this site ask them to prepare to discuss their findings at the next class meeting. Lead a discussion asking students which of the many types of memory improvement techniques do you find the most interesting?

Lecture Examples

Lecture Example 6.11: Improving Your Memory

Most students want to improve their memory skills. Use an article by Shimamura (1984) to highlight meaningfulness, organization, visualization, and attitudes in improving one's memory skills. Go to http://ego.psy.flinders.edu.au/webpages/learning/lsmnln/page1.html, a very interesting site for more information on improving memory.

Shimamura, A. P. (1984). A guide for teaching mnemonic skills. *Teaching of Psychology, 11,* 162-165.

Lecture Example 6.12: Metamemory

An effective method to improve one's memory is to become aware of it. This is called *metamemory* and refers to our awareness and knowledge of the functions and processes of our memory systems. One important aspect of metamemory is knowing what type of memory strategies to use. This ability develops and improves with age. For example, 2- or 3-year-olds do not use rehearsal to memorize. It is not until the sixth or seventh year that children can spontaneously employ rehearsal. Good students probably have a more acute sense of metamemory than poor students in the sense that they can recognize and monitor their own comprehension and memories. A recent study conducted by Reynolds et al. (1990) reported that successful tenth-grade students learned and recalled more information from a biology text because of a higher awareness of how and when to use selective attention strategy (SAS). Selective attention strategy involves task awareness, strategy awareness, and performance awareness. In this strategy, a student gives extra attention to more important information. To assess your own metamemory go to http://www.usm.maine.edu/~com/metamem.htm.

Bisanz, G. L., Vesander, G. T., & Voss, J. F. (1978). Knowledge of one's own responding and the relation of such knowledge to learning. *Journal of Experimental Child Psychology, 25,* 116-128.

Flavell, J. H., & Wellman, H. M. (1977). Metamemory. In R. V. Kail, Jr., and J. W. Hagen (Eds.). *Perspectives on the development of memory and cognition.* Hillsdale, NJ: Lawrence Erlbaum.

Reynolds, R. E., et al. (1990). Differences in the use of selective attention by more successful and less successful tenth-grade readers. *Journal of Educational Psychology, 82,* 749-759.

Lecture Example 6.13: How Good is Your Memory?

Pose the following question to the class, "Do you think your memory is above or below average?" Have the students in a small class write their answers on a piece of paper and turn it in, then tally these responses for the next class. In a larger section, have a show of hands, but have the students close their eyes to avoid social influence on their decision. In many classes you will find *most* students will believe that they are below average. Statistically, most students cannot be below average. Pursue *why* they feel inadequate in this area. Lead a discussion in which students try to identify any problems they might have with recall.

7 Cognition and Language

Chapter-at-a-Glance

Chapter Outline	Instruction Outline	Multimedia
Imagery and Concepts: Tools of Thinking p. 228 Imagery: Picture This—Elephants with Purple Polka Dots • Concepts: Our Mental Classification System (Is a Penguin a Bird?)	**Demonstration COG 1, 4** **Lecture Examples** 7.1 **Diversity Topic** 7.1 **Learning Objectives** 7.1-7.4 **Test Questions** 1-33	*PsychScience: Concept Formation* **No Digital Image Archive Avaliable for this Section** **No Cognition or Language Transparencies for this Section** **Web Sites** http://www.haverford.edu/psych/CogPsycpage.html Cognitive Psychology Resources at Haverford College on the Web http://www.psych-web.com/selfquiz/ch07mcq.htm Self Quiz
Deductive and Inductive Reasoning p. 233	**Demonstration COG 3** **Lecture Examples** 7.2 **Learning Objectives** 7.5 **Test Questions** 34-40	**Web Site** http://www.ozemail.com.au/~caveman/Creative/ Creativity Web
Decision Making: Making Choices in Life p. 234 The Additive Strategy • Elimination of Aspects • Heuristics and Decision Making • Framing Alternatives to Influence Decisions	**Demonstration COG 2, 7** **Lecture Examples** 7.3-7.5 **Learning Objectives** 7.6-7.10 **Test Questions** 41-50	**Web Site** http://mellers1.psych.berkeley.edu:80/sjdm/ The Society for Judgment and Decision
Problem Solving: Beyond Decision Making p. 238 Approaches to Problem Solving: How Do We Begin? • Impediments to Problem Solving: Mental Stumbling Blocks • Artificial Intelligence • Creativity: Unique and Useful Productions	**Demonstration COG 5, 8, 10, 11** **Lecture Examples** 7.7-7.9 **Critical Thinking Forum** 7.3 **Journal Entry** 7.1 **Diversity Topic** 7.2 **Learning Objectives** 7.11-7.15 **Test Questions** 51-96	*PsychScience: Problem Solving* Video Disc I Segments 3 & 13 **Web Site** http://ai.iit.nrc.ca/misc.html Artificial Intelligence Subject Index

Chapter Outline	Instruction Outline	Multimedia
Language p. 243 The Structure of Language • Animal Language • Language and Thinking • Bilingualism	Demonstration LANG 1, 2, 3 Lecture Examples 7.10-7.13, Critical Thinking Forum 7.4, 7.5 Diversity Topics 7.3-7.4 Learning Objectives 7.16-7.19 Test Questions 97-143	**Transparency:** MEM 9 **Web Site** http://www.lake.de/home/lake/ruban/buc_intro.html Bilingualism

What's New in Chapter 7

New Content

- An overview of cognition
- Formal and natural concepts
- Logical thinking
- Syllogisms
- Heuristics
- Decision making
- Bilingualism

Organizational Changes

- This new chapter is a full, new chapter built around the portions of the Second Edition's Chapter 7 that deal with cognition and language.
- The original Chapter 7's discussions of intelligence and creativity are now in Chapter 8.

New Special Features

- New chapter opening vignette—Deep Blue
- New *Try It's*
- New *Apply It* on avoiding bad decisions
- Revised *Remember It's*

New Key Terms

- cognition
- formal concept
- natural concept
- analogy heuristic
- surface structure
- deep structure
- reasoning

- inductive reasoning
- decision making
- additive strategy
- heuristic
- syllogism
- deductive reasoning
- availability heuristic
- representativeness heuristic
- framing

Learning Objective Questions

7.1 What is meant by cognition and what specific processes does it include?
7.2 What is imagery?
7.3 What is a concept?
7.4 What is the difference between a formal and a natural concept?
7.5 What is the difference between deductive and inductive reasoning?
7.6 How is the additive strategy used in decision making?
7.7 When is the elimination-by-aspects strategy most useful?
7.8 What is the availability heuristic?
7.9 What is the representativeness heuristic?
7.10 What is framing?
7.11 What are three basic approaches to problem solving?
7.12 What is an algorithm?
7.13 What are three heuristics used in problem solving?
7.14 How do functional fixedness and mental set impede problem solving?
7.15 What is artificial intelligence?
7.16 What are the four important components of language?
7.17 How does language in trained chimpanzees differ from human language?
7.18 In general, does thought influence language more or does language influence thought more?
7.19 When is the best time of life to learn a second language and why?

Chapter Overview

The chapter opens with a vignette about Kasparov and Deep Blue and their historic chess match. The authors then discuss a brief overview of cognition. Next, the methods that have been developed to study the nature of mental imagery and associated concepts are presented. Then the chapter turns to formation and classification of concepts, and formal and natural concepts prototypes are discussed. New information on inductive and deductive reasoning is presented. The decision-making strategies of additive and elimination-by-aspect are then reviewed. The chapter turns to heuristics and decision making, which includes availability and representativeness heuristic. A major new discussion of framing and how it influences decision is presented.

The three basic approaches to problem solving—trial and error, algorithms, and heuristics—are presented and the reasons they are important tools utilized in solving problems are discussed. Impediments to problem solving, including functional fixedness and mental set, can interfere with effective problem solving. The area of artificial intelligence is presenting new challenges to psychology in its efforts to create expert systems and computer systems that imitate thought.

The concluding section of the chapter explores the basic structures of language including phonemes, morphemes, syntax, semantics, and surface and deep structure. Animal language and the relationship between language and thought are also explored in an updated section. A new section on bilingualism and the most opportune time to learn a new language, as well as the problems associated with older people learning a new language concludes this section. The chapter concludes with a new Apply It! called *Avoiding Bad Decisions*.

Key Terms

additive strategy (p. 234)
algorithm (p. 239)
analogy heuristic (p.241)
artificial intelligence (p. 242)
availability heuristic (p. 235)
cognition (p. 228)
concept (p. 231)
decision making (p. 234)
deductive reasoning (p. 233)
deep structure (p. 245)
exemplars (p. 233)
formal concept (p. 232)

framing (p. 237)
functional fixedness (p. 241)
heuristic (p. 235)
imagery (p. 229)
inductive reasoning (p. 234)
language (p. 244)
linguistic relativity hypothesis (p. 248)
means-end analysis (p. 240)
mental set (p. 241)
morphemes (p. 244)
natural concept (p. 222)

neural networks (p. 270)
phonemes (p. 244)
problem solving (p. 238)
prototype (p. 232)
psycholinguistics (p. 244)
reasoning (p. 233)
representativeness heuristic (p. 236)
semantics (p. 245)
surface structure (p. 245)
syllogism (p. 233)
syntax (p. 245)
trial and error (p. 239)
working backwards (p. 240)

Annotated Lecture Outline

A. Imagery and Concepts: Tools of Thinking

Classroom Demonstrations and Handouts

Demonstration COG 1: Concepts and Rock 'n' Roll

Objective: To illustrate concepts using music.
Materials: A variety of music forms such as rock, gospel, rap, classical, and blues.
Procedure: Play the music for your students and ask them to classify the individual songs into

groups (concepts). Are these types of music artificial concepts or natural concepts? Are there songs your students would consider as prototypes of the various types of music?
Conclusions: Discuss the rules and dimensions employed to decide group membership. Music based upon attributes like style, instruments, vocals, or beat can be assigned to different musical concepts.

Demonstration COG 4: Learning a Concept

Objective: To demonstrate concept learning.
Materials: 3x5 index cards
Procedure: Draw one square and one triangle on each index card. The figures should vary in size (large/small), color (green/red), and position (up/down). The fourth concept is, of course, shape. Select one student to learn the concept you have chosen but not revealed from the four possibilities. Give the student feedback after each card as to whether his or her response was correct. For instance, you have selected size as the relevant concept. If the student selects a large, blue, triangle on the card, tell the student the choice is wrong (since you secretly selected small). See how many cards it takes the student to discover the relevant concept. You may want to repeat this exercise using a different concept for at least two other students.
Conclusion: Discuss how concept formation is an important, but often difficult, task.

Lecture Examples

Lecture Example 7.1: Our Amazing Mind

We are capable of performing many complex mental acrobatics. Hunt (1982) has put some of these abilities in perspective. For example, each of your students has a mind with more than fifty times the storage capacity required to memorize and recall every single telephone number in the United States. Another example is that despite the fact that there are between 50,000 and 75,000 words in the average vocabulary, we are able to search it very rapidly and efficiently to answer a questions like "What seven-letter word ending in 'y' means 'a group of interacting individuals living in the same region and sharing the same culture'?" To describe the logic and reasoning that we automatically do in milliseconds to solve an analogy like "Acorn is to oak as infant is to . . ." would take between twenty to fifty articles.

Hunt, M. (1982). *The universe within: A new science explores the human mind.* New York: Simon & Schuster.

Diversity Topic

Diversity Topic 7.1: Classification

Is classification universal or culture-specific? Have students classify different types of stimuli, such as a group of colors, a set of facial expressions showing emotion, etc. Also, have the class engage in sorting tasks with different types of stimuli. Then give a presentation on universal and culture-specific aspects of these tasks.
Discussion/Description: Cross-cultural research has shown some universals in classification of

objects or events that have commonality in experience across cultures, such as colors or facial expressions. Some evidence for cultural differences have been found for sorting tasks, although the effects of schooling have not been explained or eliminated in this research. If students can engage in a discussion about why they believe some tasks are universal while others are culture-specific, the discussion will greatly supplement their learning in this area.

Matsumoto, D. (1994). *People: Psychology from a cultural perspective*. Pacific Grove, CA: Brooks Cole.

Matsumoto, D. (1996). *Culture and diversity: A world of difference*. Pacific Grove, CA: Brooks Cole.

Berry, J. W., Poortinga, Y. H., Segall, M. H., & Dasen, P. R. (1992). *Cross-cultural psychology: Research and applications*. Cambridge: Cambridge University Press.

B. Deductive and Inductive Reasoning

Demonstration COG 3: Reasoning

Objective: To expose students to deductive and inductive reasoning.
Materials: Internet access
Procedure: Go to http://cate.santarosa.edu/philo/tutorial/first.htm and explore three different links. This site is a philosophy site but will be of interest to the students.
Conclusions: Have each student investigate this site and prepare to discuss their findings at the next class meeting. Lead a discussion using the following questions. Which of the many types of reasoning do you use? What is meant by inductive validity? After exploring this page, do you have a better understanding of reasoning?

Lecture Examples

Lecture Example 7.2: Deductive and Inductive Reasoning

Go to http://trochim.human.cornell.edu/kb/dedind.htm and you will find a discussion of deductive and inductive reasoning. Use these examples in your lecture to help the students understand this concept.

C. Decision Making: Making Choices in Life

Demonstration COG 2: Availability Heuristics

Objective: To demonstrate the potential shortcoming of availability heuristics.
Materials: **Handout COG 2**
Procedure: When people judge the relative frequency of objects or events, they are often

influenced by the relative availability or accessibility of such events in their own memories. Distribute **Handout COG 2** and ask the students to so indicate their answers to the questions. Their estimates are influenced by the availability heuristic if they indicate that the number of words beginning with *r* or *k* is greater than the number of words with those letters appearing third. This is because first letters are more useful cues than third letters for referencing and accessing items in one's personal word collection. It is easier to generate (i.e., make available) words that begin with the letters. Actually, words with those letters appearing third are far more numerous. Similarly, their estimate of the number of women faculty on campus should be positively correlated with the number of female professors they have actually had.
Conclusions: This exercise should help demonstrate that subjective ease of generation often leads to inaccurate estimates. Use http://www.psych.utah.edu/~psych312/lect16.htm, for a reference for heuristics.

Demonstration COG 7: Cognitive Psychology

Objective: To allow the students to explore cognitive sites on the Internet.
Materials: Internet access
Procedure: Go to http://casper.beckman.uiuc.edu/~c-tsai4/cogsci/. This site contains links to information on general topics for decisions making, artificial intelligence, psychology, language and linguistics, and neuroscience. Assign the students to explore several of the links.
Conclusions: Students could write a short summary of their experiences at this site.

Lecture Examples

Lecture Example 7.3: Decision Making and Hitting a Fastball

For a major league baseball player, accurately deciding whether to hit a pitch is quite impressive. Not only does the decision involve perception, it demands complex cognitive processes. Consider that the ball is traveling 90 miles per hour and takes only 40/100th of a second to travel from the pitcher's mound to the catcher. A physicist has calculated that thirteen variables are involved in hitting a baseball, and since the direction of errors can be positive or negative, there are actually twenty-six "roads" to failure. The batter has roughly 0.31 seconds to decide whether to hit a pitch; during that time span, the ball travels about 36 feet. If the batter starts to swing 3/1000th of a second too soon or too late, the ball will be missed.

Allman, W. F. (1985, April). The swing's the thing. *Science,* 6(3), 86-87.

Lecture Example 7.4: Heuristics

Go to http://socrates.berkeley.edu/~psy001/psych1tl3.html, a site that can be used in your lecture development for heuristics. This short but informative article should help you with this lecture.

Lecture Example 7.5: Syllogisms

Go to http://www.clearcf.uvic.ca/writersguide/Pages/LogSyll.html and you will find a discussion of syllogisms. Use these examples in your lecture to help the students understand this concept.

D. Problem Solving: Beyond Decision Making

Classroom Demonstrations and Handouts

Demonstration COG 5: Breaking Sets in Problem Solving

Objective: To demonstrate how psychological set (e.g., stating the problem) can interfere with the generation of solutions to problems.
Materials: **Handout COG 5**
Procedure: Ask students to think about a problem; the problem may be a corporate problem (e.g., crime or pollution) or a personal problem (e.g., poor grades). Using **Handout COG 5**, each student should reword or describe the problem in several different ways. This may open some doors in terms of solutions. Next, students should develop at least two solutions to the problem.
Conclusions: Each different formulation of the problem suggests variations of its most appropriate solution. Tell students that people generate far fewer options than the total number of possible solutions judged worthy of consideration.

Demonstration Intro 8: Critical Thinking How Many Squares Are There?

Critical thinking requires careful assessment and objective examination. As you are discussing critical thinking, present your students with **Handout Intro 7**. Ask them how many squares they see. A typical response is 16. Request your students to reevaluate their answer. Are there more than 16 squares? Did your students practice critical thinking?

Demonstration COG 10: Artificial Intelligence

Objective: To allow the students to explore cognitive sites on the Internet.
Materials: Internet access
Procedure: Go to http://www.sjdm.org/sjdm/jdm-links.shtml. This site contains links to information on artificial intelligence, psychology, language and linguistics, and neuroscience. Assign the students to explore several of the links.
Conclusions: Students could write a short summary of their experiences at this site.

Demonstration COG 11: Cognitive Psychology

Objective: To allow the students to explore cognitive sites on the Internet.
Materials: Internet access
Procedure: Go to http://casper.beckman.uiuc.edu/~c-tsai4/cogsci/. This site contains links to information on general topics for artificial intelligence. Assign the students to explore several of the links.
Conclusions: Students could write a short summary of their experiences at this site.

Lecture Examples

Lecture Example 7.7: Functional Fixedness

It is important to be able to look at a problem from several different points of view to avoid functional fixedness. Would Robinson Crusoe have survived if he had not learned to adapt to his island environment with the provisions at hand? Similarly, Air Force pilots are trained to rid themselves of functional fixedness in survival training. If a downed pilot fails to think of an unpalatable insect as a source of nourishment, he might starve to death. Ask your students to think of other examples of problem solving from literature or real life that illustrate the importance of overcoming functional fixedness. Use http://pangaea.pratt.edu/~jlampin/LEC9.html as a reference for functional fixedness.

Lecture Example 7.8: Are Machines Intelligent?

Waldrop (1987) suggests several answers to the question "Can a machine really think?" He focuses on two assertions made by those who answer that a machine cannot feel or be aware. He suggests that discoveries about the chemical basis of emotion imply that emotions must be serving biological functions (e.g., focusing our attention and helping us decide what is important). If we can discover those functions, it is possible that a computer could carry out these tasks. In addressing the second point, that a machine cannot be aware, Waldrop describes the debate between the computationalists and the holists that took place in 1980 in *Behavioral and Brain Sciences* (1983). The holists suggest that computers' ability to simulate human thought and intelligence does not mean they can duplicate it. A computer program that uses rules to manipulate abstract symbols cannot be aware because the symbols don't really mean anything. The computationalists reply that humans themselves use formal rules for thinking, and it may be impossible to distinguish between merely manipulating rules and true understanding. Use http://id001.wkap.nl/ as a reference for machine intelligence.

Searle, J. (1980). Minds, brains, and programs. *The Behavioral and Brain Sciences, 3,* 417-457.

Waldrop, M. (1987). *Man-made minds: The promise of artificial intelligence.* New York: Walker and Company.

Lecture Example 7.9: Hypertext

A new computer software program, envisioned in 1945 by Vannevar Bush and developed by Ted Nelson, attempts to imitate the brain. Hypertext, or hypermedia as it is sometimes called, mimics the way in which the brain stores and retrieves information. When we think of last summer, for example, some of our memories are non-sequentially linked together. We might recall a volleyball game at a beach party. A memory linked to that memory might consist of how the sand slowed you down and how it felt to block a spike. "The crowd went wild...that reminds me of the time that I was watching the World Series when the Twins hit a grand slam. Boy, that was spectacular!" Although still not a perfect match, Hypertext gives software authors the ability to develop new techniques in computer-assisted instruction. For an example of hypertext, see http://quarles.unbc.edu/midsummer/info.html.

Conklin, J. (1987). Hypertext: An introduction and survey. *Computer, 20,* 17-41.

HyperCard in Higher Ed. (November/December 1988). *Tech Trends for Leaders in Education and Training,* 33(6), 13-15.

Smith, K. E. (1988, March). Hypertext: Linking to the future. *Online, 12*(2), 32-34.

Diversity Topic

Diversity Topic 7.2: Problem Solving

How universal are problem-solving abilities? Give students a brief presentation on the limitations of such abilities to familiar concepts, situations, and technologies that have been found in cross-cultural research.

Discussion/Description: Cross-cultural research has indicated considerable cultural differences in people's abilities to solve various problems typically used in psychological experiments. However, research has also shown that those differences may be solely a function of the degree of familiarity of people of other cultures with the types of problems presented. Asking people of some cultures to engage with a human-made contraption to solve a certain problem may be as unfamiliar to them as it would be to have American students track animals via smells and footprints. Differences in problem-solving ability obtained using such culturally unequivalent methods of testing may show only differences in the degree of familiarity; it may not be a function of problem-solving abilities at all.

Matsumoto, D. (1994). *People: Psychology from a cultural perspective.* Pacific Grove, CA: Brooks Cole.

Matsumoto, D. (1996). *Culture and diversity: A world of difference.* Pacific Grove, CA: Brooks Cole.

Berry, J. W., Poortinga, Y. H., Segall, M. H., & Dasen, P. R. (1992). *Cross-cultural psychology: Research and applications.* Cambridge: Cambridge University Press.

E. Language

Classroom Demonstrations and Handouts

Demonstration LANG 1: What Is Language?

Objective: To invite students to define language.
Materials: Instructor
Procedure: Hunter (1981) suggests that you use no verbal language to communicate a number of requests to your students. According to Hunter, you should arrive late to class to insure that the

students are talking. Ask students to be quiet and to pay attention without using verbal language. (Hunter writes, "clap hands, or books, together loudly and place finger over lips; if absolutely necessary, but only then, write QUIET in large letters on the board." Your students should now do some type of stunt (e.g., stand, hop, clap, or sing). Next, students should get into groups to discuss what language is. However, you must indicate these requests nonverbally! After they are grouped, perform a short mime routine (e.g., sleeping and being awakened by a phone call; bowling; fishing with intense struggle but only catching a minnow). Ask the students in the discussion groups to propose a definition of language and determine whether what you were doing constitutes language and communication. In addition, pose these questions: Is American Sign Language a real language? Is crying a real language?

Conclusions: Exposure to psycholinguistics becomes more meaningful for students after contemplating what language and communication are. For more on defining language, see http://lang.ots.dk/.

Hunter, W. J. (1981). Language and communication: Defining language can leave you speechless. In L. T. Benjamin, Jr. and K. D. Lowman (Eds.). *Activities handbook for the teaching of psychology*, (Vol. 1) (pp. 103-104). Washington, D.C.: American Psychological Association.

Demonstration LANG 2: Guest Speaker: Speech Pathologist

Objective: To expose students to speech disorders.
Materials: Speech pathologist
Procedure: Invite a speech pathologist to talk to your class on how language is acquired and the problems that he or she experiences in his or her profession. Have the students prepare questions of interest for the guest. Use http://jobguide.deet.gov.au/JobGuideOnline/Text/Jobs/238611.html as a starting point for your demonstration.

Demonstration LANG 3: Language and Linguistics

Objective: To allow the students to explore cognitive sites on the Internet.
Materials: Internet access
Procedure: Go to http://casper.beckman.uiuc.edu/~c-tsai4/cogsci/language.html. This site contains links to information on general topics for language and linguistics. Assign the students to explore several of the links.
Conclusions: Students could write a short summary of their experiences at this site.

Lecture Examples

Lecture Example 7.10: Speech Errors

Long regarded as unimportant, slips of the tongue and other speech errors are now receiving scientific attention in the hopes of better understanding language and speech production. Speech errors are most common when the speaker is tired or stressed.

They seem to occur in somewhat logical ways and leave intact the rest of the sentence in terms of syntactic and phonological structure. Here are some common speech errors with examples:

> *Exchange:* Finally, you're here; but better nate than lever (*late/never*).
> *Shift:* The quarterback throw the balls as he is tackled (*throws/ball*).
> *Anticipation:* The mawn needs mowing (*lawn/mowing*).
> *Perseveration:* He is a regular Don Duan (*Don Juan*).
> *Blend:* I am going to bake some cars (*cookies/bars*).

Fromkin, V. A. (1980). *Errors in Linguistic Performance*. New York: Academic Press.

Lecture Example 7.11: Language in the Courtroom

Students often have a very keen interest in language and the courtroom. This interest may be generated from the endless hours of courtroom drama on commercial TV, Court TV, or the infamous OJ trial. Select a current case of local or national interest to explain the role of language on the outcome of the case.

Lecture Example 7.12: Language and the Brain

Now would be a good time to review the brain's role in language in your lectures. Discuss Broca's and Wernicke's areas and how they are central to the production and comprehension of language. Then discuss the role of the motor cortex and somatosensory cortex with the vast amount of brain devoted to the lips, tongue, and mouth. Finally describe how all of the brain's areas must work in close coordination for language to be produced and comprehended.

Lecture Example 7.13: Language and Thought

Infantile amnesia refers to the finding that rarely, if ever, do we have memories of events prior to the acquisition of verbal abilities. This data indicates that thought appears to be determined by language capabilities. Ask the students if they agree with this hypothesis. Also ask what types of thought might not be bound by language limitations?

Diversity Topics

Diversity Topic 7.3: Language and Thought

How does language affect thought? Ask people in class who are multilingual to comment on how they perceive things similarly or differently when speaking different languages. Then, give a brief presentation on the effects of language on personality tests and judgments of emotion as reviewed in Matsumoto (1996).
Discussion/Description: There is a considerable amount of evidence to show that responses on personality tests and judgments of facial expressions differ as a function of language within the same people, i.e., multilinguals. These differences suggest differences in world view and mindset that people adopt when speaking different languages. Given that most American students are monolingual, they generally find this research fascinating.

Matsumoto, D. (1996). *Culture and diversity: A world of difference*. Pacific Grove, CA: Brooks Cole.

Diversity Topic 7.4: Language

How do you address people around you? Your boss at work? Teachers? Younger brothers and sisters? Older brothers and sisters? Do a quick survey in class about terms of address, and discuss how these are intimately related to culture.

Discussion/Description: Terms of address are related to culture. In the American culture, we tend to address people by their first name or by pronouns such as "you" and "I." This is because our individualistic culture fosters a view of everyone as separate, autonomous individuals who are basically equal. Students call their teachers by their first name, even in preschool, which would be unthinkable in many other cultures. Many other languages have elaborate systems for terms of address, and these systems reflect elaborate cultural systems regarding interpersonal relationships. In Japanese, for example, there is a different term and pronoun for almost every type of status and relationship difference that exists.

Matsumoto, D. (1996). *Culture and diversity: A world of difference*. Pacific Grove, CA: Brooks Cole.

8 Intelligence and Creativity

Chapter-at-a-Glance

Chapter Outline	Instruction Outline	Multimedia
The Nature of Intelligence p. 256 The Search for Factors Underlying Intelligence • Intelligence: More Than One Type?	**Demonstration** INTELL 3, 4, 5 **Lecture Example** 8.1, 8.9 **Critical Thinking Opportunity** 8.1 **Critical Thinking Forum** 8.1 **Learning Objectives** 8.1-8.2 **Test Questions** 1-30	**Transparency** MEM 8 **Digital Image Archive** PSME010-011 **Web Site** http://www.netlink.co.uk/users/vess/mensal.html The Intelligence Page
Measuring Intelligence p. 260 Alfred Binet and the First Successful Intelligence Test • Intelligence Testing in the United States • Requirements of Good Tests: Reliability, Validity, and Standardization • The Range of Intelligence • Intelligence and Neural Speed and Efficiency	**Student Chalkboard** INTELL 2-3 **Demonstration** INTELL 1, 6, 7 **Lecture Examples** 8.2-8.10 **Critical Thinking Opportunity** 8.2 **Learning Objectives** 8.3-8.12 **Test Questions** 31-87	*Discovering Psychology: Testing and Intelligence* **Web Site** http://www.brain.com/ The five minute IQ test.
The IQ Controversy: Brainy Dispute p. 266 The Uses and Abuses of Intelligence Tests • The Nature-Nurture Controversy: Battle of the Centuries • Intelligence: Is It Fixed or Changeable? • Expectations, Effort, and Academic Achievement—A Cross-cultural Comparison	**Demonstration** INTELL 2 & 12, BIO 11 **Lecture Example** 8.11, 8.12 **Critical Thinking Forum** 8.2 **Learning Objectives** 8.18-8.17 **Test Questions** 88-114	*Psychology and Culture* Ch. 23 **Video Disc II** Segment 20 **Web Site** http://www.cycad.com/cgi-bin/Upstream/Issues/psychology/IQ/index.html Many links to controversial individuals and concept in IQ
Emotional Intelligence p. 274 Personal Components of Emotional Intelligence • Interpersonal Components of Emotional Intelligence	**Demonstration** INTELL 8, 9 **Lecture Examples** 8.13 **Test Questions** 115-124	**PsychScience** Concept Formation **Web Site** http://trochim.human.cornell.edu/gallery/young/emotion.htm#emotions Emotional Intelligence

Chapter Outline	Instruction Outline	Multimedia
Creativity: Unique and Useful Productions p. 277 The Creative Process • The Nature of Creative Thinking • Measuring Creativity: Are There Reliable Measures? • Characteristics of the Creative Person • Savant Syndrome: A Special Form of Creativity	Demonstration INTELL 10, COG 6, 8 Lecture Examples 8.14 Journal Entry 8.1 Test Questions 125-138	Web Site http://www.wismed.com/foundation/islands.htm Savant Syndrome

What's New in Chapter 8

A new, separate chapter devoted to intelligence and creativity!

New Content

- Intelligence and neural speed and efficiency
- Emotional intelligence
- The creative process
- The nature of creative thinking
- Characteristics of creative people
- Savant syndrome

Expanded Content

- Theories of multiple intelligences (Gardner, Sternberg)
- Twin studies
- Creativity in general

Organizational Changes

- This new chapter is built around the portions of the Second Edition's Chapter 7 that deal with intelligence and creativity.
- The original Chapter 7's discussions of cognition and language can now be found in the new Chapter 7.
- The material on Alfred Binet has been integrated within the text.

New Special Features

- Revised *Remember It's*

New Key Terms

- intelligence
- emotional intelligence
- divergent thinking
- savant syndrome
- triarchic theory of intelligence

Learning Objective Questions

8.1   What factors underlie intelligence, according to Spearman and Thurstone?
8.2   What types of intelligence did Gardner and Sternberg identify?
8.3   What is Binet's major contribution to psychology?
8.4   What is the Stanford-Binet Intelligence Scale?
8.5   What does IQ mean, and how has the method for calculating it changed over time?
8.6   What did Wechsler's tests provide that the Stanford-Binet did not?
8.7   What do the terms reliability, validity, and standardization mean?
8.8   What are the ranges of IQ scores considered average, superior, and in the range of mental retardation?
8.9   According to the Terman study, how do the gifted differ from the general population?
8.10 What two criteria must one meet to be classified as mentally retarded?
8.11 What is the relationship between intelligence and the efficiency and speed of neural processing?
8.12 Of what are intelligence tests good predictors?
8.13 What are some abuses of intelligence tests?
8.14 How does the nature-nurture controversy apply to intelligence?
8.15 What is behavioral genetics, and what are the primary methods used in the field today?
8.16 How do twin studies support the view that intelligence is inherited?
8.17 What are Jensen's and Herrnstein and Murray's controversial views on race and IQ?
8.18 What kinds of evidence suggest that IQ is changeable rather than fixed?
8.19 What are the personal components of emotional intelligence?
8.20 What are the interpersonal components of emotional intelligence?
8.21 What is creativity?
8.22 What are the four stages in the creative process?
8.23 What kinds of tests have been used to measure creativity, and how good are they as predictors of creativity?
8.24 What are some characteristics of creative people?

Chapter Overview

This chapter combines the topics of intelligence and creativity. The authors examine attempts to define intelligence by Spearman, Thurstone, Gardner, and Sternberg. Gardner's theory of multiple intelligences and Sternberg's triarchic theory of intelligence both suggest that there must be several kinds of intelligence. The emphasis then shifts to Alfred Binet who pioneered the intelligence test as a tool to predict the performance of children in school. The intelligence quotient was developed to express, numerically, the relative performance of an individual on intelligence tests. Binet's original test was modified and translated for use in the United States as the Stanford-Binet test. The development of adult scales, like the Wechsler test, and the development of group testing are also discussed. In order for a test to be considered acceptable, it must meet the criteria of reliability, validity, and standardization. Lewis Terman's study of over 1,500 students with high IQs began in 1921 and continues today. The gifted individuals have received few resources in the educational system. Mental retardation is then defined. The authors then discuss the relationship between intelligence and neural speed and efficiency.

Problems with how intelligence tests have been applied and with the apparent cultural biases they reflect have formed the basis of a set of controversies about intelligence testing. One problem is with the abuse of tests, and another concerns whether intelligence is a result of genetics or the environment. Race and IQ, the controversial views of Jensen and Herrnstein and Murray are then discussed.

The topic of emotional intelligence is then developed and includes discussions of the personal components of emotional intelligence. The discussion then turns to the area of interpersonal components of emotional intelligence.

The chapter then turns to a discussion of creativity and its unique and useful productions. In this discussion, the four stages of the creative process are outlined, as well as the nature of creative thinking. The authors expand a discussion on the reliability of measuring creativity and the characteristics of the creative person. The chapter concludes with a discussion of the Savant syndrome.

Key Terms

adoption method (p. 268)
aptitude test (p. 262)
behavioral genetics (p. 268)
creativity (p. 277)
culture-fair intelligence test (p. 267)
deviation score (p. 261)
divergent thinking (p. 277)
emotional intelligence (p. 274)
fraternal twins (p. 268)
g factor (p. 257)

heritability (p. 268)
identical twins (p. 268)
intelligence (p. 256)
intelligence quotient (IQ) (p. 261)
mainstreaming (p. 264)
mental retardation (p. 264)
nature-nurture controversy (p. 267)
norms (p. 261)
primary mental abilities (p. 257)
reliability (p. 262)

savant syndrome (p. 279)
standardization (p. 262)
Stanford-Binet Intelligence Scale (p. 261)
triarchic theory of intelligence (p. 258)
twin study method (p. 268)
validity (p. 262)
Wechsler Adult Intelligence Scale (WAIS-R) (p.61)

Annotated Lecture Outline

A. The Nature of Intelligence

Classroom Demonstrations and Handouts

Demonstration INTELL 3: What Is Intelligence?

Objective: To challenge students to think about the definitions of intelligence.
Materials: **Handout INTELL 3**
Procedure: There are two activities worthy of attention. In the first activity, students are to write down their own definition of intelligence as well as ten behaviors that signify intelligence. Follow-up with a discussion of how the students' definitions compare to the professional psychologists' definitions. Sternberg (1982) found general agreement between the two. However, the amateur group's definitions tend to be, in general, related to practical problem-solving ability, verbal ability, and social competence. The experts focused on verbal intelligence, problem solving, and practical intelligence. The second activity, described by Laura E. Beck, requires students to think about the definition of intelligence as a function of age. Ask the class to develop a list of five traits and behaviors that are indicative of intelligence in a 6-month-old, 2-year-old, 10-year-old, 20-year-old, 50-year-old, and 80-year-old. Next, compare the lists of traits generated from these two activities. Are there similarities? Differences?
Conclusions: From this activity, discuss the problems of defining intelligence. See http://clem.mscd.edu/~psych/intro/cncpintl.htm for more information on the definition of intelligence.

Sternberg, R. J. (April, 1982). Who's intelligent? *Psychology Today, 16*, 30-39.

Demonstration INTELL 4: Intelligent or Dumb?

Objective: To address the stereotypes that some students hold involving "intelligent" and "dumb" people.
Materials: **Handout INTELL 4**
Procedure: Ask students to construct lists, using **Handout INTELL 4**, of attributes for intelligent and unintelligent individuals. Examine the stereotypes of dress, speech, skin color, vocation choices, popularity, and athletic prowess.
Conclusions: Most of us have stereotypes regarding who is "intelligent" and who is "dumb"; these stereotypes affect the interactions that we have with these individuals.

Demonstration INTELL 5: Multiple Intelligences

Objective: To relate Gardner's theory of multiple intelligences to examples generated by students.
Materials: **Handout INTELL 5a**; **Handout INTELL 5b**
Procedure: After discussing Gardner's theory of multiple intelligences, have your students generate items that measure his concept of interpersonal intelligence. First, have students think of people they know who exemplify the types of intelligences presented on **Handout INTELL 5a**. Next, on **Handout INTELL 5b**, ask them to think of the individual named who has interpersonal

intelligence and to describe two behaviors that the person does that represent this high, interpersonal intelligence. After that, develop some test items that you could use that measure interpersonal intelligence.

Conclusions: When students take part in trying to come up with examples of multiple intelligences, they get a more thorough appreciation of the theory. Use http://www.newhorizons.org/crfut_gardner.html for information on Gardner and his theories.

Lecture Examples

Lecture Example 8.1: Multiple Intelligences

According to Gardner (1983) people display many different kinds of intelligences, not just one or two. Of all Gardner's types of intelligences, linguistic intelligence is the most widely shared and the one most studied by psychologists. It shows up in speaking (e.g., choosing just the right word), analyzing, remembering, explaining, and convincing. Gardner also proposes that musical intelligence is one of the earliest forms of intelligence to arise. It is described as the appreciation of melody, rhythm, timbre, and tone quality of early songs, such as lullabies. Logical-mathematical intelligence arises as the child begins to manipulate objects, and it moves from the concrete to the abstract with development. Spatial intelligence is the ability to mentally rotate and examine objects. The ability to use the body in differentiated and skilled ways, as in athletics, dance, or mime, is called body intelligence. If you have a well-developed sense of identity and know yourself and your feelings, then you have high intrapersonal intelligence. Interpersonal intelligence, however, deals with the ability to understand others, including how they feel, what motivates them, and how they interact with others. McKean argues that savants are a good illustration of how brain damage can affect one form of intelligence but not another. Consider following up this lecture with Demonstration INTELL5, on multiple intelligences. Use http://www.newhorizons.org/crfut_gardner.html for information on Gardner and his theories.

Gardner, H. (1983). *Frames of mind: The theory of multiple intelligences.* New York: Basic Books.

McKean, K. (1986, January). Intelligence and new ways to measure the wisdom of man. *Current,* 15-23.

B. Measuring Intelligence

Classroom Demonstrations and Handouts

Student Chalkboard INTELL 2: Subtests of the Stanford-Binet

Student Chalkboard INTELL 3: Subtests of the WISC-R

Demonstration INTELL 1: Reliability and Validity of a Historical Measure of Intelligence

Objective: To demonstrate the importance of reliability and validity in measuring individual

differences.
Materials: **Handout INTELL 1**
Procedure: First tell your students of S. G. Morton's attempt to measure intelligence. He filled the cranial cavities of human skulls from different races to measure intelligence. He used sifted white mustard seeds to fill these skulls and then poured back in a graduated cylinder to read the skull's volume in cubic inches. Morton concluded that whites are the most mentally worthy race because they have the largest average skull volume. Morton unconsciously misinterpreted the data to fit his strong *a priori* convictions. Notwithstanding the manipulation of data, the method produced unreliable results because the seeds did not pack well and the seeds varied in size. Remeasurements varied sometimes by more than five percent. After describing this to students, ask them to discuss the reliability and validity of this method. Place students in groups of five and provide each student with a copy of **Handout INTELL 1**.
Conclusions: Reliability and validity are mainstays of psychological testing, and this activity should help students come to an appreciation and understanding of these concepts.

Gould, S. (1981). *The mismeasure of man*. New York: Norton.

Demonstration INTELL 6: Guest Speaker: School Psychologists

Objective: To expose students to the work of school psychologists.
Materials: None
Procedure: Arrange for a local school psychologist to guest lecture to your class. Many important and far-reaching decisions are made on the basis of test scores of one type or another. A prevalent use of test scores is the assignment of "exceptional" students to various educational programs, such as programs for learning disabilities, behavior disorders, or retardation. At the other end of the spectrum, students can be assigned to gifted and talented programs. Having a school psychologist visit a class session will let your students hear firsthand what tests are used, how they are administered, and how students are selected for programs. This session will also give you an opportunity to talk about testing as a possible area of employment in the field of psychology. Use http://lserver.aea14.k12.ia.us/SWP/ahance/Psychaction.html as a reference.

Demonstration INTELL 7: Intelligence on the Internet

Objective: To allow the students to explore intelligence on the Internet.
Materials: Internet access
Procedure: Go to http://psychology2.semo.edu/PY531/chap8/index.htm. This site contains links to the major figures and concepts in the area of intelligence and intelligence testing. Assign the students to explore several of the links.
Conclusions: Students could write a short summary of their experiences at this site. Their understanding of intelligence and intelligence testing will be enhanced.

Lecture Examples

Lecture Example 8.2: Sample Intelligence Tests

In your lecture on the various tools used to measure intelligence (e.g., Wechsler's scales, K-ABC), bring the actual tests to class to show students. Read a couple of practice items from the GRE application booklet to give your students a sense of the types of questions used.

Lecture Example 8.3: Reliability and Validity

Try explaining reliability and validity using a calculator as an analogy. A calculator with good reliability means that each time you key in 2 + 2 = you get 4 and each time you push 2 x 3 = you get 6. Validity, on the other hand, might mean that the "divide" button really performs division. In other words, the sign on the button actually tells what the button does.

Lecture Example 8.4: Rating Test Reliability and Validity

As you lecture on the concepts of reliability and validity, relate the terms to tests with which students are familiar. Point out that all tests, no matter what the purpose or format, must be both reliable and valid. Ask students to rate the reliability and validity of their psychology exam, an eye chart test, a driver's license test, etc.

Lecture Example 8.5: The Range of Skills

IQ tests do not tap the full spectrum of intellectual competencies, including the child's ability to use environmental and personal resources in adapting to the world. For example, although interventions do not substantially raise the IQ's of mildly retarded individuals, "there is good reason to believe that interventions can enhance the functional abilities, learning strategies, adaptive skills, and social competencies of children whose measured IQ is low. Our goal should be to provide optimal environments to facilitate such learning and development" (Weinberg, 1989, p. 103).

Weinberg, R. A. (1989). Intelligence and IQ: Landmark issues and great debates. *American Psychologist, 44*, 98-104.

Lecture Example 8.6: Lewis Terman

Terman said, "The gifted children as a group exceeded the best standards at that time for American-born children in growth status as indicated by both height and weight. ...The combined results of the medical examinations and the physical measurements provide a striking contrast to the popular stereotype of the child prodigy so commonly depicted as pathetic, creative, overserious and undersized, sickly, hollow-chested, stoop-shouldered, clumsy, nervously tense and bespectacled." (Terman, 1925, pp. 6-8). Use http://www.gseis.ucla.edu/courses/ed191/assignment1/leeman.html as a reference for this lecture example.

Terman, L. M. (1925). *Genetic studies of genius, vol. 1: Mental and physical traits of a thousand gifted children.* Stanford, CA: Stanford University Press.

Lecture Example 8.7: Labeling People with Mental Retardation

You get a sense of how our perception of people with mental retardation has changed over the years by examining the terminology used to describe them. Originally, individuals with an IQ of 25 and below were referred to as "idiots." The current term for this level is "profoundly retarded" (or "custodial," to describe educability expectations). A profoundly retarded individual functions like a child between the ages of birth and 3 years of age. The term "imbecile" formerly described individuals with an IQ between 25 and 40; the current term is "severely retarded" (or "trainable"). This level of ability is akin to the functioning of a 3-to 6-year-old. The label "moderately retarded" describes people with IQ's between 40 and 55, who function at the level of 6- to 8-year-olds. "Moron" was previously used to describe individuals with an IQ of 50-70. Today the term "mildly retarded" (or "educable") is used to describe such people. These individuals function at the level of 9- to 12-year-olds, often achieving second- to fifth-grade levels in school. Many learn to read, interact with their peers, and eventually hold jobs. For more on this topic, see http://www.cqc.state.ny.us/pubmrabs.htm.

Lecture Example 8.8: Criterion-related Validity and Prediction

Students are always interested in how their college entrance exams were used to predict their academic performance. Many see the testing as a waste of time and money. Explain that the first concern in such prediction is finding a variable or variables that correlate with college grades. The testing companies have conducted correlational studies to determine the extent scores on the two major entrance exams, the ACT and SAT, predict first-semester grade point average (the criterion). The prediction is never perfect because grades are affected by many factors. Most correlations between test scores and first-semester grades are in the range of +.60.

Lecture Example 8.9: IQ Testing

Most students have taken a psychological test of some type. Ask them to describe their test experiences. Were they aware at the time why they were being tested and how the results were to be used? Were they helped or hindered by the results of the testing? Did they think they should have done better than they did? Were the tests employed fairly and impartially? Why does our society place so much emphasis on psychological testing? Describe how you felt when you took the GRE and when you received the results. Did you think you should have scored higher? For a discussion of children's IQ see http://education.apple.com/education/techlearn/revue/iqsoftware.html.

Lecture Example 8.10: Lectures on Intelligence

Use http://psychology2.semo.edu/PY531/chap8/index.htm as a source for an outline for your lectures on intelligence. This is a very rich source for information on intelligence.

C. The IQ Controversy: Brainy Dispute

Classroom Demonstrations and Handouts

Demonstration INTELL 2: Making a "Biased" Test of Intelligence

Objective: To emphasize the importance of cultural fairness in tests of intelligence by creating a culture bias test.
Materials: None
Procedure: Inform your students of the concepts of culture fair and culture bias tests. To stress the critical nature and influence of bias due to culture, ask your students to consider developing a "state-bias" or "country-bias" test of intelligence in the same spirit that Adrian Dove's "Soul Folks Chitling Test" was created. Go to http://www.silk.net/personal/bealesca/chitquiz.htm to take the test and have it scored. (In addition, consider giving the BITCH test developed by Williams [1970].) In this "bias" test, you ask questions that only a resident might know, like the name of the land grant university or the governor of the state. In addition, questions regarding the image of specific cities may be asked. End the activity with the question, "If you were a nonresident and did not know the answers to these questions and took the test, and then were placed in a 'special ed' class, how would you feel?"
Conclusions: Students will appreciate the significance of the effects of culture on testing and performance.

Dove, A. (July 15, 1968). Soul folks chitling test. (Pp. 51-52). *Newsweek*.

Williams, R. L. (1970). Black pride, academic relevance, and individual achievement. *Counseling Psychologist, 2*, 18-22.

Demonstration BIO 12: Interviewing Identical Twins

Objective: To explore twin research issues.
Materials: None
Procedure: Since identical twins share the same genetic makeup, it is possible that they share other nonphysical traits. First, construct an interview protocol focusing on interests, values, preferences, and goals; next select a set of identical twins. Separately interview each twin and then compare their responses to your questions. Are they similar?
Conclusions: Students should find that although twins are similar, they also can be quite different. Even so, they may share many non-physical interests and characteristics. What other factors might account for the similarities or differences?

Lecture Examples

Lecture Example 8.11: Twin Correlations

A meta-analysis focusing on age was conducted on the basis of 103 papers, from 1967 through 1985, that describe twin data for IQ and personality (McCartney et al., 1990). The analysis finds a tendency for twin correlations to decrease with age and for heritability to increase that is, the decrease is greater for fraternal twins than for identical twins. A developmental increase in heritability is strongest for IQ in childhood: An analysis of IQ data from the Colorado Adoption Project indicates that genetic influence on IQ increases steadily between infancy and middle childhood (Plomin & Rende, 1991).

McCartney, K., Harris, M. J., & Bernieri, F. (1990). Growing up and growing apart: A developmental meta-analysis of twin studies. *Psychological Bulletin, 107*, 226-237.

Plomin, R., & Rende, R. (1991). Human behavioral genetics. *Annual Review of Psychology, 42*, 161-190.

Lecture Example 8.12: Cheating in Science—Sir Cyril Burt

Although the Sir Cyril Burt saga is perhaps the most famous case of cheating in science, it is not an isolated incident. Many of your students are unaware of this incident. Take the time to explain how Sir Cyril Burt cheated on his data in twin studies. Students should be made aware of such cheating so they can appreciate the importance of replication in building a body of scientific knowledge. Another very interesting case is that of cold fusion at the University of Utah; two investigators lied about making the most important discovery in the history of physics—cold fusion. They were later disproved and shamed. Cheating still does occur, but science has ways of self-correcting—peer review of publications and replication. This is a good point in the course for mentioning the issue of ethics in science in the general context. Use http://www.oup-usa.org/docs/019852336X.html as a reference for this lecture example.

D. Emotional Intelligence

Classroom Demonstrations and Handouts

Demonstration INTELL 8: Emotional IQ Test

Objective: To allow students to access their emotional IQ.
Materials: Internet access
Procedure: Go to http://id46.bc.edu/Mod3/meas02/meas02.html and take the Emotional IQ Test.
Conclusions: Discuss with students the concept of Emotional IQ. Explain what each individual's pattern of scores might mean. The student will have many questions about their own scores.

Demonstration INTELL 9: Emotional Intelligence

Objective: To allow the students to explore emotional intelligence.
Materials: Internet access
Procedure: Go to http://trochim.human.cornell.edu/tutorial/young/eiweb2.htm. This site contains a detailed discussion of emotional intelligence and related measurement issues. Have the students explore several of the links.
Conclusions: Students could write a short summary of their experiences at this site.

Lecture Examples

Lecture Example 8.13: Emotional Intelligence

Based on the material in the text by Goleman on emotional intelligence, develop a short lead-in to the topic. Ask students for input and examples of what they believe to be the personal components of emotional intelligence.

E. Creativity: Unique and Useful Productions

Classroom Demonstrations and Handouts

Demonstration INTELL10: Evaluating Creativity

Objective: To allow students to evaluate their creativity on the Internet.
Materials: Internet access
Procedure: Go to http://www.routing.se/avica/rdlinks.htm and explore several of the over 300 links for creativity.
Conclusions: Discuss with the students the concept of creativity. Ask the students to develop their own definition of creativity. This can be accomplished in either a small group or in the form of a short paper.

Demonstration COG 6: How Creative Are You?

Objective: To demonstrate to students different types of creativity tests.
Materials: **Handout COG 6a**; **Handout COG 6b**; **Handout COG 6c**; a supply of Lego building blocks (you could substitute a generic brand)
Procedure: Proceed to give one or more of these creativity tests to students. If you use the Legos, make sure you give the selected subjects the same kind and quantity of Legos. Challenge them to come up with something creative within a set amount of time; the time could range from minutes to the next class meeting. Make sure that you point out that this is a fun activity and should not be taken as a scientific assessment of creativity. Dossick and Shea (1988) present some exercises for creative therapy that you might want to scan.
The second part of the activity requires that students complete **Handout COG 6a, COG 6b**, and **COG 6c**. Discuss answers given to these questions, and have students propose ways to measure creativity based on the questions.
Conclusions: Creativity might mean different things to different people—what might be creative to one person is not creative to the next. Emphasize the text's definition of creativity. Go to http://www.routing.se/avica/rdlinks.htm and you can explore over 300 links for creativity.

Dossick, J., & Shea, E. (1988). *Creative therapy: 52 exercises for groups.* Sarasota, FL: Professional Resource Exchange.

Demonstration COG 8: Creativity

Objective: To demonstrate creativity.
Materials: Internet access
Procedure: Go to http://www.ozemail.com.au/~caveman/Creative/ and explore three different links.
Conclusions: Have each student investigate this site and prepare to discuss their findings in the next class meeting. Lead a discussion using the following questions. What are the most important aspects of creativity? Can a person learn to be creative? What was the most interesting link?

Lecture Examples

Lecture Example 8.14: The Creative Process

Based on the material in the text on creativity ask students for input and examples of their definition of creativity. Make an overhead of the four stages of the creative process: Preparation, Incubation, Illumination, and Translation. Present the overhead and ask for additional examples based on the overhead.

9 Child Development

Chapter-at-a-Glance

Chapter Outline	Instruction Outline	Multimedia
Developmental Psychology: Basic Issues and Methodology p. 286 Controversial Issues in Developmental Psychology • Approaches to Studying Developmental Change	**Demonstration** DEV 4 **Learning Objective** 9.1 **Test Questions** 1-7	*Psychology and Culture*: Ch. 13 **Transparencies** DEV 1, 6 **Web Sites** http://www.earlychildhood.com/ General life experience of young children. http://idealist.com/children/ A key word search engine
Heredity and Prenatal Development p. 287 The Mechanism of Heredity: Genes and Chromosomes • The Stages of Prenatal Development: Unfolding According to Plan • Negative Influences on Prenatal Development: Sabotaging Nature's Plan	**Demonstration** BIO 9-10, 12, DEV 3 **Lecture Examples** 9.1-9.5 **Critical Thinking Forum** 9.1 **Journal Entry** 9.1 **Learning Objectives** 9.2-9.5 **Test Questions** 8-26	**Transparencies** DEV 2, 3, 5 **Video Disc III** Segments 3-11, 18, 19 **Video Disc IV** Segments 1-3 **Digital Image Archive** PSDV001-004, 011-012 **Web Site** http://www.parentsplace.com/genobject.cgi/readroom/pregnant.html Pregnancy and Early Care
Physical Development and Learning in Infancy p. 292 The Neonate: Seven Pounds of Beauty? • Perceptual Development in Infancy • Learning in Infancy • Motor Development in Infancy	**Demonstration** DEV 5 **Lecture Example** 9.6 **Learning Objectives** 9.6-9.8 **Test Questions** 27-43	**Transparencies** DEV 7-9, 14 **Video Disc I** Segment 12 **Video Disc IV** Segments 4-5 **Digital Image Archive** PSDV005a&b **Web Sites** http://www.earlychildhood.com/ Young Children http://www.efn.org/~djz/birth/birthindex.html Midwifery, Pregnancy, Birth, and Breast feeding

Chapter Outline	Instruction Outline	Multimedia
Emotional Development in Infancy p. 296 Temperament: How and When Does It Develop? • The Formation of Attachment • The Father-Child Relationship	**Lecture Examples** 9.7-9.8 **Critical Thinking Forum** 9.2 **Diversity Topic** 9.1 **Learning Objectives** 9.9-9.13 **Test Questions** 44-67	**Video Disc IV** Segment 6 **Web Site** http://rock.uwc.edu/psych/psy360/outlines/Socinf.htm Emotional Development
Piaget's Theory of Cognitive Development p. 301 The Cognitive Stages of Development: Climbing the Steps to Cognitive Maturity • Pioneers: Jean Piaget • An Evaluation of Piaget's Contribution	**Demonstration** DEV 1, 8, 2 **Lecture Example** 9.9, 9.10 **Critical Thinking Opportunity** 9.1 **Learning Objectives** 9.14-9.18 **Test Questions** 68-92	*Psychology and Culture*: Ch. 21 **PsychScience** Cognitive Development **Transparencies** DEV 11-13 **Video Disc I** Segment 15 **Video Disc IV** Segment **Digital Image Archive** PSDV007-010 **Web Site** http://155.33.221.112/pth1118/piaget.htm Outline of Piaget's Cognitive Development Stages
Vygotsky's Sociocultural View of Cognitive Development p. 307	**Lecture Example** 9.11 **Learning Objective** 9.19 **Test Questions** 93-95	**Web Site** http://rock.uwc.edu/psych/psy360/outlines/Cogearl.htm Vygotsky's Sociocultural View
Cognitive Development: The Information-Processing Approach p. 308	**Lecture Example** 9.12 **Learning Objective** 9.20 **Test Questions** 96-104	**WEB Site** http://www.babycenter.com/refcap/569.htmlCognitive Cognitive Development
Language Development p. 310 The Stages of Language Development: The Orderly Progression of Language • Theories of Language Development: How Do We Acquire It?	**Demonstration** LANG 3 **Learning Objectives** 9.21-9.22 **Test Questions** 105-119	**Video Disc I** Segment 14 **Web Site** http://crl.ucsd.edu/~bates/papers/html/bates-carnevale-1993/bates-carnevale-1993.html Review of Language Development
Socialization of the Child p. 313 Erikson's Theory of Psychosocial Development • The Parents' Role in the Socialization Process • Peer Relationships • Television as a Socializing Agent: Does It Help or Hinder?	**Student Chalkboard** DEV 2 **Demonstration** DEV 7 **Lecture Examples** 9.13-9.16 **Journal Entry** 9.2 **Diversity Topics** 9.2-9.3 **Learning Objectives** 9.23-9.26 **Test Questions** 120-138	*Psychology and Culture:* Chapters 14 & 16 **Video Disc II** Segment 21 **Video Disc IV** Segments 7-8 **Web Site** http://idealist.com/children/erk.html Erikson's Theory

What's New in Chapter 9

New Content

- The information-processing approach to cognitive development
- Metacognition
- Motherese

Expanded Content

- Temperament
- Types of attachment

New Special Features

- New *Try It*
- Revised *Remember It's*

Learning Objective Questions

9.1   What are two types of studies developmental psychologists use to investigate age-related changes?
9.2   How are hereditary traits transmitted?
9.3   When are dominant or recessive genes expressed in an individual's traits?
9.4   What are the three stages of prenatal development?
9.5   What are some negative influences on prenatal development, and during what time is their impact greatest?
9.6   What are the perceptual abilities of the newborn?
9.7   What types of learning occur in the first few days of life?
9.8   What is the primary factor influencing attainment of the major motor milestones?
9.9   What is temperament, and what are the three temperament types identified by Thomas, Chess, and Birch?
9.10 What did Harlow's studies reveal about maternal deprivation and attachment in infant monkeys?
9.11 According to Bowlby, when does the infant have a strong attachment to the mother?
9.12 What are the four attachment patterns identified in infants?
9.13 What are the typical differences in the ways mothers and fathers interact with their children?
9.14 According to Piaget, what are the stages of cognitive development?
9.15 What occurs during Piaget's sensorimotor stage?
9.16 What cognitive limitations characterize a child's thinking during the preoperational stage?
9.17 What cognitive abilities do children acquire during the concrete operations stage?
9.18 What new capability characterizes the formal operations stage?

9.19 In Vygotsky's view, how do private speech and scaffolding contribute to cognitive development?
9.20 What three cognitive abilities have information-processing researchers studied extensively?
9.21 What are the stages of language development, from cooing through the acquisition of grammatical rules?
9.22 How do learning theory and the nativist position explain the acquisition of language?
9.23 What is Erikson's theory of psychosocial development?
9.24 What are the three parenting styles discussed by Baumrind, and which did she find most effective?
9.25 How do peers contribute to the socialization process?
9.26 What are some of the positive and negative effects of television?

Chapter Overview

This chapter examines physical, emotional, cognitive, and social development from conception through the end of childhood. The chapter begins with a discussion of developmental psychology basic issues and methodologies. The discussion then turns to heredity and prenatal development. The nature of chromosomes is explored as well as the role of dominant and recessive genes in the expression and transmission of traits. The authors describe the stages of prenatal development and the negative influences on development during pregnancy.

The newborn has a number of reflexes that help it adapt to its new surroundings, and its sensory abilities begin organizing the world from the very beginning. Infants are capable of learning prior to birth. The maturation of motor skills follows a regular pattern, though the pace differs for each child.

The chapter then turns to emotional development in infancy and then how the temperament of a child may be controlled to some extent by genetics. The temperaments discussed are "easy," "difficult," and "slow-to-warm-up" (with many temperaments being too inconsistent to categorize). Another area of emotional development is the formation of attachment. Children may start to show stranger anxiety at about 6 months and separation anxiety between 12 and 18 months. Mary Ainsworth has described four patterns of attachment: secure, avoidant, resistant, and disorganized/disoriented. This section ends with a discussion of the father-child relationship.

The authors describe the basic concepts of Piaget's theory of cognitive development, including schemas and the processes of assimilation and accommodation. All four stages—sensorimotor, preoperational, concrete operations, and formal operation—are described in detail. An evaluation of Piaget's contributions ends this section.

Lev Vygotsky's sociocultural view of cognitive development is then discussed. The cognitive development information-processing approach, including the topics of attention, memory, and metacognition, are developed.

The stages of language development and the basic concepts of language are described. The authors compare the learning theory and the nativist position on the acquisition of language.

The socialization of the child is discussed in the context of the psychosocial stages identified by Erikson. This chapter describes the first four of Erikson's stages: trust versus mistrust, autonomy versus shame and doubt, initiative versus guilt, and industry versus inferiority. The authors discuss the parent's role in the socialization process in terms of authoritarian, authoritative, and permissive parenting styles. The chapter closes with a discussion of the roles of peers and television in socialization.

Key Terms

accommodation (p. 302)
assimilation (p. 302)
attachment (p. 297)
authoritarian parents (p. 316)
authoritative parents (p. 316)
autonomy versus shame and doubt (p. 314)
babbling (p. 310)
basic trust versus basic mistrust (p. 314)
centration (p. 304)
chromosomes (p. 287)
concrete operations stage (p. 305)
conservation (p. 303)
critical period (p. 290)
cross-sectional study (p. 287)
developmental psychology (p. 286)
dominant gene (p. 288)
embryo (p. 289)
fetal alcohol syndrome (p. 291)
fetus (p. 289)
formal operations stage (p. 305)
fraternal (dizygotic) twins (p. 290)
genes (p. 287)
habituation (p. 294)
identical (monozygotic) twins (p. 289)
industry versus inferiority (p. 314)
initiative versus guilt (p. 314)
longitudinal study (p. 287)
low-birth-weight baby (p. 292)
maturation (p. 295)
nature-nurture controversy (p. 286)
neonate (p. 292)
object permanence (p. 303)
overextension (p. 310)
overregularization (p. 311)
period of the zygote (p. 288)
permissive parents (p. 316)
phonemes (p. 310)
prenatal (p. 289)
preoperational stage (p. 303)
preterm infant (p. 292)
psychosocial stages (p. 314)
recessive gene (p. 288)
reflexes (p. 292)
reversibility (p. 304)
schemas (p. 302)
sensorimotor stage (p. 303)
separation anxiety (p. 299)
sex chromosomes (p. 288)
socialization (p. 314)
stranger anxiety (p. 299)
surrogate (p. 298)
telegraphic speech (p. 311)
temperament (p. 296)
teratogens (p. 289)
underextension (p. 311)
visual cliff (p. 293)

Annotated Lecture Outline

A. Developmental Psychology: Basic Issues and Methodology

Classroom Demonstrations and Handouts

Demonstration DEV 4: Baby Pictures

Objective: To show the dramatic physical changes evident in development.
Materials: Pictures that the students bring to class of themselves at a young age
Procedure: Attach the pictures to a poster located on a bulletin board. As physical development is discussed, challenge your students to fit the students' names to their baby pictures.
Conclusions: While there are similarities between our physical self at a young age and now, it will be difficult to identify students using their baby pictures. See http://hna.ffh.vic.gov.au/yafs/cis/chart/ for an index of physical changes in children.

B. Heredity and Prenatal Development

Classroom Demonstrations and Handouts

Demonstration Bio 9: Genetic Differences between People

Objective: To show physical differences that are genetic in nature (no pun intended) between people.
Materials: **Handout BIO 9**
Procedure: There are many differences between people that you can illustrate or demonstrate in your classroom. Tongue-rolling, hair color, facial dimples, and farsightedness are abilities and characteristics that are governed by dominant and recessive genes. Eye color appears to be determined by many genes (i.e., polygenetic). Singer (1987) offers several demonstrations of individual differences. One of these is the length of your index finger and ring finger. With **Handout BIO 9,** have your students carefully place their ring finger on the top line and trace an outline of their fingers. Then compare the lengths of the index and ring fingers. Take an informal survey of your students' findings. Singer (1987) writes that "in women, having an index finger that is shorter than the ring finger is a recessive trait, whereas in men, having a shorter index finger is dominant."
You may consider developing an activity using phenylthiocarbamide (PTC) strips; 7 out of 10 people can detect the bitter taste as a result of a recessive gene. Another activity is to test for red-green color blindness. See Singer (1987) for details.
Conclusions: Human variability may be the result of the interaction between genetics and environment. There are some characteristics in which genetics plays a larger role than environment.

Singer, S. (1987). Individual differences in biological bases of behavior. In V. P. Makosky, L. G. Whittemore, and A. M. Rogers (Eds.). *Activities handbook for the teaching of psychology* (Vol. 2) (pp. 289-293). Washington, D.C.: American Psychological Association.

Demonstration BIO 10: Genetic Detective

Objective: To provide students an opportunity to explore genetically expressed characteristics.
Materials: Family Characteristics (**Handout BIO 10**)
Procedure: Ask students to do some detective work by tracing some observable familial characteristic (e.g., eye color, height, widow's peak) through their family tree. Other traits like color blindness or even psychiatric disorders (e.g., bipolar disorder, schizophrenia) could be incorporated, but these are a bit more personal.
Conclusions: The simple traits expressed in family physical characteristics will illustrate the influence of genetic information in physical appearance. Discuss what characteristics may be revealed that are more psychological, but appear to pass down through the family tree. For more information, go to http://www.familytreemaker.com/.

Demonstration BIO 12: Interviewing Identical Twins

Objective: To explore twin research issues.
Materials: None
Procedure: Since identical twins share the same genetic makeup, it is possible that they share other nonphysical traits. First, construct an interview protocol focusing on interests, values, preferences, and goals; next select a set of identical twins. Separately interview each twin and then compare their responses to your questions. Are they similar?
Conclusions: Students should find that although twins are similar, they also can be quite different. Even so, they may share many nonphysical interests and characteristics. What other factors might account for the similarities or differences?

Demonstration DEV 3: Birth Weight and Smoking

Objective: To illustrate the effects of teratogens on prenatal development.
Materials: None
Procedure: There is clear evidence linking low birth-weight babies to mothers who smoke. Ask your students to find out their birth weights and whether their mothers smoked during their prenatal development. If the sample is large enough, there should be a significant difference.
Conclusions: This activity will strongly show the relationship between the prenatal environment and development. For more on teratogens, see http://www.fensende.com/users/swnymph/Midwife/medsters.html#Teratogens.

Lecture Examples

Lecture Example 9.1: Sex-Linked Traits and Genetic Defects

There is a myriad of genetic problems that your students might find intriguing. There are those that are carried on the sex chromosome such as color blindness, hairy ear rims, hemophilia, and Duchenne's muscular dystrophy. Some involve a problem in the number of chromosomes, such as

XYY syndrome, Klinefelter's syndrome (XXY), Turner's syndrome (XO), and triple X syndrome (XXX). Other disorders involving genetic abnormalities include cystic fibrosis, Tay-Sachs disease, Huntington's chorea, and sickle-cell anemia. These are illustrations of how biology can clearly affect behavior. For more on mental retardation, see http://www.dailycal.org/archive/05.01.97/news/gene.html. For more on Klinefelter's syndrome, see http://www.healthanswers.com/database/ami/converted/000382.html.

Plomin, R. (1986). *Development, genetics, and psychology.* Hillsdale, NJ: Erlbaum.

Plomin, R., Defries, J. C., & McClearn, G. E. (1989). *Behavior genetics: A primer* (2nd ed.). New York: Freeman.

Lecture Example 9.2: One Second Sooner or Later...

Tell your students that if their conception had taken place one second sooner or later, they might have been the opposite sex. They might have been born with a birth defect, had a different eye color, or even had another personality.

Lecture Example 9.3: Ultrasound Pictures

Bring pictures of sonograms to class and see if students can identify the various anatomical parts of the fetus. (You may want to make an overhead out of a sonogram.) Try contacting a local hospital or clinic for access to sample sonograms. See http://miso.wwa.com/~striker/pages/ultrasnd.htm for some pictures.

Lecture Example 9.4: Video Display Terminals and Pregnant Women

Should VDT's be added to the growing list of teratogens, and should exposure to these terminals be limited? A recent study sheds some light on this very important public health issue. Two groups of telephone operators were compared; one group used VDTs and the other did not. The number of pregnancies studied was 882. Schnorr and her associates (1991) reported that the risk of spontaneous abortions did *not* increase as a result of exposure to VDTs and the coinciding electromagnetic energy. For more on teratogens, see http://nba19.med.uth.tmc.edu/academic/devo/html/teratogens.htm#types.

Schnorr, T. M., et al. (1991). Video display terminals and the risk of spontaneous abortion. *The New England Journal of Medicine, 324,* 727-733.

Lecture Example 9.5: Drugs and Prenatal Development

Considering the devastating consequences of drug ingestion by a pregnant woman, ask your students if they feel that drug laws should be more strictly enforced for pregnant women than for men and nonpregnant women. Should there be laws against the use of tobacco, alcohol, and other teratogens by pregnant women? How do your students feel about the idea of imposing legal sanctions against mothers who give birth to babies who suffer from fetal alcohol syndrome or babies addicted to crack cocaine?

C. Physical Development and Learning in Infancy

Classroom Demonstrations and Handouts

Demonstration DEV 5: Motor and Verbal Development

Objective: To demonstrate the sequence of milestones in motor and verbal development.
Materials: Milestones of Physical Development (**Handout DEV 5a**); Milestones of Language Development (**Handout DEV 5b**); (**Handout DEV 5b** is the opposite of Student Chalkboard **LANG 1**)
Procedure: Give the handouts to the students and ask them to write in the average in which these milestones appear. As you explain the answers, point out that development and maturation are predictable and not random. You may also wish to discuss cephalocaudal and proximodistal patterns of development. Fernald and Fernald (1990) suggest that students indicate which milestones are due to maturation and which are due to training. Astor-Stetson (1990) offers a slightly different activity in which students in groups develop lists of five milestones and the ages that these are achieved.
Conclusions: Students will learn the sequence of developmental landmarks in verbal and motor development. For more information on motor development, see http://www.sla.purdue.edu/academic/hkls/undergrd/F34.htm.

Astor-Stetson, E. (1990). Implications of the milestones of development. In V. P. Makosky, C. C. Sileo, L. G. Whittemore, C. P. Landry, and M. L. Skutley (Eds.). *Activities handbook for the teaching of psychology* (Vol. 3) (pp. 113-114). Washington, D.C.: American Psychological Association.

Fernald, P. S., & Fernald, L. D. (1990). Early motor and verbal development. In V. P. Makosky, C. C. Sileo, L. G. Whittemore, C. P. Landry, and M. L. Skutley (Eds.). *Activities handbook for the teaching of psychology* (Vol. 3) (pp. 111-112). Washington, D.C.: American Psychological Association.

Lecture Example

Lecture Example 9.6: Male-Female Developmental Differences

Research supports the existence of a greater female viability after birth. Apparently girls are less prone to Sudden Infant Death Syndrome (SIDS) and to hyperactivity. Their skeletal development at birth is about one month ahead of males. However, the lymphatic tissues change in size and girls lose vision between 11 and 14 years as a consequence of rapid growth (Paludi, 1992). More information on Sudden Infant Death Syndrome can be obtained from http://sids-network.org/facts.htm.

Paludi, M. A. (1992). *The psychology of women.* Dubuque, IA: WCM Brown Benchmark.

D. Emotional Development in Infancy

Lecture Examples

Lecture Example 9.7: The "Dance" between Mother and Infant

The interaction between mother and infant has been likened to a choreographed dance. The child attempts to control the amount of stimulation he or she receives. When overstimulated, the baby disengages by looking away. When under-aroused, the baby smiles and verbalizes to attract the mother's attention. If this tactic is unsuccessful, the baby might cry or show other signs of distress. The mother also tries to capture the infant's attention by vocalizing, smiling, and touching. Brazelton and Tronick (1980) reported that within a few minutes of interaction, there are many cycles of attention and inattention.

Brazelton, T. B., & Tronick, E. (1980). Preverbal communication between mothers and infants. In D. R. Olson (Ed.), *The social foundations of language and thought*. New York: W. W. Norton.

Lecture Example 9.8: Crying

Parents often claim to be able to "read" their babies' crying to determine the babies' needs. Some developmental psychologists argue that parents aren't really reading a baby's cry but rather just interpreting the cry in the context of the situation. Another interesting topic deals with expression, pain, and crying (Grunau & Craig, 1987). An interesting article in *Discover* magazine addressed recent efforts to analyze crying as a possible early sign of Sudden Infant Death Syndrome (SIDS). More information on Sudden Infant Death Syndrome can be obtained from http://sids-network.org/facts.htm.

Angier, N. (1984, September). Medical clues from babies' cries. *Discover*, 49-51.

Grunau, R. V. E., & Craig, K. D. (1987). Pain expression in neonates: Facial action and cry. *Pain, 28*, 395-410.

Diversity Topic

Diversity Topic 9.1: Attachment

Is secure, close attachment the most preferred type of attachment across cultures? Cross-cultural research seems to suggest that it is not the most preferred in some cultures. Give a brief presentation of these differences.
Discussion/Description: Cross-cultural research has suggested, for example, that German families prefer what we characterize as ambivalent attachment; Japanese families prefer highly dependent attachment. These types of differences are ultimately related to the different types of cultures in which the children and parents are bonding.

Matsumoto, D. (1994). *People: Psychology from a cultural perspective*. Pacific Grove, CA: Brooks Cole.

Matsumoto, D. (1996). *Culture and diversity in a changing world*. Pacific Grove, CA: Brooks Cole.

E. Piaget's Theory of Cognitive Development

Classroom Demonstrations and Handouts

Demonstration DEV 1: Evaluating Baby Toys

Objective: To speculate on the role that toys have in development.
Materials: Several different types of infant/child toys
Procedure: Present the toys to the students. Invite your students to speculate on what benefits a child may gain by interacting with the toys. Moreover, examine gender-role stereotyping in toys (Lloyd, 1990). For example, do the toys encourage physical development or cognitive development? An equally important issue is what age or Piagetian stage the child should be in to benefit from the toy. Ask students to assess the safety problems of the toy. In addition, the students should be able to determine if they would recommend the toy to parents.
Conclusions: Students will find that there is a wide variety of toys available for children and their benefits vary significantly.
Follow-up Outside Class Project: Have students visit a toy store and do an analysis of their own choice of toys. They should focus on gender-role stereotyping. Ask them to look for themes in toys. They should also note the packaging and advertising labels, the placement of the toys in the store, and instructions that are biased. For more information on gender-role stereotyping, see http://www.ncet.org.uk/info-sheets/gender.html.

Lloyd, M. A. (1990). Gender-role stereotyping in toys: An out-of-class project. In V. P. Makosky, C. C. Sileo, L. G. Whittemore, C. P. Landry, and M. L. Skutley (Eds.). *Activities handbook for the teaching of psychology* (Vol. 3) (pp. 293-294). Washington, D.C.: American Psychological Association.

Demonstration DEV 8: Intellectual Development

Objective: To illustrate intellectual development using incomplete clichés and sayings.
Materials: Intellectual Development (**Handout DEV 8**)
Procedure: Your students might find this activity interesting and fun. Make several copies of **Handout DEV 8** for each student and charge them with the responsibility of finding a child or two to complete the phrases. Bring the completed phrases to class and present and discuss them.
Conclusions: Discuss the relationship between a child's level of intellectual development and his or her completed, albeit incorrect, sayings. Are there examples of animism, egocentrism, or artificialism?

Demonstration DEV 2: Observing a Child

Objective: To illustrate intellectual development using children.
Materials: A child
Procedure: Some of the most effective and enjoyable demonstrations of developmental psychology involve bringing children of various ages to class for direct observation. Sources for children can include your own family; when my daughter was younger, she spent time in my lectures when other day care was not available. Colleagues in your department or college and parents who are students in your class may also volunteer to bring in a child. If possible, try to provide a set of developmental norms relevant to each child's age so that the class can develop an assessment of the child's level of development.

For example, you can demonstrate lack of object permanence with a 1-year-old or younger infant. Allow the baby to play with and visually follow a toy. Remove the toy from sight. The infant will not search for the toy as an older child will.

Conservation tasks can be given to preschoolers. All you need are three glasses, two tall and thin and one short and squat. Start with the same amount of water in the two tall glasses. Show them to the child and get him or her to agree they both have the same amount of water. Then pour the water from one glass into the short, fat glass. Ask the child whether there is more, less, or the same amount of water in the short glass than in the tall glass. Once the principle of conservation has been acquired, the child will say there is no difference quite promptly. However, the tall, thin glass wins in the case of children who have not yet acquired conservation. This is a classic demonstration and always works.

Conclusions: Ask the students to listen to preschoolers talk; this will teach your students a great deal about language development. Leave time at the end of the class to encourage your class to ask questions of the parents.

Lecture Example

Lecture Example 9.9: Inability to Conserve

A pizza parlor waitress asked Yogi Berra how many pieces she should cut his pizza into. The customer replies, "Four...I don't think I can eat eight."

Lecture Example 9.10: Stages of development

To show the advantages and disadvantages of stage theories, ask your students to describe the typical freshman, sophomore, junior, and senior. The discussion should reveal that, while a typical class member can be described, characteristics that distinguish the classes are not mutually exclusive, nor are they necessarily observed in a given member of the class.

F. Vygotsky's Sociocultural View of Cognitive Development

Lecture Example

Lecture Example 9.11: Lev Semenovich Vygotsky

Use the site http://www.massey.ac.nz/~ALock/virtual/project2.htm to help develop a lecture on the work of Vygotsky. This site contains several relevant links for the development of the lecture.

G. Cognitive Development: The Information Processing Approach

Lecture Example

Lecture Example 9.12: Information Processing Approach

Use the site http://www.cpm.mmu.ac.uk/pub/workshop/gaylard.txt to help develop a lecture on Cognitive Development: The Information Processing Approach. This site contains several relevant links for the development of the lecture.

H. Language Development

Classroom Demonstrations and Handouts

Demonstration Lang 3: A Baby's First Words

Objective: To illustrate the stages of language acquisition.
Materials: Recorded speech of children of different ages
Procedure: Play the recorded speech to your students. Point out instances of preverbal sounds (e.g., cooing, babbling), holophrastic speech ("Milk"), and telegraphic speech ("Want milk"), as well as errors of overregulation, overextensions, and underextensions. Point out the differences between ages in regard to mean utterance length.
Conclusions: Your students will appreciate the fact that you have concrete examples of the stages of language acquisition.
Any parent can tell you that there is a lag between children's ability to *understand* a particular word and their ability to *produce* it. It is more difficult to pronounce a word than it is to simply make sense of it. In comparison with more outgoing children, shy children tend to experience more of a lag between comprehension and production, but they show sudden increases in production later on. Another revealing aspect of language development is errors of over-regularization.

There are general rules in the English language to indicate, for example, past tense (*-ed*) and plurality (*-s*). Often children use these morphological rules inappropriately, saying such things as "shutted," "goed," "drawed," and "eated." See Berko's classic study (1958) for a technique to test for overregularization.

Berk, L. E. *Child Development*. 2nd ed. Boston: Allyn and Bacon, 1991.

Berko, J. The child's learning of English morphology. *Word*, 1958, *14*, 150-177.

I. Socialization of the Child

Classroom Demonstrations and Handouts

Student Chalkboard DEV 2: Erikson's First Four Stages

Demonstration DEV 7: Videotaping Parents and Children

Objective: To expose students to the realities of parenting and the behavioral abilities of children.
Materials: **Handout DEV 7**
Procedure: Videotape interviews of different types of parents (e.g., first-time parents; single; adopting parents) and children engaged in various behaviors. For example, Piagetian theory gives us a wealth of ideas like conservation and object permanence. You may wish to observe other characteristics such as the quality of attachment (e.g. separation anxiety), temperament, or a newborn's reflexes. It is always much more dramatic to have the child visit the class, but you run the risk of him/her failing to perform. It is a good idea to record the responses and to show the class the tapes. Day-care centers on campus and off-campus as well as students with families (even your family) are good sources for children of different ages. Consult the sources below for methods. For example, Coates and Vietze (1981) and Nazzaro describe techniques to assess object permanence and conservation, respectively. Show the videos at appropriate times to students. In addition, provide them with **Handout DEV 7** when demonstrating conservation.
Conclusions: Students will appreciate these concrete examples of concepts that you are discussing in class.

Coates, D. L., & Vietze, P. M. (1981). Object permanence in infancy: Out of sight, out of mind? In L. T. Benjamin, Jr. and K. D. Lowman (Eds.), *Activities handbook for the teaching of psychology* (Vol. 1) (pp. 113-115). Washington, D.C.: American Psychological Association.

Harper, G. F., & Silverstro, J. R. (1981). Use of videocassette parent interviews in teaching developmental psychology. *Teaching of Psychology, 10*, 239-241.

Nazzaro, J. R. (1981). Conservation ability in children. In L. T. Benjamin, Jr. and K. D. Lowman (Eds.), *Activities handbook for the teaching of psychology* (Vol. 1) (pp. 24-125). Washington, D.C.: American Psychological Association.

Snellgrove, L. (1981). Sensory stimulation and infant development. In L. T. Benjamin, Jr. and K. D. Lowman (Eds.), *Activities handbook for the teaching of psychology* (Vol. 1) (pp. 116-117). Washington, D.C.: American Psychological Association.

Lecture Examples

Lecture Example 9.13: Erikson

Erikson (1963) states "The amount of trust...does not seem to depend on absolute quantities of food or demonstrations of love, but rather on the quality of the maternal relationship. Mothers create a sense of trust in their children by that kind of administration which in its quality combines sensitive care of the baby's individual needs and a firm sense of personal trustworthiness" (p. 249).

Erikson, E. H. (1963). *Childhood and society.* New York: W.W. Norton.

Lecture Example 9.14: Autonomy versus Shame and Doubt

Erikson (1980) writes "Shaming exploits an increasing sense of being small" (p. 71), and along with shame comes doubt in their ability. A child handled in this manner, Erikson (1980) states "goes through life habitually ashamed, apologetic, and afraid to be seen; or else, in a manner which we call 'overcompensatory,' he evinces a defiant kind of autonomy" (p. 73).

Erikson, E. H. (1980). *Identity and the life cycle.* New York: W. W. Norton.

Lecture Example 9.15: Initiative versus Guilt

Erikson (1980) writes "It is at this stage of initiative that great governor of initiative, namely, conscience becomes firmly established" (p. 84). If the child's initiative is continually or inappropriately discouraged or punished, the child may develop guilt. Erikson differentiates guilt from shame in the previous stage: Guilt is the voice of conscience coming from within and is felt whether anyone sees the act or not; shame exists because someone is watching the act. Erikson (1980) states "[He] becomes dissatisfied and disgruntled without a sense of being useful...this is what I call the *sense of industry.* ...He now learns to win recognition by *producing things*" (p. 91).

Erikson, E. H. (1980). *Identity and the life cycle.* New York: W. W. Norton.

Lecture Example 9.16: Parenting

After naturalistic home observations and laboratory observations, Baumrind (1967, 1971) proposed three typologies to describe parenting styles. The authoritative parent uses a rational, democratic-based approach to point out the reasons behind rules and regulations. These parents demand much of their children, but they also are warm, nurturing, and respectful of their children's rights. The authoritarian parent, on the other hand, demands strict, unquestioned obedience with little verbal give-and-take with the child. They use punishment to control their children. The third type of parent demands very little from the child.

The permissive parent gives the child almost complete autonomy in day-to-day activities. For more on parenting styles, see http://www.ecst.csuchico.edu/~kbarrett/parstyle.html.

Baumrind, D. (1967). Child care practices anteceding three patterns of preschool behavior. *Genetic Psychology Monographs, 75,* 43-88.

Baumrind, D. (1971). Current patterns of parental authority. *Developmental Psychology Monograph, 4* (No. 1, Pt. 2).

Diversity Topics

Diversity Topic 9.2: Childbearing

How do children perceive their own development, especially with relation to childrearing practices? Have students of various different cultural backgrounds discuss what their own families are like, and the specific childrearing practices that their caretakers engaged in. Have a discussion about these differences and similarities.
Discussion/Description: If students are able to talk freely about these issues in class, it should provide for a very interesting discussion. Childrearing practices vary greatly, not only from culture to culture, but from individual family to family. If you are able to solicit participation from a variety of people from different backgrounds, you should be able to glean the similarities and differences among them. What do they all foster? What do they discourage? Do they encourage a sense of autonomy or a sense of dependence? You may want to focus on a specific behavior, such as getting a scolding, and limit the presentation and discussion to that. For additional information, see http://www.bguide.com/webguide/parenting/plus/971002.fabfinds.html.

Diversity Topic 9.3: Childrearing Practice

Give students the assignment of writing a brief, two to three page "manual" on how to rear children. Have the students present their manuals in class. Initiate a discussion about the types of cultural values they begin to foster in the children.
Discussion/Description: Cultural values are engrained into children through concrete childrearing practices. Over time, these practices foster certain ways of understanding and viewing the world on the part of the recipients of these practices. This activity will bring this message home to the students, and give them an opportunity to see how culture "works" in development.

10 Adolescence & Adulthood

Chapter-at-a-Glance

Chapter Outline	Instruction Outline	Multimedia
Adolescence: Physical and Cognitive Development p. 324 Physical Development during Adolescence: Growing, Growing, Grown • Cognitive Development in Adolescence: Piaget's Formal Operations Stage	Demonstration DEV 1 Lecture Examples 10.1, 10.2, 10.3 Critical Thinking Opportunity 10.1 Journal Entry 10.1 Diversity Topic 10.1 Learning Objectives 10.1-10.4 Test Questions 1-17	**Video Disc IV** Segment 10 **Web Site** http://www.personal.psu.edu/faculty/n/x/nxd10/adolesce.htm Adolescence
Adolescence: Moral and Social Development p. 328 Kohlberg's Theory of Moral Development • Parental Relationships: Their Quality and Influence • The Peer Group • Sexuality and Adolescence • Teenage Pregnancy: Too Much Too Soon • Part-time Jobs for Adolescents: A Positive or a Negative?	Demonstration DEV 13 Lecture Examples 10.4, 10.5 Critical Thinking Forum 10.1 Journal Entry 10.2 Learning Objectives 10.5-10.10 Test Questions 18-48	*Psychology and Culture*: Ch. 10 **Transparency** PERS 7 **Web Site** http://www.awa.com/w2/erotic_computing/kohlberg.stages.html Kolberg's Moral Stages
Erikson's Psychosocial Theory: Adolescence through Adulthood p. 334 Identity versus Role Confusion: Erikson's Stage for Adolescence • Intimacy versus Isolation: Erikson's Stage for Early Adulthood • **Pioneers: Erik Homburger Erikson** • Generativity versus Stagnation: Erikson's Stage for Middle Adulthood • Ego Integrity versus Despair: Erikson's Final Stage • Erikson's Theory: Does Research Support It?	Student Chalkboard DEV 3 Demonstration DEV 14 Diversity Topic 10.2 Learning Objectives 10.11-10.14 Test Questions 49-62	**Web site** http://www.yale.edu/ynhti/curriculum/units/1991/5/91.05.07.x.html The Physiological and Psychological Development of the Adolescent
Other Theories of Adulthood p. 338 Levinson's Seasons of Life • Reinke, Ellicott, and Harris: The Life Course in Women • Life Stages: Fact or Fiction?	Student Chalkboard DEV 6 Lecture Example 10.6 Critical Thinking Forum 10.2 Journal Entry 10.3 Learning Objectives 10.15-.16 Test Questions 63-72	**Digital Image Archive** PSDV016 **Web Site** http://www.iog.wayne.edu/APADIV20/lowdiv20.htm American Psychological Association Division 20: Adult Development and Aging

Chapter Outline	Instruction Outline	Multimedia
Early and Middle Adulthood p. 340 Physical Changes in Adulthood • Intellectual Capacity during Early and Middle Adulthood • Lifestyle Patterns in Adulthood • Personality and Social Development in Middle Age	**Student Chalkboard** DEV 4-5 **Demonstration** DEV 11, 12, 15 **Lecture Examples** 10.7, 10.8, 10.9 **Learning Objectives** 10.17-10.21 **Test Questions** 73-97	*Discovering Psychology Maturing and Aging* **Web Site** http://www.iog.wayne.edu/APADIV20/lowdiv20.htm American Psychological Association Division 20: Adult Development and Aging
Later Adulthood p. 345 Physical Changes in Later Adulthood • Cognitive Development in Later Adulthood • Personality and Social Development in Later Adulthood • Culture and Care for the Elderly • Death and Dying	**Demonstration** DEV 16, 17, 18 **Lecture Examples** 10.10-10.14 **Critical Thinking Opportunity** 10.2 **Critical Thinking Forum** 10.3 **Journal Entry** 10.4 **Diversity Topic** 10.3 **Learning Objectives** 10.22-10.25 **Test Questions** 98-134	**Transparencies** DEV 15 & 18 **Video Disc I** Segments 4, 16, 17 **Digital Image Archive** PSDV017, 015, 014, 103 **Web Sites** http://www.nih.gov/nia/ National Institute on Aging (NIA) http://uhs.bsd.uchicago.edu/uhs/topics/delirium.dementia.html Confusion in the Elderly

What's New in Chapter 10

New Content

- "Male menopause"
- Decisions about death
- Hospice care
- Bereavement

Expanded Content

- The midlife crisis
- Effects of various medications on Alzheimer's incidence among women
- Death and dying

Organizational Changes

- Teenage pregnancy has been integrated within text.
- Theories of adulthood are grouped together in the chapter.

New Special Features

- Revised *Remember It's*
- New *Apply It!* on relationships

Learning Objective Questions

10.1 How difficult is adolescence for most teenagers?
10.2 What physical changes occur during puberty?
10.3 What are the psychological effects of early and late maturation on boys and girls?
10.4 What cognitive abilities develop during the formal operations stage?
10.5 What are Kohlberg's three levels of moral reasoning?
10.6 What do cross-cultural studies reveal about the universality of Kohlberg's theory?
10.7 What outcomes are often associated with the authoritative, authoritarian, and permissive parenting styles?
10.8 What are some of the useful functions of the adolescent peer group?
10.9 What are some of the disturbing consequences of teenage pregnancy?
10.10 In general, what is the impact on adolescents of working more than 15 to 20 hours a week during the school year?
10.11 How does Erikson explain the fifth psychosocial stage—identity versus role confusion?
10.12 What is Erikson's psychosocial task for early adulthood?
10.13 What changes did Erikson believe are essential for healthy personality development in middle age?
10.14 What is the key to a positive resolution of Erikson's eighth stage—ego integrity versus despair?
10.15 How is Levinson's concept of life structure related to his proposed stages of development?
10.16 What did Reinke, Ellicott, and Harris's study of middle-class women reveal about major transitional periods in the life cycle?
10.17 What are the physical changes associated with middle age?
10.18 In general, can adults look forward to an increase or a decrease in intellectual performance from their 20s to their 60s?
10.19 What are some of the trends in lifestyle patterns in young adulthood?
10.20 What effect does parenthood have on marital satisfaction?
10.21 Why is middle age often considered the prime of life?
10.22 What are some physical changes generally associated with later adulthood?
10.23 What happens to mental ability in later adulthood?
10.24 What is Alzheimer's disease?
10.25 According to Kübler-Ross, what stages do terminally ill patients experience as they come to terms with death?
10.26 What are some benefits of hospice care?

Chapter Overview

Continuing the topics of Chapter 9 on human development during childhood, this chapter describes development from adolescence through adulthood to death. The most dramatic physical changes are associated with puberty when the adolescent growth spurt occurs, the secondary sex characteristics appear, and the reproductive organs in both sexes mature. The developments are very significant, with early and late maturers experiencing different psychological challenges. The period of adolescence is marked also by the attainment of Piaget's formal operations stage.

Kohlberg's theory of moral development describes three levels of moral reasoning; preconventional, conventional, and postconventional, which Kohlberg tied to cognitive development. The quality, influence, and importance of parental relationships, peer groups, sexuality, and teenage pregnancy are discussed. The positive and negative aspects of part-time jobs for teenagers are explored.

Erikson's psychosocial theory of adolescence and adulthood is explored. Erikson's work on describing identity versus role confusion, intimacy versus isolation, generativity versus stagnation, and ego integrity versus despair is outlined in detail. The section ends with a discussion of whether the research supports Erikson's theory.

The authors discuss other theories of adulthood offered by Levinson (including the notion of seasons of life) and by Reinke, Ellicott, and Harris (relating women's development to phases in the family cycle).

Early and middle adulthood is then explored. The physical changes that occur in adulthood are marked first by a physical peak in early adulthood and then a gradual decline. The major biological event for women is menopause, occurring late in the period called middle adulthood. Intelligence does not decline but changes its nature through the accumulation of knowledge and skills. Lifestyle patterns in adulthood are then explored in detail. This section concludes with personality and social development in middle age.

The changes of later adulthood include a continued physical decline, which in turn may hamper cognitive abilities; however, intellectual decline is not significant. Diseases of later adulthood include senile dementia and Alzheimer's disease. Social development and adjustment in later adulthood are then explored. The major adjustment problems include retirement and the loss of a spouse. The chapter then turns to cultural differences in care for the elderly. The authors explore the work of Elisabeth Kübler-Ross, including her views on the stages of death and dying. The chapter concludes with a section on the benefits of hospice care.

Key Terms

adolescence (p. 324)
adolescent growth spurt (p. 325)
Alzheimer's disease (p. 348)
conventional level (p. 328)
crystallized intelligence (p. 347)
ego integrity versus despair (p. 337)
fluid intelligence (p. 347)
formal operations stage (p. 326)
generativity versus stagnation (p. 336)
identity versus role confusion (p. 334)
imaginary audience (p. 327)
intimacy versus isolation (p. 335)
life structure (p. 338)
menarche (p. 325)
menopause (p. 341)
mid-life crisis (p. 338)
personal fable (p. 327)
postconventional level (p. 329)
preconventional level (p. 328)
presbyopia (p. 340)
puberty (p. 325)
secondary sex characteristics (p. 325)
senile dementia (p. 348)

Annotated Lecture Outline

A. Adolescence: Physical and Cognitive Development

Classroom Demonstrations and Handouts

Demonstration DEV 1: Childhood Memories and Artifacts

Objective: To get students thinking about their own development and artifacts that played a role.
Materials: **Handout DEV 1**
Procedure: A couple of days before carrying out this activity, ask your students to bring some object or artifact from their childhood (e.g., toys, blankets, a picture, a book) to class. If a student lives far away, an early childhood memory may be substituted. On the day of the activity, each student is to "show and tell" the object or to share the memory. This is based on an activity described by Beers (she has other ideas so you may wish to consult the source).
Conclusions: The conclusion of this activity is that students actively consider their own development in the context of the topics and theories presented in lecture and textbook.

Beers, S. E. (1987) "Show and tell" for developmental psychology. In V. P. Makosky, L. G. Whittemore, and A. M. Rogers (Eds.). *Activities handbook for the teaching of psychology* (Vol. 2) (pp. 393-94). Washington, D.C.: American Psychological Association.

Lecture Examples

Lecture Example 10.1: When I Hit Puberty

Consider sharing your own personal reactions to puberty and to those identity crises that adolescents typically experience. In addition, tell your students about classmates you grew up with who illustrate some of the concepts from this chapter (such as late-maturing males or Erikson's stage of identity versus role diffusion). For a site containing information on girls and puberty, see http://www.chmc.org/aboutchi/infoline/girls.htm, or for boys, see http://www.chmc.org/aboutchi/infoline/boys.htm.

Lecture Example 10.2: Age of Menarche

In the past 150 years, the average age of menarche has declined in Western countries. In 1840 the average age in Norway was about 17 years; today it has dropped to nearly 12 years. The United States has experienced a similar trend. In 1900 the mean age of menarche was about 14.2 years; today it has fallen to about 12.5 years (a drop of about four months per decade). In part, this decline can be attributed to improved medical care and nutrition. Some researchers believe that a critical body weight must be met before puberty. Frish and Revelle (1970) suggest that 17 percent body fat content is necessary for menstruation. For an article on menarche, see http://endo.edoc.com/jcem/v82n10/3239-abs.html.

Frish, R. E., & Revelle, R. (1970). Height and weight at menarche and a hypothesis of critical body weights and adolescent events. *Science, 169,* 397-399.

Lecture Example 10.3:

Ask students to speculate on the consequences when a 12-year-old boy is introduced to sexual intercourse by a 32-year-old woman. This happened in Washington state—the woman was a schoolteacher and the boy was a student. She was imprisoned for the crime of rape, then, after being released, was apprehended at 3:00 a.m. in a parked car with the same boy. She later revealed that she was pregnant. The woman could spend many years in prison for this ongoing crime. What do your students think? Is this a crime or misplaced love? Many of the students will probably rate this as a positive experience for the boy. Now reverse the sex roles and ask the question again. Student responses could reveal double standards of society's attitudes toward the sexual development of boys and girls.

Diversity Topic

Diversity Topic 10.1: Rites of Passage

Many cultures have coming of age rituals, but they often differ in their content, age of celebration, and meaning. Have students describe some of their own experiences, drawing notes of similarities and differences among them.
Discussion/Description: This activity, of course, depends on the degree to which there is a

culturally diverse student population in the class. Some cultures have celebrations as early as age 10 or 12; others wait until age 20. Some have elaborate ceremonies, others do not. Some people think that the "sweet sixteen" parties that used to be prominent in American culture have been replaced by a focus on obtaining a driver's license as a coming of age ritual in the U.S.

B. Adolescence: Moral and Social Development

Classroom Demonstrations and Handouts

Demonstration DEV 13: Dear Mom and Dad

Objective: To allow students to communicate developmental issues from a personal perspective.
Materials: **Handout DEV 13**
Procedure: Described by Junn (1989), this activity requires your students to write to one or both parents. In this letter, students are to raise several issues, such as the impact parents had on their lives, three of the most important strengths and weaknesses possessed by their fathers and mothers, and how these strengths and weaknesses affected areas of development (e.g., moral development, intellectual development). Junn suggests that the students thank their parents for "something special."
Conclusions: Students will gain a different perspective of their own parents and their own development by taking part in this activity.

Junn, E. N. (1989)."Dear Mom and Dad": Using personal letters to enhance students' understanding of developmental issues. *Teaching of Psychology, 16,* 135-139.

Lecture Examples

Lecture Example 10.4: Moral Development

Suggest to your students that they are faced with moral decisions every day, from small ones (like whether to borrow a roommate's shirt without asking) to more significant ones (like registering for the draft). Rest (1983) describes a comprehensive, interactive model of moral development. He stresses that the need for morality in society arises because people live in groups, and it becomes necessary to balance conflicting needs of different individuals and groups. He proposes a four-component model:

> **Component 1—Interpreting the situation.** In this component, possible courses of action are identified in situations that affect the welfare of someone else. Many factors complicate the delineation of alternatives. People often have trouble imagining different possibilities and often lack an understanding of how their actions affect others.

Component 2—Figuring out what the ideally moral course of action would be. Given that a person is aware of alternative courses of action in a situation and of how these actions affect others, in this component these considerations are integrated and the person figures out what ought to be done.

Component 3—Selecting among valued outcomes to intend to take the moral course of action. Typically, a person is aware of the different outcomes that would be produced by different actions. For example, motives elicited in a student asked to show his exam to another student during a test might include a motive to resist temptation, a motive of affiliation, or a motive of need achievement. A person may formulate a course of action other than a moral one.

Component 4—Executing and implementing what one intends to do. Good intentions do not necessarily produce good deeds. In this component, the person figures out the sequence of concrete actions, working around impediments and unexpected difficulties, overcoming fatigue and frustration, resisting distractions, and not losing sight of the goal.

Rest, J. (1983). Morality. In P. Mussen (Ed.), *Handbook of child development* (Vol 3). New York: Wiley.

Lecture Example 10.5: Reaching the Highest Moral Level

People at the postconventional level of morality tend to behave more morally than those at the preconventional level. In one study, Krebs and Kohlberg (Kohlberg, 1975) found that although 70 percent of those at the preconventional level and 50 percent of those at the conventional level cheated when given the opportunity, only 15 percent at the postconventional level did so. For more on moral development, see http://www.aggelia.com/htdocs/kohlberg.shtml.

Kohlberg, L. (1985). *The psychology of moral development*. San Francisco: Harper & Row.

C. Erikson's Psychosocial Theory: Adolescence through Adulthood

Classroom Demonstrations and Handouts

Student Chalkboard DEV 3: Erikson's Last Four Stages

Demonstration DEV 14: Media Examples of Erikson's Stages

Objective: To understand Erikson's stage theory.
Materials: Erikson and the Media (**Handout DEV 14**)
Procedure: After discussing Erikson's eight stages of psychosocial development, assign your students to search for examples of the stages. Have them record the examples on **Handout DEV 14**. Good sources include cartoons, comics, television, and "real-life."

Conclusions: Your students will understand and appreciate Erikson's theory by finding examples of the stages. For more on the work of Erikson, see http://www.haverford.edu/psych/ddavis/erikson1.html.

Diversity Topic

Diversity Topic 10.2: Erikson's Psychosocial Stage for Adolescence: Identity versus Role Confusion

Have students complete the simple self-description task described in the Appendix to this annotation. Then provide background information concerning cultural differences in self-construals and how these differences should impact self-identity.

Discussion/Description: Erikson's fifth stage of psychosexual development, Identity versus Role Confusion, is described well here, particularly in terms of how this conflict is brought to a head during this period of development, and the types of questions and issues individuals will deal with in conjunction with this stage. Yet, this conflict begs the question of the meaning of self-identity and self-concept, and whether this is the same across cultures. Indeed, there is a considerable amount of cross-cultural research that indicates that people of different cultural backgrounds have quite different self-construals. One often cited, theoretical framework for understanding cultural differences in self-construals is provided by Markus and Kitayama's (1991) work on independent versus interdependent self-construals, and Matsumoto's (1996) work on how individualism versus collectivism as a cultural dimension influences these self-construals. People with interdependent self-construals, for example, see themselves as fundamentally connected with others around them; consequently, they are less autonomous and unique, and the boundaries between them and others are more porous. This basic difference in self-construal should lead to fundamental and profound differences in how they identify or describe themselves in tasks such as the one suggested in this annotation. In short, people with independent self-construals tend to describe themselves in terms of personal characteristics, attributes, or adjectives; people with interdependent self-construals tend to describe themselves in terms of roles, positions, or status. For more on the work of Erikson, see http://www.haverford.edu/psych/ddavis/erikson1.html

Markus, H. R., & Kitayama, S. (1991). Culture and the self: Implications for cognition, emotion, and motivation. *Psychological Review, 98*, 224-253.

Matsumoto, D. (1996). *Culture and diversity: A world of difference.* Pacific Grove, CA: Brooks Cole Publishing Co.

D. Other Theories of Adulthood

Classroom Demonstrations and Handouts

Student Chalkboard DEV 6: Charting Developmental Stages and Ages

Lecture Example

Lecture Example 10.6: Vaillant versus Levinson

Vaillant found that men in their forties become more introspective and begin to reassess their lives. Although the reassessment is common at this age, a *mid-life crisis* is not. He found that the "crisis is the exception, not the rule" (Vaillant & Vaillant, 1990, 223). His subjects usually did not experience great turmoil or make drastic changes in their lives. Of course, we hear about the exceptions—the middle-aged executive who escapes the rat race walking away from a six-figure income, or the same executive running away from his wife and kids to start a new life—but Vaillant did not find an epidemic of such escapism in his study.

Vaillant, G. E., & Vaillant, C. O. (1990). Natural history of male psychological health, XII: A 45-year study of predictors of successful aging at age 65. *American Journal of Psychiatry, 147,* 31-37.

E. Early and Middle Adulthood

Classroom Demonstrations and Handouts

Student Chalkboard DEV 4: Changes from Young Adulthood to Late Adulthood: Chart I

Student Chalkboard DEV 5: Changes from Young Adulthood to Late Adulthood: Chart II

Demonstration DEV 11: Decade Word Association

Objective: To examine the kinds of ideas students have about various ages.
Materials: Decade Association (**Handout DEV 11**)
Procedure: Give each student a copy of **Handout DEV 11** and ask them to write quickly four words that come to their minds as they imagine what life is like for people in each decade. Then, ask them to list the decade it was easiest to think of associations for and which one was the most difficult. Next, ask them to estimate how many people they know from each decade. Point out the relationship between familiarity with actual people of different ages and the words used to describe them. Are the words used to describe people aged 50-59 and those aged 40-49 based upon numerous experiences with several individuals, or are they based upon just a couple of individuals?

Conclusions: This activity can provide a basis for discussing ageism, developmental milestones, and stereotypes.

Rebelsky, F. (1981). Life span development. In L. T. Benjamin, Jr. and K. D. Lowman (Eds.), *Activities handbook for the teaching of psychology* (Vol. 1) (pp. 131-132). Washington, D.C.: American Psychological Association.

Demonstration DEV 12: Life Path

Objective: To get students to think about development across the entire life span.
Materials: Life Path (**Handout DEV 12**)
Procedure: Ask your students how long they want to live. Probe into reasons given for the various ages. Next, using **Handout DEV 12**, have your students estimate and predict how old they will be (were) when some of life's milestones will (have) occur(red). For example, at what ages will they marry, have their first child, reach the peak in their profession, retire, and, finally, die? You may extend this activity by having them estimate their life expectancy based on actuarial and life insurance data. There are several methods available (e.g., Schultz, 1978, Woodruff-Pak, 1988).
Conclusions: Students will realize that development and important life events are not limited to the first few years of life, but that they occur in all phases of life.

Schultz, R. (1978). *The psychology of death, dying, and bereavement.* New York: Random House.

Woodruff-Pak, D. (1988). *Psychology and aging.* Englewood Cliffs, NJ: Prentice-Hall

Demonstration DEV 15: Dear Son/Daughter

Objective: To allow students to communicate and to understand better the importance and struggles of adolescence.
Materials: Children Letter (**Handout DEV 15**)
Procedure: Instruct your students to imagine that they have a child who is about to enter adolescence. Since the student has already "successfully" passed through adolescence, he or she can advise the child about what to expect with regard to sexuality, physical changes, and emotional changes. An alternative would be to form male and female groups, and have both groups write separate letters to a son and to a daughter.
A somewhat different version of this activity is offered by Junn (1989) who suggests that students write to their future or real child on his or her eighteenth birthday. In this letter, the "parent" should attempt to address such issues as (a) the reasons for having this child, (b) the qualities you hope this child to possess, and (c) issues of discipline, moral development, sex-role development, and personality development.
Conclusions: Students will gain a different perspective of their own conflicts by taking part in this activity. If you decide to form groups, determine if "fathers" give different advice than "mothers".

Charlesworth, J., & Slate, J. (1986). Teaching about puberty: Learning to talk about sensitive topics. *Teaching of Psychology, 13*, 215-217.

Junn, E. N. (1989). "Dear Mom and Dad": Using personal letters to enhance students' understanding of developmental issues. *Teaching of Psychology, 16*, 135-139.

Lecture Examples

Lecture Example 10.7: Why Have Children?

Various studies have examined the motives for having and not having children. As an introduction to Levinson's early adulthood stage, consider posing this question to your students: What are the pros and cons of having children? Follow up with what researchers have found regarding the decision.

Campbell, F. L., Townes, B. D., & Beach, L. R. (1982). Motivational bases of child bearing decisions. In G. L. Fox (Ed.), *The childbearing decision*. Beverly Hills, CA: Sage.

Lecture Example 10.8: Marital Happiness

A survey conducted at the University of Chicago (cited in Glenn, 1987) revealed that the percentage of married people reporting that they were "very happy" declined among 25- to 39-year-olds. In 1970, 31 percent more "married" than "never married" claimed to be "very happy"; in 1986 the difference was only 8 percent. This change was found to be due partly to an increase in happiness of the never-married male and a decrease in happiness of the married female. Why? Glenn (1987) states "Since most women stay in the labor force after they marry, the biggest change in their lives after marriage may be an increase in responsibilities" (p. 21).

Glenn, N. D. (1987, October). Marriage on the rocks. *Psychology Today,* 20-21.

Lecture Example 10.9: Aging and Cognitive Functioning

Point out that many cognitive abilities, particularly mental speed, begin to decline in middle adulthood (about age 55). In light of this fact, should the trend toward extending the age for mandatory retirement be reversed? This consideration is a political/economic decision not a psychological one. What would be the social consequences of lowering the retirement age? Of raising it? Is the idea of a specific mandatory retirement age, as was enforced until Ronald Regan became president, reasonable?

F. Later Adulthood

Classroom Demonstrations and Handouts

Demonstration DEV 16: Guest Lecturer: Elderly Person

Objective: To dispel myths and stereotypes students have regarding the elderly.
Materials: None
Procedure: Ask an emeritus faculty member or some other senior citizen who has remained productive to give a guest lecture in your class. Make inquiries into how the individual has kept active and productive; request that the speaker debunk for the students their commonly held stereotypes of the elderly. Or ask a representative from the local senior citizen center to visit the class and comment on individuals who frequent the center as well as the role that the center plays in the lives of people.
Conclusions: Contrary to popular stereotypes about the elderly, many senior citizens remain healthy and actively involved in various endeavors.

Demonstration DEV 17: Guest Lecturer: Gerontologist

Objective: To dispel myths and stereotypes students have regarding the elderly.
Materials: None
Procedure: Ask a gerontologist from the community to give a guest lecture in your class. This individual will be able to discuss the most recent findings in the field of aging.
Conclusions: Contrary to prevalent stereotypes about the elderly, many senior citizens remain healthy and actively involved in various endeavors. Ask this person to describe what he/she thinks the outlook for old age will be by the time your students are of retirement age.

Demonstration DEV 18: Getting Old

Objective: To demonstrate old age.
Materials: None
Procedure: This demonstration helps students experience advanced aging. You will need a roll of plastic wrap, some cotton, and some tape. The simulation of blurred vision can be achieved by having students tape a length of plastic wrap around their head covering their eyes. They can put cotton in their ears to simulate impaired hearing and place tape around their joints to simulate arthritis. Send the students out of the classroom. They should have a guide to help them. Navigating the familiar territory outside the classroom will be more difficult than they might have imagined.
Conclusions: Discuss what it felt like to be old after all of the students have returned to the classroom and have discarded the plastic wrap, cotton, and tape. Ask the students to discuss how this exercise has helped them realize that it is not easy being old.

Lecture Examples

Lecture Example 10.10: Empathizing with People of Different Ages

It is important for students to be able to empathize with people of ages different than themselves. As you talk about life events, such as the empty nest syndrome, mid-life crisis, or widowhood, try prefacing your discussions with "How would you feel...." For example, in discussing the impact of the empty nest syndrome, you might say, "After spending the last 20 years raising four children, they're gone, and you're stuck with an empty, 5-bedroom house."

Lecture Example 10.9: They Just Keep On Running

Ask students for examples of senior citizens who have kept fit and active. Johnny Kelley completed his sixty-first Boston Marathon in 1992 at age 84. Kelley trains for one hour every day, with a two-hour run every two or three weeks. Doctors say that Kelley's blood pressure is 100, while the average for his age is 183. Johnny is still active in the Boston Marathon, although he does not run it any more.

Lecture Example 10.10: Euthanasia, Dr. Jack Kevorkian

What would you do if you were diagnosed with a terminal illness, an illness that makes death painful and prolonged? Would you consider euthanasia? This is a hotly debated issue with good reason. For some opponents of euthanasia, the very word invokes visions of involuntary murder and pulling the plug needlessly on someone's life. Euthanasia may take one of the following three forms: (1) Death with dignity allows a terminally ill patient to die naturally, to forgo an artificial prolonging of their life with machines, and to abstain from extraordinary means to keep a person alive. (2) Mercy killing, sometimes perceived as synonymous with euthanasia, means actively causing someone's death through lethal injection or other means that speeds up death. (3) The final form that euthanasia may take is death selection, which is the killing of a person deemed to be socially useless or causing a burden to society. This topic should make for a lively discussion in class. See http://www.iaetf.org/ for the negative side of this debate.

Cawley, M. A. (1977). Euthanasia: Should it be a choice? *American Journal of Nursing, 77,* 859-861.

Lecture Example 10.13: Adjustment to Fetal or Perinatal Death

Your students might be interested in a study that examined how mothers reacted to and coped with the death of a child. Graham et al. (1987) interviewed 58 women who had recently experienced a fetal or perinatal death. The interview focused on such variables as attribution of blame, depression, desire to see pictures of the child, and the effects of having older children. The article suggests some guidelines for helping a grieving mother.

Graham, M. A., Thompson, S. C., Estrada, M., & Yonekura, M. L. (1987). Factors affecting psychological adjustment to a fetal death. *American Journal of Obstetrics and Gynecology, 157,* 254-257.

Lecture Example 10.14: Alzheimer's Disease

Students may consider Alzheimer's disease and senility to be the same and to see both as inevitable consequences of old age. Develop a lecture to distinguish the differences. Use http://www.mhsource.com/hy/adunravel.html as a source for this lecture.

Diversity Topic

Diversity Topic 10.3: Elder Care

This is an excellent annotation, and this discussion could be brought into cross-cultural perspective. Have students discuss this issue in class and draw conclusions about possible cultural differences underlying the variety of responses. Also, have the students turn the tables around—when they are elderly, how do they want to be cared for?
Discussion/Description: People of individualistic cultures will tend to foster the view that each person is on his or her own, and thus they will not be responsible for the care of their aging parents. People of collectivistic cultures, however, will see it more of their duty to care for the elderly. These cultures also typically view the elderly differently, giving them higher status with a more accepted family and extended family group. These types of cultural differences are prevalent around the world.

11 Motivation and Emotion

Chapter-at-a-Glance

Chapter Outline	Instruction Outline	Multimedia
Introduction to Motivation p. 358	**Learning Objective** 11.1 **Lecture Examples** 11.8 **Test Questions** 1-8	**Transparency** MOTIV 1 **Web Site** http://lucs.fil.lu.se/Staff/ Christian.Balkenius/Thesis/ Chapter06.html Motivation and Emotions
Theories of Motivation p. 359 Instinct Theories of Motivation • Drive-Reduction Theory: Striving to Keep a Balanced Internal State • Arousal Theory: Striving for an Optimal Level of Arousal • Maslow's Hierarchy of Needs: Putting Our Needs in Order	**Student Chalkboard** MOTIV 1 **Demonstration** MOTIV 1 & 7 **Diversity Topic** 11.1 **Learning Objectives** 11.2-11.5 **Test Questions** 9-25	**Transparencies** MOTIV 6, 9 **Digital Image Archive** PSMO001, 006, 009 **Web Site** http://sol.brunel.ac.uk/~jarvis/bola/motivation/masmodel.html Abraham Maslow
The Primary Drives: Hunger and Thirst p. 365 Thirst: We All Have Two Kinds • The Biological Basis of Hunger: Internal Hunger Cues • Other Factors Influencing Hunger: External Eating Cues • Understanding Body Weight: Why We Weigh What We Weigh • Dieting: A National Obsession • Eating Disorders: Tyranny of the Scale	**Demonstration** MOTIV 2 **Lecture Examples** 11.2-11.5 **Journal Entry** 11.1 **Diversity Topic** 11.2 **Learning Objectives** 11.6-11.14 **Test Questions** 26-60	**Transparencies** MOTIV 2, 5 **Video Disc II** Segment 18 **Digital Image Archive** PSMO002 **Web Site** http://members.aol.com/edapinc/home.html Eating Disorders
Social Motives p. 373 The Need for Achievement: The Drive to Excel • Fear of Success • Work Motivation	**Demonstration** MOTIV 6 **Lecture Example** 11.6, 11.7 **Critical Thinking Opportunity** 11.1 **Journal Entry** 11.2 **Diversity Topic** 11.3 **Learning Objectives** 11.15-11.18 **Test Questions** 61-75	**Transparency** PERS 3 **Video Disc II** Segment 19 **Web Site** http://choo.fis.utoronto.ca/FIS/Courses/LIS1230/LIS1230sharma/motive4.htm Social Motives

Chapter Outline	Instruction Outline	Multimedia
The What and Why of Emotions p. 377 Motivation and Emotion: What Is the Connection? • The Components of Emotions: The Physical, the Cognitive, and the Behavioral • Theories of Emotion: Which Comes First, the Thought or the Feeling? • The Polygraph: Lie Detector or Emotion Detector?	Student Chalkboard EMOT 1 Demonstration EMOT 1, 6 Lecture Examples 11.8-11.11, Critical Thinking Forum 11.1 Learning Objectives 11.19-11.24 Test Questions 76-97	*Discovering Psychology: Motivation and Emotion* **Transparencies** EMOT 1B2 **Digital Image Archive** PSEM001-002 **Web Site** http://emotion.ccs.brandeis.edu/emotion.html Emotion Home Page
The Expression of Emotion p. 381 The Range of Emotion: How Wide Is It? • The Development of Facial Expressions in Infants: Smiles and Frowns Come Naturally • Facial Expressions for the Basic Emotions—A Universal Language • Cultural Rules for Displaying Emotion • Emotion as a Form of Communication	Demonstration EMOT 4, 5 Diversity Topic 11.4 Learning Objectives 11.25-11.27 Test Questions 98-113	*Psychology and Culture*: Ch. 25 **Web Site** http://trochim.human.cornell.edu/gallery/young/emotion.htm#emotions Motivation and Emotions
Experiencing Emotion p. 386 The Facial-Feedback Hypothesis: Does the Face Cause the Feeling? • Emotion and Rational Thinking • Gender Differences in Experience of Emotion • Love: The Strongest Emotional Bond	Lecture Example 11.12 Learning Objectives 11.25-11.29 Test Questions 114-135	**Digital Image Archive** PSEM003

What's New in Chapter 11

New Content

- Work motivation

Organizational Changes

- Eating disorders is now integrated within the text.

New Special Features

- New chapter opening vignette—Princess Diana
- New *Apply It* on happiness
- Revised *Remember Its*

New Key Terms

- anorexia nervosa
- bulimia nervosa
- industrial/organizational (I/O) psychologist
- work motivation
- Lazarus' theory

Learning Objective Questions

11.1 What is the difference between intrinsic and extrinsic motivation?
11.2 How do instinct theories explain motivation?
11.3 How does drive-reduction theory explain motivation?
11.4 How does arousal theory explain motivation?
11.5 How does Maslow's hierarchy of needs account for human motivation?
11.6 Under what conditions do the two types of thirst occur?
11.7 What are the roles of the lateral hypothalamus and the ventromedial hypothalamus in the regulation of eating behavior?
11.8 What are some of the body's hunger and satiety signals?
11.9 What are some nonbiological factors that influence what and how much people eat?
11.10 What are some factors that account for variations in body weight?
11.11 How does set point affect body weight?
11.12 Why is it almost impossible to maintain weight loss by cutting calories alone?
11.13 What are the symptoms of anorexia nervosa?
11.14 What are the symptoms of bulimia nervosa?
11.15 What is Murray's contribution to the study of motivation?
11.16 What is the need for achievement?
11.17 What are some characteristics shared by people who are high in achievement motivation?
11.18 What is work motivation and what are two effective techniques for increasing it?
11.19 What are the three components of emotions?
11.20 According to the James-Lange theory, what sequence of events occurs when an individual experiences an emotion?
11.21 What is the Cannon-Bard theory of emotion?
11.22 According to the Schachter-Singer theory, what two factors must occur in order for a person to experience an emotion?
11.23 According to Lazarus, what sequence of events occurs when an individual feels an emotion?

11.24 What does a polygraph measure?
11.25 What are basic emotions?
11.26 How does the development of facial expressions of different emotions in infants suggest a biological basis for emotional expression?
11.27 Why is emotion considered a form of communication?
11.28 What is the facial-feedback hypothesis?
11.29 How does Sternberg's triangular theory of love account for the different kinds of love?

Chapter Overview

The chapter begins with a definition of motivation and then moves to a discussion of the differences between intrinsic and extrinsic motivation. Early theories of motivation attributed motives to instincts, but this approach has been replaced by a number of competing theories. The competing theories include drive-reduction theory, arousal theory, and Maslow's hierarchy of needs. The primary drives of thirst and hunger are described in detail, including biological and psychological factors in the motivations to drink and eat. A discussion of dieting, body weight, and the eating disorders anorexia and bulimia nervosa ends this section of the chapter.

Social motives refer to motivations relevant to success in interactions with others. The need for achievement has been studied in detail, and characteristics of achievers have been identified. Also, the question of whether achievement motivation can be developed in a person has been explored. Issues regarding gender and the fear of success are also investigated. This section ends with a discussion of work motivation.

Emotions prepare us to respond adaptively to our environment by communicating feelings and intentions to others and by working closely with motivation in directing behavior. Physical, cognitive, and behavioral components have been recognized in emotions. The authors describe the James-Lange, Cannon-Bard, Schachter-Singer, and Lazarus theories of emotion. Problems with the polygraph as a lie detector are explained.
The expression of emotion is defined in terms of the range of emotion. Facial expressions of emotion appear to be biologically determined rather than learned. Research has suggested that these expressions are universal. Cultural rules for the display of emotions and emotions as a form of communication are explored.

The final section of this chapter deals with experiencing emotions. The interpretation of emotion may be influenced by the facial expression, a situation that has led to the facial-feedback hypothesis. This view suggests that if we make a happy face, we are more likely to experience happiness. The concepts of emotions, rational thinking, and gender differences in emotions are explored. The chapter concludes with a discussion of love and Sternberg's theory of love.

Key Terms

anorexia nervosa (p. 370)
arousal (p. 361)
arousal theory (p. 361)
basic emotions (p. 381)
bulimia nervosa (p. 370)
Cannon-Bard theory (p. 378)
consummate love (p. 389)
display rules (p. 381)
drive (p. 361)
drive-reduction theory (p. 360)
emotion (p. 377)
extrinsic motivation (p. 359)
facial-feedback hypothesis (p. 386)
fat cells (p. 369)
hierarchy of needs (p. 362)
homeostasis (p. 361)
incentive (p. 358)
Industrial Organizational (I/O) psychology (p. 375)
instinct (p. 369)
instinct theory (p. 360)
intrinsic motivation (p. 359)
James-Lange theory (p. 378)
lateral hypothalamus (LH) (p. 365)
Lazarus Theory (p. 379)
metabolic rate (p. 369)
motivation (p. 358)
motives (p. 358)
polygraph (p. 379)
primary drive (p. 365)
Schachter-Singer theory (p. 379)
self-actualization (p. 364)
sensory deprivation (p. 362)
set point (p. 369)
stimulus motives (p. 361)
triangular theory of love (p. 389)
ventromedial hypothalamus (VMH) (p. 365)
Work motivation (p. 375)
Yerkes-Dodson law (p. 362)

Annotated Lecture Outline

A. Introduction to Motivation

Lecture Examples

Lecture Example 11.1: Intrinsic vs. Extrinsic Motivation

Use http://www.und.ac.za/users/clarke/kzb/motiv.htm as a source to develop a lecture on intrinsic vs. extrinsic motivation.

B. Theories of Motivation

Classroom Demonstrations and Handouts

Student Chalkboard MOTIV 1: Comparing Motivation Theories

Demonstration MOTIV 1: Motives behind Daily Activities

Objective: To demonstrate the variety of motives in our lives.
Materials: **Handout MOT 1**
Procedure: Using **Handout MOT 1**, ask your students to make a list of twenty activities that they've done in the last forty-eight hours. After completing the list, have the students classify each item by its motive source. Sources of motives might include biological, need for arousal, social needs, self-actualization, need for achievement, intrinsic, and cognitive. You might even want to expand the list of motives to include financial, political, and religious sources.
Conclusions: This activity will sensitize students to the spectrum of motives that determine behaviors. Some behaviors might be explained by using more than one theory of motivation.

Demonstration MOT 7: Sensation Seeking

Objective: To test whether you are a high or a low sensation seeker.
Materials: **Handout MOT 7**
Procedure: To test students' sensation-seeking tendencies, try the shortened version of one of Marvin Zuckerman's earlier scales that are presented in **Handout MOT 7**. For each of the 13 items, students should circle the choice, A or B, that better describes their feelings. To score the results, assign one point for each of the following circled items: 1A, 2A, 3A, 4B, 5A, 6B, 7A, 8A, 9B, 10B, 11A, 12A, and 13B. Ask the students to compare their totals with the following norms:

- 0-3   Very low
- 4-5   Low
- 6-9   Average
- 10-11 High
- 12-13 Very high

For more on sensation seeking, see
http://www.nida.nih.gov/NIDA_Notes/NNVol10N4/MeasureSens.html.

Zuckerman, M. (1978, February). The search for high sensation. *Psychology Today*, pp. 38B46. American Psychological Association, 1978.

Diversity Topic

Diversity Topic 11.1: Maslow

Have students discuss the potential cultural biases underlying Maslow's theory.
Discussion/Description: Maslow's theory may be especially applicable to people of individualistic cultural backgrounds. The highest point to which Maslow suggests people can ascribe is self-actualization, which implies that such individual development is at the pinnacle of this type of motivation. Again, the individualism vs. collectivism dichotomy provides a framework that challenges such a view in two ways. First, such individual development may not be the ultimate endpoint of motivation in collectivistic cultures, which generally have much less focus on individuals. Second, even if self-actualization is a recognized goal, it may be defined in different ways in different cultures.

These differences may be interesting to discuss in class. For more on Maslow's theories, see http://www.connect.net/georgen/maslow.htm.

C. The Primary Drives: Hunger and Thirst

Classroom Demonstrations and Handouts

Demonstration MOTIV 2: Body-Mass Index

Objective: To determine students' body-mass indexes.
Materials: **Handout MOT 2**
Procedure: Provide each student with a copy of **Handout MOT 2**. Direct them to locate their weight on the left side and their height on the right side. Connect the two points with a straight line.
Conclusions: If the line passes through a position on the Body-Mass Index higher than 27, the student is overweight. If it the index number exceeds 35, the student is considerably overweight.

Lecture Examples

Lecture Example 11.2: Food and Society

Food provides more than nourishment and sustenance in our culture. For example, when someone new moves into the neighborhood, food might be brought over as a sign of welcome. At funerals, food is used to console the family. Children are taught that eating food can be a sign of obedience to parents. Some parents demand that their children clean their plate regardless of hunger, and then reinforce the children for doing so. Ask your students for more examples of social meaning and food.

Lecture Example 11.3: Diet Relapse

Recidivism rates are high for most addictive behaviors, including overeating. Most people who lose weight tend to gain it back within three months. Considerable attention has been directed to the role of situations in diet relapse. Alan Marlatt and his associates (Cummings, Gordon, & Marlatt, 1980) found that most relapses occurred in situations in which negative emotional states (e.g., depression, anxiety, or boredom) prevailed. Marlatt has also proposed a mechanism to account for high rates of relapse following a single lapse or slip. The Abstinence Violation Effect (AVE) refers to the realization that the dieter's image as an abstainer or dieter is not consistent with overeating or slips of the dieting regimen. The individual then attributes the cause of the relapse to some personal weakness. If this attribution occurs, the dieter will not have much confidence or self-efficacy to resist eating the next time the situation arises. For most dieters, then, one independent mistake becomes a full-blown relapse.

Cummings, C., Gordon, J. R., & Marlatt, G. A. (1980). Relapse: Prevention and prediction. In W. R. Miller (Ed.), *The addictive behaviors: Treatment of alcoholism, drug abuse, smoking, and obesity* (pp. 291-321). Oxford, England: Pergamon Press.

Marlatt, G. A., & Gordon, J. R. (1985). *Relapse prevention*. New York: Guilford Press.

Lecture Example 11.4: Set Point

In a study of overeating using prisoners as volunteers, subjects, who were of normal weight, were fed high-calorie meals several times a day and were asked to eat as much as possible. Intake ranged as high as 8,000 calories per day. Despite their sedentary lifestyles, the prisoners exhibited only modest weight gains throughout the experiment and had no trouble reducing their weight to previous normal levels after the experiment. The study indicated that normal weight individuals and obese individuals appear to react quite differently to an increase in food intake.

Lecture Example 11.5: Anorexia and Bulimia

Develop a lecture on obesity by discussing other eating disorders such as anorexia and bulimia. The bulk of the evidence concerning anorexia and bulimia favors learning and interpreting the motivation involved. New data indicates the role of the hypothalamus. Use http://www.ruf.rice.edu/~rucc/services/bul_anor.html to help develop this lecture.

Diversity Topic

Diversity Topic 11.2: Eating Journal

Have students try to categorize their responses for Journal Entry 11.1 according to whether they are doing college "for themselves" as opposed to for "other factors," such as their parents wishes, community pressures, etc. Then have a discussion about how these differences are observed as a function of cultural background.

Discussion/Description: As Markus and Kitayama (1991) have described, people of different self-construals, which differ according to culture, will have considerably different achievement motivations. People with independent senses of self, related to individualistic cultures, tend to have motivations for school that are more related to personal success. People with interdependent senses of self, related to collectivistic cultures, tend to have motivations for school that are more related to fulfilling familial or social obligations. These types of differences, should they emerge in class, would be interesting to explore, and would provide the platform for the discussion of these cultural influences.

D. Social Motives

Classroom Demonstrations and Handouts

Demonstration MOTIV 6: Level of Achievement

Objective: To demonstrate the level of aspiration and achievement motivation depends on several variables.
Materials: Two coffee cans; sixty marbles
Procedure: Ask for four volunteers and have them leave the room. Tell the remaining students that you want to test three hypotheses: 1) that group standards influence level of aspiration; 2) that level of aspiration remains close to actual performance, with a tendency to be above rather than below it; and 3) that success leads to an increase in level of aspiration and failure leads to a decrease. Bring the volunteers into the room one at a time. Have each one stand facing a table with two coffee cans three feet apart placed on it, one can with sixty marbles, the other empty. Ask the volunteer to transfer as many marbles as possible from the full can to the empty in thirty seconds, using only one hand and transferring only one at a time. Tell the first two volunteers, "most college students place about fifteen marbles in the empty can during a thirty-second interval." For the other two volunteers, substitute "thirty-five marbles" for "fifteen marbles." Ask the volunteer to estimate the number they expect to transfer. Have them do the task. When time is up, tell them their score, and inform them of a second trial. Again ask for the expected number to be transferred, and have them repeat the tasks. If possible, control for gender.
Conclusions: Discuss the results and support for each hypothesis stated at the onset of the activity.

Fernald, P. S., & Fernald, L. D., Jr. (1981). Level of aspiration. In L. Benjamin & K. Lowman (Eds.), *Activities handbook for the teaching of psychology* (Vol. 1) (pp. 183-184). Washington, D.C.: American Psychological Association.

Lecture Example

Lecture Example 11.6: Asian Motivation

Our traditional stereotype of the Asian American is that of a hard-working individual with a broad social network of support. The stereotype generally holds true: Asian students are among the best in the best American colleges and universities, and Asian (and especially Japanese) business endeavors in the United States rarely seem to fail. Community networks provide social and economic support, and children work hard in school so that they will not shame the family. As a result they tend to excel in areas requiring intense concentration and mental rigor such as the areas of math and science (Tsai and Uemura, 1988).

Tsai, M., & Uemura, A. (1988). Asian Americans: The struggles, the conflicts, and the successes. In P. A. Cunningham & K. Quina (Eds.), *Teaching a psychology of people: Resources for gender and sociocultural awareness*. Washington, DC: American Psychological Association, pp. 125-133.

Lecture Example 11.7: Work Motivation

Use http://psych.fullerton.edu/king/MOT.html as a basis for a lecture on work motivation. Many students have part-time jobs while attending college and will enjoy this lecture.

Diversity Topic

Diversity Topic 11.3: Asian Motivation

The description of Asian people in Lecture Example 11.3 forms a common stereotype of them. Have students discuss this stereotype. Is it accurate—that is true—for most people they know? Are there exceptions to this? (Of course there are.) What are the implications of such exceptions? What are the limitations of descriptions based on stereotypes?
Discussion/Description: While stereotypes are not the main focus of this chapter, this Diversity Topic provides the basis by which such a discussion can occur. The instructor may lead the class in such a discussion, discussing pros and cons of stereotypes, as well as instances when the stereotypes are true and not. This could also lead to discussions of the limitations of stereotypes to describe people, as well as to our own perception and interpretation processes. Triandis has a good discussion of stereotypes, including sociotypes stereotypes that are generally true for over 90% of the people they describe.

Triandis, H. C. (1994). *Culture and social behavior*. New York: McGraw Hill.

E. The What and Why of Emotions

Classroom Demonstrations and Handouts

Student Chalkboard EMOT 1: Theories of Emotion

Demonstration EMOT 1: Emotions and Their Causes

Objective: To determine the causes of several basic emotions.
Materials: **Handout EMOT 1**
Procedure: Using **Handout EMOT 1**, ask students to picture in their mind the time last year when they were a) the most angry and b) the happiest.
Conclusions: Make sure they indicated what provoked their emotion so they can analyze whether their experiences are consistent with the interruption theory of Mandler. They should also point out their physical sensations and thoughts.

Demonstration EMOT 6: To Tell the Truth

Objective: To demonstrate the nonverbal cues of deception.
Materials: **Handout EMOT 6a**; **Handout EMOT 6b**; five to ten volunteers to answer verbally the questions on Handout EMOT 6a in front of the class
Procedure: You and the volunteers should decide which student(s) should lie on which question(s). After determining who lies and when, give half of the remaining students Handout EMOT 6b, which describes nonverbal cues of deception; the other half is not given information on deception cues. Ask your "subjects" to sit in desks or chairs in front of the class and to answer each question. The student subjects are likely to answer quickly, so try to slow them down so the "judges" have time to analyze and record apparent deception. After all the questions have been answered, have the judges go back through the questions and identify the liar. Ask for a count of correct responses by your judges. Debrief all participants. This activity is loosely based upon a study done by Greene et al. (1985).
Conclusions: Does it matter if the judges knew the nonverbal cues of deception? Can we detect when someone is lying? This is also a good opportunity to review research methodology and the apparent shortcomings of this "experiment."

Greene, J. O., O'Hair, H. D., Cody, M. J., & Yen, C. (1985). Planning and control of behavior during deception. *Human Communication Research, 11*, 335-364.

Lecture Examples

Lecture Example 11.8: Children and the Schachter-Singer Theory

When children first learn to walk, they fall often. After falling, a child will immediately look at you for information about what has just occurred. If you respond by running to soothe the child and show facial expressions of concern or fear, the likely response will be crying. However, if you respond without panic and encourage the child to get up, he or she will be more likely to shake off the fall and continue playing. Use http://www-white.media.mit.edu/vismod/demos/affect/AC_research/emotions.html, in the preparation of the lecture.

Lecture Example 11.9: Other Deception Cues

Research has shown that the most likely source of nonverbal deception cues is, in fact, the least valid. Most people would guess that the face is the best place to look to determine lying. Unfortunately, liars also know this and train their faces accordingly. In general, people who are lying show more leg and foot movements, laughter, and smiling. Also associated with deception are fewer hand gestures, head nods, and eye contacts. For some interesting material on body language go to http://www.collegegrad.com/book/15-8.html.

Ekman, P. (1985). *Telling lies: Cues to deceit in the marketplace, politics, and marriage*. New York: Norton.

Lecture Example 11.10: When Do Emotions Occur?

The theories of emotion in this chapter focus primarily on how emotions come to be experienced. Mandler (1980) deals with when they occur. He asserts that many, if not all, emotional states arise out of the interruption of ongoing psychological events. He sees the emotion system as a "troubleshooting" system, one that alerts the individual to important events in the environment. An interruption draws attention, which then leads to arousal and a cognitive appraisal of the situation by the individual. Responses include trying to complete the action sequence with renewed vigor and substituting a new response. Use Demonstration **EMOT 1**, which requires students to think about the causes of anger and happiness.

Mandler, G. (1980). The generation of emotion: A psychological theory. In R. Plutchik & H. Kellerman (Eds.), *Emotion: Theory, research, and experience: Vol. 1: Theories of emotion.* New York: Academic Press.

Lecture Example 11.11: Classic Theory of Emotions Lecture

Use the material at http://www-white.media.mit.edu/vismod/demos/affect/AC_research/emotions.html to develop a lecture on emotions. This site contains information on theories of human emotion. The following descriptions should also help:

James-Lange Theory:

According to this theory, actions precede emotions and the brain interprets said actions as emotions. A situation occurs and the brain interprets the situation, causing a characteristic physiological response. This may include any or all of the following: perspiration, heart rate elevation, facial. and gestural expression. These reflexive responses occur before the person is aware that he is experiencing an emotion; only when the brain cognitively assesses the physiology is it labeled as an "emotion."

Cannon-Bard Theory:

Cannon and Bard opposed the James-Lange theory by stating that the emotion is felt first, and then actions follow from cognitive appraisal. In their view, the thalamus and amygdala play a central role by interpreting an emotion-provoking situation and simultaneously sending signals to the ANS (autonomic nervous system) and to the cerebral cortex, which interprets the situation cognitively.

Schachter-Singer Theory:

Schachter and Singer proposed a two-factor theory: 1.) First, a person must experience physiological arousal. 2.) Then, the person must cognitively interpret the physiological arousal, so the person can come up with a label for the specific emotion.

The Lazarus Theory:

The theory that an emotion-provoking stimulus triggers a cognitive appraisal, which is followed by the emotion and the physiological arousal.

F. The Expression of Emotion

Classroom Demonstrations and Handouts

Demonstration EMOT 4: Watching TV with No Sound

Objective: To reveal the importance of nonverbal communication.
Materials: A videotape of a television show (sitcoms from the 1960s work well)
Procedure: Remind your students of our reliance on nonverbal cues. Suggest that they can determine a great deal about the interaction of people by just relying on body language, posture, and facial expressions. Show a portion of the television show with the sound off. Ask students to determine what is transpiring between the characters. Then replay the scene again but this time with the sound on.
Conclusions: Were the initial judgments valid? Do nonverbal cues give us information that is correct?
Follow-Up Outside Class Project: Ask students to clip five pictures from magazines of individuals displaying different emotions. Show these pictures to ten people asking them to identify the emotion portrayed in the picture and the parts of the face and body they used to make their judgment.

Demonstration EMOT 5: Cultural Differences

Objective: To illustrate that despite similarities between cultures in expressing some emotions, dramatic differences do exist.
Materials: **Handout EMOT 5**
Procedure: Klineberg (1937) found several unique emotional expressions in Chinese literature published in the 1930s. Some expressions, as you can see, are very similar to the way we express the emotion, and others are unique:

1. Every one of his hairs stood on end and the pimples came out on the skin all over his body. (Fear)
2. He drew one leg up and stood on one foot. (Surprise)
3. He clapped his hands. (Disappointment or worry)
4. He raised one hand as high as his face and fanned his face with the sleeve. (Anger)
5. They stuck out their tongues. (Surprise)

6. He gnashed his teeth until they were all but ground to dust. (Anger)
7. Her eyes grew round and opened wide. (Anger)
8. His face was red and he went creeping alone outside the village. (Shame)
9. He laughed a great ho-ho. (Anger)
10. He scratched his ears and cheek. (Happiness)
11. She stretched the left arm flatly to the left and the right arm to the right. (Joy)

Give students a copy of **Handout EMOT 5** and challenge your students to guess what emotion is being portrayed. Students really enjoy this activity.
Conclusions: Many of Klineberg's sentences have pretty much the same meaning in our culture as they did in China in the 1930's, some have opposite meanings, and still others have no significance with regard to our interpretation of the expressed emotion.

Efron, D. (1972). *Gesture, race, and culture*. Highlands, NJ: Humanities Press.

Klineberg, O. (1937). Emotional expression in Chinese literature. *Journal of Abnormal and Social Psychology, 13*, 517-520.

Diversity Topic

Diversity Topic 11.4: Display Rules

Have students complete a brief assessment of their display rules, and then discuss the results, especially in terms of their implications for cultural differences in display management.
Discussion/Description: This Diversity Topic builds on an existing one. We have studied display rules extensively. An important part of this activity would be the discussion, and the reasons why people think they have the display rules that they do.

Matsumoto, D. (1990). Cultural similarities and differences in display rules. *Motivation and Emotion, 14*, 195-214.

G. Experiencing Emotion

Lecture Examples

Lecture Example 11.12: Facial Management Techniques

We are quite adept at regulating the emotions we display facially. In fact, facial management techniques are probably learned at a very young age. Ekman and Friesen (1969) have identified four ways in which we manage our facial expression. When we do not express our true emotion, we are using masking as when a father receives an abhorrently colored tie on Father's Day and displays pleasure at the gift. The exaggeration of an expression is called intensification. For example, after a surprise party is leaked to the honoree, she might still act very surprised. The opposite may also hold true and is called deintensification. When you are attracted to someone, you may downplay your expression because it may not be "cool" to show great interest. The fourth technique, neutralization, describes not showing any emotional expression (e.g. a "poker face"). Ask your students to identify which technique they use in social situations. For more references to this work, see http://robotics.stanford.edu/users/castello/ekman.html.

Ekman, P., & Friesen, W. V. (1969). Nonverbal leakage and clues to deception. *Psychiatry, 32*, 88-106.

12 Human Sexuality and Gender

Chapter-at-a-Glance

Chapter Outline	Instruction Outline	Multimedia
What Makes a Male, a Male and a Female, a Female? p. 396 The Sex Chromosomes: X's and Y's • The Sex Hormones: Contributing to Maleness and Femaleness	Lecture Example 12.14 Learning Objective 12.1 Test Questions 1-10	**Transparencies** DEV 16-17 **Video Disc III** Segments 27-28 **Web Site** http://www.nextwave.org/ehr/books/ Your Genes, Your Choices
Gender-Role Development p. 397 Environmental Influences on Gender Typing • Psychological Theories of Gender-Role Development	Lecture Examples 12.1-12.2 Learning Objectives 12.2-12.5 Test Questions 11-35	*Discovering Psychology: Sex and Gender* **Web Site** http://server1.admin.gatech.edu/fac/steve/p-girl/gid.htm Gender Identity
Gender Differences: Fact or Myth? p. 401 Gender Differences in Cognitive Abilities • Gender Differences in Social Behavior and Personality • Adjustment and Gender-Role Typing: Feminine, Masculine, or Androgynous? • Gender Stereotyping—Who Wins? Who Loses?	Lecture Examples 12.3-12.4 Critical Thinking Forum 12.1 Learning Objectives 12.6-12.7 Test Questions 36-56	**Web Site** http://www.students.haverford.edu/wmbweb/writings/cegender.html Gender Differences
Sexual Attitudes and Behavior p. 407 The Kinsey Surveys: The First In-depth Look at Sexual Behavior • Sexual Attitudes and Behavior Today: The New Sexual Revolution • Sexual Desire and Arousal: Driving the Sex Drive • Child Sexual Abuse	Demonstration MOT 3 Lecture Examples 12.5-12.7 Critical Thinking Opportunity 12.1 Critical Thinking Forum 12.2 Journal Entry 12.1 Learning Objectives 12.8-12.11 Test Questions 57-86	**Web Site** http://www.cc.columbia.edu/cu/healthwise/ FAQ's, Go Ask Alice

Chapter Outline	Instruction Outline	Multimedia
Sexual Orientation p. 413 What Determines Sexual Orientation: The Physiological or The Psychological? • Research Findings on the Developmental Experiences of Gay Men and Lesbians • Social Attitudes toward Gays: From Celebration to Condemnation	**Demonstration SEX 1** **Lecture Example** 12.8 **Learning Objectives** 12.12-12.14 **Test Questions** 87-108	**Web Site** http://www.virtualcity.com/youthsuicide/discuss.htm Sexual Orientation
Sexual Dysfunctions p. 417 Sexual Desire Disorders: From Disinterest to Aversion • Sexual Arousal Disorders • Orgasmic Disorders • Sexual Pain Disorders	**Lecture Examples** 12.9-12.11 **Learning Objectives** 12.15-12.17 **Test Questions** 109-115	**Web Sites** http://www.cityscape.co.uk/users/ad88/sex.htm Sexual Disorders http://text.nlm.nih.gov/nih/cdc/www/91txt.html Impotence
Sexually Transmitted Diseases: The Price of Casual Sex p. 419 The Bacterial Infections • The Viral Infections • Acquired Immune Deficiency Syndrome (AIDS) • Protection against Sexually Transmitted Diseases: Minimizing the Risk	**Lecture Examples** 12.12-12.13 **Critical Thinking Forum** 12.4-12.5 **Learning Objectives** 12.18-12.23 **Test Questions** 116-138	**Video Disc II** Segment 24 **Web Site** http://www.webboy.com/hcphu/stdlist.htm Common Sexually Transmitted Diseases

What's New in Chapter 12

New Content

- Biological influences on gender typing
- Gender differences in social behavior and personality
- Child sexual abuse
- Genital warts

Expanded Content

- Gender differences in cognitive ability

Organizational Changes

- A new section on viral STDs has been added.

New Special Features

- Revised *Remember Its*

New Key Terms

- sex
- genital warts

Learning Objective Questions

12.1   What are the biological factors that determine whether a person is male or female?
12.2   What is gender typing, and what role do biological influences play in it?
12.3   What are the environmental factors that contribute to gender typing?
12.4   What are three theories of gender-role development?
12.5   For what cognitive abilities have gender differences been proven?
12.6   What gender differences are found in social behavior and personality?
12.7   Do good adjustment and high self-esteem seem to be related to masculine, feminine, or androgyny traits?
12.8   What were the famous Kinsey surveys?
12.9   According to Masters and Johnson, what are the four phases of the human sexual response cycle?
12.10 What are the male and female sex hormones, and how do they affect sexual desire and activity in males and females?
12.11 What psychological and cultural factors influence sexual arousal?
12.12 What is meant by sexual orientation?
12.13 What are the various biological factors that have been suggested as possible determinants of gay or lesbian sexual orientation?
12.14 What does the study by Bell, Weinberg, and Hammersmith reveal about the developmental experiences of gay men and lesbians?
12.15 What are two sexual desire disorders and their defining features?
12.16 What are the sexual arousal disorders and their defining features?
12.17 What are the three orgasmic disorders and the defining features of each?
12.18 What are the major bacterial infections and viral infections known as sexually transmitted diseases?
12.19 Why do chlamydia and gonorrhea pose a greater threat to women than to men?
12.20 Why is genital herpes particularly upsetting to those who have it?
12.21 What happens to a person from the time of infection with HIV to the development of full-blown AIDS?
12.22 How is AIDS transmitted?
12.23 What are the most effective methods of protection against sexually transmitted diseases?

Chapter Overview

The first determinant of biological sex is the sex chromosomes. The presence or absence of androgens during the first trimester determines whether male or female genitals, the primary sex characteristics, develop. During puberty, the genitals mature and the secondary sex characteristics appear.

The chapter then turns to gender-role-development. Biological influences on gender typing are explored next. Environmental influences on gender typing include parental sex-role expectations and strong peer influences. The psychological theories of gender-role development include social learning theory, cognitive developmental theory, and gender-schema theory.

The cognitive differences between genders, in areas such as verbal, math, and spatial abilities and the expression of aggression, result from both biological and environmental influences. Gender differences in social behavior and personality are discussed in terms of differences in aggression and personality differences. The current view of gender roles includes the notion of androgyny, the combination of desirable male and female characteristics. Adjustment and gender typing are explored. This section concludes with a discussion of gender stereotyping.

Next, the authors describe attitudes toward sexual behavior as well as the details of the human sexual response. A discussion of the Kinsey surveys and the new sexual revolution opens this section. Data from surveys indicate the changing attitudes toward sexual behavior. Sexual desire and arousal are the next topics in this section. The phases of the sexual response cycle as described by Masters and Johnson are given in detail, as is a discussion of the hormonal and psychological factors at work in sexual arousal. Child sexual abuse ends this section.

Both physiological and psychological factors influence sexual orientation. LeVay found possible connections to the structure of the hypothalamus in gay males. Other researchers have explored genetic connections, conditions in the family, and gender role. The topic of developmental experiences of gay men and lesbians is discussed. Social attitudes toward gay and lesbians are then explored, concluding this section.

The chapter then provides a description of the common sexual dysfunctions including sexual desire disorders, sexual arousal disorders, orgasmic disorders, and sexual pain disorders.

The concluding section of the chapter explores the various sexually transmitted diseases, including the bacterial infections—chlamydia, gonorrhea, syphilis; and the viral infections—genital herpes, genital warts, and acquired immune deficiency syndrome (AIDS). Protection against sexually transmitted diseases and minimizing the risk of contracting an STD are discussed. Protecting yourself from rape is the topic of the *Apply It!*

Key Terms

acquired immune deficiency syndrome (AIDS) (p.421)
androgens (p. 397)
androgyny (p. 404)
chlamydia (p. 418)
cognitive developmental theory (p. 400)
coitus (p. 407)
dispareunia (p. 418)
estrogen (p. 410)
excitement phase (p. 409)
female sexual arousal disorder (p. 418)
gender (p. 397)
gender identity (p. 400)
gender roles (p. 397)
gender typing (p. 398)
gender-schema theory (p. 400)
genital herpes (p. 420)
genital warts (p. 420)
genitals (p. 397)
gonads (p. 396)
biological sex (p. 396)
gonorrhea (p. 420)
HIV (human immunodeficiency virus) (p. 421)
male orgasmic disorder (p. 418)
orgasm phase (p. 409)
pelvic inflammatory disease (PID) (p. 418)
plateau phase (p. 409)
premature ejaculation (p. 418)
primary sex characteristics (p. 397)
progesterone (p. 410)
resolution phase (p. 410)
secondary sex characteristics (p. 397)
sex chromosomes (p. 4396
sexual orientation (p. 413)
sexual response cycle (p. 409)
sexually transmitted diseases (STDs) (p. 418)
social learning theory (p. 399)
syphilis (p. 420)
testosterone (p. 410)
vaginismus (p. 418)

Annotated Lecture Outline

A. What Makes a Male, a Male and a Female, a Female?

Lecture Examples

Lecture Example 12.14: X and Y Chromosomes

Use the following sites to develop a lecture on the X and Y sex chromosomes.
For a microscope picture, see http://phoenix.mcet.edu/humangenome/resources/images/xy.html.
For material on the Y chromosome, see
http://www.ornl.gov/TechResources/Human_Genome/publicat/hgn/v4n4/01map.html and for material on the Human Genome project, see
http://www.ornl.gov/TechResources/Human_Genome/.

B. Gender-Role Development

Lecture Examples

Lecture Example 12.1: Biology and Sex-Role Development

Can sex-role development be explained strictly in terms of environmental influences, or are biological factors at work as well? It has long been recognized that girls generally have higher verbal skills, while boys typically do better in math and spatial relations. Some researchers suggest that greater brain lateralization in males is a contributing factor to these differences in ability. Others believe that differences in the level of androgen (the male sex hormone) at a critical period in prenatal development can affect brain organization.

Lecture Example 12.2: Single-Parent Homes

Of children born in the late 1970s or early 1980s, 40 to 50 percent will spend an average of five years in single-parent homes. In 90 percent of these homes, children live with their mother as a result of divorce. Such children may experience a series of marital transitions because 80 percent of divorced fathers and 75 percent of divorced mothers remarry, usually within 3 to 5 years (Clarke-Stewart, 1989). For more on sex roles and advertising, see http://www.aber.ac.uk/~ednwww/Resdeg/merris05.html.

Clarke-Stewart, K. A. (1989). Infant day care: Maligned or malignant. *American Psychologist, 44,* 266-273.

C. Gender Differences: Fact or Myth?

Lecture Examples

Lecture Example 12.3: Aggression

In a review of 72 studies on sex differences in aggression, Ann Frodi and colleagues (1977) found that males engage in more physically aggressive behavior and have more dreams involving aggression. But females can be as aggressive when they believe it is justified and when they have the means to be so. Females tend to identify and empathize with the victim of aggression and are more likely to feel guilty if they use aggression. For more on studies of female aggression and violence, see http://www.csc-scc.gc.ca/crd/fsw/fsw23/fsw23e05.htm. For more on males, see http://www.aacap.org/journal/october/1322.htm.

Lecture Example 12.4: Sexual Double Standard

Has the double standard been erased completely? Men are still more likely than women to hold more permissive attitudes about sex. Men are more likely to say that it is right to have sex with any partner and less likely to believe that sex should be reserved for someone you love. But both men and women tend to apply their view, whatever it is, to both sexes (Murstein et al., 1989).

Murstein, B. I., Chalpin, M. J., Heard, K. V., & Vyse, S. A. (1989). Sexual behavior, drugs, and relationship patterns on a college campus over thirteen years. *Adolescence, 24,* 125-139.

D. Sexual Attitudes and Behavior

Classroom Demonstrations and Handouts

Demonstration MOT 3: What Is Normal Sexual Behavior?

Objective: To encourage students to think about the difficulty of defining normal sexual behavior.
Materials: **Handout MOT 3**
Procedure: With **Handout MOT 3**, students are asked to decide if certain behaviors are indicative of normal sexual behavior. Following the completion of the survey, students are to form small groups (no more than five in a group), then each group should develop a definition of normal sexual behavior.
Conclusions: Developing a definition of normal sexual behavior is not an easy task. This activity will lead to a discussion of the complexities that surround human sexuality. For a methodological analysis of sexual behavior, see http://www.icpsr.umich.edu/gss/report/m-report/meth65.htm.

Kite, M. E. (1990). Defining normal sexual behavior: A classroom exercise. *Teaching of Psychology, 17,* 118-119.

Lecture Examples

Lecture Example 12.5: Depo-Provera

Depo-Provera, an antiandrogen drug used to lower blood levels of testosterone, has gained notoriety because of its experimental use on sex offenders to lower their sex drive. Some studies have shown it to be effective in decreasing both sexual interest and activity (Berlin & Meinecke, 1981; Lunde & Hamburg, 1972). Depo-Provera is now used as a birth control method for females; see http://www.kawartha.net/~whcc/provera.htm for more information.

Berlin, F., & Meinecke, C. (1981). Treatment of sex offenders with antiandrogenic medication. *American Journal of Psychiatry, 138,* 601-607.

Lunde, D., & Hamburg, D. (1972). Techniques for assessing the effects of sex hormones on affect, arousal, and aggression in humans. *Recent Progress in Hormone Research, 28,* 627B 663.

Lecture Example 12.6: Arousal and Self Report

Julia Heiman's study (1975) indicated that the men's verbal reports of arousal were more closely correlated with their actual physical arousal. The women's reports of arousal did not reflect their measured physical arousal as closely as did the men's reports. As a side issue, see http://server.psyc.vt.edu/aabt/bt/vol26no4/GCNH.html for information on sexual arousal and arousability to pedophilic stimuli in normal men.

Heiman, J. (1975, April). The physiology of erotica: Women's sexual arousal. *Psychology Today*, pp. 90-94.

Lecture Example 12.7: Exposure Effects

Zillman and Bryant (1982, 1983) had male and female subjects view, over a six-week period, nonviolent but sexually explicit pornography that degraded women. At the end of the study, subjects became more tolerant of the deviant sex practices portrayed in the films, became less supportive of "statements about sexual equality," and became more lenient in suggesting punishment for a rapist. For more on this controversy, see http://samiam.colorado.edu/~mcclelaj/violence.html.

Zillmann, D., & Bryant, J. (1983). *Pornography and sexual aggression.* New York: Academic Press.

Zillmann, D., & Bryant, J. (1982). Pornography, sexual callousness, and the trivialization of rape. *Journal of Communication, 32,* 10-21

E. Sexual Orientation

Classroom Demonstrations and Handouts

Demonstration SEX 1: Guest Lecturer on Sexual Orientation Issues

Objective: To expose students to sexual orientation issues.
Materials: None
Procedure: Arrange for a guest speaker from your local gay and lesbian rights organization. Most campuses have a student-affiliated organization.
Conclusions: This guest speaker will have a positive effect on the students' knowledge of sexual orientation issues.

Lecture Examples

Lecture Example 12.8: Learning

Some experts suggest that perhaps a homosexual orientation is learned (McGuire, Carlisle, & Young, 1965; Gagnon & Simon, 1973; Masters & Johnson, 1979), and that early positive sexual experiences with persons of the same sex or negative experiences with persons of the opposite sex may predispose one toward homosexuality. Ask the students for input on this topic. For the latest from Virginia Masters, see http://www.vjmlc.com/home.htm. For an explanation of Masters & Johnson's theory, see http://www.sexualhealth.com/content/response.htm.

Gagnon, J. H., & Simon, W. (1973). *Sexual conduct: The social origins of human sexuality.* Chicago: Aldine.

McGuire, R. J., Carlisle, J. M., & Young, B. G. (1965). Sexual deviations as conditioned behavior: A hypothesis. *Behavioral Research and Therapy, 2,* 185-190.

Masters, W. H., & Johnson, V. E. (1979). *Homosexuality in perspective.* Boston: Little, Brown.

F. Sexual Dysfunctions

Lecture Examples

Lecture Example 12.9: Spectatoring

Some therapists believe that sexual problems may be caused by a number of psychological factors, including spectatoring. In spectatoring, an individual becomes overly concerned about giving pleasure to his or her partner. Francoeur (1991) writes that spectatoring is like "...withdrawing from our bodies and hovering over the sexual experience as an observer." This increase in self-awareness may actually lead to strong pressure that interferes with performance.

Francoeur, R. T. (1991). *Becoming a sexual person.* New York: Macmillan Publishing.

Lecture Example 12.10: Test Your Sex Knowledge

Depending on the circumstances at your school, you might want to expose your students to http://askthedoc.com/sextest.html, a test of sex knowledge. If you cannot use this test in the classroom setting, you can take the test and use the knowledge gained to develop a lecture on the topic.

Lecture Example 12.11: Glossary of Sex Terms

Use http://www.sexology.org/glossary2.htm, a glossary of sex terms, to develop your lectures for this chapter.

G. Sexually Transmitted Diseases: The Price of Casual Sex

Lecture Examples

Lecture Example 12.12: Changing Behavior to Combat HIV/AIDS

As you discuss the issue of changing people's behavior to prevent AIDS, two very important points should be made. First, while there is evidence that homosexual and bisexual males have modified their sexual behaviors and practices (for example, by using condoms), there is less reason to assume that the same kind of results can be seen in adolescent and adult heterosexuals. In fact, there is very little support for the efficacy of programs to change their behaviors. The second point involves the fact that in any modification of behavior, there are lapses and relapses. In AIDS prevention, short-term changes are of little value; lifelong changes in behavior must be achieved. Prevention campaigns must stress long-term behavior modification. For more information on HIV/AIDS, see http://www.kidsource.com/kidsource/content/news/HIV_prevent7_9_96.html. For the latest on HIV/AIDS-related research at National Institutes of Health (NIH), see http://www.hivpositive.com/f-Treatment/f-Research/oar4a2a3.htm.

Lecture Example 12.13: STDs

Use the following sites to develop a lecture on sexually transmitted diseases STDs: http://www.qal.berkeley.edu/~suggs/health/tips/std.htm and http://www.shsl.com/internet/supcourt/0000230h.html.

13 Personality Theory and Assessment

Chapter-at-a-Glance

Chapter Outline	Instruction Outline	Multimedia
Sigmund Freud and Psychoanalysis p. 431 The Conscious, the Preconscious, and the Unconscious: Levels of Awareness • The Id, the Ego, and the Superego: Warring Components of the Personality • **Pioneers: Sigmund Freud** • Defense Mechanisms: Protecting the Ego • The Psychosexual Stages of Development: Centered on the Erogenous Zones • Freud's Explanation of Personality • Evaluating Freud's Contribution	**Student Chalkboard** PERS 1-4 **Demonstration** PERS 1-3 **Lecture Example** 13.1-13.4 **Critical Thinking Opportunity** 13.1 **Journal Entry** 13.1 **Learning Objectives** 13.1-13.9 **Test Questions** 1-52	**Transparency** PERS 5 *Discovering Psychology: The Self* **Digital Image Archive** PSR003, 4, 6 009a&b **Web Site** http://plaza.interport.net/nypsan/ FreudNet
The Neo-Freudians p. 439 Carl Gustav Jung • Alfred Adler: Overcoming Inferiority • Karen Horney: Champion of Feminine Psychology	**Demonstration** PERS 4, 8 **Lecture Example** 13.13 **Critical Thinking Forum** 13.1 **Learning Objectives** 13.10-13.13 **Test Questions** 53-64	**Transparency** PERS 6 **Digital Image Archive** PSR007 **Web Sites** http://www.wynja.com/personality/ theorists.html Major Personality Theorists http://www.cgjung.com/cgjung/ Jung Home Page
Trait Theories p. 443 Gordon Allport: Personality Traits in the Brain • Raymond Cattell's 16 Personality Factors • Hans Eysenck: Stressing Two Factors • The Five-Factor Theory of Personality: The Big Five • Evaluating the Trait Perspective	**Lecture Examples** 13.5-13.9 **Critical Thinking Opportunity** 13.2 **Diversity Topics** 13.1-13.2 **Learning Objectives** 13.14-13.18 **Test Questions** 64-79	**Transparencies** PERS 1, 4 **Digital Image Archive** PSR001, 2 **Web Sites** http://fujita.iusb.edu/big5.html The Big Five Taxonomy http://www.wynja.com/personality/ theorists.html Major Personality Theorists

Chapter Outline	Instruction Outline	Multimedia
Learning Theories and Personality p. 447 The Behaviorist View of B. F. Skinner • The Social-Cognitive Theorists: Expanding the Behaviorist View	Lecture Examples 13.10-13.12 Learning Objectives 13.19-13.21 Test Questions 80-88	Web Site http://www.wynja.com/personality/theorists_kelly.html Skinner and Personality
Humanistic Personality Theories p. 449 Abraham Maslow: The Self-Actualizing Person • Carl Rogers: The Fully Functioning Person • Evaluating the Humanistic Perspective	Demonstration PERS 5, 6 Lecture Examples 13.13 Critical Thinking Opportunity 13.3 Learning Objectives 13.22-13.24 Test Questions 89-102	Transparency MOTIV 6 Digital Image Archive PSR008 Web Site http://www.wynja.com/personality/rogersffnf.html Carl Rogers and Personality
Personality: Is It in the Genes? p. 451 The Twin Study Method: Studying Identical and Fraternal Twins • The Shared and Nonshared Environment • The Adoption Method • Personality and Culture	Demonstration PERS 7 Lecture Example 13.14 Learning Objective 13.25 Test Questions 103-110	Transparency PERS 9 Video Disc II Segment 19 Web Site http://www.queendom.com/typea2.html Type A personality
Personality Assessment p. 455 Observation, Interviews, and Rating Scales • Personality Inventories: Taking Stock • Projective Tests: Projections from the Unconscious • Personality Theories: A Final Comment	Demonstration INTRO 3, PERS 9, 10 Lecture Example 13.18, 13.19 Diversity Topics 13.3-13.4 Learning Objectives 13.26-13.28 Test Questions 111-135	Web Sites http://www.2h.com/Tests/personality.phtml Personality Test http://sunsite.unc.edu/jembin/mb.pl The Keirsey Temperament Sorter

What's New in Chapter 13

New Content

- The Myers-Briggs Type Indicator

Organizational Changes

- Personality and culture have been moved to fall within the section on nature-nurture determinants of personality.

New Special Features

- Revised *Remember Its*
- New *Apply It* on Optimism

Learning Objective Questions

13.1 To what two aspects of Freud's work does the term *psychoanalysis* apply?
13.2 What are the three levels of awareness in consciousness?
13.3 What are the roles of the id, the ego, and the superego?
13.4 What is a defense mechanism?
13.5 What are two ways in which repression operates?
13.6 What are some other defense mechanisms?
13.7 What are the psychosexual stages, and why did Freud consider them so important in personality development?
13.8 What is the Oedipus complex?
13.9 According to Freud, what are the two primary sources of influence on the personality?
13.10 According to Jung, what are the three components of personality?
13.11 What are five archetypes that Jung believed have a major influence on the personality?
13.12 What did Adler consider to be the driving force of the personality?
13.13 Why is Horney considered a pioneer in psychology?
13.14 What are trait theories of personality?
13.15 How did Allport differentiate between cardinal and central traits?
13.16 How did Cattell differentiate between surface and source traits?
13.17 What does Eysenck consider to be the two most important dimensions of personality?
13.18 What are the Big Five personality dimensions in the five-factor theory as described by McCrae and Costa?
13.19 How did Skinner account for what most people refer to as personality?
13.20 What are the components that make up Bandura's concept of reciprocal determinism, and how do they interact?
13.21 What does Rotter mean by the terms *internal* and *external locus of control*?
13.22 Who were the two pioneers in humanistic psychology, and how did they view human nature?
13.23 What is self-actualization, and how did Maslow study it?
13.24 According to Rogers, why don't all people become fully functioning persons?
13.25 What has research in behavioral genetics revealed about the influence of the genes and the environment on personality?
13.26 What are the three major methods used in personality assessment?
13.27 What is an inventory, and what are the MMPI-2 and the CPI designed to reveal?
13.28 How do projective tests provide insight into personality, and what are some of the most commonly used projective tests?

Chapter Overview

This chapter examines each of the major personality theories and the evidence that supports them, as well as the main criticisms that have been offered regarding them. The chapter begins with a detailed discussion of psychoanalytic theory. The realms of conscious, preconscious, and unconscious awareness are described, as is Freud's concept of ego, id, and superego making up the structure of the personality. The defense mechanisms used by the ego to protect it from anxiety are described, including repression, projection, denial, rationalization, regression, reaction formation, displacement, and sublimation. In this chapter, the authors also describe Freud's psychosexual stages of development. These are the oral stage, the anal stage, the phallic stage, the latency period, and the genital stage. Neo-Freudians are examined: Carl Jung with his concepts of the collective unconscious and the archetype; Alfred Adler and the concept of organ inferiority; and Karen Horney and the notion of basic anxiety.

The trait theories are represented by the work of Gordon Allport, Raymond Cattell, and Hans Eysenck. The trait theories focus on identifying core traits that can be used to describe the personality. Cattell and Eysenck have employed factor analysis to reduce the number of traits to a small, manageable number. Cattell identified sixteen traits, and Eysenck identified two dimensions. The contemporary five factors theory is then detailed. The section ends with an evaluation of the trait perspective.

The behavioral view of personality suggests that our personalities reflect learned tendencies acquired through our lifetime. B. F. Skinner believed that these learned tendencies reflect patterns of reinforcement, and Bandura's social-cognitive theory has added the notion that much is learned by observing others and building a sense of self-efficacy. Rotter's locus of control is then discussed.

The humanistic personality theories are focused on the concept of self-actualization. Maslow's hierarchy of needs is discussed in this aspect, as is Carl Rogers's concept of the fully functioning person. The humanistic perspective is limited by the difficulty of developing testable concepts.

The biological perspective suggests that much of our personality is a result of genetic inheritance. A detailed discussion of twin studies is explored. A discussion of personality and culture ends this section.

The chapter concludes with an examination of techniques available to assess personality. The methods described are observation, interviews, rating scales, and three personality inventories—MMPI-2, California Personality Inventory, and the Myers-Briggs Type Indicator. Several projective tests including the Rorschach Inkblot Test, the Thematic Apperception Test, and the sentence completion method are detailed.

Key Terms

anal stage (p. 437)
archetype (p. 441)
behavioral genetics (p. 451)
California Psychological Inventory (CPI) (p. 458)
cardinal trait (p. 443)
central trait (p. 443)
collective unconscious (p. 441)
conditions of worth (p. 450)
conscious (p. 431)
defense mechanism (p. 433)
denial (p. 435)
displacement (p. 435)
ego (p. 432)
extroversion (p. 441)
five-factor theory (p. 445)
fixation (p. 436)
genital stage (p. 437)
halo effect (p. 456)
heritability (p. 452)
humanistic psychology (p. 449)
id (p. 432)
introversion (p. 441)
inventory (p. 457)
latency period (p. 437)
libido (p. 432)
locus of control (p. 448)
Minnesota Multiphasic Personality Inventory-2 (MMPI-2) (p. 457)
Myers-Briggs Type Indicator (MBTI) (p. 458)
Oedipus complex (p. 437)
oral stage (p. 437)
personal unconscious (p. 441)
personality (p. 430)
phallic stage (p. 437)
pleasure principle (p. 432)
preconscious (p. 431)
projection (p. 434)
projective test (p. 459)
psychoanalysis (p. 431)
psychosexual stages (p. 436)
rationalization (p. 435)
reaction formation (p. 435)
reciprocal determinism (p. 448)
regression (p. 435)
repression (p. 433)
Rorschach Inkblot Test (p. 459)
self-actualization (p. 450)
self-efficacy (p. 448)
source traits (p. 444)
sublimation (p. 435)
superego (p. 432)
surface traits (p. 444)
Thematic Apperception Test (TAT) (p. 460)
trait (p. 443)
trait theories (p. 443)
unconditional positive regard (p. 451)
unconscious (p. 431)

Annotated Lecture Outline

A. Sigmund Freud and Psychoanalysis

Classroom Demonstrations and Handouts

Student Chalkboard PERS 1: Freud's View of the Personality Structure

Student Chalkboard PERS 2: Freud's View of the Human Mind

Student Chalkboard PERS 3: Comparing Personality Theories: Chart I

Student Chalkboard PERS 4: Comparing Personality Theories: Chart II

Demonstration PERS 1: What Is Personality?

Objective: To challenge students to think about the definitions of personality and difficulty of constructing measures of personality.
Materials: None
Procedure: Two activities are summarized here. In the first activity, students are to write down their own definition of personality. Follow up with a discussion of how their definitions compare with the definition given in your text. The second activity, described by Benjamin (1987), requires students to think about the terms that relate to personality. Narrow down the list of terms to eight major terms, then divide the class into eight groups (this number may be changed to accommodate class size). Assign one of the terms to each of the eight groups, and tell the students to write two test items that they think will measure that characteristic of personality. Tell the students that their items will be used in a personality test composed of 16 questions. After collecting the test items, type the test, and ask students to take it themselves or to give to two people outside of class.
Conclusions: Evaluate the data and report back to students. Use the data to discuss factors involved with the definition of personality and how to go about measuring it. For additional information for this demonstration, see http://www.dur.ac.uk/~dps0dk/idp-defn.

Benjamin, L. T., Jr. (1987). Personality and personality assessment. In V. P. Makosky, L. G. Whittemore, and A. M. Rogers (Eds.). *Activities handbook for the teaching of psychology* (Vol. 2) (pp. 169-171). Washington, D.C.: American Psychological Association.

Demonstration PERS 2: Comparing Personality Theories

Objective: To increase students' awareness of their own theories of personality and their relationship to articulated theories.
Materials: **Handout PERS 2a**; **Handout PERS 2b**
Procedure: Embree (1986) suggests a demonstration that tries to increase students' consciousness of their own personal theories of personality. Embree suggests asking students to complete a questionnaire dealing with different issues in personality. You will find this questionnaire in **Handout PERS 2a**. After they complete this Handout, give students **Handout PERS 2b**, which describes how the questionnaire would be completed by Skinner, Freud, and Rogers.
Conclusions: Students can compare their responses to the prototypes. This demonstration can serve as a review, and it also helps students to determine which theory they implicitly feel the most comfortable with. For more on the major personality theories, see http://www.wynja.com/personality/theorists.html.

Embree, M. C. (1986). Implicit personality theory in the classroom: An integrative approach. *Teaching of Psychology, 13*, 78-80.

Demonstration PERS 3: Role-Playing Freudian Personality

Objective: To illustrate the different parts of personality.
Materials: **Handout PERS 3**
Procedure: Hess (1976) offers an activity to illustrate the different parts of personality in which students get in groups of three and each student "becomes" the id, ego, and superego. Several

dilemmas or scenarios are presented to students (e.g., baby-sitting a rude child; wanting a piece of cake while dieting; seeing an attractive member of the opposite sex; being the recipient of unfair criticism of your work by an adult). The list of personality structures and defense mechanisms on **Handout PERS 3** can be used to rate performance. An alternative is to ask students to "draw" the parts of personality in a cartoon. Greider writes about an activity involving role-playing defense mechanisms. Ask for volunteers to present a skit in pairs demonstrating defense mechanisms. You provide the basic plot and the participants provide the dialogue. The class is asked to identify the mechanism each skit represents.

Conclusions: As the rest of the class watches, they are asked to determine what mechanism is being portrayed. This is a very good review of defense mechanisms and can be a worthwhile break from lecturing.

Hess, A. K. (1976). The "parts party" as a method of teaching personality theory and dynamics. *Teaching of Psychology, 3,* 32-33.

Greider, J. J. (1981). Defense mechanisms. In L.T. Benjamin and K. D. Lowman (Eds.), *Activities handbook for the teaching of psychology* (Vol. 1) (p. 182). Washington, D.C.: American Psychological Association.

Lecture Examples

Lecture Example 13.1: Freud's Three Parts of Personality

An effective example to illustrate the dynamics among the id, the ego, and the superego is to tell a story. The setting of the story is a bar where a person sees an attractive member of the opposite sex. The id wants sexual gratification right then and there, no matter what the consequences. The superego, of course, prohibits it because it is wrong. The ego, working to satisfy the id, must develop a strategy that acknowledges the constraints of reality. Therefore, the ego has a plan to ask the person to dance, buy the person a drink, or start up a conversation with an opening line. This example becomes more lively if your students think of dialogue for the parts of personality.

Lecture Example 13.2: Applying Freud's Theory to Teenagers

At puberty, many students can remember being caught in the dilemma of how to express sexuality prior to marriage. Freud's interpretation of this dilemma would involve the id pushing for sexual activity at any opportunity, while the superego favors abstinence because of parental, society, and religious influences. Freud would further interpret this situation as the ego being caught in the middle of this conflict, with strong pressures both to engage in and to avoid sexual behavior. This example will be a good way to personalize your lecture.

Lecture Example 13.3: Freud and Popular Culture

Freud's theory has been widely applied outside of psychology; many creative works have been analyzed from a Freudian perspective including books, poems, films, songs, and artworks. It is popular to scrutinize the works for hidden meanings with Freudian overtones. Ask the students to give examples from soap operas, tabloid newspapers or other popular sources of Freudian interpretations. Then discuss whether these interpretations are correct or incorrect. This is a good way to introduce the relatively dry Freudian material from a modern perspective.

Lecture Example 13.4: Psychodynamic Perspectives

Psychodynamic personality theories have been soundly criticized by behaviorist and others as lacking testability, being based on inadequate evidence, and being sexist. Ask students why despite these criticisms they think the psychodynamic approach has been such a powerful force in psychology. Are theories that purport effective use in therapeutic settings and that offer insights into behavior appropriate subject matter for psychology? Psychology often portrays itself as scientific, so how can it use these unscientific therapy methods?

B. The Neo-Freudians

Classroom Demonstrations and Handouts

Demonstration PERS 4: Examining Self Concept

Objective: To examine students' self-concepts.
Materials: **Handout PERS 4**
Procedure: Students can gain a different perspective of themselves by taking the Twenty-Statement Test developed by Zurcher. Pass out **Handout PERS 4** to students and ask them to think about who they are as they answer the statement, "I am…" twenty times. After completing this part, students are to place each completed statement into one of the four categories: physical self (e.g., sex, age), social self (e.g., family, membership), reflective self (e.g., in terms of values, likes, dislike), and identity self (e.g., who you are). Which category seems to be the most common? If you have time, think about modifying this activity to have students consider the self-concept of some celebrity or other well-known person (e.g., Bill Clinton, the late Princess Diana, Jerry Seinfeld, Madonna). To assist students, limit the analysis to one aspect of the individual like social relationships, physical appearance, or morality.
Conclusions: Zurcher suggests that the best outcome is a person who has a sense of balance. For more on self-concept, see
http://www.cba.uri.edu/Scholl/Notes/Self_Concept_Model.html#Structure.

Zurcher, L. A. (1977). *The mutable self.* New York: Sage.

Demonstration PERS 8: Guest Lecturer: Neo-Freudian Therapist

Objective: To expose students to the Neo-Freudian perspective.
Materials: None
Procedure: Ask students to prepare questions to pose to the guest lecturer.
Conclusions: Students will gain valuable exposure to this perspective and can have their questions answered by this individual.

C. Trait Theories

Lecture Examples

Lecture Example 13.5: Types of Traits

As you discuss the differences among Allport's traits, ask students to generate examples that fit each type of trait. A rich source of examples is television, especially sitcoms from the 1950s and 1960s. Consider Ward Cleaver, Eddie Haskell, and Roseanne Barr as possessing specific central traits. Think about historical figures and their cardinal traits.

Lecture Example 13.6: Shyness

Shyness can be understood as a continuum. There is mild shyness; it is characterized by a person's preference to be alone but includes interaction with others, albeit with difficulty. A person who is mildly shy might be labeled a "loner." A person with more shyness, according to Zimbardo (1977), experiences embarrassment, blushing, and offensive attack syndrome. Shyness to a large part interferes with this person's daily activities. Those most severely affected by shyness have chronic shyness; social situations are avoided because of an anticipation of having to do something in front of others.

Zimbardo, P. G. (1977). *Shyness*. Reading, MA: Addison-Wesley.

Lecture Example 13.7: *Amae* and Japanese Personality

The cultural concept of *amae* refers to the dependence on or the presumption of the benevolence of another (Takeo Doi, 1962). This concept describes the attitude of children toward parents or between husband and wife. Apparently this concept governs much of the family interdependence and the respect of elders that typifies Japanese family life. Interestingly, Japanese workers have a devotion to their employers that is governed by this same pattern.

Doi, T. (1962). Amae: A key concept for understanding Japanese personality structure. In R. J. Smith & R. K. Beardsley (Eds.), *Japanese culture: Its development and characteristics*. Chicago: Aldine, Publishing.

Lecture Example 13.8: Situation and Personality

Most psychologists believe that human behavior stems from a complex interplay between situational variables and personality variables. Recent attempts to conceptualize this interaction can be presented to students as a vehicle for understanding when personality factors are most influential, as evidenced by high consistency between personality factors and behavior.

Hampson (1988) reports on several approaches to personality and consistency. The idiographic approach suggests that consistency can be found, but more narrowly than once expected.

Bem (1983) suggests that consistency can be found only for certain people exhibiting certain behaviors in certain situations. For example, he and his colleagues have found that subjects who rate themselves as consistently friendly are more likely to appear friendly across self-ratings, parental ratings, peer ratings, and behavioral observations than subjects who rate themselves as more variable in regard to friendliness. The levels-of-abstraction approach argues that consistency decreases as the abstractness of the trait increases. When an abstract trait is used, such as extraversion, measurement will be imprecise because specification of behaviors of such a broad construct will be difficult. When a less abstract trait, such as punctuality, is used, consistency will increase because it is easier to specify punctual behavior. The range of punctual behaviors is smaller than the range of extraverted behaviors.

Phares (1988) also points out that it is hard to predict the person-situation interaction because different people view the same situation from quite different perspectives. Cues trigger expectancies that certain things will happen. For example, one person might view grocery shopping, interactions with the opposite sex, and conversing with the boss as functionally equivalent because they all contain cues that arouse anxiety. To predict behavior in a given situation, one needs to know about personality characteristics and also about the subjective meaning of that situation to the individuals being studied.

Bem, D. (1983). Constructing a theory of the triple topology: Some second thoughts on nomothetic and idiographic approaches to personality. *Journal of Personality, 51,* 566-577.

Hampson, S. (1988). *The construction of personality.* London: Routledge.

Phares, E. J. (1988). *Introduction to personality.* Glenview, IL: Scott, Foresman and Company.

Lecture Example 13.9: The "Big Five" Factors of Personality

Use http://www.psych-test.com/bigfive.htm to develop a lecture on The "Big Five" Factors of Personality.

Diversity Topics

Diversity Topic 13.1: Traits

Now that students have had an orientation to the types of cross-cultural challenges and foundations of Freud's theory, they can use that information as a basis for being critical of these theories as well. Have your students discuss the cultural foundations of these theories that may provide the framework for culture bound limitations in them, as was the case for psychoanalytic conceptions of personality.
Discussion/Description: This activity will develop critical thinking skills on the part of the students. Because culture-relevant criticism exists for psychoanalytic theory but not for these other theories, students will have to use the same types of bases as discussed for psychoanalytic theory to construct criticisms and limitations of these theories. If they have difficulty engaging

with this task, the instructor may wish to lead them through with guiding questions, such as "What type of information would you need to know in order to make a decision about the cultural relativity of this theory?"

Diversity Topic 13.2: Context

American psychology typically defines personality as a set of relatively enduring behavioral characteristics. However, other cultures that depend much more highly on context (Hall, 1966) challenge this basic notion of personality, as it is natural that people behave in entirely different ways in different contexts. Discuss these possibilities with your class.

Discussion/Description: Context-specific differences in behaviors that are readily observed in high context cultures would be the basis of judgments of abnormality, hypocrisy, or some other negative attribute. In American psychology, there is an underlying current of "relatively stable attributes across time and context" that we have in our notions of personality. These notions are culture bound, and do not necessarily exist in other cultures. These types of fundamental differences provide the basis for considerable intercultural conflicts, because attributions are made about people on entirely different bases.

Hall, E. T. (1966). *The hidden dimension.* New York: Doubleday.

D. Learning Theories and Personality

Lecture Examples

Lecture Example 13.10: Reciprocal Determinism

From the social learning perspective, Bandura (1977) has postulated a concept called reciprocal determinism that molds our personality. Radical behaviorism totally ignores cognitive variables so that the environment is the sole cause of behavior. So-called environmental determinism analyzes how changing the environment can cause a change in behavior or personality: $B = I(E)$, behavior as a function of the environment. Some schools of thought argue that personality (i.e., behavior) is the result of a unidirectional interaction: $B = I(C, E)$, behavior as a function of our cognitions and the environment. A shortcoming of this approach is that it ignores the abilities of behavior to change the environment as well as cognition to change how we perceive and evaluate our environment. Another approach contends that cognitive and environmental factors do interact as they produce behavior: $B = I(CE)$. Again behavior is believed not to influence the environment. Reciprocal determinism asserts that all three variables, cognition, overt behavior, and the environment, are interdependent and interactive. In other words, our personality is explained by a continual interaction of environmental, cognitive, and behavioral determinants. Each variable determines the other variables. For more on Social Learning Theory, see http://www.dcwi.com/~scherer/papers/band.htm.

Bandura, A. (1977). *Social learning theory.* Englewood Cliffs, NJ: Prentice Hall.

Lecture Example 13.11: Perceived Control

Researchers have also found that the actual degree of control in a situation is not as important as the perception of control. Phares (1988) discusses much of the research on perceived control including a study done by Langer and Rodin (1976). They showed that much of the physical and mental deterioration observed among elderly people in nursing homes may be a result of loss of control. When the environment was changed to facilitate perceptions of control for certain residents of a nursing home, they became more alert and happy, and they felt better than a comparison group for whom no changes had been made. Phares discusses the huge volume of research associated with Rotter's locus of control, including its theoretical foundation, its psychometric qualities, and its relationship to other psychological variables. For example, internals are more likely to work to stay healthy than externals. For a Locus of Control Scale, see http://www.cl.uh.edu/edu/orgbeh/orgpub/survey/locus.html.

Langer, E., & Rodin, J. (1976). The effects of choice and enhanced personal responsibility for the aged: A field experiment in an institutional setting. *Journal of Personality and Social Psychology, 34,* 191-198.

Phares, E. J. (1976). *Locus of control in personality.* Morristown, NJ: General Learning Press.

Phares, E. J. (1988). *Introduction to personality.* Glenview, IL: Scott, Foresman and Company.

Lecture Example 13.12: The Behavioral Perspectives on Personality

An ongoing debate in psychology concerns just who or what is in control of our behavior. This debate has been contested since the 1920s. Skinner places control in the environment, asserting that free will or self-control is an illusory construct. Do your students agree or disagree? Are theories that are derived from empirical observations in "artificial" laboratory settings appropriate subject matter for psychology? Develop a lecture on this topic.

E. Humanistic Personality Theories

Classroom Demonstrations and Handouts

Demonstration PERS 5: Student Gripes

Objective: To discuss the complaints and gripes of students in the context of Maslow's hierarchy of needs.
Materials: **Handout PERS 5**
Procedure: Ask students to list their complaints, then relate them to the hierarchy. Students might list physiological needs (dorm food, not enough sleep), safety needs (walking alone at night, apartment security), and so on.

Conclusions: Does experiencing minor complaints impede one's self-actualization? For a discussion of Maslow's Hierarchy of Needs, see http://www.connect.net/georgen/maslow.htm.

Demonstration PERS 6: Peak Experiences

Objective: To allow students to describe a peak experience in their lives.
Materials: None
Procedure: Ask students to describe a peak experience in their life. Give them a day or two to think about this assignment. To help get them started, read Abraham Maslow's thoughts on peak experiences to the students:

> I would like you to think of the most wonderful experiences of your life; happiest moments, ecstatic moments, moments of rapture, perhaps from being in love, or from listening to music or suddenly "being hit" by a book or painting, or from some great creative moment. First list these. And then try to tell me how you feel in such acute moments, how you feel differently from the way you feel at other times, how you are at the moment a different person in some ways (Maslow, 1962, p. 67).

After students have had a time to think and list these peak experiences, put them in groups of no more than five where they share those experiences they wish to.

Conclusions: Students will increase their comprehension and appreciation of the idea of peak experiences. For a discussion of Maslow's Hierarchy of Needs, see http://www.connect.net/georgen/maslow.htm.

Maslow, A. H. (1962). *Toward a psychology of being.* Princeton, NJ: D. Van Nostrand.

Polyson, J. (1985). Students' peak experiences: A written exercise. *Teaching of Psychology,* 12, 211-213.

Lecture Examples

Lecture Example 13.13: Humanistic Perspectives

Humanistic personality theories have been soundly criticized by behaviorists and others as lacking testability, being based on inadequate evidence, and being sexist. Ask students why, despite these criticisms, they think the psychodynamic approach has been such a powerful force in psychology. Are theories that purport effective use in therapeutic settings and that offer insights into behavior appropriate subject matter for psychology? Psychology often portrays itself as scientific, but then how can it use these unscientific therapy methods?

F. Personality: Is It in the Genes?

Classroom Demonstrations and Handouts

Demonstration PERS 7: Theories of Personality and TV

Objective: To use different theoretical orientations to describe and explain personalities.
Materials: None
Procedure: Television characters can give us a good opportunity to describe their personalities in the context of some theory. Polyson (1983) suggests that students select a character and write a brief essay describing and explaining the character's behavior from a theoretical perspective. The essay should include very specific examples of what the character said or did. For example, does the behavior lead you to believe the character has high or low self-esteem? This could be done as a collaborative learning exercise. An extension of this activity might include analyzing internationally known figures like Bill Clinton, Saddam Hussein, or Boris Yeltsin from a specific theoretical orientation.
Conclusions: Students will become more familiar with the various theories of personality by applying what they know to explain the personality of an individual.

Polyson, J. (1983). Student essays about TV characters. *Teaching of Psychology, 10,* 103-104.

Lecture Examples

Lecture Example 13.14: Genetic Influences on Personality

Research has sought to establish biological links to a number of personality variables. For example, the gender and hormonal differences associated with aggression strongly hint that aggression has a biological link. There are many more indications of biological influences on personality than were previously thought. Ask the students to develop a list of possible links for discussion in the next class period.

G. Personality Assessment

Classroom Demonstrations and Handouts

Demonstration INTRO 3: The Barnum Test of Personality

Objective: To make students understand the importance of scientific rigor, the effect of Barnum statements, and to question the validity of common sense.
Materials: The "Barnum Test of Personality" (**Handout INTRO 3a**); one personality description written with Barnum statements (**Handout INTRO 3b**)
Procedure: One reason for the apparent validity of astrological descriptions of personality is their inclusion of Barnum statements: statements that are so general, they can not miss the target. On

the first day of class, mention that besides teaching, you conduct research. One of your projects involves the development of a personality test and you would like the students to take it. With a poker face, explain that this is optional, but if they consent to it, a description of their personality will be written based upon their responses. Please note that the more "official" the personality test looks, the stronger the effect. Collect the personality tests and hand out the descriptions on the next day of class (of course, all of the personality descriptions are identical). Caution that because of confidentially, they should not reveal their description to anyone.

Conclusions: After several minutes, ask to see a show of hands of those who believe their description to be 1) totally accurate, 2) mostly accurate, 3) somewhat accurate, or 4) totally inaccurate. Follow up with a debriefing, focusing on why deception was required, the Barnum statements, and why pseudopsychologies are not valid. The pseudopsychologies do not use research methods nor do they adhere to the values adopted by scientists. This is a variation of a number of other demonstrations of pseudopsychology's illusory validity (Ward & Grasha, 1986).

Ward, R. A., & Grasha A. F. (1986). Using astrology to teach research methods to introductory students. *Teaching of Psychology, 13*, 143-145.

Demonstration PERS 9: Tests of Personality

Objective: To expose student to the variety of personality tests.
Materials: Internet access
Procedure: Go to http://www.2h.com/Tests/personality.phtml. Have students select two of the personality tests at this site. Have each student complete the personality test and be prepared to discuss the test. Lead a discussion of the reliability and validity of the tests taken by the students.
Conclusion: The students will gain an understanding of the mechanisms of personality testing. They will also see that not all personality tests are valid or worthwhile measures.

Demonstration PERS 10: Guest Lecturer: Projective Techniques Therapist

Objective: To expose students to the Projective Techniques.
Materials: None
Procedure: Arrange for a therapist who uses projective techniques to be a guest lecturer. Projective techniques are intuitively appealing because they seem to offer the promise of being able to tap unconscious motives and personality traits. These personality techniques have not been well received by many psychologists because of their apparent lack of standardization, reliability, validity and objective scoring procedures. Ask your guest to discuss standardized procedures and scoring techniques that have been developed for the most unstructured of the projective devices, the Rorschach inkblot test. Ask students to prepare questions to pose to the guest lecturer.
Conclusions: Students will gain valuable exposure to this perspective and can have their questions about this well known test answered by your guest lecturer.

Diversity Topics

Diversity Topic 13.3: Psychological Assessment

There is a small but growing amount of literature showing how personality assessment in multilinguals differ according to the language in which the test is taken. Discuss the implications of such findings to our conceptions of personality.

Discussion/Description: First of all, these types of findings challenge our traditional notions of personality by suggesting that there is not necessarily a "core" to personality that produces stability and consistency in other cultures as it does in ours. This notion is compounded by the fact that monolingual Americans are the minority in the world in their ability to speak only one language. If people from other cultures can speak multiple languages, this points to the possibility of personality being a relatively fluid and dynamic entity, shifting and changing as languages, and presumably underlying culture, changes.

Diversity Topic 13.4: Tests

Bring a personality test to class and allow students to get a feel for it (by administering it partially, or allowing them to inspect it, etc.). Then have a discussion about potential cultural biases that underlie the construction of the test. See http://www.2h.com/Tests/personality.phtml for a large selection of personality tests.

Discussion/Description: This activity, similar to those in the chapter on intelligence, exposes students to the cultural biases and limitations of testing. Just as those biases and limitations were true for intelligence, they are also true for assessments of personality. Alternatively, this activity may be assigned as a homework assignment or as a project due at a later date.

14 Health and Stress

Chapter-at-a-Glance

Chapter Outline	Instruction Outline	Multimedia
Two Approaches to Health and Illness p. 468	Lecture Example 14.1 Learning Objective 14.1 Test Questions 1-6	Web Site http://psych.wisc.edu/faculty/pages/croberts/topic12.html Stress and Health
Theories of Stress p. 469 Hans Selye and the General Adaptation Syndrome • Richard Lazarus's Cognitive Theory of Stress	Lecture Examples 14.2, 14.23 Learning Objectives 14.2-14.3 Test Questions 7-36	Transparency HEALTH 2 Web Site http://www.w3.org/vl/Stress/ Virtual Library of Stress
Sources of Stress: The Common and the Extreme p. 473 Everyday Sources of Stress • Stress in the Workplace • Catastrophic Events and Chronic Intense Stress	Demonstration HEALTH 1 Lecture Examples 14.4, 14.5, 14.6 Journal Entry 14.1 Learning Objectives 14.4-14.10 Test Questions 37-56	Transparency HEALTH 1 Video Disc II Segment 21 Digital Image Archive PSHL001 Web Site http://www.queendom.com/soc_anx2.html Social Anxiety Test
Coping with Stress p. 478 Problem-Focused and Emotion-Focused Coping • Religion and Coping with Negative Life Events • Proactive Coping: Dealing with Stress in Advance	Lecture Example 14.17 Learning Objectives 14.11 Test Questions 57-66	Video Disc II Segment 22 Digital Image Archive PSHL002 Web Site http://www.ivf.com/stress.html Coping with Stress
Evaluating Life Stress: Major Life Changes, Hassles, and Uplifts p. 480 Holmes and Rahe's Social Readjustment Rating Scale: Adding Up the Stress Score • The Hassles of Life: Little Things Stress a Lot	Demonstration HEALTH 2, 3 Lecture Examples 14.18, 14.9 Diversity Topic 14.1 Learning Objectives 14.12-14.13 Test Questions 67-82	Digital Image Archive PSHL005 Web Site http://www.cl.uh.edu/edu/orgbeh/orgpub/survey/srs.html Holmes and Rahe's Scale

Chapter Outline	Instruction Outline	Multimedia
Health and Disease p. 483 Responding to Illness • Coronary Heart Disease: The Leading Cause of Death • Cancer: A Dreaded Disease • Health in the United States • The Immune System: An Army of Cells to Fight Off Disease • Personal Factors Reducing the Impact of Stress and Illness	**Demonstration** HEALTH 4, 5, 6, 7 **Lecture Examples** 14.10, 14.11 **Critical Thinking Opportunity** 14.1 **Diversity Topic** 14.2 **Learning Objectives** 14.14-14.17 **Test Questions** 83-121	**Transparencies** HEALTH 3-5 **Video Disc II** Segment 23 **Digital Image Archive** PSHL003, 7 **Web Site** http://www.endo-society.org/pubaffai/factshee/stressrd.htm Endocrinology and Stress-Related Disease
Your Lifestyle and Your Health p. 492 Smoking: Hazardous to Your Health • Alcohol: A Problem for Millions • Exercise: Keeping Fit Is Healthy	**Demonstration** LEARN 9 **Lecture Examples** 14.12, 14.13, 14.14 **Critical Thinking Forum** 14.1-14.2 **Learning Objectives** 14.18-14.21 **Test Questions** 122-133	**Web Site** http://www.northwesternmutual.com/games/longevity/longevity-main.html The Longevity Game

What's New in Chapter 14

New Content

- Hostility's role in stress
- Stress in the workplace

New Special Features

- New chapter opening vignette—the aftermath of Oklahoma City
- New *Try It's*
- Revised *Remember It's*

New Key Terms

- burnout

Learning Objective Questions

14.1 How do the biomedical and biopsychosocial models differ in their approaches to health and illness?
14.2 What is the general adaptation syndrome?
14.3 What are the roles of primary and secondary appraisal when a person is confronted with a potentially stressful event?
14.4 How do approach-approach, avoidance-avoidance, and approach-avoidance conflicts differ?
14.5 How do the unpredictability of and lack of control over a stressor affect its impact?

14.6   For people to function effectively and find satisfaction on the job, what nine variables should fall within their comfort zone?
14.7   What are some of the psychological and health consequences of job stress?
14.8   What is burnout?
14.9   How do people typically react to catastrophic events?
14.10 What is posttraumatic stress disorder?
14.11 What is the difference between problem-focused and emotion-focused coping?
14.12 What was the Social Readjustment Rating Scale designed to reveal?
14.13 What roles do hassles and uplifts play in the stress of life according to Lazarus?
14.14 What are the Type A and Type B behavior patterns?
14.15 What aspect of the Type A behavior pattern is most clearly linked to coronary heart disease?
14.16 What are the effects of stress and depression on the immune system?
14.17 What three personal factors are associated with health and resistance to stress?
14.18 What constitutes an unhealthy lifestyle, and how serious a factor is lifestyle in illness and disease?
14.19 Why is smoking considered the single most preventable cause of death?
14.20 What are some health risks of alcohol abuse?
14.21 What are some benefits of regular aerobic exercise?

Chapter Overview

The area of health psychology is devoted to developing ways to make people healthier primarily through the understanding of and the lessening of the impact stress has on our lives. The chapter now discusses theories of stress. The first is Hans Selye's general adaptation syndrome with the following stages: alarm, resistance, and exhaustion. These are described in detail along with criticisms of the theory. The second is Lazarus's cognitive theory of stress, which makes the distinction between primary appraisal and secondary appraisal. Sources of everyday stress include stress in the workplace, stress due to catastrophic events, and chronic stress.

Coping with stress is the next section of this chapter. It includes a discussion of problem-focused and emotion-focused coping. The authors then explore religion and coping with negative life events. Part of this section includes an exploration of proactive coping, dealing with stress in advance.

Evaluating life stress with its major life changes, hassles, and uplifts is discussed. The evaluation of stressors includes the use of scales such as the Holme's and Rahe's Social Readjustment Rating Scale (SRRS). This section then turns to the hassles of life's "little things" that cause a lot of stress, and this is followed by stress uplifts, the positive experiences in life.

Health and disease is the next topic in this chapter. First, the authors explore responding to illness and the factors that effect illness, such as when one becomes aware of symptoms, the conditions that lead a person to seek treatment, and the conditions that influence compliance with the prescribed regimen for healing. Second, coronary heart disease and its contributing factors are discussed. Life-style and its influence on health, particularly the concept of Type A Behavior

Pattern's relationship to increased coronary heart disease, is examined. Third, cancer and its effects on the American population are explained and the effects of personality and stress on cancer rates are discussed. The text then describes variations in the quality of health and the leading health risk factors among different cultural and ethnic groups in the United States. An in-depth discussion of stress and how it impacts the immune system and contributes to poor health and illnesses concludes this section.

Personal factors and how they can reduce the impact of stress and illness are then explored in depth. The factors include optimism and pessimism, psychological hardiness, and social support.

Lifestyle has a dramatic influence on health through habits like smoking and excessive alcohol consumption. When these factors are combined with poor exercise habits, illness is even more likely. The importance of regular aerobic exercise is stressed. The chapter concludes with an examination of exercise and stress management.

Key Terms

aerobic exercise (p. 495)
alarm stage (p. 470)
approach-approach conflict (p. 472)
approach-avoidance conflict (p. 427)
avoidance-avoidance conflict (p. 472)
biomedical model (p. 468)
biopsychosocial model (p. 468)
controlled drinking (p. 495)
coping (p. 478)
decision latitude (p. 476)
emotion-focused coping (p. 478)

exhaustion stage (p. 470)
general adaptation syndrome (GAS) (p. 470)
hardiness (p. 491)
hassles (p. 482)
health psychology (p. 468)
lymphocytes (p. 488)
posttraumatic stress disorder (PTSD) (p. 476)
primary appraisal (p. 470)
proactive coping (p. 479)
problem-focused (p. 478)
psychoneuroimmunology (p. 489)

resistance stage (p. 470)
secondary appraisal (p. 472)
sedentary lifestyle (p. 484)
Social Readjustment Rating Scale (SRRS) (p. 480)
social support (p. 491)
stress (p. 469)
stressor (p. 470)
Type A behavior pattern (p. 484)
Type B behavior pattern (p. 484)
uplifts (p. 483)

Annotated Lecture Outline

A. Two Approaches to Health and Illness

Lecture Example

Lecture Example 14.1: Biomedical and Biopsychosocial Models

Develop a lecture on the similarities and differences in the two models based on the definition in the text. Use http://psychweb.syr.edu/sbm/sisterorg.html as a reference.

B. Theories of Stress

Lecture Examples

Lecture Example 14.2: Strain, Not Stress

Hans Selye coined the term *stress*. However, on reflection, he claims that because English was his second language, he incorrectly used the word stress. A better, more descriptive word in his judgment is *strain*. For more on Hans Selye see http://www.stressdoctor.com/selye.htm.

Lecture Example 14.3: Approach-Avoidance Conflicts

Life consists of many decisions that are difficult to make because there are good points and bad points to each alternative. These decisions represent multiple approach-avoidance conflicts. For example, take the decision of whether to marry a certain individual. On one hand, marriage has its benefits (approach factors), such as love, security, affiliation, and sex. However, marriage also has its drawbacks (avoidance factors), such as feelings of being tied down, giving up one's ability to change relationships easily, increased responsibility, and fear of a stale relationship. Ask the students for other examples of approach-avoidance conflicts.

C. Sources of Stress: The Common and the Extreme

Classroom Demonstrations and Handouts

Demonstration HEALTH 1: Exploring Stressful Life Events

Objective: To give students an opportunity to explore stressful life events through personal contact.
Materials: None
Procedure: Ask students to interview someone who has recently experienced a stressful life event (that is, injury or illness, marriage, divorce, retirement, pregnancy and birth, moving, etc.). The interview should focus on psychological effects, physical reactions, and coping strategies. What advice does the interviewee have for people about to experience the same event? These interviews should generate lively discussion.
Conclusions: Students become more familiar with the reality of stress and the consequences even positive stress can have. Use http://www.caper.com.au/adultsurvresult.htm as a reference.

Lecture Examples

Lecture Example 14.4: Examples of High Demand/Low Control Jobs

Researchers have found that jobs with high demand but low control are most stressful. One study found that the most stressful occupations (using stress-related illness as the measure) include construction workers, secretaries, laboratory technicians, waiters and waitresses, machine operators, farm workers, and painters.

Lovato, C. Y. (1990). Maintaining employee participation in workplace health promotion programs. *Health Education Quarterly, 17,* 73-88.

Smith, M., Colligan, M., Horning, R. W., & Hurrel, J. (1978). *Occupational comparison of stress-related disease incidence.* Cincinnati: Cincinnati National Institute for Occupational Safety and Health.

Lecture Example 14.5: Stress in the Workplace

An issue of the *American Psychologist* (Vol. 45, Oct. 1990) focused on stress in the workplace. One article (Sauter, Murphy, & Hurrell, 1990) discusses the National Institute for Occupational Safety and Health's proposal to address the effects of workplace stress. The report emphasizes improving working conditions and making mental health services available to employees. It suggests examining workload, work pace, work schedule, and career security factors as ways to reduce stress. Another important component is job content; according to the authors, "...narrow, fragmented, invariant, and short-cycle tasks that provide little stimulation, allow little use of skills or expression of creativity, and have little intrinsic meaning for workers have been associated with job dissatisfaction and poor mental health." Therefore, one strategy for alleviating workplace stress would be to provide "...meaning, stimulation, and an opportunity to use skills." For more on workplace stress, see http://unum.com/dislab/insight41/swork.htm.

Keita, G. P., & Jones, J. M. (1990). Reducing adverse reaction to stress in the workplace: Psychology's expanding role. *American Psychologist, 45,* 1137-1141.

Sauter, S. L., Murphy, L. R., & Hurrell, J. J., Jr. (1990). Prevention of work-related psychological disorders: A national strategy proposed by the National Institute for Occupational Safety and Health (NIOSH). *American Psychologist, 45,* 1159-1161.

Lecture Example 14.6: Posttraumatic Stress Disorder

Use http://www.queendom.com/ptsd.html to develop a lecture on posttraumatic stress disorder. The range of events that trigger posttraumatic stress disorder is thought to be much broader in women than in men, and, in fact, the disorder is thought to be more prevalent in women than in men. Ask students to speculate on possible reasons for these differences. Could learning histories or genetic differences explain the ability to deal with stressors?

D. Coping with Stress

Lecture Examples

Lecture Example 14.7: Stress and Coping

Use http://www.yorku.ca/faculty/academic/schwarze/stress.htm to develop a theory-based lecture on stress and coping.

E. Evaluating Life Stress: Major Life Changes, Hassles, and Uplifts

Classroom Demonstrations and Handouts

Demonstration HEALTH 2: The Social Readjustment Rating Scale

Objective: To allow students to take the SRRS and to determine the amount of change in their lives.
Materials: **Handout HEALTH 2**
Procedure: Ask students to determine which of the items in the scale were experienced in the last twelve months. Each item may be counted only once, even if it occurred more often. Next, they should tally the "life change units." There appears to be a relationship between the score on this scale and the likelihood of illness in the immediate future. Rahe (1972) found that scores between 0 to 100 were associated with 1.4 illnesses reported in a six-month period. Scores between 300 and 500 and between 500 to 600 were correlated with 1.9 and 2.1 illnesses, respectively. An ancillary activity is to take the scale and ask students to assign a value to indicate their own judgments of stress. Tell students that the most stressful event or situation should be given a 100 and anything that is half as stressful is given a 50. Take an informal survey of the events and situations judged to be the top ten stressors by your students.
Conclusions: You should reiterate some of the criticisms that have been levied against the scale, especially the role of cognitive appraisal. You should also caution students of the inappropriateness of making cause-effect statements with correlations. The scale is often misused to make "cause-effect" predictions of health and illness. Use http://www.cl.uh.edu/edu/orgbeh/orgpub/survey/srs.html to take the SRRS and have it scored.

Holmes, T. H., & Rahe, R. H. (1967). The social readjustment rating scale. *Journal of Psychosomatic Research, 11*, 214.

Rahe, R. H. (1972). Subjects' recent life changes and their near-future illness reports. *Annals of Clinical Research, 5*, 250-265.

Demonstration HEALTH 3: Students' Daily Hassles

Objective: To determine students' hassles.
Materials: **Handout HEALTH 3**

Procedure: Allow students to work in groups to generate a list of hassles that are present in their lives using **Handout HEALTH 3**. Students should be as specific as possible in identifying the hassle. Next, ask students to rank order the hassles in terms of importance to them. (You may modify this activity, by administering to students the Hassles Scale which consists of 117 annoying and irritating events [Kanner et al., 1981].)

Conclusions: As each group gives examples of hassles, identify any recurring hassles that are common to most students.

Kanner, A. D., Coyne, J. C., Schaefer, C., & Lazarus, R. S. (1981). Comparison of two modes of stress measurement: Daily hassles and uplifts versus major life events. *Journal of Behavioral Medicine, 4,* 1-39.

Lecture Examples

Lecture Example 14.8: Avoiding Stress?

Avoidance is not the key to coping with stress. In fact, some stress is actually quite adaptive and motivating. Stress is here to stay; as Hans Selye said, "To be totally without stress is to be dead." Strategies that help us to manage our reactions to stress are the best and most effective ways to cope. For more on Hans Selye, see http://www.stressdoctor.com/selye.html.

Lecture Example 14.9: Planning Your Life

If we are to accept the basic premise of the Social Readjustment Rating Scale, we should heed the advice of Lloyd et al. (1980). They suggest that for people to have control over the major events of their lives, the events should be spread out over time. For example, don't marry, move, buy a house, change jobs, change churches, and change social activities all in one year!

Lloyd, C., Alexander, A. A., Rice, D. G., & Greenfield, N. S. (1980). Life change and academic performance. *Journal of Human Stress, 6,* 15-25.

Diversity Topic

Diversity Topic 14.1: Stressors

Have students make their own rank orders of the life events listed in the SRRS table (**Handout HEALTH 2**) in order of severity of stress they think the events produce. Then, have a discussion about the possible differences. See how these differences appear to be related to in terms of student characteristics, such as SES, culture, ethnicity, gender, etc.

Discussion/Description: This activity accomplishes several goals. First, it would allow the students to act upon this material, rather than be passive recipients of this information. Second, it would allow them to see the degree to which this material is relevant to themselves. Third, it would allow students and instructors to see whether there are possible cultural differences in the nature of stress.

F. Health and Disease

Classroom Demonstrations and Handouts

Demonstration HEALTH 4: Exploring the Effects of Illness

Objective: To give students an opportunity to explore the effects of illness through personal contact.
Materials: None
Procedure: Ask students to interview someone who is recovering (or has recently recovered) from an illness or injury. The interview should explore the person's attitudes over the course of the injury or illness, beginning with symptoms and diagnosis through treatment and recovery. How did the person's attitudes change during this period? What was the nature of the patient-physician relationship? Did the patient follow medical advice completely? Was there some advice they thought to be less helpful or actually useless? What are the long-term effects of the illness or injury (both psychological and physical)?
Conclusions: This experience should help students come to a better sense of the reality of injury and illness, especially if they have interviewed someone with a severely debilitating illness or injury.

Demonstration HEALTH 5: Health Beliefs and Coping

Objective: To test students' vulnerability to stress.
Materials: **Handout HEALTH 5**
Procedure: Distribute **Handout HEALTH 5** to students and have them complete the form. They should be able to use the instructions at the bottom of the handout to compute their stress-vulnerability score.
Conclusions: Ask students to discuss how accurate they believe this brief assessment actually is. Should some of them be having serious, stress-related illnesses? Why or why not?

Demonstration HEALTH 6: Guest Lecturer on Emergency Room Stress

Objective: To expose students to the individuals who work in stressful environments.
Materials: None
Procedure: Arrange to have an emergency room doctor or nurse guest lecture to your class. Ask students to prepare questions to pose to the guest lecturer.
Conclusions: Students will gain valuable exposure to a career choice that involves tremendous stress.

Demonstration HEALTH 7: Type A Personality

Objective: To expose students to a Type A Personality Test.
Materials: None
Procedure: Go to http://www.queendom.com/typea2.html. Ask students to take the Type A Personality Test at the above site before your lecture on Type A Personality and Health.

Conclusions. You will have a chance to discuss the range of score that students achieve and types of intervention methods available at your school that can help change risk factors for these scores.

Lecture Examples

Lecture Example 14.10: Seeking Medical Care

Mechanic (1978) has found that the nature of an illness may contribute to how one responds to the illness. The more perceptible and obvious the symptoms, the more likely it is that medical care will be sought. If the symptom is thought to be severe, the individual will probably seek care. (Of course, this perception of the patient's own symptoms might not match the judgment of a trained professional.) The third factor is the degree to which the symptoms disrupt a person's daily activities. The fourth variable is the frequency of the symptoms. Frequent and persistent symptoms are likely to motivate a person to seek medical care. In Mechanic's view, the symptoms impart information to the subject regarding the nature of the illness.

Mechanic, D. (1978). *Medical sociology* (2nd ed.). New York: Free Press.

Lecture Example 14.11: Minority Health

The living conditions experienced by different ethnic minority groups, combined with genetic factors, lead to different health problems and require different intervention techniques appropriate to the population. For example, a study in Los Angeles County revealed sex and age adjusted mortality rates per 100,000 persons for coronary heart disease of the following groups: African Americans, 472; Whites, 429; Hispanics, 390; Japanese, 255; Chinese, 157; Koreans, 143; and Filipinos, 84. Promoting health would require an understanding of the conditions that lead to these patterns and sensitivity to the cultural reasons that may contribute to the health problems.

Castro, F. G., & Magaña, D. (1988). A course in health promotion in ethnic minority populations. In P. A. Cunningham & K. Quina, Eds.), *Teaching a psychology of people: Resources for gender and sociocultural awareness,* (pp. 94-101), Washington, DC: American Psychological Association.

Diversity Topic

Diversity Topic 14.2: Personal Factors and Compliance

Have the students rate people in their family who span a broad age range on the degree to which the family members would be willing to seek help when apparently needed and comply with treatment regimens when prescribed. Get a sampling of these results to show, hopefully, the variability that exists. Then have a discussion concerning the reasons for why this variability exists.
Discussion/Description: This activity would allow the students to apply this material to their own lives. Also, it would allow students and instructors to examine the degree to which the variability mentioned above is related to student and target person characteristics, such as personality, ethnicity, culture, age, SES, etc.

G. Your Lifestyle and Your Health

Classroom Demonstrations and Handouts

Demonstration LEARN 9: Self-Management

Objective: To apply principles of learning to one's personal life to achieve a goal.
Materials: **Handout LEARN 9a**; **Handout LEARN 9b**
Procedure: Students are to identify a specific goal that is realistic but challenging and relevant to them. Students are to attempt to apply what they have learned about regulation to change some annoying habit or to achieve a desired goal. Specific goals might include losing two pounds per week, increasing studying by ten hours a week, stopping fingernail biting, or running twenty miles per week. The students will find out that some behaviors are reactive, that is, a particular behavior's frequency changes when it is monitored, like watching what you eat. Students must indicate a goal for the week and then plot actual performance. Give students **Handout LEARN 9a** as an example and give several copies of **Handout LEARN 9b** to each student to plot their data. **Handout LEARN 9b** will provide accurate and immediate feedback to the students.
Conclusions: By using the principles of learning, students will be able to see the effects of applying the principles of this chapter to their own lives.

Lecture Examples

Lecture Example 14.12: The Need for Health Psychology

According to Knowles (1977), "Over 90 percent of us are born healthy and suffer premature death and disability only as a result of personal misbehavior and environmental conditions." See this APA site for more information http://freud.apa.org/divisions/div38/pubs.html.

Lecture Example 14.13: Improving Medical Care or Lifestyles?

The high incidence of premature death leads most people to believe that dramatic changes are needed to improve the delivery of health care, such as more doctors or more hospital beds. It appears, however, that most premature deaths are due to lifestyle, not to the inadequacy of health care. In the case of automobile fatalities, pathological lifestyles account for 75 percent of these fatalities; only 5 percent are due to the health-care system. Overall it is believed that behavioral pathogens (e.g., personal habits, lifestyles) are responsible for nearly 50 percent of all premature deaths and that smoking and excessive use of alcohol account for 20 percent of all premature deaths.

Breslow, L., Fielding, J. E., & Lave, L. B. (Eds). (1980). *Annual Review of Public Health, 1,* 1-411.

Lalonde, M. (1974). *A new perspective on the health of Canadians.* Ottawa: Canadian Government Printing Office.

Lecture Example 14.14: Health-Impairing Lifestyles

Ask students for examples of their attempts to overcome health-impairing lifestyles only to find ourselves backsliding into their old habits. Some students will volunteer that they find new lifestyles to be accompanied by new risks to their health and well-being. An example might be a smoker who switched to "smokeless" tobacco. Ask for other examples and use them for your lecture on this topic. Ask the students how their lifestyles would change if they attempted to avoid all health-risking behaviors?

15 Psychological Disorders

Chapter-at-a-Glance

Chapter Outline	Instruction Outline	Multimedia
What Is Abnormal? p. 502 Perspectives on the Causes and Treatment of Psychological Disorders • Defining and Classifying Psychological Disorders	Demonstration ABN 1, 2, 4, 6 Lecture Examples 15.1-15.7 Journal Entry 15.1 Diversity Topic 15.1 Learning Objectives 15.1-15.3 Test Questions 1-23	*Discovering Psychology: Psychopathology* *Psychology and Culture*: Ch. 40 Transparency ABN 1 Digital Image Archive PSAB001, 006, 010 Web Sites http://www.mentalhealth.com/p.html MentalHealth.Com http://uhs.bsd.uchicago.edu/dr-bob/tips/dsm4n.html DSM-IV Codes
Schizophrenia p. 507 The Symptoms of Schizophrenia: Many and Varied • Types of Schizophrenia • The Causes of Schizophrenia	Demonstration ABN 3 Lecture Examples 15.8-15.13 Critical Thinking Opportunity 15.1 Diversity Topic 15.2 Learning Objectives 15.4-15.6 Test Questions 24-47	Transparency ABN 6 Video Disc II Segment 27 Digital Image Archive PSAB008 Web Site http://www.pslgroup.com/SCHIZOPHR.HTM Doctor's guide to schizophrenia
Mood Disorders p. 512 Depressive Disorders and Bipolar Disorder: Emotional Highs and Lows • Causes of Major Depressive Disorder and Bipolar Disorder • Suicide and Gender, Race, and Age	Lecture Examples 15.14-15.16 Learning Objectives 15.7-15.9 Test Questions 48-68	*Psychology and Culture*: Ch. 41 Transparency ABN 3 Video Disc II Segment 25 Video Disc IV Segment 10 Digital Image Archive PSAB003-005, 009 Web Site http://bipolar.cmhc.com/ Bipolar Disorder

Chapter Outline	Instruction Outline	Multimedia
Anxiety Disorders: When Anxiety Is Extreme p. 519 Generalized Anxiety Disorder • Panic Disorder • Phobias: Persistent, Irrational Fears • Obsessive Compulsive Disorder	**Demonstration** ABN 5, 7, 8 **Lecture Examples** 15.17-15.20 **Learning Objectives** 15.10-15.14 **Test Questions** 69-98	**Transparencies** ABN 2, 5 **Video Disc II** Segment 26 **Digital Image Archive** PSAB002, 007 **Web Sites** http://www.sonic.net/~fredd/phobia1.html The Phobia List http://lexington-on-line.com/naf.html National Anxiety Society
Somatoform and Dissociative Disorders p. 525 Somatoform Disorders: Physical Symptoms with Psychological Causes • Dissociative Disorders: Mental Escapes	**Lecture Examples** 15.21, 15.22 **Journal Entry** 15.1 **Learning Objectives** 15.15-15.17 **Test Questions** 99-117	**Web Site** http://www.tezcat.com/~tina/dissoc.shtml Dissociation Page
Other Psychological Disorders p. 528 Sexual and Gender Identity Disorders • Personality Disorders: Troublesome Behavior Patterns	**Lecture Example** 15.23 **Lecture Example** 15.26 **Journal Entry** 15.2 **Learning Objectives** 15.18-15.19 **Test Questions** 118-128	**Web Site** http://www.healthguide.com/personality/ Personality Disorders

What's New in Chapter 15

New Content

- Negative effects of "labeling" disorders

Expanded Content

- Biological factors in etiology of schizophrenia

Organizational Changes

- The chapter has been reorganized to follow the order of DSM-IV.

New Special Features

- New *Try It*
- Revised *Remember It*s

Learning Objective Questions

15.1 What criteria might be used to differentiate normal from abnormal behavior?
15.2 What are five current perspectives that attempt to explain the causes of psychological disorders?
15.3 What is the DSM-IV?
15.4 What are some of the major positive and negative symptoms of schizophrenia?
15.5 What are the four subtypes of schizophrenia?
15.6 What are some suggested causes of schizophrenia?
15.7 What are the symptoms of major depressive disorder?
15.8 What are the extremes of mood suffered by those with bipolar disorder?
15.9 What are some suggested causes of major depressive disorder and bipolar disorder?
15.10 When is anxiety normal, and when is it abnormal?
15.11 What are the symptoms of panic disorder?
15.12 What are the characteristics of the three categories of phobias?
15.13 What do psychologists see as probable causes of phobias?
15.14 What is obsessive compulsive disorder?
15.15 What are two somatoform disorders, and what symptoms do they share?
15.16 What are dissociative amnesia and dissociative fugue?
15.17 What are some of the identifying symptoms of dissociative identity disorder?
15.18 What are the sexual and gender identity disorders?
15.19 What characteristics are shared by most people with personality disorders?

Chapter Overview

Defining abnormal behavior remains a difficult task. The criteria for defining abnormal behavior includes: how the person's culture considers behavior to be abnormal, whether the behavior causes personal distress, whether the behavior is maladaptive, whether the person is a danger to self or others, and whether the person is considered legally responsible for his or her behavior. Five perspectives on the causes and treatment of abnormal behavior are the biological, psychodynamic, learning, cognitive, and humanistic perspectives. The *Diagnostic and Statistical Manual of Mental Disorders, Fourth Edition* (the *DSM-IV*) classifies mental disorders according to major categories. The text details the major *DSM-IV* categories of mental disorder, defining symptoms and using examples.

Schizophrenia is the most serious of the mental disorders and is characterized by loss of contact with reality, hallucinations, delusions, inappropriate or flat affect, disturbances in thinking, withdrawal from normal social contacts, and other bizarre symptoms. The text then differentiates between positive and negative symptoms of schizophrenia. The types of schizophrenia currently recognized are catatonic, disorganized, paranoid, and the catch-all category of undifferentiated. A number of causes have been implicated, including genetic causes and excessive dopamine activity.

Mood disorders include major depression, seasonal affective disorder (SAD), and bipolar disorder, which includes cycles of manic and depressive behavior. The causes of mood disorders include genetic inheritance, neurotransmitter imbalances, inappropriate thought patterns, the repression of aggressive or negative feelings, and stress. To end this section, the authors examine factors that affect the causes of suicide and suicide prevention.

Anxiety disorders are distinguished by feelings of severe anxiety that can be experienced in generalized anxiety, panic disorder, phobic disorders, or obsessive compulsive disorders, marked by obsessions (ideas that will not go away) and compulsions (strong urges to repeat certain acts again and again). This section ends with a discussion of the causes of obsessive compulsive disorder.

Somatoform disorders include hypochondriasis and conversion disorder. Dissociative disorders include dissociative amnesia, dissociative fugue, and dissociative identity disorder (formerly, multiple personality). Many who suffer dissociative identity disorder were victims of extreme physical or sexual abuse as children.

The chapter then discusses sexual and gender identity disorders, and concludes with a discussion of personality disorders.

Key Terms

agoraphobia (p. 521)
antisocial personality disorder (p. 530)
anxiety (p. 519)
anxiety disorders (p. 519)
bipolar disorder (p. 515)
catatonic schizophrenia (p. 510)
compulsion (p. 523)
conversion disorder (p. 526)
delusion (p. 509)
delusion of grandeur (p. 509)
delusion of persecution (p. 509)
diathesis-stress model (p. 511)
disorganized schizophrenia (p. 510)

dissociative amnesia (p. 526)
dissociative disorder (p. 526)
dissociative fugue (p. 526)
dissociative identity disorder (p. 527)
DSM-IV (p.505)
first-degree relatives (p. 515)
gender identity disorders (p. 529)
generalized anxiety disorder (p. 520)
hallucination (p. 508)
hypochondriasis (p. 525)
inappropriate affect (p. 509)
major depressive disorder (p. 512)
manic episode (p. 515)
mood disorders (p. 512)
neurosis (p. 505)

obsession (p. 523)
obsessive compulsive disorder (OCD) (p. 523)
panic attack (p. 520)
panic disorder (p. 520)
paranoid schizophrenia (p. 510)
paraphilia (p. 529)
personality disorder (p. 529)
phobia (p. 521)
psychosis (p. 507)
schizophrenia (p. 507)
seasonal affective disorder (SAD) (p. 513)
sexual dysfunction (p. 528)
social phobia (p. 521)
somatoform disorders (p. 525)
specific phobia (p. 522)

Annotated Lecture Outline

A. What Is Abnormal?

Classroom Demonstrations and Handouts

Demonstration ABN 1: What Is Abnormal?

Objective: To expose students to the problem of identifying normal and abnormal behavior in a series of vignettes.
Materials: **Handout ABN 1**
Procedure: This activity may be done by students in groups or individually. Give each student a copy of **Handout ABN 1**. For each item, the students should indicate whether they believe the behavior described is normal or abnormal. After the handout has been completed, ask your students to identify the criterion they used to determine abnormality.
Conclusions: The identification of abnormal behavior is a difficult task. One must consider context, culture, and era among other criteria. For example, item 12 states "Luke often urinates on the street." A clear case of abnormal behavior, right? What if Luke is a Golden Retriever? What about Alana in item 11? Does it matter if Alana is Muslim and living in Saudi Arabia? For a description of "what is abnormal," see http://www.thomson.com/brookscole/psychology/brochures/dworetzky/d16c.htm.

Demonstration ABN 2: Guest Speaker on Mental Health

Objective: To expose students to authorities on the topic of mental health and to inform students of local efforts to help people in need.
Materials: None
Procedure: If you are pressed for time, consider inviting only one of the people mentioned here. Individuals to consider include a member of the local Mental Health Association, Mental Health Clinic, or University/College Counseling Center. You may even find an individual who has lived with and conquered some mental disorder (e.g., phobia, major depression) and who is willing to share their experiences with your class. This can be a most effective way to reiterate the importance of remembering that these are "real people" who suffer from the disorders.
Conclusions: Depending on your purpose for having the guest speaker, students will appreciate the personal account of overcoming mental illness or helping those with a disorder.

Demonstration ABN 4: Deviant Behavior

Objective: To have students reflect on behavior they themselves engage in that may be considered deviant.
Materials: **Handout ABN 4**
Procedure: Ask students to describe one or more of their behaviors that others (or themselves)

may consider deviant. Have them complete **Handout ABN 4**. Willing students can share with the entire class, or the class can be divided into small groups. Ask students to assess the deviance of individual behaviors. Does this mean that the student who commits this behavior is now a deviant? *Conclusions:* Students should come to the realization that deviant behavior is something that everyone does and that "deviance" is a powerful label in our society. Committing a deviant behavior does not make one abnormal or deviant. For information on *Annual Editions: Deviant Behavior*, see http://www.dushkin.com/annualeditions/0-697-37236-7.mhtml.

Demonstration ABN 6: Trip to a State Mental Hospital

Objective: To expose students to a state mental hospital.
Materials: None, or hospital consent form
Procedure: Ask for a list of individuals who would like to take a field trip to a state mental hospital. If your class is small, all interested individuals can visit. If the class is too large, you can select certain students to visit. Selecting visitors is difficult. I try to select by major or have the students write a short paragraph of why this trip would enhance their college experience or career.
Conclusions: Lead a discussion the next class day following the trip. I use the examples of behavior discussed in this period throughout the remainder of the course. Many students think this trip is the best part of the psychology class. Others base career decisions on this trip. Use this trip in conjunction with **ABN 3**, which is a trip to a private psychiatric hospital. Compare and contrast the types of treatment the clients received.

Lecture Examples

Lecture Example 15.1: Perspectives on Abnormality

In the 1500s and 1600s, great witch-hunts were common in Europe and in some American colonies as well. The official witch-hunts ended long ago, but the idea of casting out demons by exorcism is still alive and has been the theme of some popular novels and movies, such as *The Exorcist*. The oldest explanation for mental disturbances, possession by evil spirits or demons, is still firmly held by some people in our society.

Lecture Example 15.2: The Medical Model

Our culture has largely accepted the medical or disease model to explain abnormal behaviors. Give evidence of how the medical model has biased our language. For example, when you use the following terms, you are using terms from medicine: symptoms, sick, hospital, prognosis, patient, and treatment.

Lecture Example 15.3: *DSM-IV* and Its Diagnostic Criteria

The diagnostic criteria of the *DSM-IV* might be somewhat troublesome for students to understand. Get a copy of the *DSM-IV* and show that the criteria for the disorders were established by committees; in fact, open the manual to the pages listing committee membership.

Point out that, like all work done by committees, the criteria were produced with compromises. Diagnostic criteria have been changed for a specific disorder in *DSM-III-R*. In other words, nothing is written in stone when it comes to diagnostically defining abnormal behaviors. Order the DSM-IV on disk at http://www.tetondata.com/DSMFLhome.html or at http://web1.wing.net/mhc/dsm.html.

Lecture Example 15.4: "On Being Sane in Insane Places"

Rosenhan's (1973) classic study is a must for all introductory lectures. Students may be interested in further details about the quality of care received by the pseudopatients. Rosenhan found that attendants and nurses spent only about 11% of their time outside of the cage. Physicians came into the ward only 6.7 times per day. When pseudopatients approached staff members and asked direct questions about their care, psychiatrists averted their heads and walked away 71% of the time and stopped to talk only 4% of the time, while nurses walked away 88% of the time and stopped to talk only 5% of the time. See Rosenhan, D. L (1973). On Being Sane in Insane Places. *Science, 173,* 25-258, for a detailed look at the classic. For a detailed description of this article, see http://netra01.colchsfc.ac.uk/~psychlgy/rosenhan.htm.

Lecture Example 15.5: Personal Definitions of Abnormality

In your introductory lecture on abnormal behavior, explain that the definition and diagnosis of abnormal behavior necessarily involves value judgments. Raise the question *whose* values should be used in these judgments? Should society or a political party be allowed to determine the limits of normal behavior, or should such judgments be made by mental health experts?
Does society have the right to interfere with the activities of cults or other organizations whose values differ from the majority? Ask for discussion of both sides of this question.

Lecture Example 15.6: Personal Attitudes toward Psychological Disorders

When a friend complains about physical illness we are usually quick to suggest that the person see a doctor. When someone complains about psychological distress or when we see someone exhibit abnormal behaviors, we are usually quick to leave that person's company, or we are reluctant to suggest that the person seek the help of a mental health professional even if this person is a friend. What are some of the causes of these reactions to psychological problems? Are such reactions likely to change in the future, particularly after this set of lectures? Revisit this question at the end of your lectures.

Lecture Example 15.7: Prevalence Rates of Psychological Disorders

Some estimates say that perhaps as high as one-third of the U.S. population would be diagnosed as abnormal according to the *DSM-IV* criteria. Ask your students if they think this estimate is reasonable. What is the justification for their answers? Are the real figures lower or higher? One reason these estimates are difficult to formulate is that many people do not report their symptoms. What do your students think are the major differences between people who do not report symptoms and the people who do seek treatment?

Diversity Topic

Diversity Topic 15.1: Diversity and Diagnoses

Bring in the DSM-IV criteria for diagnosis of any disorder (e.g., depression). Have the class engage in a discussion on how this criteria of diagnosis is related to our own culture and society. Then draw distinctions between this relationship and other cultures to illustrate the culture-bound nature of DSM and its definitions of abnormality.

Discussion/Description: The DSM was developed to be as objective and reliable as possible. Nevertheless, it is impossible to develop a culture-free diagnostic system because culture serves as the baseline template for all of our work and products, even those that we think are culture-free. This activity challenges students and instructors to find ways in which the DSM criteria are bound to our own American culture, illustrating this close relationship. If there are people in the class experienced with other cultures, they may be able to comment on how the DSM is applicable or not to other cultures. The important aspect about this activity is that the questions are raised, not necessarily that answers are found.

B. Schizophrenia

Classroom Demonstrations and Handouts

Demonstration ABN 3: A Visit to a Private Psychiatric Facility

Objective: To expose students to the real-life setting of a private psychiatric facility and to its professionals.
Materials: None
Procedure: Arrange for your students to tour a private mental hospital or psychiatric facility in your area. Encourage your students to ask questions about the populations the facility serves, the types of therapies used, and the daily routine of the residents. Do the mental health workers tend to subscribe to the medical-biological model? Stress to your students that any patients they encounter have their right to privacy.
Conclusions: Students will now approach their study of abnormal psychology from a different perspective. They should see that there is help for individuals with behavioral and emotional problems, and they will understand that mental institutions are not dungeon-like places where straitjackets are routinely used. Use this trip in conjunction with **ABN 6**, which is a trip to a state psychiatric hospital. Compare and contrast the types of treatment the clients received.

Lecture Examples

Lecture Example 15.8: Schizophrenia—A Sane Response to an Insane World

British psychiatrist R. D. Laing has presented his most unusual notion—that schizophrenia is a sane and rational response to an insane world. In his view, the schizophrenic takes a psychological "trip," and Laing sees the trip as "valid, meaningful, and potentially beneficial—a possible growth experience through which the individual can become a better, more coping human being" (Mehr, 1983, p. 317). Apparently not many schizophrenic patients who have taken the "trip" share his view. Dory Previn (1980), who recovered from her psychosis, stated "Insanity is terrific on the 'Late Show'...but in the real world it's shit (p. 64).

Mehr, J. (1983). *Abnormal psychology.* New York: Holt, Rinehart & Winston.

Previn, D. (1980). *Bog-Trotter.* New York: Doubleday.

Lecture Example 15.9: Delusions

Some delusions are found far more frequently in schizophrenia than in other psychotic disorders. These are thought broadcasting, thought insertion, and thought withdrawal. With thought broadcasting, the individual believes that his or her thoughts are broadcast to the outside world for all to hear as they occur. Thought insertion involves the belief that another's thoughts are being inserted into one's head. In thought withdrawal, the individual believes that thoughts are being stolen or withdrawn by some mysterious force.

Lecture Example 15.10: Schizophrenic Speech and Thought Disorders

"They had an insinuating machine next door" was one patient's way of "explaining how her neighbors were bothering her" (APA, 1987, p. 402). Another schizophrenic speech disorder is clang associations, where word associations are based on rhyming or similar sounding words. One schizophrenic patient, when asked why he was hitting his head and waving his arms, replied, "That's to keep the boogers from eatin' the woogers" (Calhoun, Acocella, & Goodstein, 1977, p. 279).

American Psychiatric Association (1987). *Diagnostic and Statistical Manual of Mental Disorders.* (Third Edition—Revised). Washington D.C.: America Psychiatric Association.

Calhoun, J. F., Acocella, J. R., & Goodstein, L. D. (1977). *Abnormal psychology: Current perspectives* (2nd Ed.). New York: CRM/Random House.

Lecture Example 15.11: Schizophrenia and Dopamine

The possible link between schizophrenia and dopamine came to light in a roundabout way. Researchers found that amphetamines taken in high doses cause a significant rise in the level of dopamine in the brain, and that people abusing amphetamines often develop symptoms much like those seen in schizophrenia. Also, when schizophrenic patients are given the drug L-dopa, which the body converts into dopamine, their symptoms get worse. Furthermore, drugs found to be effective in reducing the symptoms of schizophrenia block dopamine action (Iverson, 1979; Torrey, 1983).

Iverson, L. L. (1979). The chemistry of the brain. *Scientific American, 241,* 134-147.

Torrey, E. F. (1983). *Surviving schizophrenia: A family manual.* New York: Harper & Row.

Lecture Example 15.12: Abnormal Behavior in the College Student

During your introductory lecture on defining abnormal behavior, define what constitutes deviant behavior. Ask the students for input and try to arrive at a consensus. Assign the students to engage in a public act of deviant behavior. Emphasize that the act cannot be illegal, dangerous (to the student, an observer, or the public), or against school rules. Since the students have just had your lecture on defining abnormality they should have a good idea of the types of behaviors you are expecting. Have the students go in pairs, one as the "deviant" and one as an observer who will take notes on the reactions of others in the environment. Ask the students to reverse these roles. Tell the students to concentrate on their feelings as they behave abnormally and, ask the observer, to concentrate on the reactions of others. During the next class period, lead a discussion on what constitutes deviant behavior. This is likely to be more lively and productive in eliciting insightful comments regarding people who engage in abnormal behavior.

Lecture Example 15.13: "Crazy" student

Arrange with a graduate student, GTA or trusted undergraduate to come to the first class meeting that you discuss abnormal psychology. Have the student sit in the front row of the class. During the first few minutes of the class, have the student start to act abnormally. This could include strange body movements, talking to oneself, talking to an inanimate object, or any other behaviors you might think abnormal. After several minutes of this disruptive abnormal behavior, ask the disruptive student if there is a problem. At this point have the student jump up and start to scream stereotypical, schizophrenic speech. Act concerned and ask again if there is anything you can do to help. Have the student become more agitated and run from the room. After a few minutes when the class has calmed down, explain what just happened. Ask the students how they reacted to this individual. How did they feel—afraid? Did they want to help or hide? Use this interaction when you lecture on defining abnormal behavior and schizophrenia.

Diversity Topic

Diversity Topic 15.2: Schizophrenia

Have students discuss the possible reasons for why the researchers in this section obtained the results they did, and the possible implications of such findings. What is it about African Americans that allow them to be diagnosed more as schizophrenic? What is it about Euro and Hispanic Americans that allow them to be diagnosed more frequently as depressed?
Discussion/Description: The underlying basis for this activity is the same as the previous one. Allowing the students to have a discussion on this topic will allow them to get hands on experience in dealing with material presented in the text, rather than allowing them to be passive

recipients of this type of knowledge. The findings here are interesting, and should lead to interesting discussions that touch on topics such as sociocultural contexts, cultural relativity in definitions of abnormality, cultural relativity in research on abnormality, stereotypes, and the like. Instructors will be tested on their skills in leading the discussions and to ensure that negative stereotypes do not dominate. Instructors should try to focus the discussion on what aspects of African, Hispanic, and Euro American lifestyles and cultures that may contribute to these diagnoses, or research findings.

C. Mood Disorders

Lecture Examples

Lecture Example 15.14: Depression and Suicide

Depression has been characterized as the common cold of psychopathology because of its high incidence. About 13 percent of people in the United States experience serious depression of some type. One way to introduce a lecture on depression is to point out that suicide ranks second after accidents as a cause of death among college students. An estimated 10,000 students try to commit suicide each year. Since more than half of those attempting suicide are depressed, it is important to understand the dynamics of depression. Most students already know what depression feels like if they ever felt discouraged about the future, isolated from other people, or dissatisfied with some part of their life. Most people use the words "depression" and "depressed" for minor blues, but the text primarily focuses on major depression.

Persons with mild depression experience fewer symptoms, and the depression lifts after a few hours or a few days. At the severe end is major depression, with at least four symptoms lasting for two weeks or more. It is generally thought that a genetic or physiological predisposition is a likely cause in most severe cases of major depression. In discussing suicide, Meyer and Salmon (1988) provide a portrait of the typical person who attempts suicide: an unmarried white female who had an unstable childhood with a history of stressful events. In contrast, the typical person who commits suicide is an unmarried, divorced, or widowed white male over 45-years-old with a history of physical or emotional disorders and alcohol abuse. Meyer and Salmon also provide a list of facts and fables about suicide that is useful for dispelling students' misconceptions. For example, though untrue, it is widely believed that suicide is inherited and that all suicidal individuals are mentally ill. Meyer and Salmon also discuss behavioral clues that appear to predispose an individual to suicide, as well as several suicide prevention measures at the societal and individual level.

Meyer, R., & Salmon, P. (1988). *Abnormal psychology*. Boston: Allyn and Bacon.

Lecture Example 15.15: Suicide at Holidays

"After examining 188,047 suicides occurring between 1973 and 1979—One set of holidays (Memorial Day, Thanksgiving, and Christmas) was associated with an unusually low risk of suicide before, during, and after the holiday. Another set of holidays (New Year's Day, July 4th, and Labor Day) was associated with a low risk of suicide before the holiday and a high risk just afterwards. Almost all demographic groups experienced a low risk of suicide around the holidays: whites, blacks, males, females, retired persons, and persons of working age" (Phillips and Wills, 1987).

Phillips, D. P., & Wills, J. S. (1987). A drop in suicides around major national holidays. *Suicide and Life-Threatening Behavior, 17,* 1-12.

Lecture Example 15.16: SAD PERSONS

Just one of the many tragedies of suicide is that many people will respond with disbelief, saying that the person "seemed just fine." There have been attempts to try to predict suicide using personality tests like the MMPI; these predictions are often incorrect (Clopton, Post, & Lande, 1983). Even if some effective, scientific, predictive measure were available, the general public might not know about it or, worse yet, might be unable to recall it. An acronym has been devised by Patterson, Dohn, and Patterson (1983) to summarize the risk factors of suicide: "SAD PERSONS."

- S: SEX—Females are more likely to attempt suicide, but males are more often successful.
- A: AGE—Young and old people are more likely to attempt suicide.
- D: DEPRESSION—Depression is often a precipitant in suicide.
- P: PREVIOUS ATTEMPT—A history of suicide attempts increases the risk for suicide in the future.
- E: ETHANOL ABUSE—Abuse of alcohol is found in some who commit suicide.
- R: RATIONAL THOUGHT—Not thinking clearly or rationally is a risk factor.
- S: SOCIAL SUPPORTS LACKING—Not having people to talk to and confide in increases the risk.
- O: ORGANIZED PLAN—A person who has a concrete, organized plan is more likely to attempt suicide.
- N: NO SPOUSE—Single people are at higher risk than married people.
- S: SICKNESS—Being ill puts people at high risk.

Clopton, J. R., Post, R. D., & Lande, J. (1983). Identification of suicide attempters by means of MMPI profiles. *Journal of Clinical Psychology, 39,* 868-871.

Patterson, W. M., Dohn, H., & Patterson, G. A. (1983). Evaluation of suicidal patients: The SAD PERSONS scale. *Psychometrics, 24,* 343-349.

For more information on the other depression, see http://2022.com/w&el/sad.html.

D. Anxiety Disorders: When Anxiety Is Extreme

Classroom Demonstrations and Handouts

Demonstration ABN 5: Art and Insanity

Objective: To expose students to examples of art influenced by psychological disorders.
Materials: Art pieces produced by individuals experiencing a variety of disorders (e.g., Vincent van Gogh's paintings; Munch's "The Cry")
Procedure: Present the art works to students to illustrate the effects of behavior disorders. Look at any abnormal textbook and you will probably find some very good samples.
Conclusions: Students will understand the devastating effects of psychological disorders.

Demonstration ABN 7: Writing a Case History

Objective: To provide an activity to students to strengthen their understanding of mental disorders.
Materials: None
Procedure: The students form groups of no more than five. Each group must select one of the disorder classifications (e.g., anxiety disorders) to work with. The group will develop a basic case study of some fictitious person including references to age, sex, and occupation. Then, each member of the group will choose a specific disorder to finish the case study with indications of onset and symptoms. At the next class meeting, the group is reconvened and each person reads their case.
Conclusions: This is a creative way for students to learn about these disorders. The disorders become more tangible when put in the context of an individual experiencing the relevant symptoms.

Demonstration ABN 8: Diagnosing Disorders

Objective: To challenge students to use their knowledge to make diagnoses of disorders.
Materials: Clinical audiocassettes of client-therapist interview from McGraw-Hill or Clinical Cassettes (3017 Scottsdale Road, Scottsdale AZ 85251); Summary of Major DSM-IV Categories (**Handout ABN 8**)
Procedure: In diagnosing a disorder, students are presented with case studies of individuals displaying different psychopathologies. You may wish to use actual audiotapes or just read them from a textbook or casebook (e.g., Peterson, 1989). Sometimes these case studies are presented in dialogue form; if so, have students read the therapist and patient parts. The students should summarize the presented symptoms of the client and to make a diagnosis. This activity also could also be staged as a competition between groups, complete with prizes.
Conclusions: This activity is an excellent review of disorders and their symptoms. Order the DSM-IV on disk at http://www.tetondata.com/DSMFLhome.html, or at http://web1.wing.net/mhc/dsm.html.

Peterson, C. (1989). *Casebook and study guide to accompany Abnormal Psychology*. New York: Norton.

Sue, D., Sue, D., Sue, S. (1993). *Understanding abnormal behavior*. Boston: Houghton Mifflin Company.

Lecture Examples

Lecture Example 15.17: Panic Chemistry

Research indicates a connection between panic disorder and body chemistry. It was discovered that excessive exercise could actually bring on a panic attack in some panic-disorder patients as far back as the 1940s. (Fishman & Sheehan, 1985). Why? Exercise increases the level of lactate in the blood, and panic-disorder patients are highly sensitive to the substance (Liebowitz et al., 1985).

Fishman, S. M., & Sheehan, D. V. (1985, April). Anxiety and panic: Their cause and treatment. *Psychology Today, 19*, 26-30, 32.

Liebowitz, M. R., Gorman, J. M., Fyer, A. J., et al. (1985). Lactate provocation of panic attacks. *Archives of General Psychiatry, 42*, 709-719.

Lecture Example 15.18: Simple Phobia

Seligman (1971) suggests that people are biologically prepared to fear certain objects and situations that have been a threat to humankind throughout our evolutionary history. Consequently it is easier for people to develop fears of snakes or spiders than of flowers or triangles, and such fears are more resistant to extinction. This theory has been researched fairly extensively and the laboratory studies have supported the greater resistance to extinction of fear-related stimuli (McNally, 1987). Go to http://www.sonic.net/~fredd/phobia1.html for a complete listing of phobias.

McNally, R. J. (1987). Preparedness and phobias: A review. *Psychological Bulletin, 101*, 283-303.

Seligman, M. E. P. (1971). Phobias and preparedness. *Behavior Therapy, 2*, 307-320.

Lecture Example 15.19: Blood-Injury Phobia

"Some patients with blood-injury phobia avoid urgent medical procedures that could save their lives: those who become diabetic may eschew insulin injections, and those who develop cancer may shun surgery. They avoid hospitals, sick people, or viewing medical programs on television. Some patients with blood-injury phobia are prone to syncope (faint) on hearing the word 'blood,' descriptions of surgery, the sound of ambulance sirens, or newscasts reporting disasters." Go to http://www.sonic.net/~fredd/phobia1.html for a complete listing of phobias.

Marks, I. (1988). Blood-injury phobia: A review. *American Journal of Psychiatry, 145*, 1207-1213.

Lecture Example 15.20: Trichotillomania

Between one to two million Americans suffer from an obsessive urge to pull out their hair. This urge, called *trichotillomania*, is characterized by pulling out hair found over the body, including head hair, eyelashes, arm hair, and pubic hair. The person is aware of the problem and may feel embarrassed, but he or she is unable to stop the urge to pull hair. In severe cases of trichotillomania, the individual becomes bald because of the chronic hair-pulling. Antidepressants and antiobsessive medication have been found to be effective in reducing the urge to pull hair. For a graphic picture of trichotillomania, see http://203.255.31.190/chap22/atlas/htm/22-10.htm.

E. Somatoform and Dissociative Disorders

Lecture Examples

Lecture Example 15.21: Plagiarism and Multiple Personality

There are a number of intriguing issues that arise from multiple personality. If one personality commits a crime, who goes to trial? Who goes to jail if convicted? Which personality marries? Which is granted a divorce? If one personality plagiarizes, who gets kicked out of school? Strange as it may sound, the University of Illinois at Urbana-Champaign recently faced that dilemma. *The Chronicle of Higher Education* reports that the university dismissed a student who allegedly submitted plagiarized work. The student contends in his suit against the university that he suffers from multiple personality, and that one of his other personalities committed the plagiarism without informing the dominant personality (the student).

Notebook (April 17, 1991). *The Chronicle of Higher Education*, p. A35.

Lecture Example 15.22: Reading an Account of a Multiple Personality

There are several well-written and interesting accounts of individuals with multiple personality. Consider reading one of the two most widely known examples of multiple personality: *Sybil* and *The Three Faces of Eve*. For a review of *The Three Faces of Eve*, see http://endeavor.med.nyu.edu/lit-med/lit-med-db/webdocs/webfilms/three.faces.of.ev22-film-html.

Schreiber, F. R. (1973). *Sybil*. New York: Warner Books.

Thigpen, C. & Cleckley, H. M. (1985). *The three faces of Eve*. Augusta, GA: Cleckley-Thigpen Psychiatric Assocs.

F. Other Psychological Disorders

Lecture Examples

Lecture Example 15.23: Go ask Alice

For a very informative source of answers to many questions asked by students concerning sex and sexual behavior, some normal and some not see http://www.shsl.com/internet/supcourt/0000230h.html at Columbia University.

16 Therapies

Chapter-at-a-Glance

Chapter Outline	Instruction Outline	Multimedia
Insight Therapies p. 538 Psychodynamic Therapies: Freud Revisited • Humanistic Therapies • Therapies Emphasizing Interaction with Others	**Student Chalkboard** THER 1-2 **Lecture Examples** 16.1-16.6 **Diversity Topic** 16.2 **Learning Objectives** 16.1-16.5 **Test Questions** 1-33	**Transparency** THER 1 **Digital Image Archive** PSTH001, 002a&b, 004 **Web Sites** http://plaza.interport.net/nypsan/FreudNet http://healthguide.com/Therapy/PSYCHO~1.STM Psychodynamic therapy
Behavior Therapy: Unlearning the Old, Learning the New p. 545 Behavior Modification Techniques Based on Operant Conditioning • Therapies Based on Classical Conditioning • Therapies Based on Observational Learning Theory: Just Watch This!	**Demonstration** THER 2, 3, 4 **Lecture Examples** 16.7-16.13 **Learning Objectives** 16.6-16.13 **Test Questions** 34-62	**PsychScience** Behavior Modification **Web Site** http://healthguide.com/Therapy/behaviorT.stm Behavior Therapy
Cognitive Therapies: It's the Thought That Counts p. 550 Rational-Emotive Therapy: Human Misery—The Legacy of False Beliefs • Beck's Cognitive Therapy: Overcoming "The Power of Negative Thinking"	**Demonstration** THER 6 **Lecture Example** 16.14 **Learning Objective** 16.14 **Test Questions** 63-77	**Web Site** http://healthguide.com/Therapy/COGNIT~1.STM Cognitive Therapy
The Biological Therapies p. 554 Drug Therapy: Pills for Psychological Ills • Electroconvulsive Therapy: The Controversy Continues • Psychosurgery: Cutting to Cure	**Student Chalkboard** THER 3 **Lecture Example** 16.15, 16.16, 16.17 **Critical Thinking Forum** 16.1 **Journal Entry** 16.1 **Learning Objectives** 16.15-16.21 **Test Questions** 78-102	**Web Site** http://www.ambrosia.demon.co.uk/psych/ect.htm#eol ECT Therapy Page

Chapter Outline	Instruction Outline	Multimedia
Therapies and Therapists: Many Choices p. 559 Evaluating the Therapies: Do They Work? • Mental Health Professionals: How Do They Differ? • Selecting a Therapy: Finding One That Fits • Therapy and Race, Ethnicity, and Gender	Demonstration THER 1, 5 Lecture Examples 16.18-16.21 Critical Thinking Opportunity 16.1 Critical Thinking Forum 16.2-16.3 Journal Entry 16.2 Diversity Topics 16.1, 16.3 Learning Objectives 16.22-16.24 Test Questions 103-128	*Psychology and Culture*: Ch. 37, 39, 42-43 **Transparency** THER 2 **Video Disc II** Segments 28-29 **Digital Image Archive** PSTH003 **Web Sites** http://freud.tau.ac.il/~haimw/group1.html#group1 Group-psychotherapy http://www.apa.org/pubinfo/howto.html How to Choose a Psychologist

What's New in Chapter 16

New Content

- Virtual reality as therapy

New Special Features

- Revised *Remember It*

Learning Objective Questions

16.1 What are the four basic techniques of psychoanalysis, and how are they used to help disturbed patients?
16.2 What are the role and the goal of the therapist in person-centered therapy?
16.3 What is the major emphasis in Gestalt therapy?
16.4 What four problems commonly associated with major depression is interpersonal therapy designed to treat?
16.5 What are some advantages of group therapy?
16.6 What is behavior therapy?
16.7 How do behavior therapists modify behavior using operant conditioning techniques?
16.8 What behavior therapies are based on classical conditioning?
16.9 How do therapists use systematic desensitization to rid people of fears?
16.10 What is flooding?
16.11 How does exposure and response prevention help people with obsessive compulsive disorder?

16.12 How does aversion therapy rid people of a harmful or undesirable behavior?
16.13 How does participant modeling help people overcome fears?
16.14 What is the aim of rational-emotive therapy?
16.15 How does cognitive therapy help people overcome depression and anxiety disorders?
16.16 What are the three main biological therapies?
16.17 How do antipsychotic drugs help schizophrenic patients?
16.18 For what conditions are antidepressants prescribed?
16.19 How does lithium help patients with bipolar disorder?
16.20 What are some of the problems with drug therapy?
16.21 For what purpose is electroconvulsive therapy (ECT) used, and what is its major side effect?
16.22 What is psychosurgery, and for what problems is it used?
16.23 What different types of mental health professionals conduct psychotherapy?
16.24 What therapy, if any, has proved to be the most effective in treating mental disorders?
16.25 Why is it important to consider multicultural variables in the therapeutic setting?

Chapter Overview

The chapter covers the following areas of therapy: insight therapies, behavior therapies, cognitive behavior therapies, and biological therapies. The insight therapies include psychodynamic, humanistic, and Gestalt therapy. Therapies emphasizing interactions with others include interpersonal, family, and group therapies. Psychodynamic therapies depend on psychoanalytic theory, uncovering unconscious motivations that have arisen as a result of hidden conflicts and unresolved conflicts or trauma from childhood. Humanistic therapy is focused on the person and the person's desire for health and self-actualization. Carl Rogers's concept of person-centered therapy is thoroughly described, recognizing that many psychotherapists follow the basic tenets of this approach today. The work of Fritz Perls in Gestalt therapy is also examined as a method for getting in touch with one's feelings. In interpersonal therapy, which has proven effective in the treatment of depression, the therapist and the patient focus on interpersonal conflicts that have contributed to the depression, and the family is engaged in the treatment. Family and marital therapy is focused on healing relationships (among family members or between spouses), whereas group therapy works on individual problems in a setting with others who have experienced similar problems.

A variety of behavior therapies have been developed that apply principles of classical conditioning, operant conditioning, and/or observational learning theory to deal with behavior problems. Behavior modification techniques based on operant conditioning include the use of token economies, time out (in which an individual is removed from a reinforcing situation), and stimulus satiation. Techniques based on classical conditioning include the use of systematic desensitization, flooding, exposure and response prevention, and aversion therapy. Techniques based on observational learning involve modeling and are based on the belief that social skills can be acquired and fears can be overcome by observing others undertake what might be considered frightening tasks.

Cognitive behavior therapies include rational-emotive therapy and Aaron Beck's cognitive therapy. Rational-emotive therapy is confrontational, designed to challenge clients' irrational beliefs and unrealistic expectations as the real cause of their problems. Beck's cognitive therapy helps patients recognize their own automatic thoughts that are causing them misery.

Biological therapies include the use of drugs, which is the most common biological therapy, and the use of electroconvulsive therapy (ECT) and psychosurgery. The authors describe antipsychotic drugs, antidepressant drugs, lithium, and minor tranquilizers.

The chapter concludes with a comparison of the effectiveness of the different therapies and an examination of the research supporting the evaluation. The authors provide helpful insights to issues surrounding race, ethnicity, and gender since these qualities may affect the success of various therapies, and the importance of finding a compatible therapist. The chapter ends with a summary and comparison of major approaches to therapy.

Key Terms

antidepressants (p. 555)
antipsychotic drugs (p. 554)
automatic thoughts (p. 552)
aversion therapy (p. 549)
behavior modification (p. 545)
behavior therapy (p. 545)
biological therapy (p. 554)
clinical psychologist (p. 561)
cognitive therapy (p. 553)
directive therapy (p. 541)
electroconvulsive therapy (ECT) (p. 557)
exposure and response

prevention (p. 548)
family therapy (p. 543)
flooding (p. 548)
free association (p. 539)
Gestalt therapy (p. 541)
group therapy (p. 543)
insight therapy (p. 538)
interpersonal therapy (IPT) (p. 542)
lithium (p. 556)
lobotomy (p. 558)
nondirective therapy (p. 541)
participant modeling (p. 550)
person-centered therapy (p. 540)

psychiatrist (p. 561)
psychoanalysis (p. 539)
psychoanalyst (p. 561)
psychodrama (p. 544)
psychosurgery (p. 558)
psychotherapy (p. 538)
rational-emotive therapy (p. 551)
resistance (p. 539)
self-actualization (p. 540)
stimulus satiation (p. 545)
systematic desensitization (p. 547)
time out (p. 545)
token economy (p. 545)
transference (p. 539)

Annotated Lecture Outline

A. Insight Therapies

Classroom Demonstrations and Handouts

Student Chalkboard THER 1: Comparing Psychotherapeutic Approaches: Chart I

Student Chalkboard THER 2: Comparing Psychotherapeutic Approaches: Chart II

Lecture Examples

Lecture Example 16.1: Historical Overview

Describe the treatment of the mentally ill throughout history. Each era has had particular notions about etiology and treatment methods. One unusual method was trephination; it involved boring a hole into the skull of the individual. Exorcism and other ritualistic ceremonies were commonly practiced as forms of treatment. For more information of the early history of psychology and for a timetable of significant events in psychology from 1846 to 1935, see http://paradigm.soci.brocku.ca/~lward/TIME/TIME_PSY.HTML.

Reisman, J. M. (1976). *A history of clinical psychology.* New York: Irvington.

Sue, D., Sue, D., & Sue, S. (1993). *Understanding abnormal behavior* (4th ed.). Boston: Houghton Mifflin.

Lecture Example 16.2: Countertransference

The text mentions that a patient may come to develop strong feelings or attitudes toward his or her analyst. Freud believed that this transference is a critical part of the analysis. What is equally significant and potentially harmful is the analyst's feelings for the patient, called countertransference. Freud warned his colleagues about the dangers of countertransference and argued for maintaining distance from the patient. Becoming actively involved and expressing concern and support may hinder the therapy process, according to Freud. For more on countertransference, see http://www.wawhite.org/tct.html.

Davison, G. C., & Neale, J. M. (1990). *Abnormal psychology* (5th ed.). New York: John Wiley & Sons.

Lecture Example 16.3: Psychoanalysis vs. Psychotherapy

Most students will confuse the terms "psychoanalysis" and "psychotherapy" and will use them interchangeably. Make sure you stress the differences between the two: psychoanalysis is a form of psychotherapy, and other forms of psychotherapy bear very little resemblance to psychoanalysis.

Lecture Example 16.4: Other Forms of Therapy

There are many more forms of therapy available. For example, you may discuss self-help as a method in which people in need learn to help themselves or turn to nonprofessionals for assistance. Another form of self-help, called bibliotherapy, involves reading as a therapeutic approach. In fact, there is such a huge market for self-help material that many bookstores have special sections marked "Self-improvement" or "Self-help." Another form of therapy is art therapy, in which the client creates art through painting, sculpturing, or creative writing. In music therapy clients, play instruments or merely listen to music. For a listing of books on bibliotherapy, see http://www.noble.mass.edu/nobchild/biblio.htm.

Carson, R. C., Butcher, J. N., & Coleman, J. C. (1998). *Abnormal psychology and modern life.* (10th ed.)Glenview, IL: Scott, Foresman and Company.

Lecture Example 16.5: Group Therapies

Group therapy can be divided into four classes. First, there are groups that provide support for people who are friends or relatives of people with various problems (such as Alateen, a group for children of alcoholic parents). Second are groups that help people cope with physical or mental disorders (such as AIDS support groups). Third are groups that deal with addictive behaviors (such as Overeaters Anonymous, Narcotics Anonymous, and Gamblers Anonymous). Fourth are groups that help people cope with life transitions or crises (such as groups for widows or single parents). For more on Al-Anon and Alateen, see http://www.al-anon.alateen.org/.

Lecture Example 16.6: Symptom Substitution

For years, many Insight therapists have believed that treating the symptoms of a problem (as the Behavior Therapy has done) may help the client get rid of the symptoms but not the underlying problem itself. They maintain that removing a symptom will only result in another symptom appearing (symptom substitution) because the original problem still exists. Behavior therapists, on the other hand, believe that the behavior itself is the problem and seek to change that behavior. Research on this question tends to support the behaviorist position, as most studies show that overall functioning improves after the alteration of a specific behavior.

Diversity Topic

Diversity Topic 16.2: Family and Community Psychotherapy

How important is it to take into account the contexts within which behavior occur? Can individual-based psychotherapy prove to be successful when an individual returns to the family, community, or social context that reinforced the deviant behavior in the first place? What do the students think?
Discussion/Description:
This discussion will allow students and the instructor to consider the important question of how important it is to take into account the contexts within which behavior occurs. Possible responses will range from those who suggest that context means nothing to responses that suggest context means everything. An assessment and incorporation of context, of course, is exactly the message that is given by cross-cultural and multi-cultural approaches in psychology, as these approaches attempt to understand human behavior within contexts. Regardless of the outcome of this debate, simply engaging in this discussion is a success.

B. Behavior Therapy: Unlearning the Old, Learning the New

Classroom Demonstrations and Handouts

Demonstration THER 2: Anxiety Hierarchy

Objective: To construct an anxiety hierarchy.
Materials: **Handout THER 2**
Procedure: After reading about therapies based upon classical conditioning, have students choose something that makes them anxious. Ideas might include test anxiety, snakes, visits to the dentist, speaking before large groups, or asking someone for a date. Suggest that they construct an anxiety hierarchy for the experience they have chosen using **Handout THER 2.** After they have listed twelve scenes, ordered from least anxiety-provoking to most anxiety-provoking, present a description of the progressive relaxation technique. Eison recommends using a commercially prepared tape of relaxation training. Encourage students to use relaxation techniques to substitute a relaxed response for an anxious response, starting with the least anxious scene and moving gradually up to the most anxious scene. Direct the students to go back down one or two scenes once they feel anxiety, and then move up again when relaxed.
Conclusions: The components of systematic desensitization will become clearer as students relate them to a real and personal situation. As they practice systematic desensitization, students may experience a positive outcome as well. For a brief discussion of anxiety hierarchy, see http://psy1.clarion.edu/jms/cptanxhierarch.html.

Eison, J. (1987). Using systematic desensitization and rational emotive therapy to treat test anxiety. In V. P. Makosky, L. G. Whittemore, and A. M. Rogers (Eds.), *Activities handbook for the teaching of psychology* (Vol. 2). Washington, D.C.: American Psychological Association.

Demonstration THER 3: Guest Speaker on Behavior Modification

Objective: To inform students of applications of learning theory to real-life problems.
Materials: None
Procedure: Invite someone from the community who uses behavior modification in their work to speak to the class. The speaker may be a behaviorally-oriented psychologist, teacher, counselor, or group home manager. Ask the speaker to comment on the type of clients served by the techniques.
Conclusions: The students will see the relevancy of learning theory to real-world concerns and problems.

Demonstration THER 4: Self Behavior Modification

Objective: To allow students to use learning theory with real-life problems.
Materials: None
Procedure: Have each student decide on a simple behavior he or she would like to change, such

as smoking, not studying enough, eating too much, or eating junk food. Have each student develop a very simple behavior modification program to modify this behavior. Emphasize that positive reinforcement is preferable to punishment. The students could write a short paper detailing this effort.

Conclusions: Have student volunteers read the summary of their papers. Discuss with the class the principles of behavior modification demonstrated in each case. Correct any misinformation or errors in the technique. Discuss the reinforcers and why the individual program succeeded or failed.

Lecture Examples

Lecture Example 16.7: Behavior Therapy Is Not Brainwashing

Behavior therapy has been plagued by a negative public image. In fact, within a period of five years, from 1973 to 1977, behavior therapy was portrayed in 27 articles in the *New York Times* as psychosurgery, brainwashing, and torture. Not surprisingly, college students determined that it was appropriate only for society's outcasts, such as prisoners or the mentally retarded, and not for normal children. Woolfolk, Woolfolk, and Wilson (1977) found that when a video of a classroom token economy was called an example of behavior therapy, subjects rated it more negatively than when the video was labeled a technique of humanistic education. In further research, Kazdin and Cole (1981) contended that the negative bias against behavior therapy was due to content rather than labeling. If behavior therapy is to remain a force in mainstream psychology, it must energetically respond to the negative beliefs the public has about its techniques and must focus on its effectiveness.

Kazdin, A. E., & Cole, P. M. (1981). Attitudes and labeling biases toward behavior modification: The effects of labels, content, and jargon. *Behavior Therapy, 12,* 55-68.

Woolfolk, R. L., Woolfolk, A. E., & Wilson, G. T. (1977). A rose by any other name: Labeling bias and attitudes toward behavior modification. *Journal of Consulting and Clinical Psychology, 45,* 184-191.

Lecture Example 16.8: Applications of Operant Conditioning

Operant conditioning has been used to treat an eating disorder that involves repeated regurgitation. The patient was a chronically sick 9-month-old infant who weighed only nine pounds. Researchers noticed that the child tensed his abdomen right before vomiting; at that moment a tone was sounded followed by a mild electric shock to the leg. The shocks were given at one-second intervals and continued until the vomiting stopped. After several pairings the infant no longer vomited. A one-year follow-up revealed that the infant had experienced a 26 percent gain in weight.

Lecture Example 16.9: In Vivo vs. Traditional Systematic Desensitization

In vivo exposure to the feared object may be used in systematic desensitization. Instead of imagining the steps in the anxiety hierarchy, the client actually experiences the steps in real situations. This has generally been effective in treating phobias. Use http://www.magma.ca/~kuvasz/fear.htm to help develop your lecture on this topic.

Lecture Example 16.10: Aversion Therapy

Alcoholism has been treated using aversion therapy, based on classical conditioning. A drug called Antabuse, which interacts with consumed alcohol to cause intense nausea and vomiting, is given to the alcoholic. Antabuse has no effects as long as the alcoholic abstains from drinking alcohol. The alcoholic learns to associate the taste of alcohol and related cues (CS) with the reactions of vomiting and nausea (UCR); the UCS is the combination of the drug and alcohol. In time, the individual develops an aversion to drinking alcohol. The same principle may be applied to smoking-cessation treatment. An electric shock when a smoker smokes or touches a cigarette has been used. A more effective technique called rapid smoking involves instructing the smoker to inhale on a cigarette every six to eight seconds until it is impossible to continue. Aversion therapy has also been used with homosexuals seeking therapy to change their sexual orientation. The basic procedure is to present an aversive stimulus contingent upon penile volume to pictorial stimuli. For a discussion of another use of aversion therapy with the disorder autism, see http://www.judgerc.org/Documents/Aversives/MediaCoverage/NPRTranscript.html.

Davison, G., & Neale, J. (1990). *Abnormal psychology.* New York: John Wiley & Sons.

Sue, D., Sue, D., & Sue, S. (1993). *Understanding abnormal behavior* (4th ed.). Boston: Houghton Mifflin Company.

Lecture Example 16.11: Preparing for Hospitalization

Observational learning can be used to prepare children for surgery or other invasive medical procedures. Children scheduled for elective surgery participated in a study examining the effectiveness of a film depicting a peer being hospitalized. The film shows the procedures and the anxiety they generate in the model, who ultimately overcomes and copes with the negative emotional state. Children who viewed the film displayed significantly less anxiety prior to and following the surgery (Melamed and Siegel, 1975).

Melamed, B. G., & Siegel, L. J. (1975). Reduction of anxiety in children facing hospitalization and surgery by use of filmed modeling. *Journal of Consulting and Clinical Psychology, 43,* 511-521.

Pinto, R. P., & Hollandsworth, J. G., Jr. (1989). Using videotape modeling to prepare children psychologically for surgery: Influence of parents and costs versus benefits of providing preparation services. *Health Psychology, 8,* 79-95.

Lecture Example 16.12: Systematic Desensitization

After your introductory lectures on systematic desensitization, the students will understand the rationale underlying the technique of systematic desensitization. However, these concepts and principles are acquired more easily and are retained more efficiently if the students have been actively involved in the material.

Have your class actually devise a hierarchy of anxiety-producing items for a systematic desensitization case to make the material more meaningful. For an example, see http://www.healthguide.com/Therapy/sysdesens.htm. You can then present a fictitious case to the class, or you can ask for student volunteers who have phobias that they would not mind sharing. The latter alternative tends to elicit greater participation because one of the students is highlighted and directly involved. After the hierarchy has been constructed, simulate how the technique of deep muscle relaxation is taught, as well as a typical treatment session. If you are not an expert in this area, arrange for a guest lecture on this topic.

Lecture Example 16.13: Biofeedback

Being hooked up to a biofeedback unit and being able to control their own physiological processes will help students understand this technique. Try to locate one that you can borrow at your own institution or contact a private practice psychologist.

After a brief session in which it may take several trials for your subjects to become used to the equipment and begin to be able to approximate the desired response you can, discuss the problems with calibration of this equipment. You can also discuss the problem of signal/noise in this procedure. This would also be a good place to introduce the lie detector used by police and to discuss how individuals can learn to "beat" the lie detector.

C. Cognitive Therapies: It's the Thought That Counts

Classroom Demonstrations and Handouts

Demonstration THER 6: Irrational Beliefs and Cognitive Errors

Objective: To involve students by examining irrational beliefs and cognitive errors common in test taking.
Materials: None
Procedure: Eison (1987) has developed a listing of irrational beliefs based upon Rational Emotive Therapy that are typical of the types of thoughts students experience while taking examinations. Present these irrational beliefs to students and ask them to develop more rational alternatives, which Eison provides. Moreover, ask students to look at Beck's cognitive-behavior therapy for depression, specifically the examples of illogical thinking presented in the textbook. Ask students to develop examples of self-statements based upon these tendencies that lead to depression.
Conclusions: Although not a substitute for professional counseling, it may alert students to possible causes of and solutions to test anxiety. For more on cognitive-behavioral therapy, see http://www.gallaudet.edu/~11mgourn/cbt.html.

> Eison, J. (1987). Using systematic desensitization and rational emotive therapy to treat test anxiety. In V. P. Makosky, L. G. Whittemore, and A. M. Rogers (Eds.), *Activities handbook for the teaching of psychology* (Vol 2). Washington, D.C.: American Psychological Association.

Lecture Example

Lecture Example 16.14: Beck and Ellis

Use http://www.gallaudet.edu/~11mgourn/cbt.html to develop a lecture on Beck and Ellis and their approaches to Cognitive-Behavioral therapy.

D. The Biological Therapies

Classroom Demonstrations and Handouts

Student Chalkboard THER 3: Psychopharmacological Drugs

Lecture Example

Lecture Example 16.15: Early ECT

Back in the dark ages it was widely believed that severely disturbed people could somehow be frightened or shocked back to sanity. Early "therapists" used a wide range of "shocking" methods. Patients were seized in the middle of the night and dumped into icy water, frightened with unexpected loud noises, and terrified by numerous inventive techniques such as the "spinning chair."

Lecture Example 16: Unilateral ECT, a More Modern Approach

A newer technique of unilateral ECT, in which current is administered to only one hemisphere of the brain, is an attempt to minimize the negative effect of memory disturbance. At present, the data concerning this technique are mixed. While some research supports the idea that memory disruption is lessened, it also appears that unilateral ECT may be less effective than bilateral ECT in alleviating depression. For many links on this controversial topic, see http://www.i1.net/~juli/studies.html.

Lecture Example 16.17: Effectiveness of Drug Therapies

Tell the students that there are several individuals in the classroom who are currently on drug therapies to modify their behavior. You could even be one of them. For each type of drug therapy presented in the text, there is considerable debate over its effectiveness and safety. Ask students to speculate on why such debates are so difficult to resolve. How can the medical community assure the general population that drug therapies are safe and effective? What are the methods used to assess the therapeutic effectiveness of drug therapies? How do your students react to the suggestion that just as many (minor) psychological problems go into remission without therapeutic drug intervention as with it?

E. Therapies and Therapists: Many Choices

Classroom Demonstrations and Handouts

Demonstration THER 1: Psychotherapists

Objective: To present students with the chance to question professional psychotherapists.
Materials: None
Procedure: Ask psychotherapists to come to your class to discuss their work. Invite therapists from the major theoretical orientations; in fact, choosing therapists with contrasting orientations can be especially effective in highlighting differing points of view. Encourage your students to ask questions about techniques, the importance of psychological tests, training, and issues of effectiveness.
Conclusions: The material from the lecture and text will be reinforced as your students listen to these mental health professionals.

Demonstration THER 5: Role-Playing: Therapists

Objective: To expose students to the process used by therapists.
Materials: A prepared set of case studies describing behaviors of psychiatric patients or disturbed normal individuals (abnormal psychology texts or case books are a good source)
Procedure: Have the students work in small groups to develop a therapy session. Have the students diagnose each case according to the categories discussed in the text. Let the individual groups present the role playing to the entire class.
Conclusions: Students will be exposed to the different types of therapies and grain insight into what to expect if they are ever in need of therapy.

Lecture Examples

Lecture Example 16.18: Training Psychologists to Prescribe Drugs

In treating behavioral disorders, psychologists must rely on techniques that are not pharmacological. That may be changing, at least in the military. A plan was recently proposed to the U.S. Department of Defense to train military psychologists to prescribe psychotropic drugs. There would be a 2-month training period followed by a year of supervision. One reason for this apparent departure from tradition is the significant shortage of psychiatrists in the military. By allowing psychologists to prescribe drugs, it is hoped that the burden of prescribing drugs may be lessened. Of course, the medical profession has objected, contending that psychologists lack the appropriate medical and clinical residence education. For a discussion of the types of drugs psychologists would like to prescribe, see http://www.psych.org/pub_pol_adv/meds.html.

A survey of 246 psychologists found that most are neutral regarding prescription privileges (Massoth et al., 1990). However, some expressed concern that prescription privileges would lead to higher malpractice insurance premiums and necessitate additional training.

Massoth, N. A., McGrath, R. E., Bianchi, C., & Singer, J. (1990). Psychologists' attitudes towards prescription privileges. *Professional Psychology, 21,* 147-149.

Lecture Example 16.19: The Mental Health Double Standard

Mental health workers are not exempt from possessing gender stereotypes. Clinicians' perception of an ideal, mentally healthy female is quite different from their perception of an ideal, mentally healthy male. Broverman et al. (1970) evaluated the responses of psychiatrists, clinical psychologists, and social workers in defining mental health criteria for females and males. According to Broverman et al., a mentally healthy female is characterized as being more submissive, emotional, and easily hurt and less autonomous, objective, and aggressive than her male counterpart. In fact, her male counterpart is very much like a well-adjusted adult whose gender is not specified. However, stereotypes held by clinicians are diminishing.

Consider preceding this lecture with an activity that simulates Broverman et al's study. Give students a list of personality traits. Ask them to indicate which traits describe "mature, healthy, socially competent..." (males, females, adults). One-third should have "male" in the blank, another third should have "female," and the remainder should have "adult." Compare the differences.

American Psychological Association. (1981). Sex role stereotypes and mental health. In L. T. Benjamin, Jr., & K. D. Lowman (Eds.), *Activities handbook for the teaching of psychology* (Vol. 1) (pp. 141-142). Washington, DC: Author.

Broverman, I. K., Broverman, D. M., Clarkson, F., Rosenkrantz, P. S., & Vogel, S. R. (1970). Sex role stereotypes and clinical judgments of mental health. *Journal of Consulting and Clinical Psychology, 34,* 1-7.

Lecture Example 16.20: We Need to Talk, I am a Schizophrenic

Ask your students to discuss how they would feel about an individual they had been dating for several months after this person told the student that they were schizophrenic, but were in remission and taking drugs to alleviate the symptoms of schizophrenia. Lead a group discussion on how the stigma of having a mental disorder can affect the perception of an individual. Many students will become prejudiced toward the person even though they have been dating him/her for several months.

Lecture Example 16.21: Licensing Psychologists

Licensing is required in most states to advertise oneself as a psychologist. To cover this topic it would probably be best to discuss the licensing requirements and standards for your state. These requirements can be found on the Internet by searching your state government site. In addition, if your state regulates the types of services that psychologists and other health-care professions can provide, these restrictions should be covered. See http://www.asppb.org/reqs.htm for entry requirements to the professional practice of psychology in the United States and Canada.

Diversity Topics

Diversity Topic 16.1: Definitions of Psychotherapy

Present students with a case vignette from the DSM casebook or similar source. Then, have a discussion concerning possible ways in which therapy should occur—individual, family, community level, behavioral, psychodynamic, etc. Get students' preferences and opinions, not only about a preferred mode of treatment, but also preferred outcomes. Relate the discussion to cultural (and individual) differences in preferred modes of treatment and outcomes. *Discussion/Description:* Psychotherapy as generally described, and as is presented in this book, is usually focused on individual improvement. However, people of different cultures will have different views on what the exact goals of psychotherapy are or should be. Some cultures, for example, focus not so much on the growth and development of the individual per se, but rather on the repairing and restoring of interpersonal relations. Other cultures focus on the expelling of demon spirits from the body and psyche. Of course, these different modes of treatment are related to different fundamental ways of viewing people and personality, and this discussion could be linked to the previous discussion of personality and culture.

Sue, D., Sue, D., & Sue, S. (1993). *Understanding abnormal behavior* (4th ed.). Boston: Houghton Mifflin Company.

Matsumoto, *People and Cultural Diversity*.

Diversity Topic 16.3: Attitudes Regarding Psychotherapy

While psychotherapy is common and well accepted in this culture, it does not enjoy the same rank and privileges in other cultures. Discuss this difference, and the possible reasons why it exists. *Discussion/Description:* Psychotherapy appears to be much better accepted in individualistic cultures such as our own. In collectivistic cultures, however, psychotherapy is not common, nor does it have a good reputation. I believe that this difference occurs because of the focus on individual growth and development in individualistic cultures; thus, psychotherapy fits right into the social milieu. In collectivistic cultures, however, psychological problems are viewed in the context of shame and humility. People who need psychotherapists bring dishonor to their families. The entire social network is also different in these cultures, and they often find other ways of dealing with problems (such as engaging that network, alcoholism, etc.). Nevertheless, the difference in attitude regarding psychotherapy is an important distinction to make, and one students should be introduced to. Indeed, this variation in attitudes exists within the U.S. as well.

17 Social Psychology

Chapter-at-a-Glance

Chapter Outline	Instruction Outline	Multimedia
Introduction to Social Psychology p. 570	Lecture Example 17.1 Test Questions 1-4	**Web Site** http://paradigm.soci.brocku.ca/~lward/PUBS/MEAD_038.HTML Historical Review of Early Social Psychology
Social Perception p. 571 Impression Formation: Sizing Up the Other Person • Attribution: Our Explanation of Behavior	Demonstration SOCIAL 1, 2 Lecture Example 17.2 Critical Thinking Opportunity 17.1 Critical Thinking Forum 17.1 Diversity Topic 17.1 Learning Objectives 17.1-17.3 Test Questions 5-12	**PsychScience** Impression Formation **Transparencies** MOTIV 3, 8 **Digital Image Archive** PSSC017a&b **Web Site** http://www.psych.bangor.ac.uk/deptpsych/courses/BryanProj/Group1/start_co.htm Attribution
Attraction p. 573 Factors Influencing Attraction: Magnets That Draw Us Together • Romantic Attraction • Mate Selection: The Mating Game	Demonstration SOCIAL 13, 8 Lecture Examples 17.3, 17.4 Critical Thinking Opportunity 17.2 Critical Thinking Forum 17.2 Journal Entry 17.1 Diversity Topics 17.2-17.3 Learning Objectives 17.3-17.6 Test Questions 13-32	**Transparency** SOCIAL 6 **Digital Image Archive** PSSC005a&b, 006, 009 **Web Site** http://pw1.netcom.com/~bkursine/Love.html The Love Test
Conformity, Obedience, and Compliance p. 578 Conformity: Going Along with the Group • Obedience: Following Orders • Compliance: Giving In to Requests	Lecture Examples 17.5-17.8 Critical Thinking Forum 17.3-17.4 Journal Entry 17.2 Diversity Topic 17.4 Learning Objectives 17.7-17.9 Test Questions 33-52	**Transparencies** SOCIAL 13B14 **Web Site** http://netra01.colchsfc.ac.uk/~psychlgy/milgram.htm Milgram

Chapter Outline	Instruction Outline	Multimedia
Group Influence p. 582 The Effects of the Group on Individual Performance • The Effects of the Group on Decision Making • Social Roles	Journal Entry 17.3 Lecture Examples 17.9, 17.10 Diversity Topics 17.5-17.6 Learning Objectives 17.10-17.12 Test Questions 53-64	**Digital Image Archive** PSSC011, 012-015 **Web Site** http://oak.cats.ohiou.edu/~ch670694/groupthinkex.html Groupthink
Attitudes and Attitude Change p. 586 Attitudes: Cognitive, Emotional, and Behavioral Patterns • Persuasion: Trying to Change Attitudes	Demonstration SOCIAL 3-4 Lecture Example 17.11 Critical Thinking Opportunity 17.3 Journal Entry 17.4 Learning Objectives 17.13-17.16 Test Questions 65-80	**PsychScience** Attitude Scales **Transparencies** SOCIAL 1-2, 12 **Digital Image Archive** PSS 002, 012 **Web Site** http://www.inlink.com/~dhchase/ofshe.htm Attitude Change
Prejudice and Discrimination p. 590 The Roots of Prejudice and Discrimination • Discrimination in the Workplace • Combating Prejudice and Discrimination • Prejudice: Is It Increasing or Decreasing?	Demonstration SOCIAL 5, 6, 7 Lecture Example 17.12 Critical Thinking Forum 17.5 Diversity Topic 17.7 Learning Objectives 17.17-17.21 Test Questions 81-104	*Psychology and Culture*: Ch. 12, 29, 33 **Transparencies** SOCIAL 3B4 **Video Disc II** Segment 31 **Digital Image Archive** PSSC003, 004 **Web Site** http://www.faa.gov/acr/wkdiscr.htm Workplace Discrimination
Prosocial Behavior: Behavior That Benefits Others p. 596 The Bystander Effect: The More Bystanders, the Less Likely They Are to Help • People Who Help in Emergencies	Demonstration SOCIAL 9 Lecture Example 17.13-17.15 Critical Thinking Opportunity 17.4 Learning Objective 17.22 Test Questions 105-112	*Psychology and Culture*: Ch. 24 **Transparency** SOCIAL 7 **Video Disc II** Segment 30 **Digital Image Archive** PSSC007 **Web Site** http://www.humboldt.edu/~spo1/altru.htm Prosocial Behavior
Aggression: Intentionally Harming Others p. 598 Biological Factors in Aggression: Genes, Hormones, and Brain Damage • Aggression in Response to Frustration: Sometimes but Not Always • Aggression in Response to Aversive Events: Pain, Heat, Noise, and Crowding • The Social Learning Theory of Aggression: Learning to Be Aggressive	Demonstration MOTIV 4, DEV 10 Lecture Examples 17.16, 17.17 Learning Objectives 17.23-17.29 Test Questions 113-128	*Psychology and Culture*: Ch. 25 **Digital Image Archive** PSSC008 **Web Site** http://www.ttacev.org/Articles/Origins%20of%20Violence%20and%20Aggression.html Aggression

What's New in Chapter 17

New Content

- Effects of crowding on aggression

New Special Features

- Revised *Remember It*s

New Key Terms

- crowding
- density

Learning Objective Questions

17.1 Why are first impressions so important and enduring?
17.2 What is the difference between a situational attribution and a dispositional attribution for a specific behavior?
17.3 How do the kinds of attributions people tend to make about themselves differ from those they make about other people?
17.4 Why is proximity an important factor in attraction?
17.5 How important is physical attractiveness in attraction?
17.6 Are people, as a rule, more attracted to those who are opposite or to those who are similar to them?
17.7 What did Asch find in his famous experiment on conformity?
17.8 What did Milgram find in his classic study of obedience?
17.9 What are three techniques used to gain compliance?
17.10 Under what conditions does social facilitation have either a positive or a negative effect on performance?
17.11 What is social loafing, and what factors lessen or eliminate it?
17.12 How are the initial attitudes of the group likely to affect group decision-making?
17.13 What are the three components of an attitude?
17.14 What is cognitive dissonance, and how can it be resolved?
17.15 What are the four elements in persuasion?
17.16 What qualities make a source most persuasive?
17.17 What is the difference between prejudice and discrimination?
17.18 What is meant by the terms in-group and out-group?
17.19 How does prejudice develop, according to the social learning theory?
17.20 What are stereotypes?
17.21 What are several strategies for reducing prejudice and discrimination?

17.22 What is the bystander effect, and what factors have been suggested to explain why it occurs?
17.23 What biological factors are thought to be related to aggression?
17.25 What is the frustration-aggression hypothesis?
17.26 What kinds of aversive events and unpleasant emotions have been related to aggression?
17.27 What is the difference between density and crowding?
17.28 What are some psychological effects of crowding?
17.29 According to social learning theory, what causes aggressive behavior?

Chapter Overview

Social psychology attempts to explain how the real or imagined presence of others influences the behavior of individuals. Social perception refers to the impressions we form of others as we try to understand their behavior. Impression formation is influenced by factors of appearance, and the first impression often has a strong influence over later judgments. Some specific traits, like the perception of being a warm or a cold person, can color our whole impression of a person. Fundamental to understanding others is the manner in which we attribute causes and behaviors. The chapter examines the concept and research on attributional biases.

Attraction is governed by a number of factors: proximity, liking through association, reciprocal liking, physical attractiveness, and similarity. The matching hypothesis has been applied to romantic attraction, suggesting that successful romance requires similarity between the individuals. The process of selecting a mate is discussed in detail.

The classic studies by Asch on conformity, by Milgram on obedience, and by other researchers on compliance are presented in the discussion. The major sales techniques of foot-in-the-door, door-in-the-face, and low-balling are described in their role in gaining compliance.

Group influence is another type of social influence; social facilitation is any positive or negative effect on performance due to the presence of others. One explanation for the effect is that people experience heightened arousal in social settings that can result in either increased or decreased performance. Social loafing is also discussed in this section. The effects of groups on decision making, which can lead to either polarization of the group or to a style of decision making called Groupthink, is then explored. This section ends with a discussion of social roles.

The chapter then turns and focuses on the traditional area of the study of the relationship between attitude and attitude change. The first topic in this section covers the relationship between attitudes and behavior. The topic of cognitive dissonance, which is one of the consequences of inconsistencies between attitudes and behavior, is discussed. The methods of changing attitudes through persuasion are also described.

The roots of prejudice and discrimination are explored in terms of realistic conflict theory, in-groups versus out-groups, social learning theory, and social cognition theory. The next topic in this section covers discrimination in the workplace and is followed by a section on combating prejudice and discrimination.

This section concludes with a discussion on whether prejudice is increasing or decreasing.

The chapter then turns to a discussion of prosocial behavior. The bystander effect and the concept of the diffusion of responsibility are examined closely. A discussion of people who help in emergencies ends this topic.

The chapter ends with a discussion of the causes of aggression. Theories of aggression are examined, including the influence of biological factors, aggression in response to frustration and to aversive events, and the social learning theory of aggression.

Key Terms

aggression (p. 598)
altruism (p. 597)
attitude (p. 586)
attribution (p. 572)
audience effects (p. 583)
bystander effect (p. 596)
coaction effects (p. 583)
cognitive dissonance (p. 597)
compliance (p. 581)
confederate (p. 571)
conformity (p. 578)
contact hypothesis (p. 294)
crowding (p. 601)
density (p. 601)
diffusion of responsibility (p. 596)
discrimination (p. 590)
dispositional attribution (p. 572)

door-in-the-face technique (p. 581)
foot-in-the-door technique (p. 581)
frustration (p. 599)
frustration-aggression hypothesis (p. 599)
fundamental attribution error (p. 572)
group polarization (p. 584)
groupthink (p. 584)
halo effect (p. 575)
in-group (p. 590)
low-ball technique (p. 582)
matching hypothesis (p. 576)
mere-exposure effect (p. 573)
naive subject (p. 571)
norms (p. 578)

out-group (p. 590)
persuasion (p. 588)
prejudice (p. 590)
primacy effect (p. 571)
prosocial behavior (p. 597)
proximity (p. 573)
realistic conflict theory (p. 590)
roles (p. 585)
scapegoating (p. 601)
self-serving bias (p. 572)
situational attribution (p. 572)
social cognition (p. 591)
social facilitation (p. 583)
social loafing (p. 583)
social psychology (p. 570)
stereotypes (p. 591)

Annotated Lecture Outline

A. Introduction to Social Psychology

Lecture Examples

Lecture Example 17.1: Introduction to Social Psychology

Use http://www.psych.nwu.edu/psych/people/faculty/roese/social/sweb.htm as a reference to develop an introductory lecture for social psychology.

B. Social Perception

Classroom Demonstrations and Handouts

Demonstration SOCIAL 1: Attribution to Solve Problems

Objective: To become more familiar with attribution theory.
Materials: Using Attribution to Solve Problems (**Handout SOCIAL 1a**); How We Answer the Question: "Why?" (**Handout SOCIAL 1b**)
Procedure: Give each student **Handout SOCIAL 1a** and **Handout SOCIAL 1b**. The examples of **Handout SOCIAL 1a** provide students with a question they want to answer. They must examine the pattern of consistency, distinctiveness, and consensus in each example before they can do so. In addition, it may be helpful that students receive **Handout SOCIAL 1b** to serve as a guide.
Conclusions: Students will become more knowledgeable about attribution theory and the sources of information used.

Demonstration SOCIAL 2: Fundamental Attribution Error and Self-Serving Bias

Objective: To demonstrate fundamental attribution error and self-serving bias.
Materials: Sources of Bias in Attribution (**Handout SOCIAL 2**)
Procedure: Present **Handout SOCIAL 2** to your students and ask them to complete the sentences. Collect the completed sentences for analysis. If the class is small enough, do the data analysis in class. If that is not possible, show the results in the next class. Separate the statements into "I" and "They" categories. Code each statement completion into either a "Dispositional Cause" or a "Situational Cause" category. For example, "Allan was late for work because...he hates to get up in the morning (code dispositional), or his alarm clock failed to go off (code situational). If you do this in class, have the students help with the coding. Display the results on the blackboard in a 2 x 2 table.
Conclusions: Since the fundamental attribution error asserts that we over-attribute behavior to dispositional causes, the results should show a greater number of dispositional explanations than situational explanations for "They" categories. Our (i.e., "I" category) own success, according to the self-serving bias, should be attributed more to dispositional causes than situational, while our failures are attributed to situational causes. To view an attributional theories map, go to http://www.psych.bangor.ac.uk/deptpsych/courses/BryanProj/Group1/sub_theo.htm.

Lecture Examples

Lecture Example 17.2: Attribution and Its Uses

At first, students may be put off by attribution theory because they don't understand why it is important to analyze the underlying causes of others' behavior, and they don't realize how often they do it automatically in everyday life. A few examples would be helpful. For instance, if a student misses a class and needs to borrow someone's lecture notes, he probably uses attributions to decide whom to ask. If he knows the person sitting next to him scored an A on the last exam, that very few others scored an A on the exam (low consensus), that this person always gets As in this class, whether tests are multiple choice or essay (high consistency), and that this person gets As in most classes (low distinctiveness), then he will probably be eager to borrow notes from her. He has made an internal attribution for her high grades. Her performance is due to ability and/or consistent effort and conscientiousness, so she probably takes terrific notes. Other examples might include a study by Wilson and Linville (1982) who found that incoming freshmen often attribute difficulties with their studies to stable, internal causes. When they are trained to think of their low grades as due to more temporary causes, such as adjustment to the new environment, their grades improve and they are less likely to drop out than students who have not experienced this realignment of attribution. For more on attribution theory, see http://uts.cc.utexas.edu/~mdixon/theory.html, or for more on attribution theory and motivation, go to http://www.cmhc.com/psyhelp/chap4/chap4k.htm.

Wilson, T., & Linville, P. (1982). Improving the academic performance of college freshmen: Attribution therapy revisited. *Journal of Personality and Social Psychology, 42*, 367-376.

Diversity Topic

Diversity Topic 17.1: Gazing and Its Effects

In our culture, we are socialized to look people directly in the eye, to pay attention, etc. In other cultures, such gaze behavior may be arrogant and challenging. The existence of such differences has been the source of intercultural conflict in interpersonal relationships. Discuss how and why these types of differences may exist.
Discussion/Description: Gaze behavior may be related to dominance/submissiveness, and it may be related across subhuman species. How we deal with gaze behavior is a function of cultural background, and different cultures will deal with these behaviors in different ways. In the individualistic American culture, for example, we are socialized to look one straight in the eye, to stand up for oneself, etc. This is no doubt related to the fact that our culture fosters a sense of a unique and autonomous self. Other cultures, however, do not foster this type of gaze behavior. Thus, what may be deferential for other cultures (e.g., looking away when talking) may be interpreted as rude or impolite by us, when it is not true.

C. Attraction

Classroom Demonstrations and Handouts

Demonstration SOCIAL 13: Attractiveness and Influence

Objective: To illustrate physical attraction on other personality variables.
Materials: Attractiveness Rating Scale (**Handout SOCIAL 13**); a slide of an attractive person; a slide of an unattractive person (same sex as the other slide)
Procedure: Present the slides to your students and ask them to rate each slide using **Handout SOCIAL 13**. Collect the rating sheets, sum the scores for each student for each slide, and then calculate the mean rating for each slide. The results should show a tendency for students to attribute the more desirable traits to the physically attractive person reflected by the larger mean score of the attractive slide.
Conclusions: Discuss why, given information only about the person's physical appearance, we tend to "see" more or less desirable traits. Question the students about the implications of these findings for matters such as attitudinal change and interpersonal behavior. Ask them to think of any differences in how they might interact with attractive and unattractive people.

Demonstration SOCIAL 8: Ideal Date

Objective: To help students understand concepts of attraction
Materials: 3" x 5" index cards
Procedure: Pass out a 3" x 5" index card to each student. Have the students list the characteristics they feel their ideal date should possess. These characteristics should be listed in terms of words and phrases, not complete sentences. Students should list as many characteristics as possible in five minutes.
Conclusions: In discussing the characteristics students have listed, you might want to ask questions such as: How many students listed physical characteristics first? How many listed some degree of higher education as a characteristic? Since you are in a college classroom, this may well reflect a similarity factor. Could it reflect proximity? How many listed personality factors were similar to their own? Different from their own? Again, the influence of similarity could be discussed.

Lecture Examples

Lecture Example 17.3: Grooming and Endorphins

Research indicates that endorphins may be produced in the brains of monkeys during grooming. Endorphins are the body's own morphinelike substances that can reduce pain and lead to feelings of pleasure. Lawren (1990) and his associates assert that grooming and other forms of touch may be a biological need, one so important that the body insures its occurrence by producing these endorphins. The next step is to determine if endorphins are produced in the human brain during grooming. One could speculate that abnormally high levels of endorphins are being produced in the case of trichotillomania.

Lawren, B. (1990, August). The roots of grooming. *Omni, 12,* 26.

Lecture Example 17.4: Breaking Up

Various factors contribute to the breakup of a relationship. Since many college students are probably experiencing their first serious relationships, this is an appropriate lecture. Breakups before marriage are generally due to inequality in the relationship, age differences, and differences in educational goals, intelligence, and physical appearance (Hill, Rubin, & Peplau, 1976). Another study reported commitment, self-disclosure, self-esteem, and satisfaction in the relationship to be factors that contribute to breakups (Hendrick, Hendrick, & Adler, 1988).

Hendrick, S., Hendrick, C., & Adler, N. (1988). Romantic hardships: Love, satisfaction, and staying together. *Journal of Personality and Social Psychology, 54,* 980-988.

Hill, C., Rubin, Z., & Peplau, L. (1976). Breakups before marriage: The end of 103 affairs. *Journal of Social Issues, 32,* 147-168.

Diversity Topics

Diversity Topic 17.2: Smiling

Present the results from Matsumoto and Kudoh (1993) that showed how smiling faces were interpreted quite differently between the U.S. and Japan. Alternatively, you might want to get some smiling and neutral faces on slides and replicate a small version of this study in class. *Discussion/Description:* In this study, American subjects found smiling faces to be more attractive and intelligent than neutral faces, which was not true for Japanese subjects. American subjects also found smiling faces to be more sociable and friendly to a much larger degree than did the Japanese subjects. These types of findings question whether smiles have the same connotations in other cultures as they do in the U.S.

Matsumoto, D., & Kudoh, T. (1993). American-Japanese cultural differences in attributions of personality based on smiles. *Journal of Nonverbal Behavior, 17,* 231-243.

Diversity Topic 17.3: Love

How important is love in a marriage? Discuss the implications of this question after a presentation of arranged marriages that are prevalent in many cultures of the world.
Discussion/Description: In many cultures of the world, parents and other family and community members arrange marriage partners for the youth. Oftentimes, these decisions are made years in advance of the marriage, and have nothing to do with love. These decisions are typically made on the basis of family standing, occupation, etc. There is considerable evidence that divorce rates for these types of marriages are considerably lower than love-marriages. Why?

One person from such a culture commented to me that it was very easy to understand why "Americans marry the person they love. We love the person we marry."

D. Conformity, Obedience, and Compliance

Lecture Examples

Lecture Example 17.5: Presenting Asch's Study

Rather than lecturing on Asch's study in the traditional way, walk through the experiment as if the students were the subjects. Ask students to speculate on what they would have done if they had been subjects in the experiment. Would they have conformed and responded with what they knew to be the correct answer?

Lecture Example 17.6: Introducing Obedience

Here is an excellent way to demonstrate obedience to authority. Tell, do not ask, your students to stand up, raise their arms, and spin around in a circle. Alternatively, give students a "quiz" and then tell them to rip their papers up. How many students obeyed? As you introduce the topic, refer to examples of too much obedience to authority (e.g., soldiers shooting civilians who attempted to escape East Berlin or Nazi concentration camps), and then ask students whether they have obeyed an authority figure. Are people who are willing to obey authority figures without question mindless, robotlike people? More activities are presented by Hunter (1981) and Lutsky (1987). For a discussion on obedience, see http://www.statewave.com/tiers_1_4/AUTHRITY.HTM.

Hunter, W. J. (1981). Obedience to authority. In L. T. Benjamin, Jr., & K. D. Lowman (Eds.), *Activities handbook for the teaching of psychology* (Vol. 1). Washington, DC: American Psychological Association.

Lutsky, N. (1987). Inducing academic suicide: A demonstration of social influence. In V. P. Makosky, L. G. Whittemore, & A. M. Rogers (Eds.), *Activities handbook for the teaching of psychology* (Vol. 2). Washington, DC: American Psychological Association.

Lecture Example 17.7: Milgram's Study: Would You Continue?

As you describe the procedures of the Milgram study, keep asking students whether they would have continued the study if they had been the subject. Before you tell your students the percentage of Milgram's subjects who administered the maximum amount of "shock," ask for a show of hands in response to the question "How many of you would have given the maximum amount of shock?" Typically most students report that they would not. Next suggest that most of them are not telling the truth, since 65 percent of Milgram's subjects administered the maximum shock level. For a detailed description of Milgram's experiments, see http://netra01.colchsfc.ac.uk/~psychlgy/milgram.htm

Lecture Example 17.8: Milgram's Study: Follow-up

Milgram conducted approximately 20 versions of his classic obedience experiment and found compliance rates ranging from 0% to 93%. Milgram determined that four factors influence obedience. The first factor is the emotional distance of the victim. When the learner was in another room and could not be heard, compliance was high. As the teacher was brought into closer contact with the victim, compliance dropped. This is a negative correlation between victim distance and obedience. Second, closeness and legitimacy of the authority. Compliance was highest when the authority figure had high status and was physically present. When the experimenter was absent or a student assistant ran the study, obedience declined. Third, institutional authority influenced obedience. Obedience declined when the experiment was moved away from Yale. Finally, group influence was a factor in obedience. If confederate teachers refused to participate in the experiment, obedience declined. After the experiment, only 1% of the subjects said they were sorry to have participated, while 84% were glad that they had taken part. For a detailed description of Milgram's experiments, see http://netra01.colchsfc.ac.uk/~psychlgy/milgram.htm

Diversity Topic

Diversity Topic 17.4: Conformity, Compliance, and Obedience

What do students feel about conformity, compliance, and obedience? Is it good or bad? Divide the class in half, and have a debate concerning the morality of these constructs, with one group arguing that they are good, while the other group argues they are bad.
Discussion/Description: In my experience, most students have a negative bias against these constructs. I believe that this is related to the fact that the American culture discourages conformity, compliance, and obedience, because they are antithetical to individualism. Other cultures, however, value these constructs, both in terms of terminal values and in development. This difference makes for interesting differences, and possible conflicts, in social relations between people of different cultures.

E. Group Influence

Lecture Examples

Lecture Example 17.9: Group Pressure and Bad Behavior

Ask your students to remember the worst thing they did in high school. Stole something, shoplifted, underage drinking, and fighting are good examples. After the students have had some time to think of their own example, ask them if they were alone or with friends when they did this bad behavior. Ask for a show of hands. Most will indicate they were with friends. Use this as a lead-in for your lecture on peer pressure.

Lecture Example 17.16: Effect of the Group

Ask students if they play golf; many will indicate that they do. Then ask what is the most difficult shot in golf. Many will offer answers that range from sand shot, shot over water, putting, or the drive. Usually, someone will mention the first shot off the first tee. The effects of a group of friends and other golfers makes the first tee shot by far the hardest in golf. If you play, you can relate some of your worst shots and then ask for students' input. Use this as a starting point for your lectures on group facilitation effects.

Diversity Topics

Diversity Topic 17.5: Social Loafing

All students have had some experience working in groups for class or extracurricular projects. They will undoubtedly have observations about social loafing and its counterpart, social striving. Let students have a discussion about these observations, and examine their attributions about the causes of these effects. What makes some people strive, while others loaf, in work groups?
Discussion/Description: The basis of this activity is the same as described in the previous annotation. A caution that instructors should be aware of concerns the possibility that students make race- or ethnicity-based interpretations of loafing or striving. These would be detrimental to the discussion. Instead, they should focus on the psychological and social characteristics of people to produce the behaviors that occurred. Why did they occur, and how are those behaviors ingrained and reinforced?

Diversity Topic 17.6: Social Striving

Research across cultures has shown that social loafing may not occur as it has within work groups here in research conducted in the U.S. Instead, some researchers have found the opposite effect—social striving—when people are put into groups. Give a brief presentation of these studies and findings here.
Discussion/Description: It has been thought that these effects are related to individualism versus collectivism. Social loafing seems to have occurred in our individualistic culture because individual efficiency reduces in social situations. In collectivistic cultures, however, teamwork and group productivity tends to increase because people are used to working in groups, and prefer it. Thus, the opposite findings were obtained. However, as mentioned in the text under the topic of social facilitation, social striving has been found in some studies in the U.S. in recent years as well. In any case, there may not be as many negative consequences to group work as has been considered in the past under social loafing.

F. Attitudes and Attitude Change

Classroom Demonstrations and Handouts

Demonstration SOCIAL 3: Attitudes and Advertising

Objective: To analyze the components of television/print advertisements in the context of the dimensions of an attitude.
Materials: Videotapes of five commercials or five print ads (if you use the latter, make sure you have enough copies for every student.)
Procedure: This activity works well with students working in groups. Ask them to analyze the extent to which the advertisements appeal to the viewer's intellect or cognitions, their emotions or feelings, and their physical actions. Those that appeal to our intellect usually emphasize facts about the product or research-based comparisons with other products (e.g., "More dentists recommend..."; "In a taste test..."). Emotional appeals will stress fear, excitement, and fun associated with the product (e.g., the freedom of owning XYZ car; winning a million dollars). If an ad appeals to our actions then we are urged to try the product or service (e.g., coupons; loss leaders in grocery stores"; "hurry—only for a limited time..."; "limited supplies").
Conclusions: Participants in this activity will see how their attitudes are subtly influenced by commercials and advertisements.

Kasschau, R. A. (1981). Attitude change and advertisements. In L. Benjamin, Jr. and K. Lowman (Eds.), *Activities handbook for the teaching of psychology* (Vol. 1). Washington, D.C.: American Psychological Association.

Demonstration SOCIAL 4: Persuasion and Social Issues

Objective: To discuss with your students the role that social psychology can play in addressing social issues.
Materials: None
Procedure: There are a number of serious social issues that challenge us today. Social psychology has a long history of involvement in research pertinent to many pressing issues. Medical researchers are far from a cure for AIDS, and prevention is the most effective approach available at present to combat the spread of the disease. As a result, the media are currently infused with messages about "safer sex" and "safe intravenous drug use." We see a similar dilemma with drug use, drinking and driving, and seat belt use. Put your students into groups and give them the challenge of how one might go about designing persuasive programs to address these concerns. Remind them of the variables of persuasion such as the source, message, and target audience. The elaboration-likelihood model would be relevant.
Conclusions: Your students can apply what they have learned about persuasion in attempting to solve social problems. This activity makes the topics more relevant and powerful in changing the world.

Lecture Example

Lecture Example 17.11: Preventing Smoking in Adolescents

There has been a shift in media campaigns designed to prevent youth from smoking cigarettes. The original strategy was to communicate fear by showing diseased lungs or taped messages by people such as Yul Brynner, who contracted lung cancer because they smoked. However, a more recent tactic is to use what Petty and Cacioppo call peripheral processes. Antismoking messages now focus on the social and financial disadvantages of smoking. For instance, in one ad spot, a group of adolescents fall over as an approaching teen says "Hi" with her smoke-odor breath. Another commercial shows the effects of smoking on the smoker's clothes, and another illustrates the monetary drawbacks to smoking as a cigarette machine is filled with quarters.

Petty, R. E., & Cacioppo, J. T. (1981). *Attitudes and persuasion: Classic and contemporary approaches.* Dubuque, IA: William C. Brown.

Petty, R. E., and Cacioppo, J. T. (1985). The elaboration likelihood model of persuasion. In L. Berkowitz (Ed.), *Advances in experimental social psychology* (Vol. 19). New York: Academic Press.

G. Prejudice and Discrimination

Classroom Demonstrations and Handouts

Demonstration SOCIAL 5: Headbands and Stereotypes

Objective: To help students learn the impact of stereotypes and the effect of how others see us.
Materials: Headbands made from construction paper with names written on them—see **Handout SOCIAL 5** for ideas
Procedure: Randomly distribute the headbands to students; if you have a small class, you could give each student a headband. In large classes, you should select a small group to participate while other students do another activity, or put the large class into groups in which one or two members wear the headbands. Those who wear the headbands should not know what they say. So, as you distribute the headbands, caution students not to look at them. The class is told to treat those wearing headbands as the label on the headband reads. Those wearing headbands must try to figure what their headbands are labeled.
Conclusions: Ask students how they felt as people interacted with them. Were the interactions stereotypical, that is, based upon some prevailing stereotypes? Did any student feel prejudice towards anyone or feel prejudice from others? Based upon these reactions, how might we develop images of ourselves and how might they develop?

Demonstration SOCIAL 6: Common Stereotypes

Objective: To expose some common stereotypes.
Materials: **Handout SOCIAL 6**
Procedure: This activity comes from Engle and Snellgrove (1981) and it involves having students fill in the blank to a number of statements. The statements are general stereotypes with the ethnic, gender, and racial name removed (e.g., _____ are great lovers). Consult the source for the complete list or be adventuresome and develop your own statements. The authors also suggest eliciting examples of regional or geographic stereotypes. For example, from the stereotypical perspective of Midwestern students, most people that live in the East are arrogant, want to keep you lost, and avoid eye contact. People living in the Midwest, like the Dakotas, are viewed as still fighting the Indians, living in tepees, or lacking indoor plumbing. Further extend the activity by asking for stereotypes of various occupations (e.g., NFL linebackers, used car salesmen, farmers).
Conclusions: Even those students who see themselves as educated and sophisticated will acknowledge that they possess stereotypes. For common Latino stereotypes, see http://www.ucr.edu/classes/fvc/fvc143/tropicana5.htm. For common stereotypes of Canadians, see http://flash.lakeheadu.ca/~bhatia/ca.html. For German-British stereotypes, see http://rcswww.urz.tu-dresden.de/~english3/Jana/stereot.htm#order.

Engle, T. L., & Snellgrove, L. (1981). Stereotypes. In L. T. Benjamin, Jr. and K. D. Lowman (Eds.), *Activities handbook for the teaching of psychology* (Vol. 1). Washington, D.C.: American Psychological Association.

Demonstration SOCIAL 7: Stereotyping through Time

Objective: To demonstrate stereotyping and how it has changed.
Materials: Stereotyping (**Handout SOCIAL 7a**); **Handout SOCIAL 7b**
Procedure: This activity is based upon the study done by Katz and Braly (1933) and is to be used as an introduction to a discussion of stereotyping. Give students **Handout SOCIAL 7a**, which lists several racial and ethnic groups. Ask students to indicate two adjectives for each group. These adjectives are on the same handout. The adjectives can be used to describe more than one group. Then compare the students' results with those found by Katz and Braly in 1933 and Gilbert in 1951. These findings are on **Handout SOCIAL 7b**.
Conclusions: Discuss with students their results and the concept of stereotyping. Have stereotypes changed since the times of these two studies? If so, what accounts for the changes? Relate student responses to your text's discussion of methods of reducing prejudice.

Anonymous. (1981). Stereotyping. In L. T. Benjamin, Jr. and K. D. Lowman (Eds.), *Activities handbook for the teaching of psychology* (Vol. 1) (pp. 145-146). Washington, D.C.: American Psychological Association.

Gilbert, G. M. (1951). Stereotype persistence and change among college students. *Journal of Abnormal and Social Psychology, 46,* 245-254.

Katz, D., & Braly, K. (1933). Racial stereotypes of one hundred college students. *Journal of Abnormal and Social Psychology, 28,* 280-290.

Lecture Example

Lecture Example 17.12: Stereotyping

It is impossible to process all the information about people that bombards us every day. To simplify the social world and this massive amount of information, we automatically place individuals into cognitive categories like male or female, friendly or hostile, and adult or child. Stereotyping occurs when people in a given category are assumed to possess a set of attributes that are associated with the category. Recent work suggests that the cognitive processes involved in categorization contribute to the development and perpetuation of stereotypes. Rothbart et al. (1984) discuss several psychological mechanisms associated with categorization: (1) the perception of the in-group superiority, (2) the tendency for a group to be perceived as more heterogeneous by in-group than by out-group members, (3) the tendency to exaggerate differences between one's own and other groups, and (4) the tendency for different groups to differentially encode the same event in accordance with existing expectancies and goals.

Rothbart, M., Dawes, R., & Park, B. (1984). Stereotyping and sampling biases in inter-group perception. In J. Eiser (Ed.), *Attitudinal judgment.* New York: Springer-Verlag.

Diversity Topic

Diversity Topic 17.7: Stereotyping

After students have completed Demonstration **SOCIAL 7**, engage in a discussion about the formation and maintenance of stereotypes using principles of psychology they have learned throughout the book.
Discussion/Description: This activity goes beyond the current **SOCIAL 7** activity, and attempts to explain stereotypes as a normal outgrowth of other basic psychological processes. This approach will help students to diffuse the emotion surrounding stereotypes. In addition, this approach should help students to loosen the hold that stereotypes may have on them in their social interactions. The material in the reference cited below needs to be followed carefully.

H. Prosocial Behavior: Behavior That Benefits Others

Classroom Demonstrations and Handouts

Demonstration SOCIAL 9: Guest Speaker on Local Efforts to Help Those in Need

Objective: To acquaint students with local efforts to assist the homeless, poor, and others in need.
Materials: None

Procedure: Many organizations, such as hospitals, churches, clubs, and government agencies, provide assistance to individuals. Invite a representative from one of these groups to come to class and discuss the organization's programs. Who are they trying to reach? How are they trying to help? And, if appropriate, what can your students do to assist them?

Conclusions: This activity will serve to raise the consciousness of students regarding local programs that promote prosocial behavior.

Lecture Example

Lecture Example 17.13: Diffusion of Responsibility

It is commonplace to be solicited for funds by a variety of organizations, whether they involve environmental funds, blankets for flood victims, victims of El Nino, or food and medicine for children. Our decision not to contribute may be due in part to diffusion of responsibility rather than to indifference or insensitivity. "George will do it." The responsibility is spread over an audience of thousands, so little responsibility falls on any one individual. The problem is, will George do it?

Lecture Example 17.14: Bystander Effects: Kitty Genovese

Research on the bystander effect was stimulated by a real-life event: the highly publicized murder of Kitty Genovese. In 1964, Kitty Genovese was attacked, left for dead, attacked again, and killed over the period of an hour in the view of 38 of her neighbors in Queens, New York. During that time, not a single person called the police or otherwise intervened in any way. Your students will probably be shocked and indicate that they think "those people" or "New Yorkers" are bad and uncaring. A more recent incident in Denver, Colorado involved a cab driver who was killed while others watched and did not report the incident.

Lecture Example 17.15: Bystander Effects

Ask your students to imagine themselves in dire need in a public place for example, falling and breaking their leg in a shopping mall during last minute December holiday rush or having car trouble on a busy freeway in a major city. Ask the class what actions would they take to decrease the likelihood of the bystander effect? Ask your students to volunteer any experiences they have had with bystander effect.

I. Aggression: Intentionally Harming Others

Classroom Demonstrations and Handouts

Demonstration MOT 4: Defining Aggression

Objective: To introduce the students to the difficulty of defining aggression.
Materials: **Handout MOT 4**

Procedure: Before lecturing on aggression motivation, give each student a copy of **Handout MOT 4**. Ask them to read each statement and decide whether or not the situation can be defined as aggression. Record their opinions with a show of hands for each item.

Conclusions: Discussion can center on how the context influences whether we tend to call something "aggression." If a behavior seems justified (e.g., a soldier shooting an enemy, a woman kicking a would-be rapist), we tend to label it "self-defense" even though it fits the psychological definition of human aggression (i.e., behavior intended to harm another).

Benjamin, L. T., Jr. (1988). Defining aggression: An exercise for classroom discussion. *Teaching of Psychology, 12*, 40-42.

Demonstration DEV 10: Assess the Violence in Children's Cartoons

Objective: To illustrate the level and intensity of violence depicted in cartoons for children.
Materials: Videotape of several types of children's cartoons; **Handout DEV 10**
Procedure: This is best presented in your discussion of television as a socializing agent. Present the cartoons to your students. Ask them to count the number of acts of violence and record them on **Handout DEV 10**. Clearly, you must define what constitutes a violent act; consider explicit versus implicit acts. Some of the older cartoons are just as violent as the cartoons of today. At the end of each cartoon, determine the number of acts of violence committed per minute. Vandendorpe (1987) suggests a number of variations to the original intent of this activity. One is to observe other children's shows like *Sesame Street* and *Mr. Rogers* for examples of cognitive skills, demographic data on models, and social skills.
Conclusions: Make sure you ask the students what they think children are learning from watching cartoons of this nature. Typically, responses might mention that violent behavior is acceptable in solving interpersonal problems and that one-upmanship is acceptable. For some examples of commentary on this topic, see http://tiger.towson.edu/~sdavis1/cartoons.html or http://www.naeyc.org/.

Eron, L. D., Lefkowitz, M. M., Huesmann, L. R., & Walder, L. D. (1972). Does television violence cause aggression? *American Psychologist, 27*, 253-263.

Sherman, B., & Dominick, J. R. (1986). Violence and sex in music videos: TV and rock'n'roll. *Journal of Communication, 36*, 79-93.

Vandendorpe, M. (1987). Television as teacher: Studying the media's message. In V. P. Makosky, L. G. Whittemore, and A. M. Rogers (Eds.). *Activities handbook for the teaching of psychology* (Vol. 2) (pp. 101-102). Washington, D.C.: American Psychological Association.

Lecture Examples

Lecture Example 17.16: Aggression with a Familial Basis

A notion that has gained attention recently is the likelihood that extreme aggression has a familial basis. The issue is one of nature versus nurture. If aggression is due to genetic influences, we might be able to locate a gene that controls its expression or some physiological correlate. But perhaps aggression is a result of modeling influences, for example, children imitating their violent parents. Ask students for their opinions.

Pines, M. (1985, July). Aggression: The violence within. *Science Digest*, 36-39, 68.

Lecture Example 17.17: Rodney King and Mass Violence

Within hours of the verdict acquitting four police officers of charges related to the videotaped beating of Rodney King, one of this century's most deadly riots in the United States broke out. Although clearly an expression of frustration felt by the many who identified with King, to what extent was the violence also a result of opportunism? Identify other factors at work in the riots. Were people influenced by diffusion of responsibility? What other effects were present?

Appendix A Statistical Methods

Appendix-at-a-Glance

Appendix Outline	Instruction Outline	Multimedia
Descriptive Statistics p. 607 Measures of Central Tendency • Describing Data with Tables and Graphs • Measures of Variability • Range • The Standard Deviation • The Normal Curve • The Correlation Coefficient	**Demonstration STAT 1, 4, METHODS 3-4** **Lecture Examples A.1-A.5** **Diversity Topic A.1**	*Discovering Psychology: Understanding Research* **Web Site:** http://www.spss.com/StatsWeb/ Statistics on the Web
Inferential Statistics p. 614 Statistical Significance	**Demonstration STAT 2-3** **Lecture Example A.6** **Diversity Topics A.2-A.3**	**Web Site:** http://www.cas.lancs.ac.uk/glossary_v1.1/main.html Statistic Glossary

Annotated Lecture Outline

A. Descriptive Statistics

Classroom Demonstrations and Handouts

Demonstration STAT 1: Greyhound Strike

Objective: To make the measures of central tendency more relevant.
Materials: **Handout STAT 1**, which includes several sets of fictitious data. One set of data describes the individual salaries of fifty bus drivers and the average dollar amount of fringe benefits; a frequency distribution would be appropriate. The second set of data summarizes the salary and fringe benefits of drivers from four rival companies; this data set includes mean, median, mode, and standard deviation.
Procedure: Shatz (1988) suggests this activity in which a strike by Greyhound drivers serves as the setting. Divide the class into a labor group and management group. Labor opposes a salary cut and management supports a cut. Allow the two groups to negotiate a contract. Both labor and management have access to these two sets of data. The task of both groups is to "massage" the data to defend their positions. Consult Shatz for more detail.

Conclusions: This activity requires students to apply what they know about descriptive statistics to make decisions.

Shatz, M. (1988). The Greyhound strike: Using a labor dispute to teach descriptive statistics. In V. P. Makosky, L. G. Whittemore, & A. M. Rogers (Eds.), *Activities handbook for the teaching of psychology*. Washington, D.C.: American Psychological Association.

Demonstration STAT 4: Collecting Data

Objective: To generate, collect, and analyze student data.
Materials: Calculator
Procedure: Generate, collect, and analyze real in-class data using descriptive statistics (e.g., mean, mode, median, and standard deviation), correlation, and some basic inferential statistics (e.g., independent samples t-test). You could ask for simple (albeit boring) variables (e.g., shoe size), or consider more lively variables (see Hettich, 1985).
Conclusions: Rather than just lecturing about these various statistics, students take a more active approach in their learning.

Beers, S. E. (1987). Descriptive statistics. In V. P. Makosky, L. G. Whittemore, and A. M. Rogers (Eds.), *Activities handbook for the teaching of psychology* (Vol. 2). Washington, D.C.: American Psychological Association.

Hettich, P. (1985). The student as data generator. In L. T. Benjamin, R. S. Daniel, & C. L. Brewer (Eds.), *Handbook for teaching introductory psychology*. Hillsdale, NJ: Lawrence Erlbaum.

Demonstration METHODS 3: Classroom Correlation

Objective: To understand correlations.
Materials: Correlation (**Handout METHODS 3**)
Procedure: This is a relatively simple activity to perform in which the correlation between two variables is plotted. Select two variables that are innocuous and lend themselves to easy data collection. Two time-honored variables are students' height and shoe size. Collect the data and plot the data on a graph. If you have time, you may want to compute Pearson's *r* on the data. Students record their hypothesized correlations on **Handout METHODS 3**.
Conclusions: Ask students to speculate on the relationship between height and shoe size. Stress the fact that we cannot show cause and effect relationships with correlation.

Demonstration METHODS 4: Correlation versus Causation

Objective: To compare correlation and causation.
Materials: Correlation Versus Causation (**Handout METHODS 4**)
Procedure: Ask students to provide a possible cause and effect relationship using the blank spaces in Part B, 1) on the handout (do not allow height and shoe size if you have used **Demonstration METHODS 3**). Students then should volunteer their causal relations, and other

students can offer prior causes of both factors, thus illustrating that sometimes causation is only apparent. In Part B, 2) students are to provide additional correlated factors with a hypothesized third, possibly causal factor, similar to that illustrated in Part A, 2).

Conclusions: Quite a number of apparent causal relations should be offered, some may be quite correct. Discuss the kind of research needed to demonstrate a causal relationship, and how these intervening variables must be eliminated.

Lecture Examples

Lecture Example A.1: Statistics as a Language

Students probably have an "innate" disdain for statistics. This might be lessened if you tell them that statistics is a language. Like any other language, it has a unique vocabulary to learn and syntax to understand. Alternatively, they can think about statistics as a drug to be administered to treat an illness. As psychologists, we are presented with a research problem with variables of a certain type of measurement (e.g., symptoms). Which statistical technique (e.g., drug therapy) is most appropriate? For example, we certainly do not want to use a mean for a variable that has a nominal level of measurement, just as physicians would not want to prescribe a laxative for an ingrown toenail.

Lecture Example A.2: Descriptive Statistics

Descriptive statistics allow one to summarize large quantities of data with one or two numbers. Beers (1987) recommends that the instructor select a variable with a large variation, such as height. Tell students to calculate their height in inches and then in unison report the heights out loud. Next say, "That sounded just like what data look like when they are first gathered. Data are just a pile of numbers waiting to be organized." This provides a good rationale for using descriptive statistics.

Beers, S. E. (1987). Descriptive statistics. In V. P. Makosky, L. G. Whittemore, & A. M. Rogers (Eds.), *Activities handbook for the teaching of psychology*. Washington, DC: American Psychological Association.

Lecture Example A.3: Cruisin'

A group of college students decided to go on a cruise for spring break. The travel agent said the average age of the other passengers was 22. When the students boarded the cruise ship, they found that the other passengers were not even close to that age. The travel agent wasn't lying, but he did forget to mention that the trip was a special cruise for grandparents and their young grandchildren. The average age was indeed 22, but the range was 2 to 90 years of age.

Lecture Example A.4: Statistics and Multiculturalism

Measures of central tendency are often misused when applied to comparisons of overall population and minority groups within the population. A tendency for a minority group to have different average scores *does not mean* that any one individual performs in accordance with the group tendencies. When they are not fully understood, these measures can actually reinforce stereotypes. Ironically, measures of variability are intended to guard against overemphasis on central tendency.

Lecture Example A.5: Correlation and Cause-Effect

As you are discussing correlation, emphasize a basic point: Correlation does not show a cause-effect relationship. Make the point by speculating about correlations between two unrelated variables. For example, there is probably a positive correlation between the number of bars and the number of traffic lights in a city. If correlation showed a cause-effect relationship, we would have to conclude that more bars cause more traffic lights, or vice versa. Of course a third variable, namely, city size, accounts for the correlation. (Incidentally, a special type of correlation called path analysis does in fact show cause- effect relationships.)

Diversity Topic

Diversity Topic A.1: Cultural Variability

Say you did a study that showed that Hong Kong Chinese people gave significantly lower intensity ratings than Americans did to a series of facial expressions of emotion. How would the students interpret the results?
Discussion/Description: Similar types of results have been interpreted in the past according to how the Chinese sample learned to deamplify their responses to emotional stimuli. But, this interpretation suggests that the Americans have the "correct" score, and the Chinese have a mistaken score, because they learned to change their response. This is a biased interpretation. In actuality, the Americans may have learned to exaggerate their response. Or, the "true" intensity may actually be higher or lower than both the Americans and the Chinese. This type of subtle difference in wording is a blanket cover for many cultural biases in the interpretation of cross-cultural differences that occur in research.

B. Inferential Statistics

Classroom Demonstrations and Handouts

Demonstration STAT 2: Representative Sample

Objective: To demonstrate the importance of representative samples in research as well as to show the effect of increasing sample size.
Materials: **Handout STAT 2**
Procedure: Identify a "population" (e.g., everyone sitting in the two rows next to the windows). Calculate the mean age of that population. Next, draw a sample of 10 percent from the population and determine the mean age. Compare the two means. Increase the size of the sample gradually and note how the sample mean becomes a more accurate statistic of the population mean. Your last sample should be the entire population.
Conclusions: Psychologists rely heavily on inferential statistics and acknowledge the importance of representative samples and sample sizes.

Demonstration STAT 3: Randomization

Objective: To demonstrate the importance of random assignment of subjects to groups.
Materials: None
Procedure: Subject differences between groups are leveled by random assignment. The purpose of randomization is demonstrated in an activity by Stang (1981). Students should count off in sixes. On the board, write the numbers 1 through 6 and under each appropriate column, write the height in inches of the students in each number group. Calculate the mean of each group. The odd groups should be combined into one as well as the even groups into one single group. The means from the two collapsed groups should be very similar, while the means of the original six are probably more less similar.
Conclusions: The activity illustrates that random assignment provides for very similar groups and that as the sample size increases the more similar the groups become. Stang recommends examining the groups for extraneous variables such as sex difference. Next, assign subjects to groups using a prior selection; for example, males in one group and females in the other group and calculate mean heights.

Stang, D. J. (1981). Randomization. In L. T. Benjamin, Jr. and K. D. Lowman (Eds.), Activities handbook for the teaching of psychology (Vol. 1). Washington, D.C.: American Psychological Association.

Lecture Examples

Lecture Example A.6: Lying with Statistics

An adage says there are three kinds of lies: "lies, damned lies, and statistics." There is a general belief that anything can be proven with statistics. In other words, statistics can be manipulated in such a way that both sides of an argument are supported. Huff (1954) has written a very interesting and insightful book on how statistics are used and abused. One notable way to deceive by using statistics is to incorrectly construct graphs. Show students examples of how incorrect graphs can distort information. Another excellent source is Kimble (1970).

Huff, D. (1954). *How to lie with statistics.* New York: W. W. Norton.

Kimble, G. (1970). *How to use and abuse statistics.* Englewood Cliffs, NJ: Prentice Hall.

Diversity Topic

Diversity Topic A.2: Interpretation

People of different cultures will learn to prefer to use different parts of a rating scale. This tendency is called a cultural response set. When you do a study and obtain differences, how do you know that the differences that you obtained are reflective of true differences on the construct being rated, or merely a product of cultural preferences in how to use scales?
Discussion/Description: In actuality, there are a couple of ways to detect whether cultural response sets are at work in a data set. And, there are several ways to deal with them in data analysis. These topics may be beyond the purview of introductory psychology, but their existence is germane to this topic.

Diversity Topic A.3: Subject Selection

In cross-cultural research, the selection of subjects is a particularly tricky issue. There are two questions that need to be raised: (1) are the subjects adequate representatives of the groups they are supposed to represent? (2) are the samples equivalent on all other subject characteristics other than what they are supposed to vary on? Give a brief presentation of some of the difficulties inherent in this research process.
Discussion/Description: Use an example such as a cross-cultural study with a group of Americans, French, and Indians from Bombay. How are we to know that the samples in each country are adequate representatives of their respective cultures? To answer this question, we would have to know what their respective cultures are, measure that characteristic in the individuals, and establish that they are the same. In addition, how can we compare these individuals? For example, university students who serve as research subjects in India typically are of a considerably higher social class in India, because entrance in universities in India is much more restrictive than either in the U.S. or France. If differences are found, how are we to weed out the potential confounding influence of social class in this example?

Part Three

Handouts and Transparency Masters

STUDENT CHALKBOARD INTRO 1

Perspectives in Psychology

Use the chart to identify the main views of each perspective or historical school and at least one early leader.

School	Early Leader	Main Focus
Structuralist		
Functionalist		
Behaviorist		
Cognitive		
Physiological		
Sociocultural		
Psychodynamic		

©1999 Allyn & Bacon

Handout INTRO 3a

Demonstration INTRO 3: The Barnum Test of Personality

Carefully read each statement and then indicate your degree of agreement using this scale:

   1 = strong agreement

   2 = some agreement

   3 = little agreement

   4 = no agreement at all

_____ a.   I like spending time with other people.

_____ b.   I have realistic dreams and goals.

_____ c.   People are only looking out for their own interests.

_____ d.   I have frequent nightmares.

_____ e.   I prefer to use humor to cope with stress.

_____ f.   When I get nervous, I have problems thinking clearly.

_____ g.   I worry about how I spend my time.

_____ h.   My feet and hands are usually cold.

_____ i.   I'd like to travel around the world.

If you give consent to analyze your responses, please sign below. A printed copy of the analysis describing your personality will be made available to you.

_____   _____
Signature   Date

©1999 Allyn & Bacon

Handout INTRO 3b

Demonstration INTRO 3: The Barnum Test of Personality

Barnum Statements

Personality Description for

_____
(name of student)

According to your responses, you are an outgoing, gregarious, and warm person who enjoys socializing with others. At times, however, you are a somewhat introverted person who needs privacy. When the situation demands it, you can present your opinions and beliefs and assert leadership, while being a follower in other circumstances. Your ability to make quick and clear decisions is indicated, although in the past you have experienced some difficulty in making important choices.

The analysis has also revealed a sense of humor which is often apparent, but you also possess a sense of seriousness when the situation warrants it. You have an even temper and usually keep it under control, but there are times when your temper can rise and you let people know you're upset. In addition, working on practical and conceptual problems seems to bring out the best in you.

Handout INTRO 4

Demonstration INTRO 4: Commonsense Psychology Quiz

Indicate whether each statement is true or false. Then count the total number of true and false statements you answered.

T F 1. The titles "psychologist" and "psychiatrist" refer to the same profession.

T F 2. Psychologists study behavior and the mind, but not biology.

T F 3. Most psychologists believe that ESP exists.

T F 4. A person who is blind in one eye can't see depth and therefore can't fly an airplane.

T F 5. Some people never dream.

T F 6. When we sleep, the brain sleeps as well.

T F 7. Negative reinforcement is the same as punishment.

T F 8. We can't do much to improve our memory.

T F 9. Eyewitness testimony is some of the best evidence used by police and in court trials.

T F 10. In order to be creative, a person must be very intelligent.

T F 11. A person's intelligence is partially determined by brain size.

T F 12. Instinct determines many of our behaviors.

T F 13. The more motivated and aroused you are, the better your performance will be.

T F 14. We can train babies to walk at an early age.

T F 15. There is not much society can do to help the mentally retarded.

T F 16. All psychologists do is therapy.

T F 17. Shock treatment is often used for people with anxiety.

T F 18. A correlation between two variables means that one of those variables causes the other.

T F 19. Most of us would not follow instructions from an authority figure to hurt another person.

T F 20. Opposite types of people attract each other.

T F 21. A person with schizophrenia has a split personality.

T F 22. How a person shows he is happy depends on his culture and upbringing.

T F 23. Most old people have some degree of senility.

T F 24. Many people come through adolescence with emotional scars and conflicts.

T F 25. People with hypochondriasis pretend to be sick.

©1999 Allyn & Bacon

Handout INTRO 6

Demonstration INTRO 6: Seat Belt Contract

I, _____, herein known as the student, am taking Introduction to Psychology at _____ with Professor _____, herein known as the instructor. I acknowledge that I agree to the following without reservation.

I agree to wear properly a seat belt each and every time I drive or ride in an automobile. I agree that as a driver, I will verbally request all passengers to wear their seat belts properly. I understand that some passengers will not comply, but I must make a reasonable effort.

In return for doing so, the instructor will _____ _____. I agree that every time the instructor observes me or my passengers riding in an automobile without using seat belts, the instructor may _____. In this event, the instructor will discuss with me the circumstances surrounding the incident, and I will be candid and faithful in my explanation.

I understand that by properly wearing a seat belt I can reduce my chances of being seriously injured or killed in an accident; however, I understand that the probability for injury or death is not totally eliminated. In any case, I will not hold the instructor or the college liable or responsible for any unforeseen events stemming from the agreement.

_____ _____
Student signature   Date

_____ _____
Instructor signature   Date

©1999 Allyn & Bacon

HANDOUT INTRO 7

Demonstration INTRO 7: Critical Thinking Squares

Count the squares:

©1999 Allyn & Bacon

STUDENT CHALKBOARD METHODS 1

Strengths and Weaknesses of Research Methods

On the chart fill in the strengths and weaknesses of each research method.

Method	Strength	Weakness
Experiment		
Correlational Study		
Questionnaire		
Naturalistic Observation		
Case Study		

©1999 Allyn & Bacon

HANDOUT METHODS 2

Demonstration METHODS 2: Representative Sample

Sample Data

Mean Height (in inches)

Total Population: _____   _____
                    (number)

Sample Mean   10%   _____

Sample Mean   25%   _____

Sample Mean   50%   _____

Sample Mean   75%   _____

Sample Mean   100%   _____

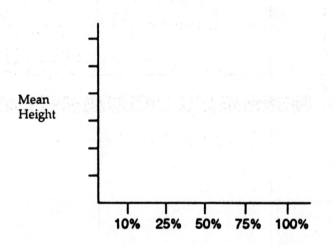

Mean Height

10% 25% 50% 75% 100%

©1999 Allyn & Bacon

Handout METHODS 3

Demonstration METHODS 3: Classroom Correlation

Correlation

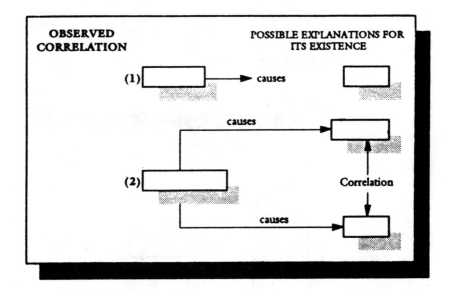

Handout Methods 4

Demonstration METHODS 4: Correlation versus Causation

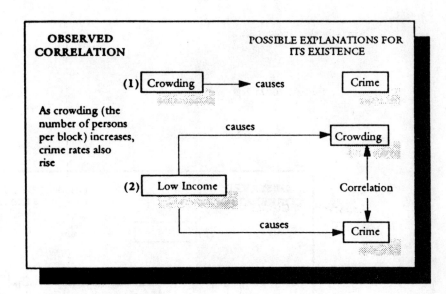

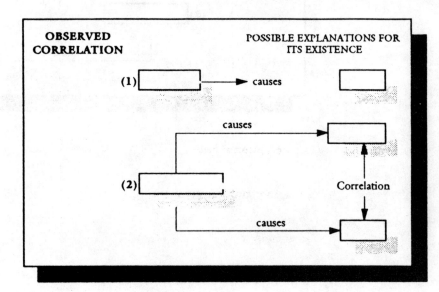

HANDOUT METHODS 5

Demonstration METHODS 5: Designing an Experiment

Cliche/Old Wive's Tale:

State it as a hypothesis:

    Populations:

    How do you select a sample?

Experimental Group:

Control Group:

Variables:

    Independent Variable:

    Dependent Variable:

Ethical Issues?

    Any deception required?

    Any minor children required?

    Other issues?

What is your next step?

HANDOUT METHODS 6

Demonstration METHODS 6: Research Ethics

Judging the Ethics of Research

Homosexual attitudes
Men are recruited to participate in an experiment on sexual attitudes, although they are not told that it is actually a study of attitudes toward homosexuality. Participants are led to believe that a "psychogalvanometer" used in the experiment is capable of detecting sexual arousal. They are also told that if the galvanometer registers arousal when an individual looks at slides of nude males, the individual is probably a latent homosexual. The galvanometer is rigged so that all participants are led to believe they are latent homosexuals. Following the experiment, the researcher informs the participants that the galvanometer was rigged, and he gives detailed information about the study and its true purpose.

very ethical ❑ ❑ ❑ ❑ ❑ very unethical

Student cheating
Without informing his students, a professor uses one of his classes for a research study of cheating behavior. True-false exams are given at various points in the semester. After each test the exams are collected, copied, and then returned to the students, who are told they will score their own tests. A comparison of student graded exams with ungraded copies will reveal instances where students cheated by changing test answers. At the end of the semester, the professor tells his class about the research project in which they had participated unknowingly.

very ethical ❑ ❑ ❑ ❑ ❑ very unethical

Racial attitude change
The purpose of the experiment is to compare the effects of different methods of reducing racial prejudice. Students with strong racial prejudice are recruited for the experiment but are not told the true purpose of the study. Instead, they are led to believe that the experiment focuses on a topic unrelated to prejudice. After the experiment is completed, participants are informed of the true purpose of the experiment and of its effect on their personal beliefs. Details of the study are discussed.

very ethical ❑ ❑ ❑ ❑ ❑ very unethical

Effects of combat stress
Inexperienced soldiers, unaware that they are actually involved in a research study of the effects of combat stress, are disoriented, isolated, given false instructions, and led to believe that they have caused artillery to fire on their own troops during final training maneuvers. Since actual ammunition is used in these maneuvers, the soldiers are led to think that real casualties have occurred and that they are responsible. When the soldiers return to their base of operations, they are told that the incident was staged as part of a research study of combat stress. The importance of the study and the details of the research are explained to the men.

very ethical ❑ ❑ ❑ ❑ ❑ very unethical

©1999 Allyn & Bacon

HANDOUT METHODS 7

Demonstration METHODS 7: Writing Informed Consent Form

Sample Informed Consent Form

I freely and voluntarily consent to be a participant in a research project entitled "_____" to be conducted at Big State Research University in the semester of 199__ with Professor _____ as the principle investigator. I have been told that my part will require about forty-five minutes.

The purpose of this study:

    To explore _____.

The research procedures are as follows:

    Subjects _____.

I understand that no risk is involved in my participation in this research. I have been told that my responses will be kept strictly confidential. All responses will be identified only by a code number, and my individual responses will not be revealed to anyone without my permission.

I understand that I may withdraw my consent and discontinue participation in this research at any time without prejudice. I have been given the right to ask questions concerning the procedure, and any questions I have about the procedure have now been satisfactorily answered.

I have read and understand the above.

_____   _____
Witness   Participant

                                              _____
                                              Date

I have explained and described in detail the research procedure in which the subject has consented to participate.

_____   _____
Principle Investigator   Date
(or assistant)

Handout METHODS 8

Demonstration METHODS 8: Participating on an Institutional Animal Rights Committee

The following two cases are from Herzog (1990), and they illustrate the kinds of issues that must be dealt with by animal welfare committees.

Case 1:

"Professor King is a psychobiologist working on the frontiers of a new and exciting research area of neuroscience, brain grafting. Research has shown that neural tissue can be removed from the brains of monkey fetuses and implanted into the brains of monkeys that have suffered brain damage. The neurons seem to make the proper connections and are sometimes effective in improving performance in brain-damaged animals. These experiments offer important animal models for human degenerative diseases such as Parkinson's and Alzheimer's. Dr. King wants to transplant tissue from fetal monkey brains into the entorhinal cortex of adult monkeys; this is the area of the human brain that is involved with Alzheimer's disease.

"The experiment will use twenty adult rhesus monkeys. First, the monkeys will be subjected to ablation surgery in the entorhinal cortex. . . . After they recover, the monkeys will be tested on a learning task to make sure their memory is impaired. Three months later, half the animals will be given transplant surgery. . . . Control animals will be subjected to sham surgery, and all animals will be allowed to recover for two months. They will then learn a task to test the hypothesis that the animals having brain grafts will show better memory than the control group.

"Dr. King argues that this research is in the exploratory stages and can only be done using animals. She further states that by the year 2000 about two million Americans will have Alzheimer's disease and that her research could lead to a treatment for the devastating memory loss that Alzheimer's victims suffer (Herzog, 92)."

Case 2 (Herzog's Case 4):

"The Psychology Department is requesting permission from your committee to use 10 rats per semester for demonstration experiments in a physiological psychology course. The students will work in groups of three; each group will be given a rat. The students will first perform surgery on the rats. Each animal will be anesthetized. Following standard surgical procedures an incision will be made in the scalp and two holes drilled in the animal's skull. Electrodes will be lowered into the brain to create lesions on each side. The animals will then be allowed to recover. Several weeks later, the effects of destroying this part of the animal's brain will be tested in a shuttle avoidance task in which the animals learn to cross over an electrified grid.

"The instructor acknowledges that the procedure is a common demonstration and that no new scientific information will be gained from the experiment. He argues, however, that students taking the course in physiological psychology must have the opportunity to engage in small animal surgery and to see firsthand the effects of brain lesions (Herzog, 93)."

Source:

Herzog, Harold. (1990). Discussing animal rights and animal research in the classroom, *Teaching of Psychology, 17*, 90-94.

STUDENT CHALKBOARD BIO 1

The Basic Structure of the Neuron

Identify the parts of the neuron discussed in the text.

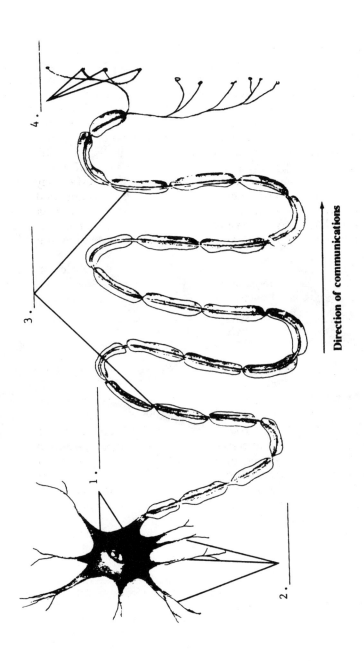

©1999 Allyn & Bacon

STUDENT CHALKBOARD BIO 2

Transmission at the Synapse

Identify the part and describe its function in the space provided.

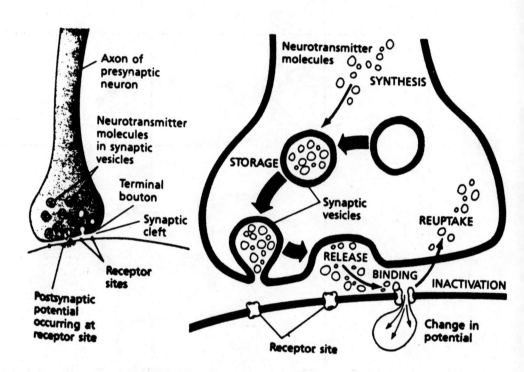

STUDENT CHALKBOARD BIO 3

Neurotransmitters

Identify where each neurotransmitter is found and the effects it has in that area on the chart below.

Neurotransmitter	Where Found	Effects
Acetylcholine		
Norepinephrine		
Dopamine		
Serotonin		
GABA		

STUDENT CHALKBOARD BIO 4

The Human Nervous System

Identify each division of the nervous system and describe its role briefly.

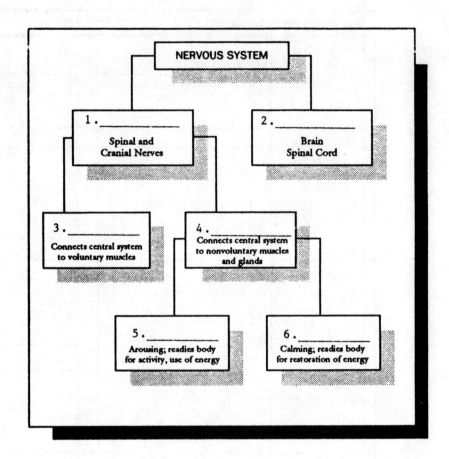

1. _____
2. _____
3. _____
4. _____
5. _____
6. _____

STUDENT CHALKBOARD BIO 5

The Autonomic Nervous System

Describe how each organ is affected by the sympathetic and parasympathetic nervous system.

Organ	Sympathetic	Parasympathetic
Adrenal Medulla		
Bladder		

Blood Vessels
  Abdomen
 	
  Muscles
 	
  Skin		

Heart		
Intestines		
Liver		
Lungs		
Pupil of Eye		
Salivary Glands		
Sweat Glands		

©1999 Allyn & Bacon

STUDENT CHALKBOARD BIO 6

The Human Brain
(Limbic System and Brain Stem)

Identify the major parts and describe their roles in the space below.

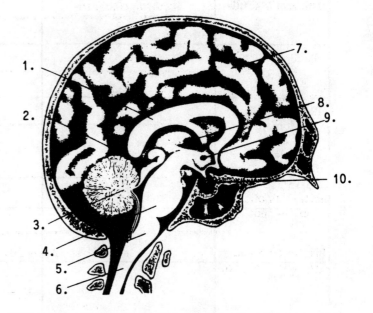

1. _____
2. _____
3. _____
4. _____
5. _____
6. _____
7. _____
8. _____
9. _____
10. _____

©1999 Allyn & Bacon

Handout BIO 3a

Demonstration BIO 3: Measuring Sympathetic Responses

Effects of Mental Activity on Physiological Responses

INSTRUCTIONS	BEATS PER MINUTE	
	Your subject's data	Your data
Relax		
Increase physical activity		
Relax		
Increase emotional excitement		

List for both you and your subject the basic situations that you imagined in the "increase" periods:

	Physically exerting	Mentally exciting
You:		
Your subject:		

©1999 Allyn & Bacon

Handout BIO 3b

Demonstration BIO 3: Measuring Sympathetic Responses

Data Graph

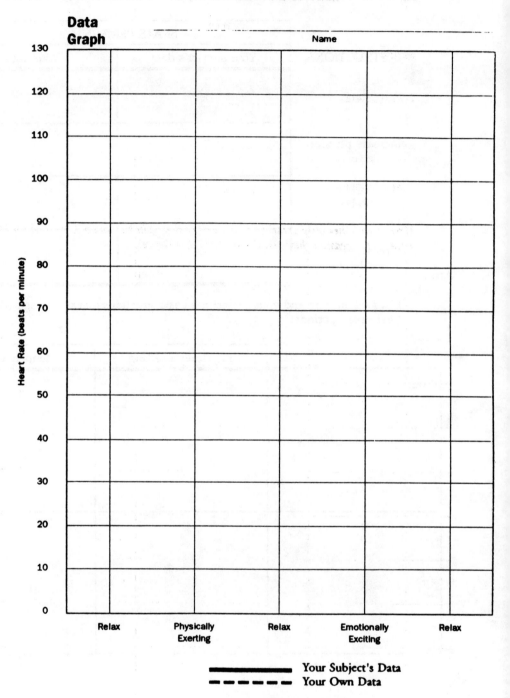

HANDOUT BIO 5

Demonstration BIO 5: Two-Point Threshold

Record the distance at which the subject reports feeling two distinct points.

	Distance
Elbow	_____
Forearm	_____
Palm	_____
Index Finger	_____

Now locate other body areas, predict whether they will be more or less sensitive than the above areas, then measure their sensitivity (that is, distance).

Area:	More than/less than which area?	Distance
_____	_____	_____
_____	_____	_____
_____	_____	_____
_____	_____	_____
_____	_____	_____
_____	_____	_____
_____	_____	_____
_____	_____	_____

©1999 Allyn & Bacon

HANDOUT BIO 7

Demonstration BIO 7: Looking Left—Looking Right

Left and Right Hemisphere Questions

1. What does the word "appetite" mean? (language).

2. How many letters are there in the word "growing"? (language)

3. What direction does the Statue of Liberty face? (spatial)

4. Name three states that border Iowa. (spatial)

5. You are walking due north and turn left and then left again and then right. What direction are you walking? (spatial)

6. How many straight lines are their in a hexagon? (spatial)

7. Which word has more letters, "publication" or "contemplation"? (language)

8. What is a synonym for "help"? (language)

HANDOUT BIO 9

Demonstration BIO 9: Genetic Differences Between People

Ring Versus Index Finger

Place your ring finger on the line. Trace all your fingers. Compare the length of your index finger and your ring finger. Which is longer?

_____

Handout BIO 10

Demonstration BIO 10: Genetic Detective

Family Characteristics

Chart physical characteristics that you know through several generations of your family (eye or hair color, for instance).

Characteristic: _____

Great-Grandparents

Grandparents

Parents and their siblings

Mother   Father

You and your siblings

You

Children

©1999 Allyn & Bacon

STUDENT CHALKBOARD S&P 1

The Structure of the Eye

Identify the parts of the eye and describe their roles in vision.

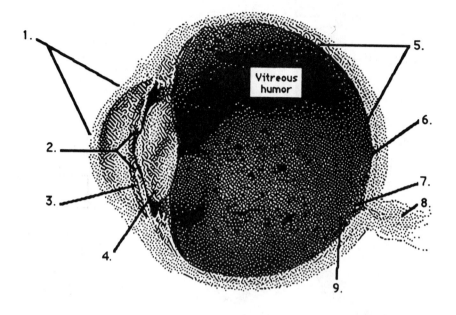

1. _____
2. _____
3. _____
4. _____
5. _____
6. _____
7. _____
8. _____
9. _____

©1999 Allyn & Bacon

STUDENT CHALKBOARD S&P 2

Left and Right Visual Image

Identify each part and describe how the image is transmitted from the left and right halves of the eyes to the visual cortex.

LEFT EYE IMAGE   RIGHT EYE IMAGE

1. _____
2. _____
3. _____
4. _____
5. _____
6. _____
7. _____
8. _____

_____
_____
_____
_____
_____
_____

STUDENT CHALKBOARD S&P 3

Anatomy of the Auditory System

Label the parts and describe their roles in hearing.

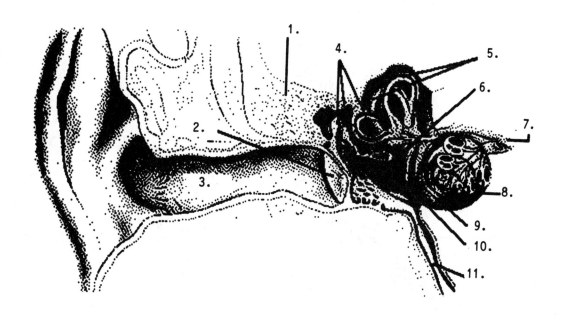

1. _____

2. _____

3. _____

4. _____

5. _____

6. _____

7. _____

8. _____

9. _____

10. _____

11. _____

©1999 Allyn & Bacon

HANDOUT S&P 4

Demonstration S&P 4: The Blind Spot

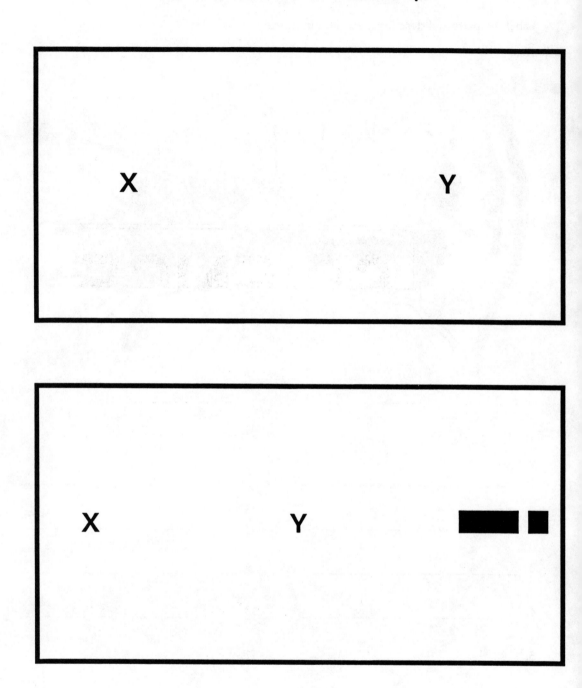

©1999 Allyn & Bacon

HANDOUT S&P 5a

Demonstration S&P 5: "What do you see?"

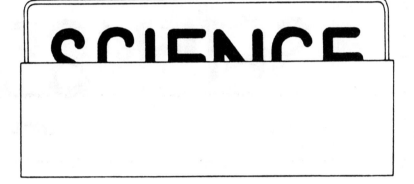

HANDOUT S&P 5b

Demonstration S&P 5: "What do you see?"

```
+------------------------------+
|                              |
|      S615N65                 |
|  1986              OPIL      |
+------------------------------+
```

©1999 Allyn & Bacon

Handout S&P 8

Demonstration S&P 8: Brightness Constancy

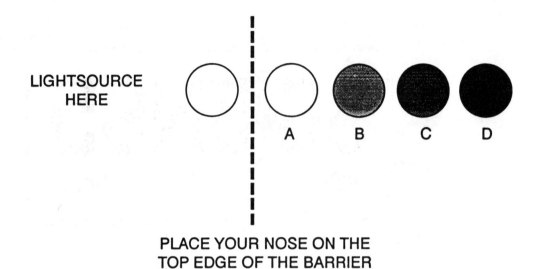

PLACE YOUR NOSE ON THE
TOP EDGE OF THE BARRIER

©1999 Allyn & Bacon

HANDOUT S&P 9

Demonstration S&P 9: Top-Down Processing Versus Bottom-Up Processing In Reading Handwriting

Handwriting Samples

I would like to get an undergraduate degree in psychology with hopes of earning a Ph.D. My area of specialty would be child psych since I really enjoy working with children.

I am especially interested in the development of a child's social relationship. As a psychologist, I would like to teach at a small university and head my own Child Research Center.

HANDOUT S&P 11a

Demonstration S&P 11: Testing Students for ESP

Zener Cards

HANDOUT S&P 11b

Demonstration S&P 11: Testing Students for ESP

Recording Sheet

Test of Precognition		Subject: _____		
Run #1		(Circle each hit)		Hits: _____
1	6	11	16	21
2	7	12	17	22
3	8	13	18	23
4	9	14	19	24
5	10	15	20	25
Run #2		(Circle each hit)		Hits: _____
1	6	11	16	21
2	7	12	17	22
3	8	13	18	23
4	9	14	19	24
5	10	15	20	25

Test of Clairvoyance		Subject: _____		
Run #1		(Circle each hit)		Hits: _____
1	6	11	16	21
2	7	12	17	22
3	8	13	18	23
4	9	14	19	24
5	10	15	20	25
Run #2		(Circle each hit)		Hits: _____
1	6	11	16	21
2	7	12	17	22
3	8	13	18	23
4	9	14	19	24
5	10	15	20	25

Test of Telepathy		Subject: _____		
Run #1		(Circle each hit)		Hits: _____
1	6	11	16	21
2	7	12	17	22
3	8	13	18	23
4	9	14	19	24
5	10	15	20	25
Run #2		(Circle each hit)		Hits: _____
1	6	11	16	21
2	7	12	17	22
3	8	13	18	23
4	9	14	19	24
5	10	15	20	25

©1999 Allyn & Bacon

STUDENT CHALKBOARD CONSC 1

Brain Activity During Stages of Sleep

Identify the stages of sleep and name the brain waves.

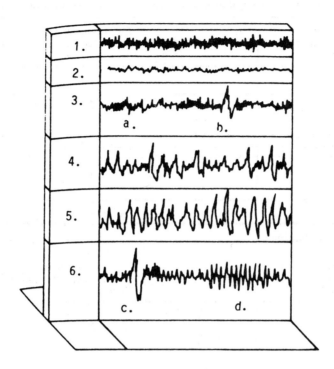

1. _____   a. _____

2. _____   b. _____

3. _____   c. _____

4. _____   d. _____

5. _____

6. _____

©1999 Allyn & Bacon

STUDENT CHALKBOARD CONSC 2

Drugs and their Effects

Describe the effects of each drug in the list.

Drug	*Effect*
Depressants	
Alcohol	
Barbiturates	
Opiates	
Stimulants	
Amphetamines	
Cocaine	
Caffeine	
Tobacco	
Hallucinogens	
Marijuana	
Mescaline	
LSD	

©1999 Allyn & Bacon

HANDOUT CONSC 2

Demonstration CONSC 2: Dream Journal

Sleep and Dreaming Record

Student Number_____   Date_____

1. Total sleep time (in hours) _____. On the time line below, block out your sleep periods, including naps.

   ```
   _____
   6:00    10:00   2:00    6:00    10:00   2:00    6:00
   p.m.    p.m.    a.m.    a.m.    a.m.    p.m.    p.m.
   ```

2. Total number of awakenings during major sleep period _____. (Do not count the final morning awakening.)

3. On the scale below, rate the quality of your night's sleep (in your opinion). Circle one of the numbers from plus four to minus four.

   ```
   bad  -4   -3   -2   -1   0   +1   +2   +3   +4   good
   ```

4. In your judgment, how many separate dreams can you recall at least a fragment of?

   _____

5. It is possible that you will recall some of your dreams better than others. Using percentages, estimate the amount of each dream recalled.

   Dream 1 _____   Dream 2 _____   Dream 3 _____   Dream 4 _____

6. How many of these dreams could you relate to presleep experiences of the dream day?

   _____

7. Did you appear as a character in the dreams you recall? In how many? _____

8. How many of your dreams were in color? _____

9. Were there stimuli in your dreams of a nonvisual nature? Check the following if appropriate.

   sound _____   taste _____   touch _____   smell _____

Benjamin, L. (1988). To sleep perchance to dream. In L. Benjamin and K. Lowman (Eds.). *Activities Handbook for the Teaching of Psychology*, Vol. 1. Washington, D.C.: American Psychological Association, 196-198. Copyright 1988 by the American Psychological Association. Adapted by permission of the publisher and author.

©1999 Allyn & Bacon

Handout CONSC 5

Demonstration CONSC 5: Antecedents and Consequences of Drug Use

Caffeine, Alcohol, and Nicotine

Day: 1 2 3 4   (circle one)
      Weekend Weekday   (circle one)

Antecedents (psychological and behavioral):
_____
_____

Consequences (psychological and behavioral):
_____
_____

Time: _____   Drug used: _____

Antecedents (psychological and behavioral):
_____
_____

Consequences (psychological and behavioral):
_____
_____

Time: _____   Drug used: _____

Antecedents (psychological and behavioral):
_____
_____

Consequences (psychological and behavioral):
_____
_____

Time: _____   Drug used: _____

©1999 Allyn & Bacon

STUDENT CHALKBOARD LEARN 1

Order of Presentation

Name the order of presentation, and describe the effectiveness of each one. Then, give an example of each.

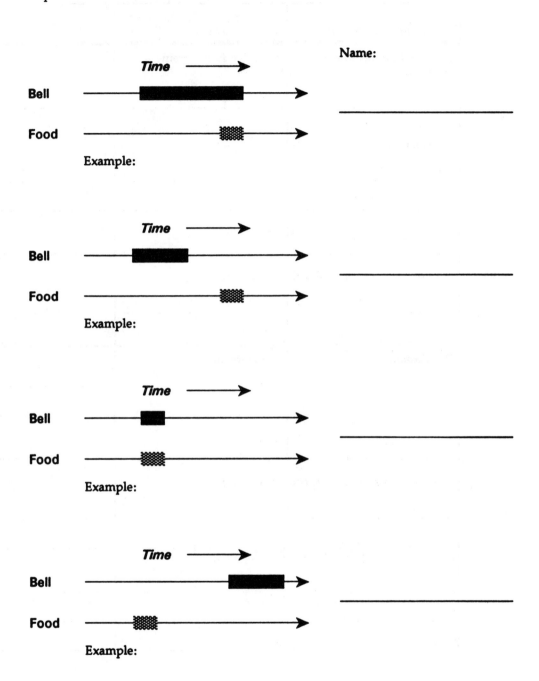

STUDENT CHALKBOARD LEARN 2

Reinforcement and Punishment

On the chart, complete the description for each kind of reinforcement or punishment.

Addition of a Stimulus	Subtraction or Withholding of a Stimulus	Effect
Positive Reinforcement	**Negative Reinforcement**	
Punishment	**Punishment**	

©1999 Allyn & Bacon

Student Chalkboard LEARN 3

Learning Theory Comparison

Describe the procedures and results, and give an example for each learning theory.

Comparison	
Classical Conditioning	
Procedure	
Result	
Example	
Operant Conditioning	
Procedure	
Result	
Example	
Observational Learning	
Procedure	
Result	
Example	

©1999 Allyn & Bacon

HANDOUT LEARN 1

Demonstration LEARN 1: Classical Conditioning in Humans

Conditioning Record

Fill in the blanks, then explain.

Puff of Air ⟶ _____ (UCR)

(CS) _____ ⟶ _____ (CR)

Explain:

Balloon Pop ⟶ _____ (UCR)

(CS) _____ ⟶ _____ (CR)

Explain:

(UCR) _____ ⟶ _____ (UCR)

(CS) _____ ⟶ _____ (CR)

Explain:

(UCR) _____ ⟶ _____ (UCR)

(CS) _____ ⟶ _____ (CR)

Explain:

©1999 Allyn & Bacon

HANDOUT LEARN 2

Demonstration LEARN 2: Learning Curve and the Backwards Alphabet

Learning Curve: Backwards Alphabet

Trial	Score
1.	
2.	
3.	
4.	
5.	
6.	
7.	
8.	
9.	
10.	
11.	
12.	
13.	
14.	
15.	

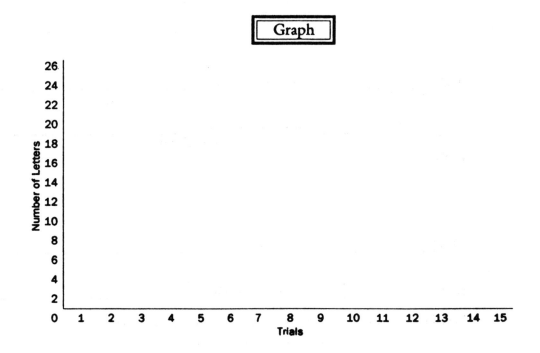

©1999 Allyn & Bacon

Handout LEARN 3

Demonstration LEARN 3: Operant Conditioning and TV Ads

Tally Record

Advertisement: _____

Paired Stimuli: _____With_____

Reinforcers: _____

_____

_____

Advertisement: _____

   red Stimuli: _____With_____

Reinforcers: _____

_____

_____

Advertisement: _____

Paired Stimuli: _____With_____

Reinforcers: _____

_____

_____

HANDOUT LEARN 4

Demonstration LEARN 4: Using Positive Reinforcement

©1999 Allyn & Bacon

Handout LEARN 8

Demonstration LEARN 8: Assess the Violence In Children's Cartoons

Violent Act Tally

Name of Cartoon: _____ Length: _____

Characters: _____ _____

_____ _____

Implicit Acts   Explicit Acts

Total: _____   Total: _____
Acts Per Minute: _____   Acts Per Minute: _____

Name of Cartoon: _____ Length: _____

Characters: _____ _____

_____ _____

Implicit Acts   Explicit Acts

Total: _____   Total: _____
Acts Per Minute: _____   Acts Per Minute: _____

©1999 Allyn & Bacon

HANDOUT LEARN 9a

Demonstration LEARN 9a: Self-Management

Sample Data Record

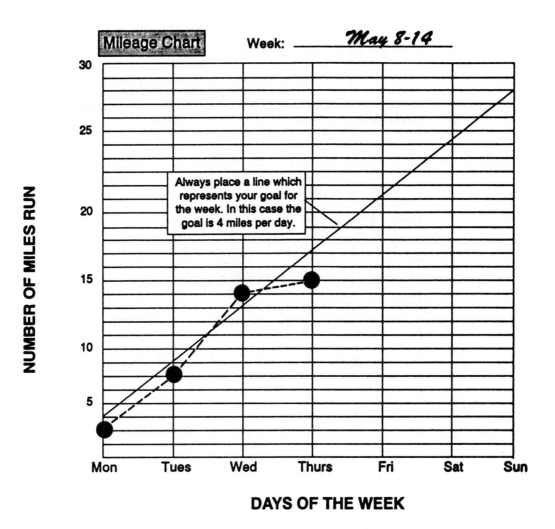

HANDOUT LEARN 9b

Demonstration LEARN 9b: Self-Management

Personal Data Record

©1999 Allyn & Bacon

STUDENT CHALKBOARD MEM 1

Model of Memory

Describe the encoding, storage, and retrieval processes for sensory memory, short-term memory, and long-term memory. Also describe the capacity and duration of information in each type of memory.

Sensory Memory	
Encoding Process	
Storage (capacity) (duration)	
Retrieval	
Short-Term Memory	
Encoding Process	
Storage (capacity) (duration)	
Retrieval	
Long-Term Memory	
Encoding Process	
Storage (capacity) (duration)	
Retrieval	

©1999 Allyn & Bacon

STUDENT CHALKBOARD MEM 2

Retention and Forgetting in Memory

Describe the processes of retention and forgetting in sensory memory, short-term memory, and long-term memory.

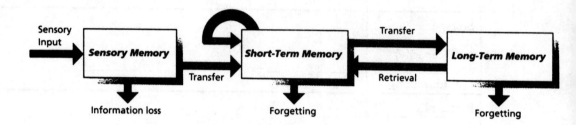

	Retention	Forgetting
Sensory		
Short-term memory		
Long-term memory		

©1999 Allyn & Bacon

Handout MEM 1a

Demonstration MEM 1: Memory and Forgetting

Group List

Group #: _____

Sense Words   Nonsense Words

_____   _____

_____   _____

_____   _____

_____   _____

_____   _____

_____   _____

_____   _____

_____   _____

_____   _____

_____   _____

_____   _____

©1999 Allyn & Bacon

HANDOUT MEM 1b

Demonstration MEM 1: Memory and Forgetting

Individual Recall List

Group #: _____

Sense Words   Nonsense Words

©1999 Allyn & Bacon

Handout MEM 2

Demonstration MEM 2: Grocery List

Grocery List Response Sheet

Recall the grocery list just read, and record your responses here.

	Word:	Correct/Incorrect
1.	_____	_____
2.	_____	_____
3.	_____	_____
4.	_____	_____
5.	_____	_____
6.	_____	_____
7.	_____	_____
8.	_____	_____
9.	_____	_____
10.	_____	_____
11.	_____	_____
12.	_____	_____
13.	_____	_____
14.	_____	_____
15.	_____	_____
16.	_____	_____

©1999 Allyn & Bacon

HANDOUT MEM 3

Demonstration MEM 3: Chunking to Increase Meaningfulness

Th era inhe lpsf arm ersgr owcro ps.

✂ ————————————————————————

The rain helps farmers grow crops.

©1999 Allyn & Bacon

HANDOUT MEM 4

Demonstration MEM 4: Short-Term Memory

HANDOUT MEM 6a

Demonstration MEM 6a: Hierarchical Organization and Recall

Minerals

emerald	marble	slate	ruby
silver	limestone	diamond	aluminum
steel	brass	bronze	iron
granite	sapphire	gold	lead
platinum	copper		

HANDOUT MEM 6b

Demonstration MEM 6b: Hierarchical Organization and Recall

Minerals

Metal			*Stones*	
rare	*common*	*alloys*	*precious*	*masonry*
platinum	aluminum	bronze	sapphire	limestone
silver	copper	steel	emerald	granite
gold	iron	brass	diamond	marble
	lead		ruby	slate

HANDOUT MEM 7

Demonstration MEM 7: Using Retrieval Cues

Recall Versus Recognition

Describe several situations where you rely on recognition memory. What retrieval cues are involved.

Describe several situations where you rely on recall memory. What retrieval cues are involved?

Describe one situation (like the supermarket) where you can use either recognition or recall. How do you manipulate the retrieval cues to chose one or the other?

©1999 Allyn & Bacon

HANDOUT MEM 8

Demonstration MEM 8: U. S. Presidents

President List

1.	Washington	22.	Cleveland
2.	J. Adams	23.	B. Harrison
3.	Jefferson	24.	Cleveland
4.	Madison	25.	McKinley
5.	Monroe	26.	T. Roosevelt
6.	J. Q. Adams	27.	Taft
7.	Jackson	28.	Wilson
8.	Van Buren	29.	Harding
9.	W. Harrison	30.	Coolidge
10.	Tyler	31.	Hoover
11.	Polk	32.	F.D. Roosevelt
12.	Taylor	33.	Truman
13.	Fillmore	34.	Eisenhower
14.	Pierce	35.	Kennedy
15.	Buchanan	36.	L. Johnson
16.	Lincoln	37.	Nixon
17.	A. Johnson	38.	Ford
18.	Grant	39.	Carter
19.	Hayes	40.	Reagan
20.	Garfield	41.	Bush
21.	Arthur	42.	Clinton

©1999 Allyn & Bacon

Handout MEM 9

Demonstration MEM 9: Creating a Déjà Vu Experience

REST	TIRED
AWAKE	DREAM
SNORE	BED
EAT	SLUMBER
SOUND	COMFORT
WAKE	NIGHT

©1999 Allyn & Bacon

Handout MEM 10

Demonstration MEM 10: Distortion and Construction in Memory

Veteran teachers will tell you how much things have changed in the past twenty years. And you will find that today's teacher has more responsibilities than ever before. For one thing, there is simply a lot more to know about teaching and learning. The knowledge explosion of the past few decades means that much more information is available to the new teacher starting out today than was available to graduates of schools of education only a few short years ago. It also means that teachers need to know more.

From the Preface of Gibson, J. T., & Chandler, L. A. (1988). *Educational psychology: Mastering principles and applications*. Boston: Allyn and Bacon

©1999 Allyn & Bacon

HANDOUT MEM 11a

Demonstration MEM 11: Eyewitness Memory

Accident Scene

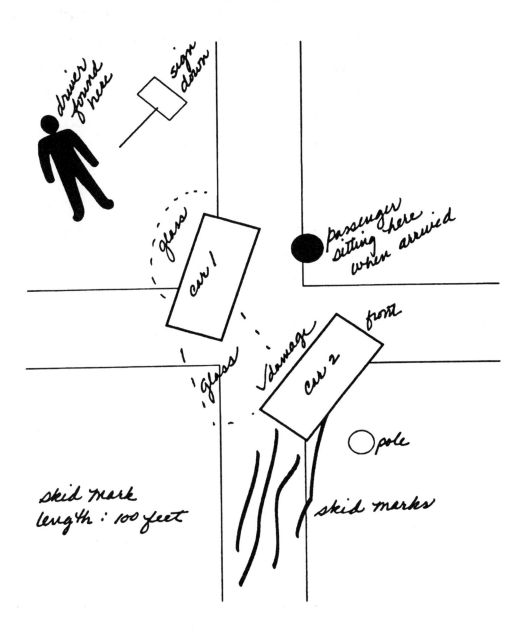

©1999 Allyn & Bacon

HANDOUT MEM 11b

Demonstration MEM 11: Eyewitness Memory

Witness Report

How fast were the cars going when they smashed into each other?

Was there broken glass on the ground?

How badly was the light pole damaged?

Was one driver intoxicated?

Were there any serious injuries?

Were the drivers not wearing their seat belts?

Handout MEM 11c

Demonstration MEM 11: Eyewitness Memory

Witness Report

How fast were the cars going when they ran into each other?"

Was there broken glass on the ground?

How badly was the light pole damaged?

Was one driver intoxicated?

Were there any serious injuries?

Were the drivers not wearing their seat belts?

HANDOUT MEM 12a

Demonstration MEM 12: Class Interruption

Student Responses

About how tall was the person?

How poorly dressed was the person?

How old was the person?

How rude was the person?

How loud was the person?

HANDOUT MEM 12b

Demonstration MEM 12: Class Interruption

Student Responses

About how short was the person?

How well dressed was the person?

How young was the person?

How polite was the person?

How quiet was the person?

©1999 Allyn & Bacon

Handout MEM 13

Demonstration MEM 13: Which One Is the Correct Drawing?

Which Penny?

©1999 Allyn & Bacon

STUDENT CHALKBOARD COG 1

Problem Solving Approaches

Describe the procedure, advantage, disadvantage, and an example of each of the types of problem-solving strategies.

Algorithms	
Procedure	
Advantages	
Disadvantages	
Example	

Heuristics	
Procedure	
Advantages	
Disadvantages	
Example	

STUDENT CHALKBOARD LANG 1

Language Achievement

Describe the language activity achieved by the age indicated (on average).

Age	Language Activity
12 weeks	
16 weeks	
20 weeks	
6 months	
12 months	
18 months	
24 months	
30 months	
36 months	

©1999 Allyn & Bacon

HANDOUT COG 2

Demonstration COG 2: Availability Heuristics

Heuristics

1. In the English language, are there more words beginning with the letter "r" or more words with the letter "r" appearing as the third letter?

   ❑ First position

   ❑ Third position

2. In the English language, are there more words beginning with the letter "k" or more words with the letter "k" appearing as the third letter?

   ❑ First position

   ❑ Third position

3. What percentage of the faculty at this university are women?

   _____ %

4. How many of your courses have been taught by female professors?

   _____ courses

©1999 Allyn & Bacon

HANDOUT COG 3

Demonstration COG 3: Solving Problems

Problem Sets

Group # _____

Problem Statement:

Proposed Solution:

©1999 Allyn & Bacon

Handout COG 5

Demonstration COG 5: Breaking Sets in Problem Solving

Think of a problem. Describe it concisely, then list four alternative ways to describe the difficulty.

Initial statement of the problem:

Alternate 1:

Alternate 2:

Alternate 3:

Alternate 4:

Describe the problem from the point of view of other parties involved:

Describe two solutions to this problem, indicating how these solutions are influenced by the particular statement of the problem you have chosen:

©1999 Allyn & Bacon

Handout COG 6a

Demonstration COG 6: Legos and Creativity

The Unusual Use Test

What atypical uses can you describe for the following everyday objects?

1. 1973 Volkswagen Bug:
   _____
   _____

2. Paper clip:
   _____
   _____

3. Tennis Racket:
   _____
   _____

4. Used Toothbrush:
   _____
   _____

5. Index Card:
   _____
   _____

6. Madonna CD:
   _____
   _____

7. Pen with no ink:
   _____
   _____

8. Floppy disk:
   _____
   _____

©1999 Allyn & Bacon

Handout COG 6b

Demonstration COG 6: Legos and Creativity

The Consequences Test

1. What would happen if the world ran out of tape?

2. What would be the results if everyone in the world looked liked Popeye?

3. What would be the consequences if a law was passed to prohibit the use of "um," "ah," and "like"?

4. What would happen if people lost the ability to put the left shoe on the left foot and the right shoe on the right foot?

5. What would be the results if everyone in the world suddenly became a Robin Leach clone?

©1999 Allyn & Bacon

HANDOUT COG 6c

Demonstration COG 6: Legos and Creativity

Abstract Figures

Identify each of the following:

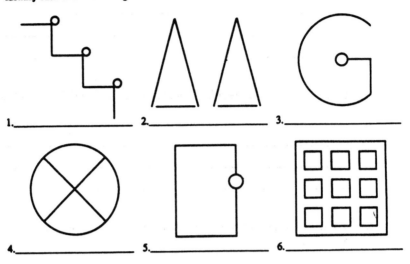

1. _____ 2. _____ 3. _____

4. _____ 5. _____ 6. _____

Complete the following drawings and tell what each represents.

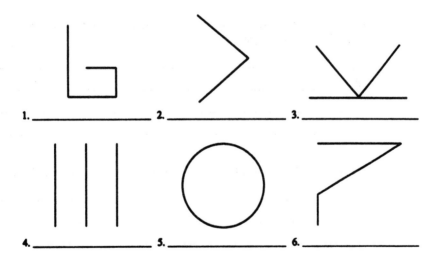

1. _____ 2. _____ 3. _____

4. _____ 5. _____ 6. _____

©1999 Allyn & Bacon

HANDOUT LANG 2

Demonstration LANG 2: Positive Versus Negative Instance

6	7	3	5	9	0	8	3	1	6	7	6	6
2	4	3	8	7	5	0	1	7	3	9	2	1
6	0	1	8	2	0	3	3	4	9	6	4	1
0	2	9	1	8	7	4	5	7	7	2	2	3
1	5	9	3	7	0	2	5	7	8	3	3	1
9	9	9	8	5	3	8	4	1	3	8	0	5
2	4	4	3	8	6	0	9	7	5	1	1	4
8	1	7	7	3	6	4	2	8	9	0	5	3
3	5	4	7	7	1	9	8	0	5	6	2	1
4	1	7	3	8	9	0	3	4	6	2	7	8
0	7	8	4	3	2	1	7	4	7	8	3	2
8	3	2	5	6	1	6	9	4	1	0	7	7
6	7	4	4	2	0	8	1	0	3	9	2	8

©1999 Allyn & Bacon

STUDENT CHALKBOARD INTELL 1

Types of Validity

Describe what each of the four types of validity can measure.

Validity	Aspect Measured
Content Validity	
Face Validity	
Predictive Validity	
Construct Validity	

©1999 Allyn & Bacon

STUDENT CHALKBOARD INTELL 2

Subtests of the Stanford-Binet

Describe the subtest named in the left-hand column.

Subtest	Description
Verbal Reasoning	
Abstract Reasoning	
Quantitative Reasoning	
Short-Term Memory	

©1999 Allyn & Bacon

Student Chalkboard INTELL 3

Subtests of the WISC-R

Describe the subtest named in the left-hand column.

Performance Section	
Picture Arrangement	
Block Design	
Digit Symbol	
Picture Completion	
Object Assembly	
Verbal Section	
Digit Span	
Vocabulary	
Information	
Comprehension	
Arithmetic	
Similarities	

©1999 Allyn & Bacon

Handout INTELL 1

Demonstration INTELL 1: Reliability and Validity of an Historical Measure of Intelligence

To test the hypothesis that intelligence differs among the races as a function of head size, S. G. Morgan, a prestigious scientist of the nineteenth century, filled the cranial cavities of human skulls of various races with sifted mustard seed. He then poured the sifted seed back into a graduated cylinder to determine the skull's volume in cubic inches.

List the problems with the *validity* of this measure of intelligence:

List the problems with the *reliability* of this measure of intelligence:

©1999 Allyn & Bacon

Handout INTELL 2

Demonstration INTELL 2: Psychology Test and Taxonomy of Objectives

Bloom's Taxonomy

1	**Knowledge**	recalling learned information that is factual
2	**Comprehension**	using factual information
3	**Application**	using learned information in new situations
4	**Analysis**	breaking down learned information into its elementary parts
5	**Synthesis**	using elementary parts and re-assembling them back into the whole
6	**Evaluation**	judging the merits of whether the learned information meets criteria or standard

After Gibson, J. T., & Chandler, L. A. (1988). *Educational psychology: Mastering principles and applications.* Boston: Allyn and Bacon. p. 432.

Handout INTELL 3

Demonstration INTELL 3: What Is Intelligence?

For each age group, list five traits that characterize intelligence.

6-month-old

1. _____
2. _____
3. _____
4. _____
5. _____

2-year-old

1. _____
2. _____
3. _____
4. _____
5. _____

10-year-old

1. _____
2. _____
3. _____
4. _____
5. _____

20-year-old

1. _____
2. _____
3. _____
4. _____
5. _____

50-year-old

1. _____
2. _____
3. _____
4. _____
5. _____

80-year-old

1. _____
2. _____
3. _____
4. _____
5. _____

©1999 Allyn & Bacon

Handout INTELL 4

Demonstration INTELL 4: Intelligent Versus Dumb

List as many characteristics as you can think of to describe intelligent and unintelligent people.

Intelligent People:

_____
_____
_____
_____
_____
_____
_____
_____
_____

Unintelligent People:

_____
_____
_____
_____
_____
_____
_____
_____
_____

©1999 Allyn & Bacon

Handout INTELL 5a

Demonstration INTELL 5: Multiple Intelligences

For each of the types of intelligence listed below, name and describe a person you know (or know of) who embodies that kind of intelligence to you.

Linguistic intelligence:

Musical intelligence:

Logical-mathematical intelligence:

Spatial intelligence:

Bodily intelligence:

Interpersonal intelligence:

Intrapersonal intelligence:

©1999 Allyn & Bacon

Handout INTELL 5b

Demonstration INTELL 5: Multiple Intelligences

Measuring Interpersonal Intelligence

Interpersonal intelligence involves understanding others—how they feel, what motivates them, and how they interact with another.

List two people you believe are high in interpersonal intelligence:

Person 1:

Person 2:

Describe two behaviors you have observed in each person that lead you to believe that they are high in interpersonal intelligence:

Person 1:   Behavior 1

                Behavior 2

Person 2:   Behavior 1

                Behavior 2

Create a test item (using either true-false or an agree-disagree continuum) that reflects the interpersonal intelligence exhibited in each of the above behaviors:

Item 1 (Person 1; Behavior 1):

Item 2 (Person 1; Behavior 2):

Item 3 (Person 2; Behavior 1):

Item 4 (Person 2; Behavior 2):

©1999 Allyn & Bacon

HANDOUT INTELL 8

Labeling People With Mental Retardation

Mental retardation Classification Scheme

Past	Present		
	Based on Educability	*Based on Severity*	
Idiot →	Custodial	Profound	(IQ 0-25)
Imbecile →	Custodial	Severe	(IQ 25-40)
Moron ⟨	Trainable	Moderate	(IQ 40-55)
	Educable	Mild	(IQ 55-70)

©1999 Allyn & Bacon

STUDENT CHALKBOARD DEV 1

Newborn Reflexes

Describe the stimuli and the responses of each of these inborn reflexes.

Reflex	Initiated by	Response
Eye blink		
Babinski		
Withdrawal reflex		
Plantar		
Rooting reflex		
Sucking response		

STUDENT CHALKBOARD DEV 2

Erikson's First Four Stages

Name, identify the age, and describe the first four stages of Erik Erikson's developmental theory.

Stage Name	Approximate Age	Important Event	Description

©1999 Allyn & Bacon

STUDENT CHALKBOARD DEV 3

Erikson's Last Four Stages

Name, identify the age, and describe the last four stages of Erik Erikson's developmental theory.

Stage Name	Approximate Age	Event	Important Description

STUDENT CHALKBOARD   DEV 4

Changes From Young Adulthood to Late Adulthood

Chart I

Use the chart to describe significant changes in the areas indicated.

Age	Physical Change	Cognitive Change
Young Adulthood 18-25		
Early Adulthood 25-40		
Middle Adulthood 40-65		
Late Adulthood 65-75		
Late, Late Adulthood 75+		

©1999 Allyn & Bacon

Student Chalkboard DEV 5

Changes From Young Adulthood to Late Adulthood

Chart II

Use the chart to describe significant changes in the areas indicated.

Age	Work Roles	Personality Development	Major Tasks
Young Adulthood 18-25			
Early Adulthood 25-40			
Middle Adulthood 40-65			
Late Adulthood 65-75			
Late, Late Adulthood 75+			

©1999 Allyn & Bacon

STUDENT CHALKBOARD DEV 6

Charting Developmental Stages and Ages

Identify the stages for each theorist.

Age	Piaget	Erikson	Levinson	Freud
1				
2				
3				
4				
5				
6				
7				
8				
9				
10				
11				
12				
16				
17				
18				
20				
25				
40				
50				
65				

©1999 Allyn & Bacon

Handout DEV 1

Demonstration DEV 1: Childhood Memories and Artifacts

Memory Record

What is your earliest memory?

What was your favorite toy? At what age? Do you recall from whom you received the toy?

What is your earliest memory of your home? Your grandparent's home?

What significant thing happened to you before you were four?

What significant thing happened to you before you were seven?

©1999 Allyn & Bacon

HANDOUT DEV 5a

Demonstration DEV 5: Motor and Verbal Development

Milestones of Physical Development

BEHAVIOR	AVERAGE AGE AT WHICH ACTIVITY IS PERFORMED
Child can raise chin from ground	1 month
Child can sit with support	4 months
Child can sit alone	7 months
Child can stand by holding onto furniture	9 months
Child can crawl	10 months
Child can walk when held by hand and led	11 months
Child can stand alone	14 months
Child can walk alone	15 months

Physical development is rapid during infancy. (Please note: large individual differences exist with respect to this aspect of development. The values shown here are only averages, and many normal infants will depart from them substantially.)

©1999 Allyn & Bacon

Handout DEV 5b

Demonstration DEV 5: Motor and Verbal Development

Milestones of Language Development

Average Age	Language Behavior Demonstrated by Child
_____ weeks	Smiles when talked to; makes cooing sounds.
_____ weeks	Turns head in response to human voice.
_____ weeks	Makes vowel and consonant sounds while cooing.
_____ months	Cooing changes to babbling, which contains all sounds of human speech.
_____ months	Certain syllables repeated (e.g., "ma-ma").
_____ months	Understands some words; may say a few.
_____ months	Can produce up to fifty words.
_____ months	Has vocabulary of more than fifty words; uses some two-word phrases.
_____ months	Vocabulary increases to several hundred words; uses phrases of three to five words.
_____ months	Vocabulary of about a thousand words.
_____ months	Most basic aspects of language well established.

HANDOUT DEV 7

Demonstration DEV 7: Videotaping Parents and Children

Two Tasks Used by Piaget

If two rows of nickels are equally spaced, four-year-olds will agree that the rows contain the same number (upper diagram). If the nickels in one row are then placed farther apart, many four-year-olds will state that this row now contains more nickels than the other. According to Piaget, this illustrates their lack of *conservation*.

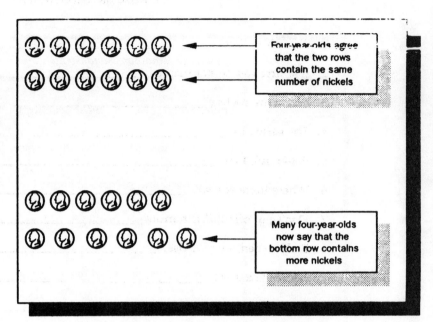

When children up to age six are shown a model similar to this one and are asked to indicate what a doll placed at different points would see, they often describe their own perspective. However, when situations more familiar to them are used (e.g., Grover driving a toy car), they can report this character's perspective accurately. Such findings indicate that young children are not as subject to *egocentrism* as Piaget believed.

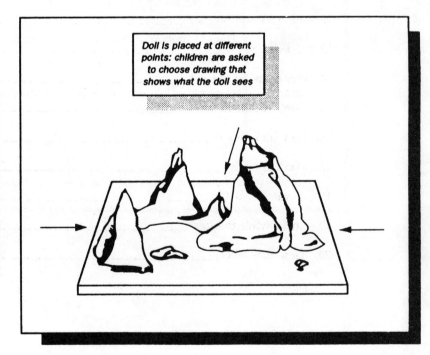

Handout DEV 8

Demonstration DEV 8: A bird in the hand . . .

Intellectual Development

1. A stitch in time _____
2. If at first you do not succeed, _____
3. Too many cooks _____
4. The early bird _____
5. Better safe than _____
6. Where there is a will _____
7. Don't put off until tomorrow _____
8. Early to bed, early to rise, _____
9. An apple a day _____
10. Don't count your chickens _____
11. Haste makes _____
12. All work and no play _____
13. A penny saved _____
14. When the cat is away _____
15. Don't cut off your nose _____
16. He who hesitates _____
17. Don't cry over _____
18. A watched pot _____
19. Strike while the iron _____
20. Time flies when _____

©1999 Allyn & Bacon

Handout DEV 9

Demonstration DEV 9: Examples of Parenting Styles

Parenting Styles

Describe two situations that show how your parent(s) tried to influence you as you were growing up. Think particularly of situations where you wanted to do something different than what they wanted to do. How were the issues resolved?

Situation 1:

Situation 2:

Based on your descriptions, what parenting style do you think best describes that used by your parents?

❏ Authoritarian ❏ Authoritative ❏ Permissive ❏ Combination

Now describe an example of a contrasting parenting style you have seen exhibited elsewhere, such as by a friend's parents, on a television show, or in a movie.

Which parenting style does this incident best represent?

❏ Authoritarian ❏ Authoritative ❏ Permissive ❏ Combination

Which parenting style do you prefer and why?

©1999 Allyn & Bacon

Handout DEV 10

Demonstration DEV 10: Assess the Violence in Children's Cartoons
(Same as Handout 5.8)

Violent Act Tally

Name of Cartoon: _____   Length: _____

Characters: _____   _____

_____   _____

Implicit Acts	Explicit Acts

Total: _____   Total: _____
Acts Per Minute: _____   Acts Per Minute: _____

Name of Cartoon: _____   Length: _____

Characters: _____   _____

_____   _____

Implicit Acts	Explicit Acts

Total: _____   Total: _____
Acts Per Minute: _____   Acts Per Minute: _____

©1999 Allyn & Bacon

Handout DEV 11

Demonstration DEV 11: Decade Word Association

Decade Association

Decade:

0–9: _____ _____ _____ _____

10–19: _____ _____ _____ _____

20–29: _____ _____ _____ _____

30–39: _____ _____ _____ _____

40–49: _____ _____ _____ _____

50–59: _____ _____ _____ _____

60–69: _____ _____ _____ _____

70–79: _____ _____ _____ _____

80–89: _____ _____ _____ _____

With which decade was it easiest to make associations? _____

With which decade was it hardest to make associations? _____

Approximately how many people do you know at the following stages?

0–9: _____

10–19: _____

20–29: _____

30–39: _____

40–49: _____

50–59: _____

60–69: _____

70–79: _____

80–89: _____

©1999 Allyn & Bacon

HANDOUT DEV 12

Demonstration DEV 12: Life Path

Life Path

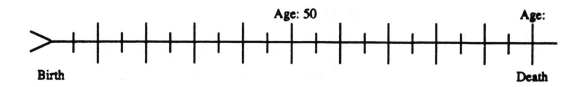

Use the number line to plot the major events in your life. Include the age you will be (or were) when each milestone is (or was) reached. You may include the following:

- graduation
- marriage
- birth of first child
- birth of subsequent children
- professional peak
- children leave home
- retirement
- death

©1999 Allyn & Bacon

HANDOUT DEV 13

Demonstration DEV 13: Dear Mom and Dad,
Parent Letter

Date: _____

Dear Mom and Dad,

_____

_____

_____

_____

_____

_____

_____

_____

_____

_____

Love,

_____

©1999 Allyn & Bacon

Handout DEV 14

Demonstration DEV 14: Examples of Erikson's Stages in the Media

Erikson and the Media

Stage	Example	Explain the characteristics that make it an example

©1999 Allyn & Bacon

HANDOUT DEV 15

Demonstration DEV 15: Dear Son/Daughter,

Children Letter

Date: _____

Dear _____,

_____

_____

_____

_____

_____

_____

_____

_____

_____

_____

_____

Love,

_____

©1999 Allyn & Bacon

Handout DEV 16a

Demonstration DEV 16: Ageism and the Elderly

List all of the words or phrases that come to mind whenever you think of "old people."

_____

_____

_____

_____

_____

_____

_____

_____

_____

_____

_____

©1999 Allyn & Bacon

Handout DEV 16b

Demonstration DEV 16: Ageism and the Elderly

When I am seventy-five years old, I will

_____

_____

_____

_____

_____

_____

_____

_____

_____

_____

_____

_____

_____

©1999 Allyn & Bacon

STUDENT CHALKBOARD MOT 1

Comparing Motivation Theories

Identify the principle theorist or theorists, what is explained, the key ideas, and the views of behavior of each of the following theories of motivation.

Theory	*Drive*	*Expectancy*	*Cognitive*	*Humanistic*
Theorist	a. b. c.	a. b.		
Explains this Activity				
Key Idea				
View of Behavior				

Handout MOT 1

Demonstration MOT 1: Motives Behind Daily Activities

List twenty activities you have done in the past forty-eight hours. Then classify each activity by its motive. Sources of motives might include: biological, need for arousal, social needs, self-actualization, need for achievement, intrinsic, or cognitive needs.

Activity	Motive
1. _____	_____
2. _____	_____
3. _____	_____
4. _____	_____
5. _____	_____
6. _____	_____
7. _____	_____
8. _____	_____
9. _____	_____
10. _____	_____
11. _____	_____
12. _____	_____
13. _____	_____
14. _____	_____
15. _____	_____
16. _____	_____
17. _____	_____
18. _____	_____
19. _____	_____
20. _____	_____

©1999 Allyn & Bacon

Handout MOT 2

Demonstration MOT 2: Body-Mass Index

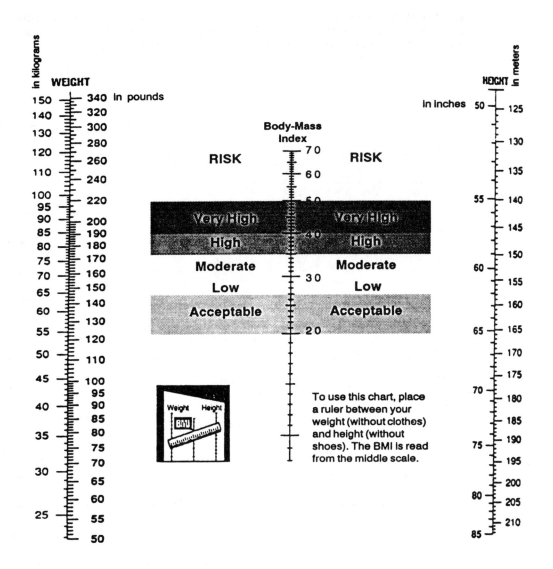

©1999 Allyn & Bacon

Handout MOT 3

Demonstration MOT 3: What is Normal Sexual Behavior?

Questionnaire for Student Evaluation of Normal Sexual Behavior

Please rate whether or not each of the following activities represents normal sexual behavior by placing either a Y (yes) or N (no) in the blank.

____ 1. Watching X-rated movie several times a week.
____ 2. Having sex with more than one person at the same time.
____ 3. Preferring oral sex over intercourse.
____ 4. Having intercourse with a member of the same sex.
____ 5. Fantasizing about having sex with a member of the same sex.
____ 6. Fantasizing about a person other than one's partner during sexual intercourse.
____ 7. Masturbating in front of a partner.
____ 8. Having sex somewhere other than a bed (e.g., floor, shower, kitchen, outdoors).
____ 9. Never engaging in masturbation.
____ 10. Becoming excited by exposing oneself in public.
____ 11. Being celibate.
____ 12. Being unable to achieve orgasm.
____ 13. Enjoying being physically restrained during sex (e.g., bondage).
____ 14. Becoming aroused by voyeurism (e.g., Peeping Toms).
____ 15. Playing with food (e.g., fruit and whipping cream) during sex.
____ 16. Dressing in the clothing of the other sex.
____ 17. Preferring that one's partner initiates sex.
____ 18. Inflicting pain during sex.
____ 19. Receiving pain during sex.
____ 20. Using sex toys (e.g., a vibrator) during sex.
____ 21. Having rape fantasies.
____ 22. Masturbating after marriage.
____ 23. Not being aroused by a nude member of the other sex.
____ 24. Being aroused by receiving an obscene phone call.
____ 25. Being aroused by making an obscene phone call.
____ 26. Engaging in sex with animals.
____ 27. Deriving sexual pleasure from seeing or touching dead bodies.
____ 28. Becoming aroused by being urinated on.
____ 29. Becoming aroused by soiling the clothing of the other sex.
____ 30. Becoming aroused by viewing or touching feces.

From Kite, M. E. (1990). Defining normal sexual behavior: A classroom exercise. *Teaching of Psychology, 17*, 118-119.

©1999 Allyn & Bacon

HANDOUT MOT 4

Demonstration MOT 4: Defining Aggression

Aggression Questionnaire

Circle the number of each statement that illustrates an aggressive act.

1. A spider eats a fly.
2. Two wolves fight for the leadership of the pack.
3. A soldier shoots an enemy at the front line.
4. The warden of a prison executes a convicted criminal.
5. A juvenile gang attacks members of another gang.
6. Two men fight for a piece of bread.
7. A man viciously kicks a cat.
8. A man, while cleaning a window, knocks over a flowerpot, which, in falling, injures a pedestrian.
9. A girl kicks a wastebasket.
10. Mr. X, a notorious gossip, speaks disparagingly of many people of his acquaintance.
11. A man mentally rehearses a murder he is about to commit.
12. An angry son purposely fails to write to this mother, who is expecting a letter and will be hurt if none arrives.
13. An enraged boy tries with all his might to inflict injury on his antagonist, a bigger boy, but is not successful in doing so. His efforts simply amuse the bigger boy.
14. A man daydreams of harming his antagonist, but has no hope of doing so.
15. A senator does not protest the escalation of bombing to which he is morally opposed.
16. A farmer beheads a chicken and prepares it for supper.
17. A hunter kills an animal and mounts it as a trophy.
18. A dog snarls at a mail carrier, but does not bite.
19. A physician gives a flu shot to a screaming child.
20. A boxer gives his opponent a bloody nose.
21. A Girl Scout tries to assist an elderly woman, but trips her by accident.
22. A bank robber is shot in the back while trying to escape.
23. A tennis player smashes his racket after missing a volley.
24. A person commits suicide.

From Benjamin, L. T., Jr. (1988). Defining aggression: An exercise for classroom discussion. *Teaching of Psychology, 12,* 40-42.

©1999 Allyn & Bacon

HANDOUT MOT 5b

Demonstration MOT 5: Measuring Achievement Motivation

Thematic Apperception Test Response

What is happening? Who are the people?

What has led to this situation?

What is being thought or what is wanted (and by whom)?

What will happen?

©1999 Allyn & Bacon

Handout MOT 7

Demonstration MOT 7: Sensation Seeking

Measuring Sensation Seeking Behavior

Circle the choice A or B that better describes your feelings.

1. A I would like a job that requires a lot of traveling.
   B I would prefer a job in one location.

2. A I am invigorated by a brisk, cold day.
   B I can't wait to get indoors on a cold day.

3. A I get bored seeing the same old faces.
   B I like the comfortable familiarity of everyday friends.

4. A I would prefer living in an ideal society in which everyone is safe, secure, and happy.
   B I would have preferred living in the unsettled days of our history.

5. A I sometimes like to do things that are a little frightening.
   B A sensible person avoids activities that are dangerous.

6. A I would not like to be hypnotized.
   B I would like to have the experience of being hypnotized.

7. A The most important goal of life is to live it to the fullest and experience as much as possible.
   B The most important goal of life is to find peace and happiness.

8. A I would like to try parachute-jumping.
   B I would never want to try jumping out of a plane, with or without a parachute.

9. A I enter cold water gradually, giving myself time to get used to it.
   B I like to dive or jump right into the ocean or a cold pool.

10. A When I go on a vacation, I prefer the comfort of a good room and bed.
    B When I go on a vacation, I prefer the change of camping out.

11. A I prefer people who are emotionally expressive even if they are a bit unstable.
    B I prefer people who are calm and even-tempered.

12. A A good painting should shock or jolt the senses.
    B A good painting should give one a feeling of peace and security.

13. A People who ride motorcycles must have some kind of unconscious need to hurt themselves.
    B I would like to drive or ride a motorcycle.

Count one point for each of the following items that you have circled: 1A, 2A, 3A, 4B, 5A, 6B, 7A, 8A, 9B, 10B, 11A, 12A, 13B. Add up your total and compare it with the norms: 0–3 Very low; 4–5 Low; 6–9 Average; 10–11 High; 12–13; Very high.

©1999 Allyn & Bacon

STUDENT CHALKBOARD EMOT 1

Theories of Emotion

Compare the James-Lange and the Cannon-Bard theories of emotion by filling in the boxes to indicate the relationships among 1) the emotion-provoking stimulus, 2) the cognitive labeling of feeling, and 3) the physiological reactions for each theory. Provide an example of how each would interpret a specific emotion.

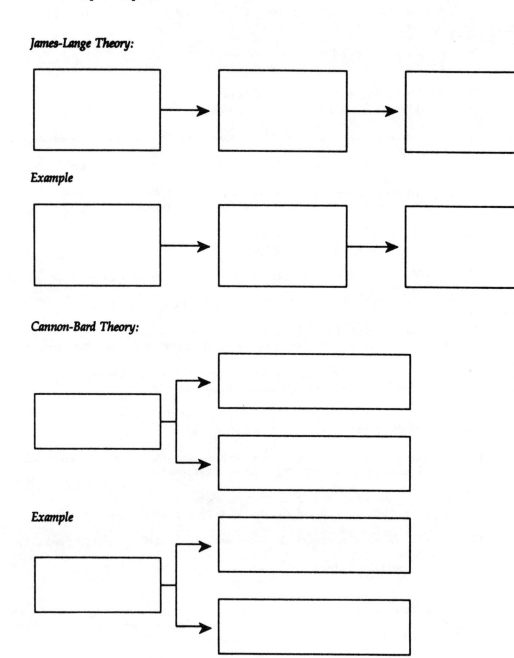

©1999 Allyn & Bacon

Handout EMOT 1

Demonstration EMOT 1: Emotions and Their Causes

Picture in your mind the time in the last year when you were most angry.

1. Describe what provoked your anger:

2. Describe the physical sensation you felt:

3. Describe the thoughts you had at the time:

Picture in your mind the time in the last year when you were the happiest.

1. Describe what provoked your happiness:

2. Describe the physical sensation you felt:

3. Describe the thoughts you had at the time:

©1999 Allyn & Bacon

HANDOUT EMOT 2

Demonstration EMOT 2: Facial Feedback Hypothesis

Cartoon Ratings as a Function of Facial Expression

Cartoon 1:

Smile Frown (circle one)

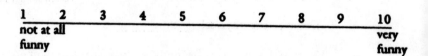

1 — not at all funny   2   3   4   5   6   7   8   9   10 — very funny

Cartoon 2:

Smile Frown (circle one)

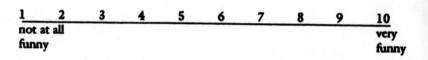

1 — not at all funny   2   3   4   5   6   7   8   9   10 — very funny

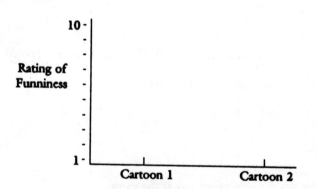

F = Average of ratings for those frowning

S = Average of ratings for those smiling

©1999 Allyn & Bacon

Handout EMOT 5

Demonstration EMOT 5: Cultural Differences in Facial Expressions

Determine what emotion is being portrayed in each of the following statements.

1. Every one of his hairs stood on end and the pimples came out on the skin all over his body. _____

2. He drew one leg up and stood on one foot. _____

3. He clapped his hands. _____

4. He raised one hand as high as his face and fanned his face with the sleeve. _____

5. They stuck out their tongues. _____

6. He gnashed his teeth until they were all but ground to dust. _____

7. Her eyes grew round and opened wide. _____

8. His face was red and he went creeping alone outside the village. _____

9. He laughed a great ho-ho. _____

10. He scratched his ears and cheek. _____

11. She stretched the left arm flatly to the left and the right arm to the right. _____

Klineberg, O. (1938). Emotional expression in Chinese literature. *Journal of Abnormal and Social Psychology, 33,* 517-520.

Handout EMOT 6a

Demonstration EMOT 6: To Tell the Truth

At least one person in the "To Tell the Truth" line will lie. It is your job to detect who is not telling the truth. Some of you will know what top look for with regard to nonverbal cues of deception, others will not.

1. In what month is your birthday?

2. How many siblings do you have?

3. What is the last digit of your student I.D. number?

4. What is your middle name?

5. What is your favorite color?

6. What is your father's first name?

7. To which political party do you subscribe?

8. Where were you born?

9. How old are you?

10. What is your shoe size?

11. Have you ever been given a speeding ticket?

12. How well do you play tennis?

©1999 Allyn & Bacon

HANDOUT EMOT 6b

Demonstration EMOT 6: To Tell the Truth

What to look for in detecting deception:

1. Hand gestures decrease.

2. More hand to face gestures.
   - mouth guard
   - nose touching
   - rubbing eye
   - neck scratch
   - ear rub

3. Body shifts increase.

4. Less eye contact.

5. More foot movements.

6. More speech errors.

7. Pitch of voice increases.

Increase:

Hand to face gestures
Shifts in body posture
Foot/leg movements
Speech errors
Voice pitch

Decrease:

Hand gestures
Eye contact

©1999 Allyn & Bacon

Student Chalkboard HEALTH 1

Sources of Work-Related Stress

Identify the sources of work-related stress in the spaces provided. Elaborate on methods of coping with each kind of stress you identify.

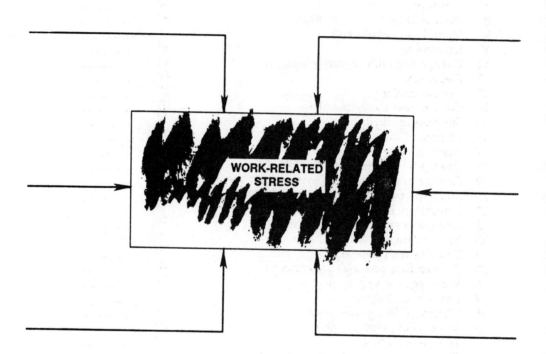

Handout HEALTH 2

Demonstration HEALTH 2: The Social Readjustment Rating Scale

Rank	Life Event	Value	Score
1	Death of spouse	100	_____
2	Divorce	73	_____
3	Marital separation	65	_____
4	Jail term	63	_____
5	Death of close family member	63	_____
6	Personal injury or illness	53	_____
7	Marriage	50	_____
8	Fired at work	47	_____
9	Marital reconciliation	45	_____
10	Retirement	45	_____
11	Change in health in family member	44	_____
12	Pregnancy	40	_____
13	Sex difficulties	39	_____
14	Gain of new family member	39	_____
15	Business readjustment	39	_____
16	Change in financial state	38	_____
17	Death of close friend	37	_____
18	Change to different line of work	36	_____
19	Change in number of arguments with spouse	35	_____
20	Mortgage over $10,000	31	_____
21	Foreclosure of mortgage or loan	30	_____
22	Change in responsibilities at work	29	_____
23	Son or daughter leaving home	29	_____
24	Troubles with in-laws	29	_____
25	Outstanding personal achievement	28	_____
26	Wife begin or stop work	26	_____
27	Begin or end school	26	_____
28	Change in living conditions	25	_____
29	Revision of personal habits	24	_____
30	Trouble with boss	23	_____
31	Change in work hours or conditions	20	_____
32	Change in residence	20	_____
33	Change in schools	20	_____
34	Change in recreation	19	_____
35	Change in church activities	19	_____
36	Change in social activities	18	_____
37	Mortgage or loan less than $10,000	17	_____
38	Change in sleeping habits	16	_____
39	Change in number of family get-togethers	15	_____
40	Change in eating habits	15	_____
41	Vacation	13	_____
42	Christmas	12	_____
43	Minor violations of the law	11	_____

Total Score: _____ Life Change Units

©1999 Allyn & Bacon

HANDOUT HEALTH 3

Demonstration HEALTH 3: Student's Daily Hassles

List the hassles you must cope with in your daily life. Group them in the following categories:

- household/living arrangement hassles
- times pressure hassles
- inner concern hassles
- health hassles
- environmental hassles
- family hassles
- financial responsibility hassles
- work hassles
- school hassles
- future/security hassles
- social hassles
- other hassles

Rank each hassle on a scale of 1 to 10 (1 = least important; 10 = most important).

	Rank		Rank
1.	_____	21.	_____
2.	_____	22.	_____
3.	_____	23.	_____
4.	_____	24.	_____
5.	_____	25.	_____
6.	_____	26.	_____
7.	_____	27.	_____
8.	_____	28.	_____
9.	_____	29.	_____
10.	_____	30.	_____
11.	_____	31.	_____
12.	_____	32.	_____
13.	_____	33.	_____
14.	_____	34.	_____
15.	_____	35.	_____
16.	_____	36.	_____
17.	_____	37.	_____
18.	_____	38.	_____
19.	_____	39.	_____
20.	_____	40.	_____

©1999 Allyn & Bacon

Handout HEALTH 5

Demonstration HEALTH 5: Health Beliefs and Coping

The following test was developed by psychologists Lyle H. Miller and Alma Dell Smith at Boston University Medical Center. Score each item from 1 (almost always) to 5 (never), according to how much of the time each statement applies to you.

_____ 1. I eat at least one hot, balanced meal a day.
_____ 2. I get seven to eight hours sleep at least four nights a week.
_____ 3. I give and receive affection regularly.
_____ 4. I have at least one relative within 50 miles on whom I can rely.
_____ 5. I exercise to the point of perspiration at least twice a week.
_____ 6. I smoke less than half a pack of cigarettes a day.
_____ 7. I take fewer than five alcoholic drinks a week.
_____ 8. I am the appropriate weight for my height.
_____ 9. I have an income adequate to meet basic expenses.
_____ 10. I get strength from my religious beliefs.
_____ 11. I regularly attend club or social activities.
_____ 12. I have a network of friends and acquaintances.
_____ 13. I have one or more friends in which to confide about personal matters.
_____ 14. I am in good health (including eyesight, hearing, teeth).
_____ 15. I am able to speak openly about my feelings when angry or worried.
_____ 16. I have regular conversations with the people I live with about domestic problems, e.g., chores, money, and daily living issues.
_____ 17. I do something for fun at least once a week.
_____ 18. I am able to organize my time effectively.
_____ 19. I drink fewer than three cups of coffee (or tea or cola drinks) a day.
_____ 20. I take quiet time for myself during the day.

_____ TOTAL

To get your score, add up the figures and subtract 20. Any number over 30 indicates a **vulnerability** to stress. You are seriously vulnerable if your score is between 50 and 75, and extremely vulnerable if it is over 75.

Source:
Miller, L. H., & Smith, A. D., Boston University Medical Center. In Wallis, C. (1983, June 6). Stress: Can we cope? *TIME*, p. 54.

STUDENT CHALKBOARD PERS 1

Freud's View of Personality Structure

Identify and describe the Id, Ego, Superego, and the realms of Consciousness and the Unconscious.

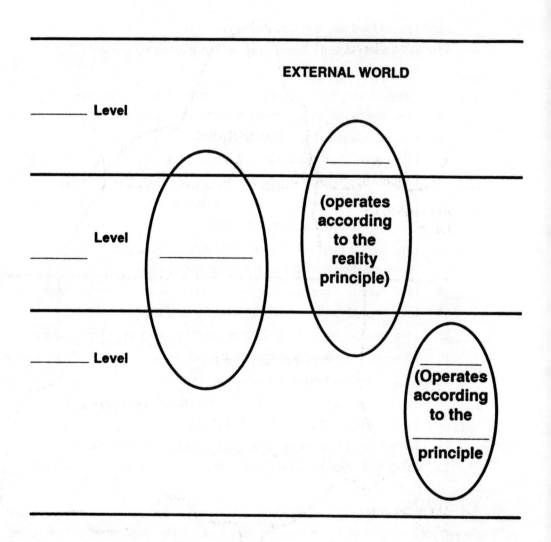

STUDENT CHALKBOARD PERS 2

Freud's View of the Mind

Identify and describe the Id, Ego, Superego, and the realms of Consciousness and the Unconscious using the metaphor of the iceberg.

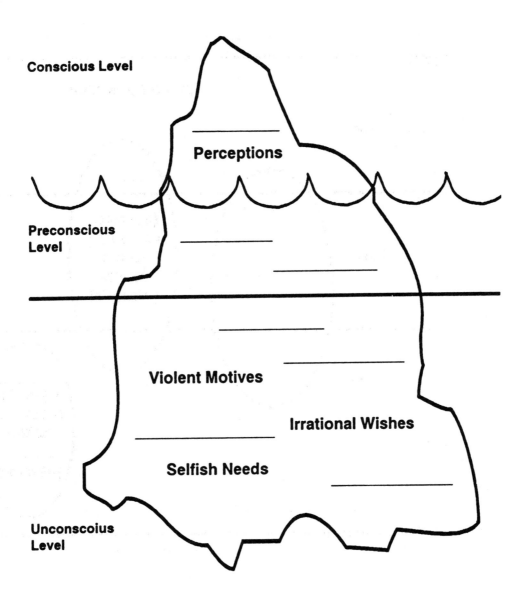

STUDENT CHALKBOARD PERS 3

Comparing Personality Theories

Chart I

Compare the personality theories on the basis of the items listed in the left-hand column.

Approach	Psychoanalytic	Humanistic
Major Proponent(s)		
Core of Personality		
Structure of Personality		
Developmental View		
Behavior Pathology Caused By:		

©1999 Allyn & Bacon

STUDENT CHALKBOARD PERS 4

Comparing Personality Theories

Chart II

Compare the personality theories on the basis of the items listed in the left-hand column.

Approach	Trait	Behavioral	Cognitive
Major Proponent(s)			
Core of Personality			
Structure of Personality			
Developmental View			
Behavior Pathology Caused By:			

©1999 Allyn & Bacon

Handout PERS 2a

Demonstration PERS 2: Comparing Personality Theories

Assumptions About Personality

		Strongly Agree				Strongly Disagree		
1.	Because each person is a unique individual, there is really no point in trying to fit everyone into a single "theory."	1	2	3	4	5	6	7
2.	It's more important to be concerned with what people do, not why they do it, if one is trying to help them change.	1	2	3	4	5	6	7
3.	Understanding how people view their own lives is very important in coming to an adequate understanding of personality.	1	2	3	4	5	6	7
4.	People (e.g. children) really do go through "stages"; the stages are real, not just a way of speaking about a behavior.	1	2	3	4	5	6	7
5.	People often are not aware of the real reasons for their behavior.	1	2	3	4	5	6	7
6.	A person must make a deliberate, conscious choice to change, or she or he can not be helped.	1	2	3	4	5	6	7
7.	If I wanted to know something about a person, a personal interview would be more useful than an objective personality test.	1	2	3	4	5	6	7
8.	A person is the product of her or his environment.	1	2	3	4	5	6	7
9.	If you understand adults, you will have no trouble understanding children.	1	2	3	4	5	6	7
10.	The focus of therapy or counseling should be to change outward behavior, not inward thoughts or feelings.	1	2	3	4	5	6	7
11.	People are usually quite consistent from one situation to another.	1	2	3	4	5	6	7
12.	What people choose or decide is an important determinant of what they do.	1	2	3	4	5	6	7
13.	Understanding people's motives is important in helping them change.	1	2	3	4	5	6	7
14.	Psychological tests provide a complete picture of personality.	1	2	3	4	5	6	7
15.	Early childhood experience largely determines adult personality.	1	2	3	4	5	6	7
16.	The current environment largely shapes what a person is and does.	1	2	3	4	5	6	7
17.	The same general laws or principles apply to all people.	1	2	3	4	5	6	7
18.	The notion of the "unconscious mind" is useful in helping people change.	1	2	3	4	5	6	7

From Embree, M. (1986). Implicit personality theory in the classroom: An integrative approach. *Teaching of Psychology, 13*, 78-80. Copyright 1986 by Lawrence Erlbaum Associates. Reprinted with permission by the publisher.

©1999 Allyn & Bacon

HANDOUT PERS 2b

Demonstration PERS 2: Comparing Personality Theories

Prototype Ratings

Item Number	Skinner	Freud	Rogers
1.	1	4	7
2.	7	1	1
3.	1	4	7
4.	1	7	4
5.	4	7	4
6.	1	4	7
7.	1	7	7
8.	7	4	1
9.	7	4	4
10.	7	1	1
11.	1	4	4
12.	1	1	7
13.	1	4	7
14.	4	1	1
15.	1	7	1
16.	7	1	1
17.	7	4	1
18.	1	7	4

©1999 Allyn & Bacon

Handout PERS 3

Demonstration PERS 3: Role-Playing Parts of Personality

Personality Structures and Defense Mechanisms

Identify who played which role, and describe the behavior that revealed the role. Also, rate the performance.

1. Id

2. Ego

3. Superego

4. Conscious

5. Unconscious

6. Repression

7. Rationalization

8. Displacement

9. Projection

10. Regression

©1999 Allyn & Bacon

HANDOUT PERS 4

Demonstration PERS 4: "Who am I? I am..."

1. I am _____.
2. I am _____.
3. I am _____.
4. I am _____.
5. I am _____.
6. I am _____.
7. I am _____.
8. I am _____.
9. I am _____.
10. I am _____.
11. I am _____.
12. I am _____.
13. I am _____.
14. I am _____.
15. I am _____.
16. I am _____.
17. I am _____.
18. I am _____.
19. I am _____.
20. I am _____.

A. Physical self (e.g., sex, age) Count ____

B. Social self (e.g., family, membership) Count ____

C. Reflective self (e.g., values, like, dislikes) Count ____

D. Identity self (e.g., who you are) Count ____

©1999 Allyn & Bacon

Handout PERS 5

Demonstration PERS 5: Student Gripes and Maslow's Hierarchy

List your top ten complaints and determine which of Maslow's needs applies to each: physiological, safety, belongingness, self-esteem, or self-actualization.

Complaints	Need
1. _____	_____
2. _____	_____
3. _____	_____
4. _____	_____
5. _____	_____
6. _____	_____
7. _____	_____
8. _____	_____
9. _____	_____
10. _____	_____

©1999 Allyn & Bacon

Handout ABN 1

Demonstration ABN 1: What Is Abnormal?

After each of the descriptions below place an "A" (for abnormal) or an "N" (for normal) based on your analysis of each person. Then, after a class discussion of the criteria for abnormality, indicate which criterion (or criteria) apples to each item.

1. Henry, editor of a medium-size city's only newspaper, does not believe that women are capable of serving on the editorial board. He has decided not to promote Karen, a well-qualified veteran of the staff, to the board. _____

2. Terry has been having terrible nightmares at least three times a week from which he wakes up shaking and sweating. _____

3. Vanda has visions and hallucinations that she often uses to guide her important decisions. _____

4. Alana always covers her face when she goes out in public. _____

5. Tanya hears voices speaking only to her whenever she turns on television, but she is not upset about it. _____

6. Sam is afraid of snakes. _____

7. Sally is vaguely dissatisfied that she is not living up to her potential. _____

8. Sandy has been plotting to assassinate the governor next time she appears locally. _____

9. Even though public transportation is easily accessible, Tom drives to work during a summer ozone alert when the mayor has asked people to use their cars as little as possible. _____

10. Mary continues to be very upset about her sister's death, even though the accident that killed her happened two years ago. She still wears dark mourning clothes and cries almost every day whenever she thinks of her sister. _____

11. Harry is so fearful of crowds that he can no longer ride the bus to work. _____

12. Luke often urinates on the street. _____

©1999 Allyn & Bacon

HANDOUT ABN 4

Demonstration ABN 4: Deviant Behavior

1. Describe the deviant behavior you chose to engage in:

2. What is it that makes you define this behavior as abnormal or deviant? Are there circumstances under which it would be normal?

3. Where did you engage in this behavior?

4. How many people observed you?

5. What were their reactions?

6. How did you feel as you engaged in this behavior? How did you feel when you observed the reactions of others?

©1999 Allyn & Bacon

Handout ABN 8

Demonstration ABN 8: Diagnosing Disorders

Summary of Major DSM-IV Categories

Type of disorder	Subtype (examples)
Disorders usually first diagnosed in infancy, childhood, or adolescence	mental retardation; attention deficit with hyper-activity; separation anxiety; eating disorders; gender identity disorder
Delirium, dementia, amnesia, and other cognitive disorders	Alzheimer's disease
Substance-related disorders	alcohol abuse and dependence; drug abuse and dependence; nicotine dependence
Schizophrenic and other psychotic disorders	schizophrenia (one of five varieties)
Delusional disorders	paranoia (one of six varieties)
Mood disorders	depression; bipolar disorders
Anxiety disorders	phobias; panic disorder; obsessive-compulsive disorder
Somatoform disorders	conversion disorder (hysterical neurosis); hypochondriasis
Dissociative disorders	psychogenic amnesia; fugue; dissociative identity disorder
Sexual disorders and gender identity disorders	paraphilias; sexual dysfunctions
Impulse control disorders	pathological gambling; pyromania; kleptomania
Personality disorders	schizoid; histrionic; paranoid; narcissistic; compulsive; antisocial; passive-aggressive
Sleep disorders	insomnia
Eating disorders	bulimia
Adjustment disorders	adjustment disorder

©1999 Allyn & Bacon

Handout ABN 9

Depression and Suicide

Depression Continuum

Mild		Severe
Minor depression (the "blues")		Major depression
Normal thought processes		Disrupted thought processes
Environmental causes most likely		Genetic or physiological causes most likely
Few symptoms		Four or more symptoms
Short duration		Two weeks or more duration

©1999 Allyn & Bacon

STUDENT CHALKBOARD THER 1

Comparing Psychotherapeutic Approaches

Chart I

Compare the psychotherapeutic approaches on the basis of the items listed in the left-hand column.

Approach	Psychoanalytic Therapy	Humanistic Therapy
View of Psychopathology		
Goal of Therapy		
Role of Therapist		
Role of Unconscious Material		
Role of Insight		
Techniques		

STUDENT CHALKBOARD THER 2

Comparing Psychotherapeutic Approaches

Chart II

Compare the psychotherapeutic approaches on the basis of the items listed in the left-hand column.

Approach	Behavior Therapy	Cognitive Therapy
View of Psychopathology		
Goal of Therapy		
Role of Therapist		
Role of Unconscious Material		
Role of Insight		
Techniques		

©1999 Allyn & Bacon

Student Chalkboard THER 3

Psychopharmacological Drugs

Identify the common drugs used in the treatment of psychological disorders.

Effect Group	Chemical Group	Generic Name	Trade Name
Antianxiety (Anxiolytics)			
Antidepressants (thymoleptics)			
Antimania (Thymoleptic)			
Antipsychotics (Neuroleptics)			

©1999 Allyn & Bacon

HANDOUT THER 2

Demonstration THER 2: Developing an Anxiety Hierarchy

Choose an experience that has tended to make you anxious in the past:
_____

Now list twelve scenes, ordered from least anxiety-provoking (1) to most anxiety-provoking (12), that are associated with this experience. For example, if you got nervous before an exam you might order scenes according to how close in time they were to the test. The first (and least anxiety-provoking) scene would be noticing on the syllabus that there is a test two weeks away. A later scene could be studying for the test the night before.

(Least anxiety)

1. _____
2. _____
3. _____
4. _____
5. _____
6. _____
7. _____
8. _____
9. _____
10. _____
11. _____
12. _____

(Most anxiety)

©1999 Allyn & Bacon

Handout THER 8

Paradigms and Treatment

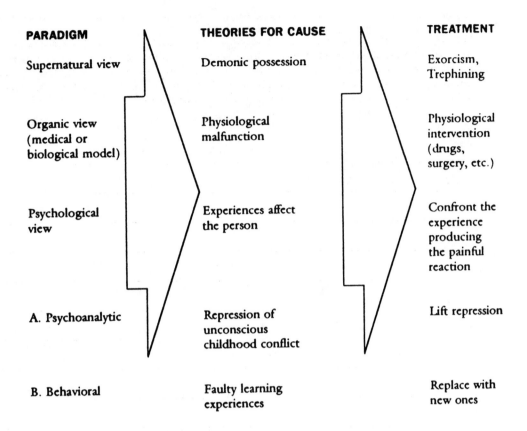

©1999 Allyn & Bacon

HANDOUT SOCIAL 1a

Demonstration SOCIAL 1: Attribution to Solve Problems

Using Attribution to Solve Problems

You need an expert for your next canoe expedition, and you are trying to decided whether Molly is your person. You observe her one day canoeing across a river. From another observer you learn that most people don't make it across this river without spill. You learn that she has made it across this river several other times without mishap. You also learn that she canoes well in calm or treacherous waters.

Consensus is **high low** (circle one)

Describe the consensus information:

Consistency is **high low** (circle one)

Describe the consistency information:

Distinctiveness is **high low** (circle one)

Describe the distinctiveness information:

Based on this information, should you take Molly on your next trip? **yes no** (circle one)

You are trying to decided whether to go see a movie. It has been recommended by a friend of yours. Todd says he has seen it several times and liked it a lot each time no matter what kind of mood he was in. He also mentions that there aren't very many movies that he likes. You have also heard from several other friends that this is a good movie.

Consensus is **high low** (circle one)

Describe the consensus information:

Consistency is **high low** (circle one)

Describe the consistency information:

Distinctiveness is **high low** (circle one)

Describe the distinctiveness information:

Based on this information, should you see this movie? **yes no** (circle one)

©1999 Allyn & Bacon

HANDOUT SOCIAL 1b

Demonstration SOCIAL 1: Attribution to Solve Problems

How We Answer the Question: "Why?"

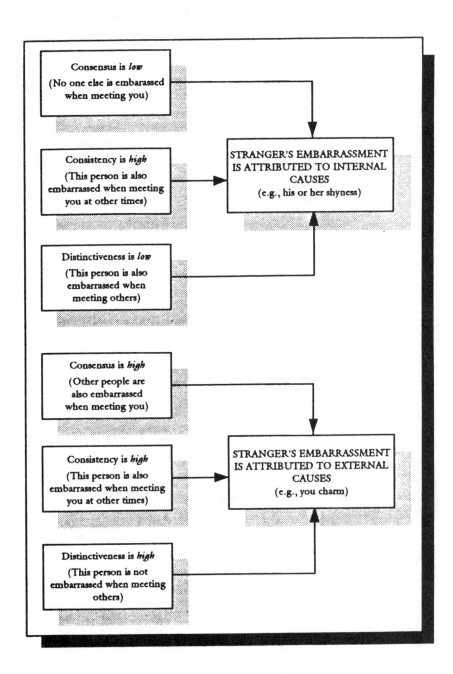

Handout SOCIAL 2

Demonstration SOCIAL 2: Fundamental Attribution Error and Self-Serving Bias

Sources of Bias in Attribution

Complete the following sentences.

1. Johnny struck another student on the playground because

2. I didn't do very well on my last exam because

3. When I get mad it is because

4. Sally was laughing at the joke Frank told because

5. When I cry it is because

6. Allan was late for work because

7. If I miss an appointment with my instructor it will be because

8. Denise flunked this class because

9. I got this job at the company because

10. Last semester my GPA was 4.0 because

©1999 Allyn & Bacon

HANDOUT SOCIAL 5

Demonstration SOCIAL 5: Headbands and Stereotypes

Ideas for Headbands Labels

Boss	Comic	Blonde	Quiet	Hot-tempered
Diseased	Chinese	Farmer	Insane	Insignificant
Wealthy	Gilligan	Arab	Retarded	Gang member
Feminist	Athletic	Nerd	Ross Perot	Roseanne
Hispanic	Irish	American	Military	George Bush
Japanese	Black	Odd	White	AIDS patient
Teacher	Drug addict	mechanic	murderer	Grandparent
Minister	Brat	Scientist	Writer	Psychologist
New Ager				

©1999 Allyn & Bacon

Handout SOCIAL 6

Demonstration SOCIAL 6: Stereotypes

1. _____ are cold and arrogant.
   a. Southerners
   b. Westerners
   c. Easterners
   d. Midwesterners

2. _____ are great lovers.
   a. Canadians
   b. Italians
   c. Eskimos
   d. Nigerians

3. _____ are industrious and obedient.
   a. The Chinese
   b. Americans
   c. Australians
   d. The Irish

4. _____ are moody.
   a. Men
   b. Women
   c. Americans
   d. Children

5. _____ are shrewd penny pinchers.
   a. Buddhists
   b. American Indians
   c. Catholics
   d. Jews

6. _____ are unsophisticated country hicks.
   a. Californians
   b. Easterners
   c. Southerners
   d. Northerners

7. People who _____ are intelligent.
   a. wear glasses
   b. wear jewelry
   c. drive American cars
   d. are tall

8. _____ are forgetful.
   a. Children
   b. Parents
   c. Adolescents
   d. Old people

9. _____ are self-centered and irresponsible.
   a. Adolescents
   b. Parents
   c. Old people
   d. Men

10. _____ are not very intelligent.
    a. Lawyers
    b. Football players
    c. Musicians
    d. Salespeople

©1999 Allyn & Bacon

HANDOUT SOCIAL 7a

Demonstration SOCIAL 7: Stereotyping

	Rank	Adjective 1	Adjective 2
Americans	___	_____	_____
Chinese	___	_____	_____
English	___	_____	_____
Germans	___	_____	_____
Irish	___	_____	_____
Italians	___	_____	_____
Japanese	___	_____	_____
Jews	___	_____	_____
Blacks	___	_____	_____
Turks	___	_____	_____

Adjectives:

artistic
cruel
extremely nationalistic
ignorant
imitative
impulsive
industrious
intelligent
lazy
loyal to family ties
materialistic
mercenary
musical
pleasure-loving
pugnacious
quick-tempered
reserved
scientifically-minded
shrewd
sly
sportsmanlike
superstitious
tradition-loving
very religious

From Anonymous (1988). Stereotyping. In L. Benjamin and K. Lowman (Eds.), *Activities handbook for the teaching of psychology, Vol. 1.* Washington, D.C.: American Psychological Association. Copyright 1988 by the American Psychological Association. Adapted by permission of the publisher.

HANDOUT SOCIAL 7b

Demonstration SOCIAL 7: Stereotyping

Katz and Braly (1933) results:

Americans	industrious (43%) and intelligent (47%)
Chinese	superstitious (34%) and sly (29%)
English	sportsmanlike (53%) and intelligent (46%)
Germans	scientifically-minded (78%) and industrious (65%)
Irish	pugnacious (45%) and quick-tempered (39%)
Italians	artistic (53%) and impulsive (44%)
Japanese	intelligent (45%) and industrious (43%)
Jews	shrewd (79%) and mercenary (49%)
Blacks	superstitious (84%) and lazy (75%)
Turks	cruel (47%) and very religious (26%)

Gilbert (1951) replication:

Americans	materialistic (37%) and intelligent (32%)
Chinese	loyal to family ties (35%) and tradition-loving (26%)
English	tradition-loving (42%) and reserved (39%)
Germans	scientifically-minded (62%), industrious (50%), and extremely nationalistic (50%)
Irish	quick-tempered (35%) and very religious (30%)
Italians	very religious (33%), artistic (28%), and pleasure-loving (28%)
Japanese	imitative (24%) and sly (21%)
Jews	shrewd (47%) and intelligent (37%)
Blacks	superstitious (41%) and musical (33%)
Turks	cruel (12%), ignorant (7%), and sly (7%)

From Anonymous (1988). Stereotyping. In L. Benjamin and K. Lowman (Eds.), *Activities handbook for the teaching of psychology, Vol. 1*. Washington, D.C.: American Psychological Association. Copyright 1988 by the American Psychological Association. Adapted by permission of the publisher.

Handout SOCIAL 8

Demonstration SOCIAL 8: Is It Easier To Be a Male or Female?

List the Advantages

Female   Male

List the Disadvantages

Female   Male

Handout SOCIAL 9

Demonstration SOCIAL 9: To Do Anything!

If you could do anything humanly possible with complete assurance you would not be detected or held responsible, what would you do?

Handout SOCIAL 10

Demonstration SOCIAL 10: What Do You Like?

List the five things you want most in a mate.

1.

2.

3.

4.

5.

©1999 Allyn & Bacon

Handout SOCIAL 11

Demonstration SOCIAL 11: Determinants of Attraction

List your three closest friends and use a scale of 1 to 10 to rate them on proximity (how close they live to you), similarity (the degree to which they are similar to you), and physical attractiveness.

Close Friend	Proximity	Similarity	Physical Attractiveness
1. _____	_____	_____	_____
2. _____	_____	_____	_____
3. _____	_____	_____	_____

Rate your own attractiveness: _____

©1999 Allyn & Bacon

Handout SOCIAL 12

Demonstration SOCIAL 12: "Birds of a Feather Flock Together"

	Self	Close Friend	Acquaintance
Serious			
Shy			
Honest			
Sensitive			
Warm			
Intelligent			
Attractive			
Creative			
Outgoing			
Kind			
Conceited			

©1999 Allyn & Bacon

HANDOUT SOCIAL 13

Demonstration SOCIAL 12: Attractiveness and Influence

Attractiveness Rating Scale

For Slide #1: Mark with an "X"

For Slide #2: Circle choice

not very intelligent	1--------2--------3--------4--------5--------6--------7	very intelligent
not very attractive	1--------2--------3--------4--------5--------6--------7	very attractive
not very competent	1--------2--------3--------4--------5--------6--------7	very competent
not trustworthy	1--------2--------3--------4--------5--------6--------7	very trustworthy
not very friendly	1--------2--------3--------4--------5--------6--------7	very friendly
not very well liked	1--------2--------3--------4--------5--------6--------7	very well liked
not well mannered	1--------2--------3--------4--------5--------6--------7	very well mannered
not very fun to be with	1--------2--------3--------4--------5--------6--------7	very fun to be with

©1999 Allyn & Bacon

HANDOUT STAT 1

Demonstration STAT 1: Greyhound Strike

Salaries of drivers for the company

Yearly Salary	Number of drivers
13,000	4
16,500	1
19,250	1
20,619	1
21,500	3
22,540	4
29,800	11
31,000	10
32,000	6
35,500	4
36,800	2
41,000	2
42,900	1

Salaries of drivers for four Competitors

Competitor A
N = 65
Mean = 31,000
SD = 3,000
Median = 31,000
Mode = 31,000

Competitor C
N = 25
Mean = 35,000
SD = 4,000
Median = 29,000
Mode = 26,000

Competitor B
N = 125
Mean = 28,000
SD = 1,500
Median = 29,000
Mode = 30,000

Competitor D
N = 75
Mean = 29,000
SD = 1,000
Median = 29,000
Mode = 29,000

©1999 Allyn & Bacon

HANDOUT STAT 2

Demonstration STAT 2: Representative Sample

Sample Data

		Mean Age
Total Population:	_____ (number)	_____
Sample Mean	10%	_____
Sample Mean	25%	_____
Sample Mean	50%	_____
Sample Mean	75%	_____
Sample Mean	100%	_____

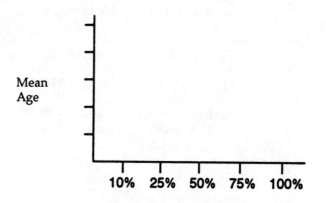

©1999 Allyn & Bacon

HANDOUT DT 6.2

Diversity Topic 6.2: Eyewitness Testimony

Have You Seen this Before?

You will now see the faces you saw earlier in this class, along with some other faces that you have not seen. Please make a judgment for each according to whether or not you believe you saw it earlier.

Face #	Yes	No
1	___	___
2	___	___
3	___	___
4	___	___
5	___	___
6	___	___
7	___	___
8	___	___
9	___	___
10	___	___
11	___	___
12	___	___
13	___	___
14	___	___
15	___	___
16	___	___
17	___	___
18	___	___

©1999 Allyn & Bacon

Handout DT 9.2

Diversity Topic 9.2: Identity

Self-Identity and Self-Concept Activity Sheet

Complete the sentences below in order to describe yourself in the ways you think are most important to you.

1. I am _____.
2. I am _____.
3. I am _____.
4. I am _____.
5. I am _____.
6. I am _____.
7. I am _____.
8. I am _____.
9. I am _____.
10. I am _____.

Now, assign each sentence a score of 1 if you described yourself using an adjective, or a personal trait or characteristic. If you used anything else to describe yourself, score that a 0. Add across the items to get a total score. People with independent self-identities will have higher scores than people with interdependent self-identities, who will tend to identify themselves according to their roles, positions, or status.

©1999 Allyn & Bacon

Handout DT 10.4

Diversity Topic 10.4: Display Rules

Display Rule Assessment
Developed by David Matsumoto

Below, you will see a table with the four social groups across the top, and a list of emotions down the left side. Please tell us what you think people should do when they feel each of the emotions listed toward someone in each of the four situations when interacting with that person. At the top of the page is a list of seven possible responses for how one may behave in those situations. You may use whatever you deem most appropriate as the basis for your responses. For example, you may use what rules you think your culture has concerning these situations. Or, you may use family rules, or your own personal rules.

Possible Responses:

1. Express the feeling as is with no inhibitions
2. Express the feeling, but with less intensity than one's true feelings
3. Express the feeling, but with more intensity than one's true feelings.
4. Try to remain neutral; express nothing.
5. Express the feeling, but together with a smile to qualify one's feelings.
6. Smile only, with no trace of anything else, in order to hide one's true feelings.
7. Some other response.

	Family	Friends	Colleagues	Strangers
Sadness				
Anger				
Shock				
Contempt				
Joy				
Aversion				
Worry				
Happiness				
Disgust				
Gloomy				
Surprise				
Hostility				
Defiance				
Fear				

©1999 Allyn & Bacon

NOTES

NOTES

NOTES

NOTES

NOTES

NOTES

NOTES